Anim
Personalities

Animated Personalities

CARTOON CHARACTERS AND STARDOM
IN AMERICAN THEATRICAL SHORTS

David McGowan

UNIVERSITY OF TEXAS PRESS 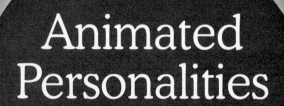 AUSTIN

Requests for permission to reproduce material from this work
should be sent to:
    Permissions
    University of Texas Press
    P.O. Box 7819
    Austin, TX 78713–7819
    utpress.utexas.edu/rp-form

♾ The paper used in this book meets the minimum requirements
of ANSI/NISO Z39.48–1992 (R1997) (Permanence of Paper).

LIBRARY OF CONGRESS CATALOGING-IN-PUBLICATION DATA

Names: McGowan, David, 1984– author.
Title: Animated personalities : cartoon characters and stardom
    in American theatrical shorts / David McGowan.
Description: First edition. | Austin : University of Texas Press,
    2019. | Includes bibliographical references and index.
Identifiers: LCCN 2018015283 | ISBN 978-1-4773-1743-3
    (cloth : alk. paper) | ISBN 978-1-4773-1744-0 (pbk. : alk.
    paper) | ISBN 978-1-4773-1745-7 (library e-book) |
    ISBN 978-1-4773-1746-4 (nonlibrary e-book)
Subjects: LCSH: Animated films—United States—History and
    criticism. | Animation (Cinematography)—United States—
    History. | Cartoon characters—United States. | Characters
    and characteristics in motion pictures.
Classification: LCC NC1766.U5 M39 2019 | DDC
    741.5/80973—dc23
LC record available at https://lccn.loc.gov/2018015283

doi:10.7560/317433

Contents

Acknowledgments

This book has grown out of my doctoral thesis, which was itself made possible by a Development Fund studentship from the Department of English and Drama at Loughborough University in the United Kingdom. I am extremely grateful to Brian Jarvis, who co-supervised the first year of my studies; the late Bill Overton, who served as my director of research; and Paul Wells and Peter Krämer for their input as examiners. My biggest thanks, however, must go to Andrew Dix, my primary supervisor, whose advice has been invaluable; my development as a scholar and a lecturer owes a great deal to his guidance.

I would also like to acknowledge the staff at the following institutions: the Pilkington Library at Loughborough University, the Jen Library at the Savannah College of Art and Design (with specific thanks to the inter-library loan coordinator Janice Shipp), the British Library, the British Film Institute Library, the Rubenstein Library at Duke University, the Library of Congress, and the Margaret Herrick Library. I am also much obliged to Anna Cooper, Pete Falconer, and Laura Sava for their help in accessing certain materials.

Although most of the archival research was done long enough ago that I was still spooling through microfilm reels, the Media History Digital Library (http://mediahistoryproject.org) has become an essential resource for studio-era film magazines. I have used their scans for a number of the images featured in this volume. I would also like to highlight several independent DVD producers: Cartoons on Film (http://cartoonsonfilm .com); Inkwell Images (http://inkwellimagesink.com); Jerry Beck (www .cartoonresearch.com/garagesale.html); and especially Thunderbean Animation (www.thunderbeananimation.com), which has made available a great deal of American animation that goes beyond the usual canons and major studio releases.

While preparing the final drafts of this manuscript, I received assistance from many individuals. Jim Burr, my sponsoring editor, has been extremely helpful throughout the lengthy process, from initial pitch to publication. Louis Bayman, Lee Clarke, and Anna Cooper each gave useful feedback during the submission stage, as did the peer reviewers who surveyed my work. My copy editor, Sally Furgeson, offered many thoughtful suggestions that have benefited every chapter. I would also like to thank the staff at the University of Texas Press, including Nancy Bryan and Sarah McGavick, who have guided the book's production.

Writing this volume has taken the best part of a decade, on and off, yet in some ways the text has been gestating for much longer. I owe a debt of gratitude to a teacher at the Bishop's Stortford High School, Mr. Patterson (this being a stage of education where first names were off-limits!), who was the first to encourage my interest in film studies as a scholarly pursuit. I would also like to thank the lecturers and staff of the Department of Film and Television Studies at the University of Warwick, where I undertook my undergraduate and master's degrees (the latter of which was supported by an award from the Arts and Humanities Research Council).

None of this would have been possible without family and friends, and my only regret is that work—and our increasing dispersal across the globe—has made opportunities for reunions more infrequent, if hopefully no less pleasurable. I recall my long-term friend Alex Roe commenting in our early teens (possibly with a little malice) that I would grow up to become an "archive historian," and it is with great annoyance that I have to admit he wasn't too far wrong. I am also obligated to mention Matt Baldwin, Lee Clarke, Emma Keeling, Lauren Pilkington, Anna Power,

Leanne Weston, and Rachel Young, as they made me promise during our undergraduate studies that I would do so if I ever wrote a book.

My parents, Jeanette and Tom McGowan, have been extremely supportive and have provided many unofficial "research grants" and "maintenance stipends" over the course of my studies. I must thank my younger brother, Tim, for his willingness to let me commandeer the family television to watch old movies and cartoons on many occasions throughout our childhood when I'm sure he would rather have watched something else. I should also apologize for my hard-fought campaign to have him named Popeye when he was born (or Olive Oyl, had he been a girl) and feel with hindsight that our parents ultimately made the right decision. I would like to dedicate this book to the memory of my grandparents, Ann and Reg Brazzier and Mary and Tom McGowan.

Finally, I must thank my wife, Laura, for her love and patience, her occasional deputization as research assistant, and her lack of shame when introducing me to people as someone who researches cartoons for a living.

Animated
Personalities

Introduction

From the 1910s until the 1970s, the American movie industry routinely produced short cartoons for theatrical exhibition. Donald Crafton suggests that, by the early 1920s, the "continuity series"—a collection of "films released under a series title [that related] the exploits and [developed] the personality of the recurring protagonist"—had become the dominant form of American short animation (*Before Mickey* 271). The cartoons that emerged from this production context spawned a vast range of animated characters, many of whom enjoyed lengthy "careers" on the big screen and have endured into the twenty-first century on television and elsewhere. Examples include Felix the Cat, Betty Boop, Mickey Mouse, Bugs Bunny, and Woody Woodpecker. This volume argues that these figures can be legitimately understood as stars.[1]

Studio-era theatrical animation with recurring characters very rarely exceeded a single reel (approximately 7–10 minutes) in length, and so these films were generally positioned as a supporting text to the main (live-action) feature.[2] Notions of cinematic stardom, however, are not exclusively

1

tied to the feature film. The Three Stooges, for instance, produced short subjects for the cinema until the 1950s, with only occasional full-length releases. The cartoon was often recognized as an anticipated aspect of the cinema program: Julian Fox estimates that "at the height of [Felix the Cat's success] over three quarters of the population of the world" had either seen his films or at least "knew him by name" (44). In 1932, Terry Ramsaye dubbed Mickey Mouse "the most famous personality of the screen," regardless of film length or medium. He also proclaimed the Mouse to be the industry's "best contributor to the creation and maintenance of the habit of attending the screen theater," implying that, if a Mickey film was playing, many went to the cinema primarily to see the cartoon rather than the feature ("Mickey Mouse" 41). One article even mentions "theater marquees on which Mickey is billed in huge letters above Greta Garbo in smaller letters" and another stating "MICKEY MOUSE. ALSO JOAN CRAWFORD AND CLARK GABLE" (Fidler 77).

Throughout the decades, the term "star" has frequently been used in popular writing (such as fan magazines and coffee-table cinema books) in conjunction with these animated creations, often with direct comparisons to live-action performers. For instance, Marcia Blitz states that critics treat Donald Duck "as if he were as real a star as Robert Redford" (10). In *Close-Ups: The Movie Star Book*, Road Runner and Wile E. Coyote are profiled alongside comedic actors such as Charlie Chaplin, Bob Hope, and Woody Allen (Brown 41–43); Mickey Mouse appears in another section that contains articles on John Wayne, Bette Davis, and James Stewart (Watkin 502–504). At least two books catalogue animated stars: *The Great Cartoon Stars: A Who's Who!* by Denis Gifford and *The Encyclopedia of Cartoon Superstars* by John Cawley and Jim Korkis. The problem with all these sources, however, is that they do not really explain why or how the characters qualify as stars. The belief that they *are* stars is well documented, but few published materials have submitted these claims to any sustained examination.

This is slowly beginning to change: during the writing of *Animated Personalities*, I found that two books—Donald Crafton's *Shadow of a Mouse* and Nicholas Sammond's *Birth of an Industry*—have emerged as rare and important examples of scholarly literature that take the concept of studio-era animated stardom seriously. This is not the main focus of either text: Crafton primarily adopts a performance studies model, discussing how the characters "act" in their films, while Sammond is concerned with the industrial context of animation production and the influence of blackface minstrelsy on character design and behavior. However, both offer provocative analysis that will be addressed throughout this volume.

The biggest obstacle to recognizing the animated star as a legitimate academic concept (rather than just using the term as a casual descriptor for a famous screen personality) seemingly concerns its incompatibility with existing research, which has tended to presuppose a corporeal subject. This is, sadly, a cross that the cartoon medium often has to bear: as Tom Gunning notes, "again and again, film theorists have made broad proclamations about the nature of cinema, and then quickly added, 'excluding, of course, animation'" ("Moving Away" 38).[3] The work of Richard Dyer—one of the first, and still one of the most influential, proponents of star studies—does not explicitly mention cartoons, and it is fair to suggest that some aspects of his model prove better suited for adaptation than others. On the positive side, Dyer argues that "authenticity is both a quality necessary to the star phenomenon to make it work, and also the quality that guarantees the authenticity of the other particular values a star embodies. . . . It is this effect of authenticating authenticity that gives the star charisma" ("*A Star Is Born*" 133). What is especially intriguing about this is his acknowledgment that most aspects of the star's persona are artificial and that the authentication process is usually one of *rhetoric*—essentially a falsification or abstraction masquerading as absolute truth ("*A Star Is Born*" 137).

In the early to mid-twentieth century, Hollywood film studios played a major role in shaping perceptions of contracted stars. Historian Ronald L. Davis notes that "a young player was expected to project what the studio considered an appropriate image, often at the expense of personal identity. In many cases a newcomer's name was stripped away and replaced by a name the studio thought would command attention on a marquee" (90). For example, "John Wayne" is merely a stage name that was imposed upon an actor called Marion Morrison. Most accounts suggest that Raoul Walsh and Winfield R. Sheehan, the director and producer of Morrison/Wayne's first starring film, *The Big Trail* (1930), chose the name without Morrison even "being party to the meeting" (Roberts and Olson 84). The name "John Wayne" thus has no more intrinsic authenticity than that of an animated character such as Mickey Mouse or Bugs Bunny. It exists primarily as a means of identifying the lead performer in a film (just like Mickey and Bugs) and has nothing to do with Morrison's life before he became a star.

Almost any element of an actor's persona, lifestyle, and even body could be substituted, reconstructed, or fabricated. For example, Heather

Hendershot notes that "star biographies recount, often with sadistic glee, how during Hollywood's Golden Age female movie star images were re-designed by studios or Svengali managers: Columbia's Harry Cohn raised Margarita Cansino's hairline with painful electrolysis, making her 'Rita Hayworth'; director Josef [von Sternberg] had Marlene Dietrich's back teeth removed to 'redefine' her cheekbones" ("Secretary" 117). While an animated character may have been entirely created on an artist's drawing board, the live-action star was often so heavily filtered through the camera's gaze, studio publicity, and even the surgeon's knife that claims to authenticity can be extremely problematic. The anthropologist Hortense Powdermaker even categorizes live-action stars as essentially "inhuman." Although they appeared to be glamorous "folk heroes to their admirers all over the world," they were "regarded by the studio as a valuable but *synthetic* product" (280, 254). Despite their apparent vitality on screen, both animated *and* live-action stars were essentially "created" and manipulated by an external source.

Dyer nonetheless argues that stars exist as human beings on at least a basic level, and it is this fundamental assumption that has the potential to automatically disqualify the status of the cartoon character. Since his first major publication on the subject in the late 1970s, Dyer's work has become the de facto reference point for virtually every subsequent academic investigation into stardom, even those branching into other national cinemas, other time frames, or other mediums and arenas (such as sport, television, and music). For instance, in the introduction to a book of essays on stars in China, Yingjin Zhang and Mary Farquhar express little surprise that many of the volume's contributors refer to Dyer's scholarship, despite the clear differences between the Chinese film industry and the classical Hollywood system (3). It is important to emphasize, however, that Dyer has encouraged modifications of his work in new contexts, noting that "the specificities of those other places where stars are to be found [should] always . . . be respected" (*Stars* 3). Neepa Majumdar's account of early female stardom in India provides a useful example of this. She argues that the system initially operated without any "discourse on the private lives" of the performers—even though this is crucial to Dyer's analysis—and notes that Indian publications were, in fact, routinely printing gossip about American actors while avoiding discussion of the homegrown stars (2). Such analysis indicates that it is possible to move away from some aspects of Dyer's theoretical model without completely destroying it or denying the subject's validity as a star. The following sections attempt to negotiate two of Dyer's major arguments that have traditionally complicated a straightforward comparison between live-action and animation. The first outlines the value of photography in authenticating the image, and the second stresses the existence of a private life as a necessity for a star.

Photography, Cinema, and Authenticity

The vast majority of the theatrical short, and later televisual, cartoons discussed in this volume were produced as "hand-drawn" animation.[4] For the most part, this involved drawings on paper and/or painted images on translucent celluloid sheets (cels). As Stephen Prince notes, notions of film realism have historically been "rooted in the view that photographic images, unlike paintings or line drawings, are indexical signs: they are causally or existentially connected to their referents" (28). Roland Barthes suggests that the photograph is a confirmation of *"what has been,"* adding, "Every photograph is a certificate of presence" (*Camera Lucida* 85, 87). Dyer echoes a similar reading position in his analysis of stardom:

> [T]he question of the star's authenticity can be referred back to her/his existence in the real world. . . . Stars are a particular instance of the supposed relation between a photograph and its referent. A photograph is always a photograph *of* something or somebody who had to have been there in order for the photograph to be taken. . . . [T]he residual sense of the subject having-been-there remains powerful. Joan Crawford is not just a representation done in paint or writing—she is carried in the person née Lucille LeSueur who went before the cameras to be captured for us. (*"A Star Is Born"* 135)

The problem with such readings is that belief in the indexical relationship between photograph and referent can become self-perpetuating. Because the photograph is considered to be a record of the subject's presence in front of the camera, we place trust in the existence of the subject; because we accept the existence of the subject, we are encouraged to believe in the authenticity of the photograph. Consequently, as Thomas Lamarre indicates, analyses of the cinema have frequently enforced "an absolute distinction between reality and illusion," which has served to either ignore or significantly devalue the cartoon (127). Barthes's and Dyer's accounts have a great deal of merit in many contexts, but there is a need to question whether the photograph or its referent are as perfectly authentic as they imply. As Susan Sontag argues, "although there is a sense in which the camera does indeed capture reality, . . . photographs are as much an interpretation of the world as paintings and drawings are." Her research shows that, as early as the mid-1840s, a German photographer had developed a method for retouching negatives. This act, Sontag contends, creates a falsified representation (*On Photography* 6, 86). From the very origins of the medium, then, there have been reasons to doubt the absolute "truth" of the photographed image, and yet a stated trust in its representational qualities has continued to persist.

Despite the illusion of movement created by live-action cinematic technology, early theorists generally reiterated the link to photography as a means of authentication. In *The World Viewed*, Stanley Cavell argues that filmmaking "overcame subjectivity in a way undreamed of by painting . . . by *automatism*, by removing the human agent from the task of reproduction." Essentially, once turned on, the camera cannot help but reproduce the world and capture the activity that is occurring independently in front of it (23, 103).

Cartoons, by contrast, do not replicate this inherent automatism—individual drawings have to be painstakingly photographed frame-by-frame to achieve the same effect of motion. The stylization of hand-drawn animation also makes no definitive claim toward the indexicality of the represented subjects. Cavell thus concludes that "cartoons are not movies . . . because we are uncertain when or to what extent our [real-world physical] laws and [metaphysical] limits do and do not apply" (168, 170). It is true that animated films often self-consciously disobey these laws—for instance, many Warner Bros. cartoons featuring Wile E. Coyote involve him running off a cliff edge and hanging in midair for a number of seconds, contemplating his fate, before gravity finally sends him plummeting to the ground. Yet live-action films are also capable of creating the *artifice* of physical laws being broken. As V. F. Perkins argues:

> The credibility of the movies comes, I believe, from our habit of placing more trust in the evidence of our eyes than in any other form of sense data: a film makes us feel like eye-witnesses of the events which it portrays. Moreover, our belief extends even to the least realistic forms of a movie because movement so strongly connotes life. The source meaning

of the term "animation" indicates that we regard a moving picture, even a cartoon, as a picture *brought to life*. . . . The powerful combination of picture and movement tempts us to disregard the involvement of our imaginations in what we see. (62–63)

Perkins alludes to the fact that the term "animation" was initially used around 1900 to refer primarily to live-action filmmaking. Although this definition has since been superseded, it reminds us that all cinema is ultimately a series of still images, captured—at least traditionally—onto film and projected in a particular sequence. Even if a live-action scene is recorded automatically by the camera, this raw footage may still be submitted to a great deal of manipulation before it is projected. As Jane M. Gaines suggests, "in the process of editing and sound-mixing, the actor's body is divorced from his or her voice; it is reorganized, gestures are recombined; other bodies 'stand in' for that of the actor; other voices are heard as his or her voice" (*Contested Culture* 35). A finished movie is likely to contain many aspects that alter or even fabricate "what has been" (to use Barthes's term). The photographic basis of live-action film might appear to authenticate this process, but in actuality, the constructed seamlessness of the moving image and sound track serve only—as in Dyer's suggestive account of the mechanisms underpinning the star system—as a *rhetoric* of authenticity.

Perkins briefly indicates in the above passage that this rhetoric can be extended even to hand-drawn cartoons. In a direct criticism of Cavell's *The World Viewed*, Alexander Sesonske makes a similar claim:

Recall those charming characters, Mickey, Pluto, Donald Duck, and the perverse objects which surrounded them, and the whirl of motion that usually erupted before the adventure was resolved. My memory is that we experienced these films in just the way that we did all others—as a world present to us while we were not present to it, in Cavell's terms, with the same immediacy and conviction, the same sense of moving through its space, the same feeling of intimate acquaintance with its inhabitants. A simpler world than others, perhaps, but just as easy, and just as hard, to remember; containing its own possibilities for recognition and revelation. (563)

Sesonske's remarks are extremely valuable in suggesting that the properties of the cinematic cartoon world can be persuasive, while at the same time different from live-action. Gunning has also argued that motion "need not be realistic to have a 'realistic' effect, that is, to invite the empathic participation, both imaginative and physiological, of viewers" ("Moving Away" 46).[5]

One can define the particular type of motion enacted by most cartoon short film protagonists as "personality animation—an art that goes beyond merely moving designs around, and emotionally involves the audience by communicating a character's individualism to them" (Canemaker, "Winsor McCay's *Little Nemo*" 33). As Anthony Kinsey elaborates, "in terms of an animated film even a square or a dot or indeed almost any non-figurative image can be given personality if it is made to behave in a way which seems to be in character with its appearance" (40). Despite the essential freedom from traditional corporeality that the medium can permit, it is significant that virtually every recurring short cartoon star was presented either as a caricatured human (such as Popeye or Mutt and Jeff) or anthropomorphized animal (i.e., a creature with human characteristics, such as Bugs Bunny or Woody Woodpecker). There appears to have been a conscious effort to keep the animated body broadly comparable to that of the live-action star. Even characters capable of elaborate physical transformations still had a recognizable default state to which they would ultimately revert—a stable appearance that could be easily publicized (and that became an even greater necessity when merchandising turned the images of stars such as Felix the Cat and Mickey Mouse into rigid designs for dolls and toys).

Several of the above quotations have made reference to the role played by an audience in responding to animation. Academia has often struggled to speak on behalf of the average viewer: the tentativeness of Sesonske's summary of his own experience of the cartoon world—and, conversely, Cavell's assuredness about what he believes it lacks—is indicative of the ongoing difficulty of reaching a consensus, even about the definition of something as fundamental as the term "animation" itself (see Beckman 1–2). Certainly, Cavell and other film critics who champion the photographic basis of live-action cinema are entitled to a personal interpretation that privileges this element. The danger with such theory is, again, its absoluteness. It can close off or deny other legitimate responses to animation, ones espoused by authors such as Perkins, Sesonske, and Lamarre (and ones that at least appear to have been shared by a sizeable portion of the wider moviegoing public). Indeed, as Lamarre indicates, certain "traditional" accounts essentially deny spectators any sense of agency, the insinuation being that "if the viewer feels that animated things are somehow alive, it is because the subject has been tricked or confounded, unable to detect the truth of the matter—that movement has been added to an object. . . . If we want to take animation seriously, we must challenge this received wisdom" (127). In developing a model for cartoon stardom, it does have to be accepted that the perception of such a figure is rendered (at least partially) as "the other," as an explicitly and *unmistakably* constructed entity. However, as Crafton suggests, rather than seeing (for instance) Betty Boop's "pen and ink" status as a "liability," it should actually be viewed as part of her "charm" in delivering many of the pleasures associated with the cinematic medium (*Shadow of a Mouse* 300). The movement of sound and image—coupled with a deliberate attempt to convey personality—can still encourage audiences to perceive life in the characters, possibly removing the need for further authentication.

The Public/Private Dichotomy

While cinema has the potential to convince us—or, at least, inspire us to play along with the conceit—that the characters exist on-screen, their presence off-screen remains in doubt. In the introduction to *Contemporary Hollywood Stardom*, Martin Barker asks: "Can [cartoon figures] be classed as 'stars' in their own right? This is a controversial issue. There are arguments that [they] cannot be stars because they do not have a life outside of the films in which they appear" (21–22). Dyer again appears to reaffirm this skepticism:

> Stars are carried in the person of people who do go on living away from their appearances in the media, and the point is that we know this. When he got home John Wayne may have become Marion Morrison again, but there was a real human being with continuous existence, that is, who existed in between all the times that he was "being" John Wayne. ("*A Star Is Born*" 135)

The suggestion is that the innate corporeality of the live-action star—the "continuous" and seemingly undeniable existence of the actor's human body over the course of his or her life—is "an in-built means of authentication," even though Dyer does acknowledge that the star's body as a site of meaning is "unstable" ("*A Star Is Born*" 135, 137). However much the basic existence of the person *suggests* coherence, the example of John Wayne highlights that a given star's life could be extremely contradictory, particularly in the relationship between public and private. Simply put, the fact that a star exists beyond his or her films means that he or she has the potential to disrupt or negate the image constructed for those films.

Richard deCordova's account of the birth of the star system in silent-era American cinema makes a distinction between the "picture personality" and the "star." DeCordova suggests that the picture personality was a transitional stage in which certain details relating to a performer were released to the audience (such as his or her name), but studios otherwise restricted "knowledge about the players to the textuality of the films they were in" (*Picture Personalities* 86). In deCordova's view, the emergence of the star occurred when public desire for knowledge about actors began focusing on their private lives in addition—and sometimes in contradistinction—to their on-screen work. Dyer emphasizes, however, that the apparent "reveal" of the star's private life was frequently just another, newer rhetoric of authenticity—the intimation being that "what is behind or below the surface is, unquestionably and virtually by definition, the truth," even if this was itself manufactured. If an actor became involved in a public scandal that called this rhetoric into question, then studios could often incorporate the supposed "truth of the exposé" into the star image as a means of re-authenticating all the other fictional elements ("*A Star Is Born*" 136). The point is not necessarily that live-action stardom reveals anything of significance that is true, but that audiences *believe* a truth exists (rooted at least partly in the actor's off-screen life) and are actively engaged in trying to uncover it.

One potential barrier to animated characters being considered as stars is the implication that everything about, for example, Mickey Mouse or Bugs Bunny is clearly defined on a surface level, entirely visible in the films, and not continued in (or contradicted by) a separate private life. Assuming, at least initially, that this is accurate—that there is nothing "behind or below the surface" to find—should this necessarily disqualify cartoon protagonists from being stars? Without denying the level of intrigue that the private sphere can bring, it should be questioned whether its significance is always as central to the live-action star image as critics such as Dyer and deCordova appear to suggest. In her essay, "Re-Examining Stardom," Christine Geraghty argues that traditional star theory has tended to over-emphasize a single, standardized relationship between the public and private, rather than acknowledge the varying conceptions of star image in different situations. She outlines three main categories—the star-as-celebrity, star-as-professional, and star-as-performer—as a means of identifying new approaches to understanding stardom. The star-as-professional seems the most analogous to animation because it focuses on figures "whose fame rests on their work in such a way that there is very little sense of a private life and the emphasis is on the seamlessness of the public persona" (187). This model, coupled with the aforementioned research into other national industries (such as Majumdar's account of early Indian filmmaking), is helpful in its suggestion that live-action actors can still be considered stars even if the audience response is primarily rooted in their films. Although this does not fully deny the existence of a private life, it downplays its significance and therefore helps to broach the fusion of star theory and animation.

In his analysis of Woody and Buzz from *Toy Story* (1995), Paul Wells goes even further and argues that the lack of a private life actually *strengthens* their star image: "Woody and Buzz[,] in . . . being wholly defined by their 'manufacture,' are invested with a sincerity, genuineness and clarity that speaks to a contemporary sensibility which embraces the needs of the *text*, and not the pursuit of the *subtext*; the requirements of the *narrative* above the invisible premises of its implications" ("To Affinity" 99). Wells asserts that there is no need to use a rhetoric to merge the basic truth of the actor's existence with the "manufactured elements" of the star persona: the *complete artifice* of Woody and Buzz serves to fully authenticate them. Audience engagement with the characters is straightforward and stable because it is entirely rooted in the narrative of the film(s). These protagonists were created specifically for the first *Toy Story* movie, and their appearances in the sequels, *Toy Story 2* (1999) and *Toy Story 3* (2010), explicitly continue the story line within this previously established world. By this logic, it would be extremely incongruous if a new film featured Woody, for instance, as a pirate, or as the villain in a sequel to Pixar's *The Incredibles* (2004), or placed him in a fully fledged musical, with no reference to his existing backstory and status as Andy's toy.

Wells focuses primarily on CG animation and the *Toy Story* films in particular, but he does briefly imply that his theory can be applied to theatrical short film stars as well:

In the pre-war era of cartooning, . . . [the] "symbolic" identity of the characters was well understood—Mickey as "John Doe," Donald as "the average irascible American," Betty as the sexually harassed "flapper," Bugs as a "wise-ass victor"—and this, in effect, was part of their currency as "stars." Their dominant traits represented something clear and meaningful in their own fictional context. ("To Affinity" 96–97)

These protagonists did generally display a broad consistency of personality across a series, but Wells arguably overstates the degree to which this generation of animated star personas can be collapsed into a "symbolic identity." The early Mickey Mouse cartoons, for instance, portray the character as rural, riotous, and somewhat mean-spirited compared to his later suburban, middle-class, good-natured "everyman" image, which had crystalized by the mid-1930s. Equally, a small number of Bugs Bunny cartoons dotted around the character's filmography show his schemes backfiring, leaving him to experience an ironic or "unhappy" ending. The living situation, profession, relationships with other characters, and many other attributes of figures such as Mickey Mouse and Popeye could change greatly from film to film. Unlike, say, the *Toy Story* stars, such as Woody and Buzz, who have comparatively fixed textual identities, studio-era cartoon stars often assumed temporary identities for the characters they "portrayed" in individual cartoons. In *Robin Hood Daffy* (1958), for example, Daffy Duck appears not as himself but as Robin Hood, with Porky Pig playing Friar Tuck.[6] A number of 1950s cartoons, such as *Cold War* (1951), begin with a title card stating, "Walt Disney Presents GOOFY," and yet the protagonist in the narrative (who certainly looks like Goofy) is actually identified as "George Geef." Flora O'Brien makes a revealing pronouncement about this confusion: "[A]s Mr. Geef, the suburban hero of the 1950s films, Goofy is seen with a wife and child. . . . Such an action would seem out of character, and we should probably see Mr. Geef as a role played by Goofy, the actor, rather than a true reflection of his real-life circumstances" (*Walt Disney's Goofy* 64). O'Brien's statement implies that cartoon stars exist in a way that transcends the specific context of their appearance in any given film, although the author unfortunately does not develop or explain the idea any further.

In a challenge to the "purity" that Wells ascribes to Woody's and Buzz's star images, Matt Hills suggests that "the sense of a star's 'ongoing life' outside textual performance is played with [in *Toy Story 2* and a number of other Pixar features], where closing digital 'out-takes' portray characters 'as if' they are actors fluffing their lines or [bursting into laughter]"

(89n3). The format of the blooper or outtake often privileges the process of transition between public and private: we see the star in performance, something goes wrong, the dramatic illusion is shattered, and the "real" person is revealed. In one outtake included in *Toy Story 2*, Woody, attempting to convey a moment of sadness in the narrative, sits down on a roll of sticky tape and accidentally gets stuck in the hole. The sincerity of his performance is undermined: he stops "acting" and begins laughing with the assembled "film crew" at his own clumsiness.[7] Whereas the outtakes in *Toy Story 2* are confined to the end credits, creating a clear distinction between the main text and these supposed glimpses "behind the scenes," one can identify many examples of studio-era cartoon stars explicitly interrupting the action of the film itself. In *Bugs Bunny Gets the Boid* (1942), the story line involves Bugs believing that he has been seriously injured, mistaking the skeletal remains of another animal for his own broken body. He starts weeping uncontrollably, but Bugs the "actor" temporarily halts this performance and deadpans to the audience, "Gruesome, isn't it?" Later, Bugs (the "character") realizes that he is not hurt and begins rejoicing. However, the "actor" once again intervenes and nonchalantly tells the audience that he knew that he was fine all along, thus undermining the emotional impact of the scene (fig. 0.1).

To reverse Wells's analysis of *Toy Story*, then, many theatrical short star-led cartoons actively pursue subtext at the expense of a coherent diegesis. The stars within these films often lack—and even appear to consciously reject—the "surface only" authenticity claims that Wells attributes to Woody and Buzz. My insinuation that this is a "conscious" decision reflects that figures such as Daffy Duck and Porky Pig are presented as having an inherent sense of personal agency that exceeds their status as stable "characters." While it is important to reiterate that any suggestion of the animated star existing beyond his or her on-screen characterization is itself an interpretive construct, the point is that those controlling the animated character routinely had their authorial role(s) denied or at least downplayed. To reiterate Dyer's terminology, it can be suggested that there was, in fact, a *rhetoric* of authenticity surrounding these cartoon stars. This implies that there *is* something "behind or below the surface," and one can attempt to authenticate the star image precisely upon this disjunction between public and private, just as with a live-action performer.

The approach was not just confined to the films themselves: many media outlets continued the illusion of animated stars living in the "real world."

FIGURE 0.1. Bugs Bunny in and out of character in *Bugs Bunny Gets the Boid* (1942).

These include fan magazine columns in which the character expresses his or her opinion on a particular subject, "interviews" with the stars in print and on television and radio, and even reports of supposed personal "appearances" at Hollywood parties and other functions.[8] A *New York Times* article on Donald Duck, for instance, mentions the actor's thwarted attempts to break into features and his desire to play Hamlet on-screen. It also claims that he and Daisy Duck—who reportedly met during the making of *Mr. Duck Steps Out* (1940), her debut in a Disney cartoon—are looking for somewhere to live together in the San Fernando Valley, but that Donald does not consider it "dignified . . . to discuss his personal affairs" with the press ("The Ascendency of Mr. Donald Duck" X4). An "interview" with Mickey Mouse in the magazine *Motion Picture Classic* similarly delves into his off-screen romances, with the Mouse noting, "I hope [this] will give my fans some idea of what we stars, apparently so carefree on the screen, have to go through in our private lives in Hollywood" (Mouse and Belfrage 69). Although one might expect a degree of absurdity to these pieces, the subject matter and writing style are generally remarkably similar to editorials about live-action stars from the same period. The average reader was undoubtedly in on the joke, but these items are rarely signaled as being anything other than just another regular article within the context of the wider publication and seldom imply that the animated basis of the star places limitations upon them. Indeed, the *Motion Picture Classic* article is particularly firm on the latter point—Mickey is quoted as saying that "it is no earthly use for jackasses and prodnoses to yell at me: 'But you're only a drawing!'" (68).

The prominence of such materials raises an important question: If Mickey *claims* to have a private life and *acts* like he has a private life, does the underlying fact that he is, really, "only a drawing" affect his star status? In a discussion of the boundaries of John Wayne's off-screen existence, Dyer suggests that, unlike Wayne, "there is no way in which Elizabeth Bennett [*sic*] can leave the pages of *Pride and Prejudice* (except to be referred to in other media texts, in parodies, speculative continuations of the story, adaptations etc.)" ("*A Star Is Born*" 135). Although it may be tempting to simply reiterate Dyer's discussion of the literary creation when considering the animated star, this does not really account for the complexities and differences between the two forms. Both Elizabeth Bennet and, for example, Mickey Mouse have undoubtedly become popular characters, extended by a variety of media sources, but cartoon protagonists from the studio era tend to be much less tied to the narrative requirements of an originating text than does Bennet in *Pride and Prejudice* (or, as noted above, Woody and Buzz in *Toy Story*). Furthermore, the reportage about Mickey Mouse (and many other animated personalities) covers a vast range of different subjects, extending well beyond the plots and settings of the films themselves.

A cartoon star's primary existence in film rather than in printed text is another point of deviation, which has a considerable impact on the way that that star can be articulated. The various cinematic and televisual adaptations, sequels, and reboots of *Pride and Prejudice* have meant that Elizabeth Bennet has been, as Hills suggests, "in different incarnations and at different moments, realized through embodied stars/celebrities," whose individual star personas will undoubtedly have influenced each version. Conversely, the body of the animated character has already been established on-screen and so is "not significantly semiotically articulated to flesh-and-blood performers" from one appearance to the next (83).

The use of the qualifier "significantly" in Hills's statement is worthy of further exploration. His study focuses on Jar Jar Binks from *Star Wars: Episode I—The Phantom Menace* (1999), another example of a computer-generated "star." Hills acknowledges the role played by voice artist Ahmed Best, but he concludes that the majority of viewer reactions "did not invoke the figure of Best," essentially treating Jar Jar as a separate entity (89n4). Such a viewpoint is arguably just as valid in relation to traditional animated characters, especially given their particular longevity. As Wayne Allwine, the third official cinematic voice artist for Mickey Mouse (following Walt Disney himself and then Jimmy MacDonald) noted: "It's really not about me. It's about Mickey. . . . I get to take this wonderful American icon and keep it alive until the next Mickey comes along. And it will one day, and that's also one of the heartbreaks of the character, of doing the job, because you know, I'm three. There's gonna be a four" ("The Voice Behind the Mouse"). Allwine passed away in 2009, and a new voice of Mickey was appointed. The intention here is not to minimize the contribution of such artists or to suggest that their input was not essential to the ongoing legacy of the characters, but just to acknowledge—as Allwine did—that animated stars have the potential to "live on," usually with little interruption, beyond any individual who worked to create them. The re-casting of Mickey's voice has considerably less impact on the overall star image than the announcement of a new actor to play a live-action Batman, James Bond, or even Elizabeth Bennet.

Many animated characters do, admittedly, endure a peculiar form of embodiment in the case of costumed actors at theme parks and other events. The various Disney resorts encourage guests to receive "autographs" from, take photographs with, and even enjoy breakfast events attended by the likes of Mickey Mouse, Donald Duck, and Goofy (Jackson, "Autographs for Tots" 208–209). Popeye and Olive Oyl appear near the themed character rides at the Universal Studios parks, while the numerous Six Flags venues across the United States permit attendees to engage with Bugs Bunny and many other *Looney Tunes* protagonists. However, Crafton notes that while human performers are "necessary vehicles" for this live experience to occur, "they are uninteresting as actors in their own right. . . . It is the character that is the authentic performer, not the living, sweating college student" inside the outfit. Once again, the cartoon star remains the primary attraction, and the human performers "are interchangeable, without uniqueness," transient and anonymous in their contribution (*Shadow of a Mouse* 84).

It cannot be denied, however, that animated characters and Elizabeth Bennet are united in their status as creations, rather than truly living beings. One can "meet" Mickey Mouse at a Disney theme park, but, for most fans this would arguably be a rather different experience from a direct encounter with a famous human star. At the same time, a case can be made that relatively few audience members will actually get the opportunity to meet any major Hollywood figure in person (even if the acceptance of their real-life existence at least acknowledges the potential to do so). For the most part, information about these stars' lives, like our engagement with cartoon characters, is relayed to us through media sources. As Paul McDonald argues, "somewhere in the world is the flesh-and-blood Brad Pitt but he is only 'present' and known to his audience as an ensemble of textual materials" (*Hollywood Stardom* 6). Significantly, Dyer has also acknowledged that these materials can "displace the individual as a guarantor of discourse. . . . At this point the authentication afforded by the ambivalent star-as-image:star-as-real-person nexus resembles nothing so much as a hall of mirrors" ("*A Star Is Born*" 136).

Being able to prove that the actor actually exists (or once existed) is a useful means of beginning the process of authentication. However, star theory, with its privileging of a human subject, often takes for granted and exaggerates this basic "truth." In response to Dyer's work, Gaines argues that live-action stardom can be so constructed that "the real person (if there is one) is more functional than real in the way that he or she is invoked as an authenticating presence" (*Contested Culture* 33). Gaines's statement that the existence of the body has more value symbolically than as a physical entity—and particularly her implication that it does not actually have to be a real entity at all—appears to justify the star claims of the theatrical short cartoon protagonist. As Joe Adamson evocatively asserts, "Bugs Bunny does not exist. But *he lives*" (*Tex Avery* 15).

It is difficult to prove how viewers truly engage with the on- or off-screen status of animated stars (or, for that matter, live-action ones). Attempts to undertake detailed audience research—such as Jackie Stacey's valuable and pioneering *Star Gazing*, which uses letters and questionnaires to collate British women's responses to female Hollywood stars of the 1940s and 1950s—can often offer only a partial account (due to the limited number of surveys that can be undertaken, the range of evidence that can be obtained, and so on). The main focus of the research for this volume has been the representation of animated stars within the films, as well as in newspapers, studio advertising, and many other surrounding media texts. While it has been possible to find some historical records of viewer responses to animation—such as letters written to fan magazines and trade reports from cinema owners about how individual films played locally—one must still acknowledge the potential for bias, fabrication, or even studio coercion. For this reason, my arguments here should be read primarily as a study of the *rhetoric* used to sell films and stars to audiences, not a definitive account of the audiences' subsequent reactions to those films and stars.

The extent to which this "illusion" was maintained is especially intriguing: such an august newspaper as the *New York Times* was not above printing "gossip" about Donald Duck, a number of prominent artists and scholars wrote articles about characters such as Mickey Mouse and Felix the Cat, and at times even government institutions and world leaders got in on the act. Lamarre nonetheless reiterates the need to avoid simplistic accounts of viewers being duped or controlled when it comes to animation (126). Recall, for instance, Max Horkheimer and Theodor W. Adorno's striking assertion that cartoons "hammer into every brain the old lesson that continuous attrition, the breaking of all individual resistance, is the condition of life in this society. Donald Duck in the cartoons and the unfortunate victim in real life receive their beatings so that the spectators can accustom themselves to theirs" (110).[9] One should certainly not posit Hollywood output as purely entertainment, but it is important to acknowledge viewers as playing an active and discriminating role in constructing culture. Crafton has boldly suggested that the audience should be deemed "coanimators . . . when they indulge their assumptions, exercise their imaginations, suspend disbelief up to a point, and fill in toons' personalities." Crucially, he acknowledges that "the same process applies to 'real' [live-action] actors on film, especially stars" (*Shadow of a Mouse* 6). Kerry O. Ferris's use of Erving Goffman's concept of "frame sophistication" offers similar insights into wider categories of stardom in that it sees the viewer *as well as* the performer (and one might broaden this to include studios, press agents, and others) as "collaborators" (and perhaps, at times, "combatants") in negotiating the real, the unreal, and everything in between (Ferris 62–63).

While a uniform summary of "animation" and its effects may remain elusive, we can highlight some of the inefficiencies of film theory that have filtered down into star studies, frequently at the expense of serious discussion about the cartoon form. Indeed, it is perhaps surprising that many accounts of stardom—which so often productively complicate existing assumptions and identify gray areas—have adopted certain "truisms" out of convenience or academic tradition. As Crafton argues, "clinging to the primacy of the physical body"—with the inherent assumptions about the role of a private life and the indexicality of live-action cinema—"is understandable, but we realize too that this very attitude is an acculturated anthropocentric practice, one that animation performance undermines and routinely discredits" (*Shadow of a Mouse* 56).

At the same time, however, I emphasize how productive existing theory can be when it is simply permitted the opportunity to be applied to animation. In the preface to *Shadow of a Mouse*, Crafton notes the difficulty of pitching a book about cartoon performance when the validity of this subject may seem "self-evident" to some and yet rejected as "balderdash" by others (xiv). In presenting variations of my research at academic conferences and elsewhere, I have experienced a similar balance between those who are immediately accepting of animated stardom and those who require a much more elaborate justification of how this concept can stand alongside the scholarship of Dyer and others. This second grouping should not be dismissed, and there remains a lot of work to be done in order to establish the viability of cartoon stardom as an ongoing area of study. It is my hope that my arguments in this book will contribute to this endeavor as much by highlighting the important continuities with current live-action scholarship as by finding areas in which it can be refined. Compared to accounts of stardom in, for example, Bollywood cinema or the pop music scene, the characters discussed in this volume possess a unique proximity to the American "golden age" figures privileged by Dyer: not only do they begin to appear on-screen at roughly the same time, but their work is also produced and released by the very same studios, viewed by the same audiences, and written about by the same publications. The Hollywood live-action and cartoon star share numerous common bonds that exceed the complications of indexicality and physical ontology.

This book is divided into three sections. "Stages of Theatrical Stardom" looks chronologically at specific periods in cinematic short animation production and discusses how characters responded to changes in the star system, the film industry, and the wider political landscape. Chapter 1 draws upon Richard deCordova's study of the emergence of live-action stardom in the early 1910s and suggests that the promotion of animated characters developed from similar contexts. Just as some producers initially created interest in the human actor by drawing upon the preexisting fame of stage performers, many early cartoon series adapted popular characters from newspaper comic strips. A number of these animated protagonists developed beyond deCordova's notion of the "picture personality," earning the label of "star" by evoking notions of a private life within surrounding publicity. A character such as Felix the Cat was featured in merchandising and was even presented socializing with live-action stars on a number of occasions during the silent period. Although newer figures such as Mickey Mouse quickly came to dominate in the early 1930s, they entered an already-established animated star system rather than being responsible for creating it.

Chapter 2 covers animation production of the 1930s and discusses the increased potential for scandal following the arrival of sound. It highlights additional examples in which fan magazines purported to delve deeper into the off-screen "lives" of these figures, focusing on romance and heartbreak in a similar manner to live-action performers. Audiences also began to speculate about the sexual desires of both human and animated stars in the form of unofficial comic books called "Tijuana bibles," which presented such figures in a variety of compromising positions—sometimes showing explicit relationships between cartoon and corporeal actors. The animators appeared to be well aware of the erotic potential of their creations, as demonstrated by the production of a pornographic cartoon, *Eveready Harton in Buried Treasure* (ca. 1928), a reported collaboration among several film studios. Even mainstream theatrical releases were capable of generating anxieties about the star's ability to misbehave. This chapter considers how wider debates surrounding content regulation, particularly the development of the Production Code guidelines, affected the industry. Characters such as Mickey Mouse and Betty Boop were significantly altered—and, for the most part, softened—over the course of the decade, but so too were the personas of live-action performers such as the Marx Brothers and Mae West. Once again, the lack of a true existence was no barrier to the perception of animated stars transgressing in much the same ways as their human counterparts.

Chapter 3 moves into the 1940s and considers how the Second World War affected cartoon production. Many performers supported the war effort by entertaining audiences (and boosting morale) through appearances in movies and cartoons. The chapter also discusses further extensions of star personas during this period, including fronting educational and propaganda campaigns. The Disney cartoon *The New Spirit* (1942), produced for the US Treasury, offers a revealing case study of the influence of cartoon stars: for instance, some members of Congress specifically praised Donald Duck for encouraging a sharp rise in tax contributions. The Army also saw the value in using animated characters in similar contexts, most notably through the recurring presence of Private Snafu, a figure who served to instruct soldiers largely by showing them what *not* to do in any given situation. The constructed nature of cartoon characters nonetheless proved to be a mixed blessing during wartime. Although they automatically sidestepped the stigma of not physically serving overseas—something used to shame certain human performers who remained at home—the extra resources needed to produce animation meant that the evocation of these figures usually came at a greater monetary cost than appearances from live-action stars. Cartoon characters also proved easier to appropriate, and the chapter highlights instances in which the Axis powers created anti-American films featuring personalities such as Mickey Mouse. At the same time, however, human beings were also often reduced to icons in propaganda—for instance, the pin-up images of female stars such as Betty Grable—highlighting that the boundaries of corporeality still remain loose and transferrable.

The second section of the book, "Conceptualizing Theatrical Animated

Stardom," shifts the focus to the studio era as a whole rather than on specific historical moments. These chapters attempt to position the animated star in relation, and at times in opposition, to existing scholarship. In chapter 4, I point to numerous similarities between the live-action slapstick comedy and the protagonist-led cartoon, with both containing aspects that deviate from the majority of classical Hollywood productions. The comedian's compatibility with star theory has rarely been discussed within academic work. Steve Seidman's 1981 volume *Comedian Comedy* still offers one of the most in-depth accounts of the unique ways in which such a figure interacts with the media. While Seidman does not make much mention of animation, a number of useful parallels can be drawn. In most genres, characters appear to exist within a self-enclosed narrative world, separate from that of the actor engaged in the portrayal. Cartoons and comedian comedies, by contrast, take inspiration from vaudeville and the conventions of live theater, where performers would often improvise and interact with the audience. The "liveness" approximated by comedic film complicates the usual boundaries between character, screen persona, and private life, implying that the "real" person is somehow interrupting the diegesis. The comedian also regularly challenges expectations of cinematic glamor, even at times moving between aspects of the human and the animal in a similar manner to anthropomorphic characters such as Bugs Bunny and Mickey Mouse. Although, as noted, all Hollywood personas are constructed to a degree, the comedian and the cartoon character make the contradictory nature of this artificiality explicit both within and outside the film texts, exhibiting behaviors not always accounted for by star studies. Comedians still tend to be automatically accepted as stars due to their live-action status, despite deviating from usual expectations in other ways. The frequent dismissal of cartoon characters speaks to a potential double standard that scholarship in this field would arguably benefit from addressing. The chapter concludes with a brief discussion of the emphasis that comic theory places upon the physicality of the body and notes that many of these stars have submitted themselves to cinematic manipulation—including actual animation—which is often ignored.

It is important to note, however, that animation studies contributed to the divide between comedian and cartoon. Writers such as Donald Crafton and Nicholas Sammond have emphasized the role played by the animator, with Sammond in particular viewing this as an explicit complication of the comic's direct address to the audience. Chapter 5 considers the dominance of auteur theory within traditions of cartoon scholarship; I argue that such readings come at the expense of a closer understanding of the animated star. Much like the live-action counterpart, the ongoing cartoon series tended to be more heavily publicized with reference to on-screen figures than to anyone behind the scenes. Walt Disney arguably enjoyed the greatest personal fame of any theatrical-era animator, but still found himself in competition with his studio's biggest creations. During the early 1930s, Disney's attempt to sever a reliance on the recurring character with the experimental *Silly Symphonies* series was thwarted by his distributors' insistence on heavily evoking Mickey Mouse in surrounding literature. The United Productions of America (UPA) studio similarly found its ambitions limited by the unintended popularity of certain protagonists—most notably, Mr. Magoo. Such examples highlight that the power relationship between creator and creation is not entirely one-sided, and, in fact, the latter was historically favored within the industry. Auteurism has encouraged valuable work that has finally brought recognition to marginalized artists. It must be acknowledged, however, that this has largely been a *retrospective* endeavor, which can (inadvertently or not) obscure the discourses available when the films were actually released. At the time of production, Hollywood frequently understated the work of the animator in favor of positing the cartoon figure as a largely autonomous "actor."

Chapter 6 builds on this notion of mythologizing labor practices, suggesting that the restrictive long-term contracts held by many live-action performers often reduced them to commodities manipulated by the studios. While both animated characters and human stars were presented as having *personal* control over their own careers, the underlying truth was usually more complicated. Live-action personnel could be cast in roles against their will, loaned out to other studios without consultation, and even evoked in advertising and merchandising campaigns, regardless of whether they endorsed the product. Although animated characters were protected by intellectual property laws rather than by employment agreements, studios sometimes fostered the illusion that these figures had signed contracts just like their human counterparts. Indeed, in this chapter, I suggest that cartoon characters arguably proved the ultimate expression of the studio-era star because of, rather than despite, the extent to which they could be controlled. During this period, some actors, such as Bette Davis and James Cagney, began to publicly challenge the conditions of the studio system, claiming overwork and lack of fair compensation, in ways that risked undermining Hollywood's own constructed representations. Cartoon stars were, by contrast, able to be presented as humble and unspoiled, with publicity frequently drawing attention to the lack of temper tantrums and salary demands. At the same time, a touch of scandal could be beneficial to the star image, and so animated figures were also permitted to masquerade as rebellious, albeit (primarily) in ways that were officially sanctioned and carefully controlled.

The slow decline of the studio system, beginning in the late 1940s, saw the top actors pursue independence, finally taking control of project choices and often negotiating impressive pay increases. For many others, however, the situation was very different. Hollywood curbed its production of B-movies, shorts, and serials, putting a lot of performers out of work. Cartoon stars, despite remaining "obedient" constructed entities, were also victims of this shift, and over the course of the 1950s, 1960s, and 1970s, each major studio abandoned the habitual creation and release of animated shorts. The final section of the book, "Post-Theatrical Stardom," considers the "afterlife" of these protagonists following the conclusion of the "golden age" of production. This later work is regularly overlooked in academic histories of animation, largely because of a perceived decline in quality. This has also been true in accounts of live-action stardom, where a focus has similarly been placed on the earlier, more celebrated works. It is only fairly recently that star studies has paid serious attention to subjects such as televisual stardom, star decline and revival, and the impact of aging upon the star's image. As such, this final section is undoubtedly more tentative than earlier sections because so much research remains to be done in both the live-action and animated spheres. I hope that these chapters will begin the process of sketching out historical and theoretical frameworks for the later periods of cartoon stardom, encouraging further work.

In chapter 7, I discuss the migration of cartoon characters to television—initially through the repetition of the existing cinematic shorts over the airwaves but subsequently in works made specifically for the small screen. Drawing on the pioneering work of scholars such as Susan Murray, Christine Becker, and Mary Desjardins, I consider the privileging of intimacy and naturalness in early television aesthetics and suggest that cartoon stars frequently reproduced—rather than parodied—many of these markers of authenticity. The characters were often presented as the hosts of their shows, emphasizing direct address and interaction in a manner that has parallels with, but also significantly transforms, the approaches used by earlier generations of cinematic comedians. Cartoon characters, like their human counterparts, were also required to deliver sponsor messages with apparent "sincerity." Although product endorsements inferred that these characters had real opinions (and thus an implicitly tangible existence), it also limited their ability to be transgressive. The need to satisfy the demands of advertisers led to direct changes to star images—including the further censoring of preexisting theatrical shorts rerun on television and the toning down of aggressive personalities in new made-for-TV series— particularly as cartoons were targeted toward younger viewers. The chapter concludes with a brief discussion of *Who Framed Roger Rabbit* (1988), posited by numerous critics as the beginning of a renaissance in the American animation industry, which offered "comeback" roles for many neglected theatrical-era characters. It will be suggested, however, that such accounts tend to use the film as a convenient milestone to jump from the "golden age" of the studio era to a discussion of celebrated contemporary works, glossing over the events between the two.

In the final chapter, I consider how certain animated stars have negotiated a prolonged existence, often stretching from the first half of the twentieth century to the present day. With Mickey Mouse, at the time of writing, almost in his nineties, and Felix the Cat gearing up for his centenary, there are challenges in finding a suitable rhetoric to account for this longevity. The chapter highlights examples in which cartoon characters have been shown as, at least to some degree, embracing their senior status. In the 1990s and early 2000s, a subset of productions placed these figures in comparatively mature roles, either acting as mentors to a newer generation of younger characters or being presented as actual parents. During this same period, however, other films and shows adopted a trend known as "babyfication," reversing the age of the protagonists, even regressing them to a childhood state. These productions call into question the expected linearity of an actor's life, but the chapter suggests that all forms of star theory need to be reconsidered in the wake of emerging digital filmmaking techniques.

The book concludes with a discussion of the "synthespian," computer-generated photorealistic human characters whose body images are frequently based upon live-action stars. The ambiguous contribution of the physical person toward the continuing evocation of his or her synthespian persona—especially in the case of posthumous performances, in which a dead actor is digitally "resurrected" for new roles—offers a suggestive parallel to the textually constructed animated star. Rather than offer an aberrant model of stardom, the theatrical-era cartoon character may actually offer a valuable precedent for understanding the future articulation of cinematic personalities.

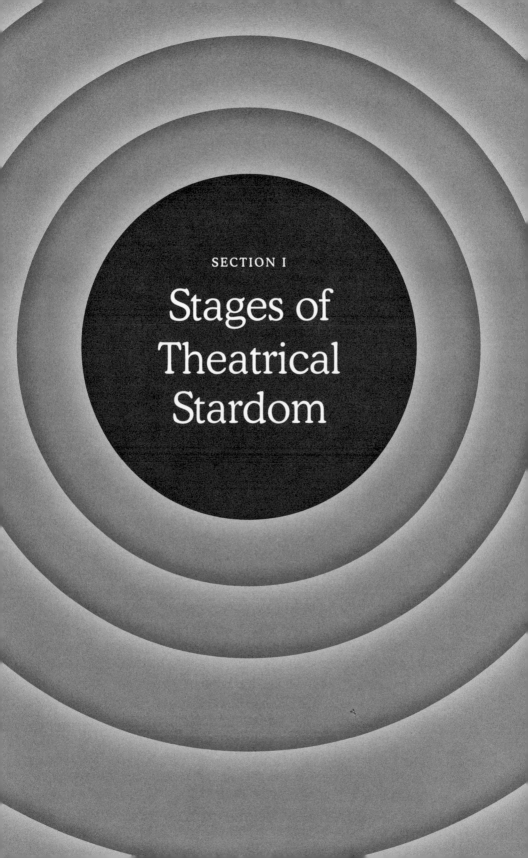

SECTION I

Stages of
Theatrical
Stardom

Chapter 1

Silent Animation and the Development of the Star System

Historical accounts of silent animation are commonly full of assumptions and gaps in knowledge. Most of the sound-era output of the major animation studios still survives, but a substantial proportion of silent cartoons are now considered lost.[1] Where prints of films do still exist, the lack of sound (and color) has prohibited their syndication on television and home video to any significant degree. As Donald Crafton suggests, "some people will no doubt be surprised to learn that there was any animation at all before Mickey [Mouse]" (*Before Mickey* xviii). Many accounts have attributed particular developments in animation to texts from the sound era, often overlooking or ignoring clear precedents in this earlier period. I argue that the animated star system was essentially fully formed by the time the movies began to speak, even if—and this is largely true of live-action as well—relatively few of these pioneering figures remain in popular memory.

Crafton's groundbreaking study of silent cartoons, *Before Mickey*, makes an important contribution to the discussion as it acknowledges the gradual emergence of popular, recurring animated protagonists during the 1910s and 1920s. However, while Crafton mentions the "hegemony of the cartoon 'star'" and notes that "in a sense the increasing emphasis on the character series in animation is the analog of Hollywood's emerging star system" (272, 298), the book does not really interrogate these pronouncements in greater detail. *Before Mickey* ultimately privileges discussions of the animator's claim to authorship, despite having argued so convincingly for an animated film market primarily distinguished by each studio's roster of characters.[2]

The role of a "creator" should certainly not be ignored, especially during the industry's formative years. As Nicholas Sammond states, the notion of the "performing animator" being an on-screen figure was fairly common in cartoons "until the coming of sound" (80–81). Many of the earliest attempts at presenting extended sequences of cinematic animation explicitly show the artist engaged in the manipulation of the drawn figures. For instance, the French cartoon *Fantasmagorie* (1908) begins with a live-action hand (seemingly that of the film's creator, Émile Cohl) sketching a clown figure, who subsequently "comes to life" through frame-by-frame animation. The hand disappears for the majority of the film, but intervenes again shortly before the conclusion, gluing the protagonist's head back onto his body after an accident. The American artist Winsor McCay frequently appeared live on stage alongside his cartoon productions and, in his most famous work, *Gertie the Dinosaur* (1914), even presented the illusion (through careful advance planning) of being able to interact directly with the animated creature. Versions of these texts created for "regular" cinema screenings (without McCay's physical presence) included dramatized live-action prologues in which the artist was shown at work manufacturing the thousands of drawings necessary to complete the film.

These examples nonetheless also contain sequences that focus primarily on the apparent vitality of the animated protagonists, at least partially separated from the framing explanation of the artist's labor. *Gertie* even shows the creature *defying* McCay's instructions on several occasions—including briefly snapping at the side of the screen as if to attack him. Sammond suggests that the theme of the cartoon character's rebellion intensified as the 1910s continued, which he views in part as a reaction to the rise of industrialized studios and the productivity measures that limited opportunities for individual artistic expression (81). The trade journal *Moving Picture World* offers a revealing synopsis of a 1916 short, unfortunately now lost, titled *Trials of a Movie Cartoonist*: "The figures that [the cartoonist] draws become rebellious and refuse to act as he wants them to, so he has a terrible time to make them do his bidding. They answer back and say that he has no right to make slaves of them even if he is their creator" ("Stories of the Films" 1544). Similarly, the Mutt and Jeff cartoon *On Strike* (1920) begins with the staff of a cinema preparing to screen a newsreel about Captain "Bud" Fisher, originator of the comic strip on which the animated series was based. The projectionist remarks: "Fisher's lucky to have those guys [Mutt and Jeff]—they're making a fortune for him." Mutt and Jeff decide to head into the auditorium to "see that reel of our boss." Fisher appears as himself in live-action footage, and the depiction of his opulent lifestyle causes Mutt to question: "Why should we work our heads off for that guy?" In response, the animated duo go on strike and resolve to make their own independent production. The resulting film has a weak plot and poorly executed animation and is heavily criticized by the audience. Realizing they have made a mistake, the characters dash back to Fisher's office. Standing outside, Mutt exclaims: "Tell him if he'll take us back, we'll work for nothing!" Jeff emerges a few moments later, however, looking bashful: "He was so glad to see me that he kissed me." Although Mutt and Jeff are shown as lacking the technical ability to produce a quality cartoon without the input of their "creator," Fisher himself is presented as equally bereft without his stars.

Recurrent examples of animated insurgency can also be found in the *Out of the Inkwell* series, produced by Max and Dave Fleischer from 1918 to 1927. The films feature another cartoon clown, drawn by a live-action artist (played on-screen by Max). The clown frequently breaks out into the "real world," often causing a great deal of mischief, and many installments see Max routinely humiliated by his creation's antics. Sammond suggests that the animated figures were the ones generally subdued by the end of the narrative. Mutt and Jeff are victims of their own hubris in *On Strike*, the Fleischer clown is consigned back to the inkwell, and so on (110). However, in a battle for screen time, the toons were undoubtedly victorious. Donald Crafton notes that this period ultimately saw the "progressive retreat of the animator behind the screen" as his or her protagonists gained more textual control (*Before Mickey* 298). Following the rise of sound filmmaking, relatively few American short cartoons evoke the creative artist as an explicit diegetic presence. It is tempting to read the above works as a convenient metaphor for the rise of the animated star. However, this trope was far more prevalent in some productions than others and was rarely all-consuming. In fact, the success of *Out of the Inkwell* in the early 1920s, and the fleeting influence that this had on competing franchises, was potentially somewhat *regressive* compared to the articulation of the cartoon protagonist in the latter stages of the previous decade. Furthermore, the narrativized battles with animators were arguably a symptom of the star's perceived agency and presence, rather than the cause (or even their ultimate means of "liberation").

Given the centrality of stardom to American mainstream filmmaking throughout much of the twentieth century, it can be surprising to discover that the promotion and/or consumption of a cinematic text in relation to its lead performers was not an immediate, automatic phenomenon coinciding with the birth of the medium. Richard deCordova suggests that, until 1907—more than a decade after the first public screening of moving pictures by the Lumière brothers—"there was no discourse on the film actor. Textual productivity was focused . . . for the most part on the apparatus itself, on its magical abilities and its capacity to reproduce the real" ("The Emergence of the Star System" 17–19). This corresponds with Tom Gunning's concept of the "cinema of attractions," which claims that early cinema regularly privileged "novelty and . . . the act of display." Although a variety of narrative forms—such as vaudeville acts, scenes from plays, and even comic strips—were adapted for the live-action screen in the early 1900s, such events, Gunning notes, "were absorbed by a cinematic gesture of presentation, and it was this technological means of representation that constituted the initial fascination with cinema" ("Now You See It" 73). The mechanical achievements of the movie camera, and the multitude of visual possibilities that it offered, were initially more important than whomever appeared in the film.

In this chapter, I argue that Richard deCordova's account of the development of stardom within silent live-action cinema offers a valuable point of comparison for the subsequent promotion of cartoon protagonists. The latter clearly draws upon the frameworks that were being established by the former, particularly in the growth of extratextual promotion that isolated the lead performers as a valuable form of product differentiation. While animation sometimes parodied the excesses of live-action at this time, it more often than not reproduced or adapted its methods in a reasonably earnest manner, and both forms ultimately went through similar transitional phases before a star system was truly established.

The Discourse on Acting: Theater and the Comic Strip

DeCordova considers the consolidation of more overtly narrative-focused live-action films to have occurred in 1907–1908, and he argues for the emergence of a "discourse on acting" during the same period. In this discourse, "the spectator regarded the actor as the primary source of aesthetic effect" (*Picture Personalities* 27, 46). He states: "This resituation signaled a new form of product individuation more in keeping with an increasingly rationalized production system: the audience's appreciation would no longer be confined to the magic of the machine or to the socio-cultural interest of the thing photographed but would involve the possibility of discriminating—at the level of performance—between specific films" ("The Emergence of the Star System" 23–24). Crafton's work discusses a similar, if somewhat belated, development within animation: a transition from trick films, "which used animated effects as gratuitous one-time novelties" in the cinema of attractions mode, toward (initially one-off, and subsequently recurring) films with protagonists, which featured "a character who initiated or was the object of the action of the film" (*Before Mickey* 260). Just as in the live-action model, where the mainstream audience's increasing awareness and enjoyment of screen acting surpassed its earlier primary engagement with cinema technology as a representational apparatus, the presence of protagonists in cartoons gradually shifted attention from the process of animation toward an interest in narrative and the on-screen figures that were enacting it.

DeCordova argues that the initial discourse around the film actor derived primarily from publicity surrounding the French Films D'Art productions in 1908: "The Films D'Art, after all, were moving pictures of theatrical plays. Because of this, it probably seemed natural (as well as expedient) to emphasize the performance of the actors involved and publicize their names. Plays were promoted and consumed in this way. The enunciative position that the theatrical actor assumed in the theater was reproduced in these films" (*Picture Personalities* 39). The adaptation of newspaper comic strips for the cinema provided a comparable starting point for the evolution of a star system within animation of the 1910s. While the "funnies" clearly lacked the prestige of the theater, films based on either comic strips or the stage drew heavily upon an intertextual relationship with a preexisting art form with an established enunciative position based around a central figure or a group of figures.

Ian Gordon argues that the comic strip, as specifically developed in the

United States in the 1890s, made a unique contribution to the tradition of comic art through "the use of continuing characters and their appearance in mass-circulated newspapers" (9). R. F. Outcault's Yellow Kid is considered the first to have achieved widespread acclaim, beginning in 1895. Although initially restricted to a minor or background figure within an ensemble series, the Yellow Kid rapidly grew in popularity and was promoted to the lead protagonist. He also demonstrated the potential for commercial exploitation beyond the strip itself: his image appeared on a range of merchandise, and he was the subject of popular songs and plays.[3] In this regard, Gordon suggests, "comic strip characters, and the celebrity status accorded them, anticipated Hollywood's creation of movie stars" (45). Indeed, even the Yellow Kid's humble origins—being plucked from "obscurity" and rising to fame—foreshadows the kind of narrative often shaped for live-action performers in fan magazines throughout the silent era.[4] The fusion of comic strips and cartoons prompted a reconsideration of animation production methods and the promotion of a main protagonist, which served to broadly standardize the American cartoon industry. Furthermore, Paul Wells suggests that these adaptations firmly advocated "the primacy of 'gags' and the evolution of a [comedic] vocabulary" that quickly became dominant within animated shorts, continuing to persist even after the form broke from its direct reliance on newspaper franchises (*Understanding Animation* 17).

Winsor McCay's *Little Nemo* (1911) marked the first cinematic realization of a comic strip using animation. It rests heavily, however, in the cinema of attractions tradition of earlier films, presenting its protagonists as enactors of spectacle without character development or a sustained narrative. The primary relevance of *Little Nemo* to animated stardom is not the articulation of its comic strip figures, but rather its aesthetic quality, which, John Canemaker argues, set "a high standard for character animation, not to be surpassed until the Golden Era of the Walt Disney studio in the mid-1930s" (*Winsor McCay* 157). Most early comic strip adaptations have stilted, low frame-rate animation and a flat, two-dimensional style, whereas McCay's films display smooth, continuous movement and depth. The fact that one of the earliest practitioners in the medium produced work of greater technical sophistication than many of his immediate successors has often led historians to dismiss much of the silent era's output as primitive and regressive. Shamus Culhane, for instance, suggests that "had these pioneers followed McCay's lead, animated cartoons would have gotten off to a flying start. But they didn't. It is as if McCay had designed the Rolls-Royce, and the others decided to build bullock carts" (3). It should be argued, however, that the relative simplicity of most other films of the period did not result from an inability to meet McCay's standard, but was, in fact, a *rejection* of it. McCay's filmmaking style was simply not sustainable in the marketplace of the 1910s, where continual pressure from exhibitors for new product led to a rapid turnover of films. McCay's films rarely turned a profit, and the number of drawings required for each production caused significant delays between new productions.

The first animated series featuring a recurring protagonist—a 1913 American adaptation of George McManus's newspaper strip *The Newly-weds* by French animator Émile Cohl—reflected a tentative effort to create regular cartoon releases, a key aspect of the newspaper comic strip form that McCay's works did not emulate. However, results appear to have been erratic, lacking a coherent aesthetic style: Crafton concludes that "Cohl was experimenting with new techniques while forging an uneasy compromise with McManus's original strip" (*Emile Cohl* 164). This was at least partly a result of the struggle to meet the demands of ongoing production. A review of the fifth film in the series, *He Loves to Watch the Flight of Time* (1913), notes the lack of animation in certain sequences: "It is plain that the caricaturist is 'getting wise.' No longer does he always draw each picture. The scene does not always 'move.' Some views are of groups which are stationary" ("Comments on the Films" 921). The series ultimately faltered, with new films appearing only sporadically in the latter half of 1913 and early 1914 before being discontinued.

Mark Langer emphasizes that "some way had to be found to facilitate the animation process" to ensure that cartoons could be cost-effective and maintain a consistent presence in the release schedule inasmuch as they were in competition with live-action films, which were often shot in a matter of days, rather than months ("John Randolph Bray" 140). Wells suggests that this was achieved primarily through the creation of studios, moving from the individual auteur, such as McCay, to a collective, almost assembly-line manufacturing process, with many employees laboring simultaneously on any given film (*Understanding Animation* 17).

The amalgamated patents of John Randolph Bray and Earl Hurd, which introduced the concept of cel animation, also revolutionized production (see Callahan). McCay, for instance, had created his early works on opaque paper, meaning that every single detail had to be copied in full from one drawing to the next. By contrast, with the Bray-Hurd system, the only thing that needed to be generated for each new frame was the specific part of the image that was going to move. This could be painted onto celluloid and placed over a separate background, which now had to be drawn only once since the transparency of the cel would not obscure the information underneath it. The cumulative effect was that cartoons *did* become considerably cheaper and more efficient to produce by the middle of the decade. In some cases, these films were being released every two weeks, or even weekly, which helped to support a "habit formation" akin to that of consuming comics (Gordon 34). Viewers could now expect to see animation as a regular part of the cinema program, just as readers of a newspaper would anticipate the presence of a new comic strip in each edition. The new methods of production both facilitated and encouraged a rise in series production, as opposed to the sporadic one-offs of the past. There were also numerous benefits to having at least one recurrent character at the center of the franchise: not only did this aid in marketing efforts, but it also permitted further economies in subsequent installments. By having the same figure appear across multiple texts, artists could reiterate certain personality traits and narrative devices—and at times even reuse existing cels and animation cycles—rather than having to develop a brand new concept with each film (Crafton, *Before Mickey* 272).

This was really valuable, of course, only if viewers actually *wanted* to see the protagonists more than once, and the intangibility and volatility of a proto-star's "appeal" has continued to frustrate Hollywood production throughout the decades. It is revealing, then, that in the early 1910s, both live-action and animated cinema initially aimed to gain legitimacy, and reduce risk, by appropriating not just the enunciative approaches undertaken in other areas of cultural production, but also some of its established individuals. Live-action targeted theatrical actors, often recreating their most famous roles (Staiger 14), and animation looked to comic strip characters. Upon the release of *Little Nemo*, the value of its association with the newspaper original was noted by the journal *Moving Picture World*: "It is one of those films which should have a natural advertising heritage in the great and wide popularity of its subject—Little Nemo is known everywhere" ("Winsor McKay [*sic*]" 900). Although McCay chose not to capitalize on his creation with further on-screen appearances, the adaptation of comic strips dominated animation production in the mid-1910s among the newly formed industrialized studios. With an already-known commodity, publicity largely reiterated the protagonist's preexisting fame rather than creating it from scratch. The 1916 animated series featuring Mutt and Jeff frequently presented this rhetoric in its surrounding materials: for example, one advertisement for the films prominently claimed that the characters were "laughed at daily by 17,000,000 people through the medium of 200 newspapers."[5] An early review suggested that a "second helping" of the protagonists in film had the potential to solidify, rather than fracture, enthusiasm for the newspaper franchise:

> Usually the people were obliged to wait until the next day before witnessing the further antics of Mutt and Jeff after they had digested the morning or evening paper in which they were running. Now they can go to the [movie theater] that afternoon or evening and see these creations in animation. The double diet won't hurt them for a long, long time. (Milne 2214)

From an advertising perspective, it appears to have been considered valuable to suggest continuity between page and screen: an announcement for the *Happy Hooligan* animated series in 1916, for instance, assures readers that "he is the same Happy that people have laughed at for years."[6]

Not all cartoon versions offered this implied fidelity, though. The *Krazy Kat* series arguably proved the most (retrospectively) contentious for historians. The surreal strip by George Herriman, in which Krazy's love for Ignatz Mouse routinely leads to the rodent projecting a brick at the eponymous protagonist's head, offered an established formula for the movies. Some installments, including *Krazy Kat Goes A-Wooing* (1916), do conform to this basic premise and comedic punch line. However, cartoons such as *Krazy Kat, Bugoloist* (1916) and *Krazy Kat and Ignatz Mouse at the Circus* (1916) suggest a blander friendship between the characters. The series was temporarily discontinued in 1918 and revived by Bray Studios in the early 1920s, which continued the trend of inconsistency in Krazy and Ignatz's relationship. By the 1925 launch of the third *Krazy Kat* film series, now distributed by Winkler Pictures, the characterizations seemingly bore little resemblance to Herriman's original text: *Bokays and Brickbatz* (1925), for example, places the protagonists in a standard cat-and-mouse chase, with Krazy showing clear aggression toward Ignatz.

The decision, then, to posit Krazy Kat as a movie star in initial advertisements for the 1916 cartoon seems oddly prescient. The copy—which does at least mimic the distinct speech patterns and gender ambiguity of the newspaper version—presents Krazy saying:

> "Ignatzes," me and you is about to make a dee-buts into them "movie pitchers" as ectors, and hobble-nobble with "stars"—Y'know what it is a "star" Ignatz? No? Well "Anita Stewart" is a "star." Also me . . . . Always before "Ignatz" my talents has been in a stationary condition but now I can wiggles my eye-brow, waggles my tails and make gestures just like "Sarahs Bernhard," and all of em—so get your old brick throwing eye in good condition "Ignatz" because when you go to work as assistant to Mr. "Krazy Ket" the leading film ectress for the "Hearst-Vitagraph News Pictorial" you don't make a mistake and bounce that brick offa the audience instead of me—Well, goodbye "Ignatz," meet me under the "lamps."[7]

Krazy truly did become an "actor" with varied roles, rather than a fixed characterization, during this period. With each resurgence of production at a new studio, the on-screen Krazy moved further away from the newspaper original toward a new identity constructed solely for the cinema.

As the films gained more exposure, the references to the popularity of the newspaper strip also became less prominent. A number of advertisements for the 1925 and 1928 revivals of *Krazy Kat* do not mention Herriman at all. A similar shift can be seen in the promotion of the *Mutt and Jeff* cartoon series. Although the producers remained obliged to credit Bud Fisher as creator of the comic, as well as erroneously implying that he also worked on the animated versions, the characters increasingly became the focal point of the film publicity, rather than their nominal author. A particularly relevant example can be found in a multi-page block of advertisements for a variety of Fox releases in *Motion Picture News* in 1919. It is possible to draw a parallel between the pages covering *Mutt and Jeff* and those advertising Fox's live-action feature, *Sacred Silence* (1919).[8] Both contain a large image of the "stars" of the film, identified by name: in the former case, Mutt and Jeff, and in the latter, William Russell. The text that credits Bud Fisher in the *Mutt and Jeff* advertisement is formatted in a similar manner to the credits for the director and screenwriter of *Sacred Silence*. The framing of Mutt and Jeff in the position usually occupied by the actor shows an important shift in the discourse between the characters and their creator (fig. 1.1). As Bud Fisher commented:

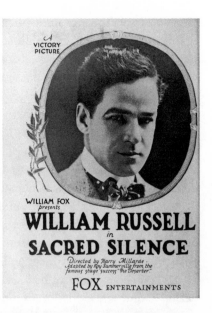

FIGURE 1.1. *Mutt and Jeff* and *Sacred Silence* (1919) advertisements, *Motion Picture News* (27 September 1919).

Having created Mutt and Jeff doesn't mean that I control their destinies—not by a long shot. They control their own destinies pretty well. In fact, Mutt and Jeff now almost control Bud Fisher. . . . I say "making motion picture cartoon stories," but in a way I don't make them. Mutt and Jeff make them. All I have to do is to give them some scenery and they supply the action. (58)

Sammond is correct when he describes the publicity of this period as "oddly contradictory" (73). Despite the fanciful nature of Fisher's comments, the interview still contains some comparatively accurate "making-of" information. However, the degree to which the cartoon personalities were already being presented as complicating, and to an extent even displacing, the real labor behind the animation is significant. Furthermore, the written discourse on live-action cinema at this time was not entirely dissimilar, also shifting uneasily between trade and technical information as well as attempting to serve the public's growing interest in the performer.

By the early 1920s, the number of newspaper adaptations began to decline in favor of studios developing original characters. Mutt and Jeff and

Krazy Kat were the sole preexisting figures to retain substantial notoriety in this next decade. Although comic strip characters enjoyed only a temporary reign as the leading protagonists of animated cinema, their influence should not be underestimated. This phase prompted the development of an industry capable of ongoing production of cost-effective cartoons and moved the focus away from the sheer novelty of the technology toward the presence of the animated "actor," just as in deCordova's concept of the theater's influence upon live-action. The established multiplicity and frequency of installments in the original newspaper strips also helped to normalize the concept of following a character across a recurring series of cartoons.

There were admittedly certain aesthetic drawbacks to this adaptation process. In the early years of the cel system, where studios such as Bray encouraged as much economization as possible, the link to the comic strip offered a partial justification for creating films that were spatially flat and dialogue-heavy. Word balloons were often displayed for an extended period of time and used as an excuse to restrict movement elsewhere on the screen since audiences would supposedly be reading the text. As the silent era wore on and the studios became more established, there was a clear attempt to refine the animation processes and improve the overall product (albeit still within profitable limits). Even before these shifts, however, early comic adaptations should not be dismissed as poor-quality works that either failed to learn from the contemporary artist Winsor McCay or failed to anticipate the quality standards of later producers such as Disney. Instead, they must be viewed as calculated attempts to establish economic (and creative) viability for ongoing cartoon production. In this regard, the studios were successful and would likely not have taken bolder steps with the animated protagonist by the end of the 1910s—a move equivalent to deCordova's concept of the burgeoning "picture personality"—were it not for this intermediary stage.

The Picture Personality

In his analysis of live-action cinema, deCordova creates a distinction between "legitimate" (theater) actors, whose fame preceded their appearances in films, and the rise of "picture personalities," whose identities were "produced and maintained largely by the cinema itself" (*Picture Personalities* 50–51). The use of newspaper characters in animation reflected a similar division in which the cinema traded upon an existing reputation and personality. Even in cases, such as that of Krazy Kat, where the relationship between the print and screen characterizations grew more complicated as time passed, there remained an intertextual link back to the comic strip origins.

The development of animated picture personalities—series characters developed specifically for the screen—overlapped somewhat with the mid-1910s newspaper adaptations, but these animated characters became dominant only in the latter half of the decade. Although animators had produced one-off films featuring newly created characters since the beginning of the medium, Bray Productions's Colonel Heeza Liar was the first to be promoted to an ongoing series.[9] It is not clear if the debut film, *Colonel Heeza Liar in Africa* (1913), was made with further entries in mind, as there were a number of months between the initial cartoon and subsequent regular releases in 1914. However, as Christopher Lehman indicates, the Colonel's potential was quickly realized, with the resultant series receiving nationwide distribution—a rare privilege at this early stage of animation history, one dominated by newspaper adaptations—via Pathé (7). The series gained an additional boost when Bray made a deal in late 1915 to release his cartoons exclusively through Paramount. A full-page advertisement in *Moving Picture World* promoted *Colonel Heeza Liar's Waterloo* (1916), the first installment under this new agreement (fig. 1.2).[10] A subsequent review of the film in *Motion Picture News* also noted that "although Heeza Liar is well and exceedingly favorably known, his appearance in a release all to himself is new, and should make a very acceptable form of comedy" (Thew 394).

DeCordova notes that the picture personality was primarily defined by the "circulation of the image," denoting "both the actor's physical image and the personality that is represented as existing within or behind it" (*Picture Personalities* 73). Although publicity for some newspaper adaptations had begun to emphasize aspects of the image, Heeza Liar's specific link to cinema severed a reliance on earlier works. Pictures of Heeza Liar were prominently displayed in much of the publicity for the series. Of particular note is a 1916 trade advertisement featuring a portrait of Heeza Liar above the following copy:

Do You Know Him?
So do all your patrons—
A murmur of mirth sweeps through your audience. The wily old Colonel Heeza Liar is dear to the hearts of grown ups and children.[11]

COL. HEEZA LIAR'S WATERLOO!
RELEASED JAN. 6th, 1916

The BRAY ANIMATED CARTOONS

Will be released EXCLUSIVELY

THROUGH THE

Paramount Pictures Corporation
BEGINNING JAN. 6th, 1916

EVERYBODY LOVES A CARTOON!!

The newspapers and magazines prove it.   These
cartoon comedies are famous the world over!

THE BRAY STUDIOS, INC.
23 EAST 26th STREET, NEW YORK

FIGURE 1.2. Advertisement for the *Colonel Heeza Liar* series, *Moving Picture World* (18 December 1915).

The premise of the advertisement is that audiences would not only recognize the Colonel through his picture alone but also be aware of his character traits and associate them instantly with humor.

Another aspect of deCordova's model for the picture personality is based on the audience's fledgling recognition of the "professional experience of the actor," which

> worked to establish intertextual connections between films. For example, note this description of Dorothy Phillips: "Miss Dorothy Phillips— Played [ingénue] leads with the Essanay Eastern stock company. Played Ruth in 'The Rosary,' or 'The Two Devotions' and Mary in 'Her Dad, the Constable.' Watch for her in the following Essanay photoplays soon to appear: 'The New Manager,' 'Love in the Hills,' 'The Gordian Knot,' etc." (*Picture Personalities* 90)

This emphasis on a filmography, rather than credits obtained in another medium (such as theater), proved an important development in the creation of the cinematic star system. In the case of animation, where critical histories have often dismissed the output of the 1910s as disposable filler, it is significant to find an article displaying a broad awareness of the Colonel's career:

> Mention the name of "Colonel Heeza Liar" to almost any one and you'll see his or her face light up and a smile spread all over it. Who doesn't know the funny little Colonel—who hasn't laughed at his antics as he hunted wild beasts in Central Africa, outwitted cannibals on the River of Doubt, cultivated his farm with the aid of some strange assistants, and hunted ghosts in Castle Clare? The Colonel's friends are legion. ("Animated Cartoons in Motion Pictures" 54)

The various "antics" described above refer to separate installments of the *Heeza Liar* series, with the implication being that many cinemagoers would have watched most, if not all, of the entries. In the cases of both Dorothy Phillips and the Colonel, therefore, one can identify examples of a discourse that encourages audiences to find continuity across a wide body of work as a means of determining the overall image of the performer.

The *Heeza Liar* series wound down in 1917, but it had been valuable in establishing the dominance of Bray Studios. The majority of its releases during the 1910s and early 1920s were entries produced as part of a series, featuring a recurring protagonist. For instance, Earl Hurd's *Bobby Bumps* series, which began in 1916, enjoyed continuous production for the rest of the decade with sporadic releases into the 1920s. Even characters that did not fully catch on with audiences, such as Clarence Rigby's Miss Nanny Goat and Wallace Carlson's Otto Luck, were piloted by Bray Studios as potential series films with more than one installment.

Although the picture personality series became increasingly common as the decade progressed, its supremacy should not be overstated. While developing these productions, a number of studios were still releasing one-off films, or series without a recurring protagonist. Technological novelty also enjoyed a brief resurgence in the early 1920s, threatening to undermine the otherwise fairly linear enunciation of the character as star. The *Out of the Inkwell* series prompted a craze for "combination cartoons," films that blended live-action footage with animation in a much more sophisticated manner than in earlier productions. As noted, such works presented a suggestively fractious relationship between the artist and the animated figure, but this came at the cost of reiterating the manufactured status of the protagonist and reducing his or her narrative range. Colonel Heeza Liar, for instance, had appeared in earlier films as an autonomous being, existing within a relatively self-enclosed world. Although the combination craze essentially brought him out of "retirement"—his discontinued series was resumed in late 1922 for two more years of approximately monthly releases in an attempt to emulate the Fleischers' success—it did so by reintroducing the artist into the equation. In *Knighthood* (1924), the Colonel ends up in a sword fight with his live-action creator, played by the animator Walter Lantz (fig. 1.3). It is only after this battle that the Colonel shifts to a fully animated space, as he recalls another improbable adventure. The end of the cartoon sees him return to the "real world" after being chased by a bee, and he jumps back into the inkwell, very much like the Fleischer clown.

An article about an earlier entry in this rebooted *Heeza Liar* series notes that "the Colonel's account of his remarkable experiences is not merely uproariously funny . . . , but sends the audience away puzzling its brains to figure out how the trick is done" ("New Effects" 3390), reintroducing a preoccupation with technological spectacle that is reminiscent of the pre-1907 cinema of attractions era. The early entries of *Out of the Inkwell* were similarly ambiguous in their focus: although the clown became the most recognizable element of the series, his personality was not strongly

FIGURE 1.3. Colonel Heeza Liar and Walter Lantz duel in the combination cartoon *Knighthood* (1924).

developed, and publicity for the series in the early 1920s emphasized the "novelty" value of the films above all else.[12] Indeed, the clown did not even receive a name—an important aspect of the picture personality—until 1923, when he was finally christened "Koko," almost five years after the series had begun (Cabarga 25).

The recurring presence of Colonel Heeza Liar and Koko the Clown in these films nevertheless reflects the importance attached to the animated protagonist by the 1920s. Studios may have developed a thirst for novelties to attract audiences to their product, but it is revealing how often picture personalities—by now an established selling point—were added to these experiments to improve their marketability. For example, *Bert Green's Animated Crossword Puzzles* (ca. 1925), one of several contemporary attempts to present on-screen puzzles for cinema attendees to solve communally, introduced two characters, Blotto and Bozo, as hosts of the films.[13] Even the Fleischers permitted Koko to move beyond his most famous role in *Out of the Inkwell* and make numerous appearances in their separate *Song*

Car-Tunes series (produced between 1924 and 1927), which guided audience sing-alongs by projecting song lyrics with an animated bouncing ball.

The combination craze dissipated by the mid-1920s, and production once again began to privilege the vitality of the cartoon personality without reference to the underlying animation process. Indeed, as the decade continued, even the *Inkwell* shorts, which had so frequently framed the character as the rebellious creation of the artist, ultimately downplayed Koko's interaction with the real world. As Sammond suggests, the notion of the modest animation unit with Max Fleischer at the drawing board was now somewhat archaic: the studio had grown rapidly over the course of the 1920s, with the day-to-day work increasingly undertaken by a group of artists (98). Producers such as Fleischer still usually took credit for the films in surrounding publicity, meaning that, like the previous newspaper adaptations, the picture personality characters were still paratextually linked with a "creator" of some description. However, as this was no longer being mediated on-screen, the animated protagonist—and his or her recognizable "image"—became an increasingly cohesive force across a series and permitted the final stage of stardom to flourish.

The Star

Although the lines between the picture personality and the star were blurred during the 1920s, I posit that Felix the Cat was the quintessential animated star persona of the silent era, whose fame significantly eclipsed that of his contemporaries.[14] As with many characters of the period, Felix the Cat had relatively humble beginnings. A last-minute request to create a cartoon for the *Paramount Screen Magazine* newsreel was made to the Pat Sullivan studio "to fill in for a tardy animator" (Canemaker, *Felix* 51). The result, *Feline Follies* (1919), animated by Sullivan employee Otto Messmer, featured the Felix prototype, provisionally named "Master Tom," attempting to woo a female cat and neglecting to guard the family home from mice. The film ends with Tom being cast out by his owner and discovering that he has fathered a large litter of kittens. Dejected, he connects a hose to a gas pipe and attempts to commit suicide. As Canemaker notes, "killing off the hero indicates how one-shot and dead-end a film Messmer and Sullivan thought *Feline Follies* would be, and how unexpected was Famous Players-Lasky's request for a series." His analysis nonetheless highlights how much of what would come to be known as Felix's persona—including his ability to transform his own tail into useful or evocative objects—was apparent in the very first film. The Cat was renamed and publicized as "Felix" from the third installment onward, consolidating the essential elements of the "image" for the picture personality (*Felix* 55–56).

The series rapidly gained momentum. *Moving Picture World* reported in 1920 that Sullivan had been signed to a long-term contract with Paramount to produce cartoons and that "outside of [Bobby] Bumps, Sullivan's cat, Felix, is among the best known character[s] of the motion picture comics and its antics have had a record run at leading houses throughout the country" ("Cartoonist Pat Sullivan" 1927). Crafton states that "it seems as though the cat's personality was understood and appreciated almost overnight" (*Before Mickey* 307), referencing a December 1920 review of a Felix short that noted that the character "emerges with his usual savoir-faire" ("Paramount Magazine" 910). Distributors also clearly recognized Felix's perceived appeal: an advertisement for the *Paramount Screen Magazine* newsreel portrayed the Cat at a typewriter with a piece of paper stating, "Not a filler—A FEATURE!"[15]

Although not a reflection on the popularity of the Felix cartoons, the closure of the *Paramount Screen Magazine* in 1921 briefly threatened to derail this momentum. However, Sullivan reclaimed the copyright on Felix and entered into a distribution agreement with Margaret J. Winkler, a pioneering distributor who had already played a role in the success of the Fleischers' *Out of the Inkwell* series. The agreement gave Felix his own releases, rather than being part of an umbrella series that included a variety of different subjects. Canemaker notes that Winkler "aggressively promoted" each new release, "papering the trade journals with a blizzard of press releases and advertisements touting the new series and star" (*Felix* 65). Such material continued to emphasize Felix's status as a personality, and this was extended by marketing the character in a variety of products across the globe. A contemporary *Film Daily* article noted the extent of the craze:

In London today Felix is the recipient of an honor in that the most popular song of the day is entitled "Felix Kept on Walking" and it is being sung by many music hall performers. There are Felix handkerchiefs, Felix toys, Felix chinaware and an actor in vaudeville is made up to resemble Felix and struts in the same manner as Felix's peculiar walk. ("The Felix Vogue" 16)

The notion of a human performer imitating Felix—as a cartoon character and an animal—reflects the fluidity of his stardom. However, it also highlights the fact that audiences were distinctly attuned to the specificities of Felix's screen image—the vaudeville routine mimicked not only his appearance but also his familiar mannerisms.

While earlier characters had inspired merchandising, it usually remained intertextually tied to their recognition from a pre-cinematic newspaper franchise. All products, spin-offs, and even unauthorized cash-ins of Felix instead originated from his emerging status as a film star. Felix became the first animated protagonist to be adapted into a major syndicated comic strip, rather than the other way around.[16] An advertisement for the strip contains the following statement, seemingly attributed to the Cat himself:

Two Years on the Screen.
Now a full page COLORED COMIC SUPPLEMENT every week in the
SUNDAY PAPERS.
DID I MAKE GOOD?[17]

Although only a brief aside, this summary of Felix's rise has parallels with deCordova's analysis of articles detailing the "success story" of contemporary live-action stars (*Picture Personalities* 98–101). These indicated an awareness of the film actor's private life—separate from his or her filmography—and marked the development from the initial picture personality model into a full-fledged star system. Indeed, a notable aspect of much of the publicity and writing about Felix is the degree to which the character is discussed as a separate, perhaps even "living," entity. A review of *Felix Saves the Day* (1922) states: "'Felix' the cat does some clever stunts and cuts some amusing capers in this animated reel. . . . Pat Sullivan is the artist and trainer, and coaches Felix from the side lines" ("Short Reels" 20). Canemaker's research has highlighted that fan journals and newspapers printed "interviews with 'Felix', as well as by-lined articles 'written' by the cartoon cat" and even photographs created to represent Felix interacting with real people. In particular, images of Felix "dancing" with actresses such as Virginia Vance and Ann Pennington toyed with his apparent off-screen persona as a jazz-loving playboy, akin to many leading men of the era (*Felix* 100–101).

DeCordova has also argued that the star persona emerged as an "idol of consumption." Film actors began to appear in advertising, which served as a reflection of their privilege and wealth (*Picture Personalities* 109–110). Felix was licensed as a representative by a number of companies during the 1920s. A particularly relevant example is the use of the Cat in advertisements for a Chevrolet car dealership in 1923 (Canemaker, *Felix* 88) since deCordova identifies numerous examples of live-action stars being publicized in relation to their automobiles. Viewed as a sign of prosperity, car ownership was also presented as a "modern recreational activity" that formed part of life outside the movie studio (*Picture Personalities* 108–109). Felix clearly amassed a great deal of extratextual material that showed him keeping pace with live-action stars, with surprisingly little mediation or self-reflexive "winking" at the audience to admit that he was, ultimately, *just* a cartoon character.

"You Ain't Heard Nothin' Yet . . .": The End of the Silent Era

Despite Felix's domination of the latter half of the silent era, the character's career ended rather abruptly following the arrival of the "talkies." The Cat's films initially resisted sound altogether and only belatedly provided Felix a minimal voice, presented as "an annoying whine" (Canemaker, *Felix* 130). The new technology brought rapid and monumental change, and half-hearted attempts to capitalize on the craze were generally dismissed in favor of a new generation of stars—in particular, Mickey Mouse. The majority of cartoon personalities of the silent era endured into the 1930s only as cheap reissues of older films with poorly constructed sound tracks. The lack of a detailed list of such releases within either scholarly or fan discourse highlights the relative lack of interest in these recycled works. Characters whose films had helped the cartoon become a recognized art form were relegated to low-end cinema programs before disappearing entirely. Nonetheless, the animated star system was essentially fully formed by the time the movies began to speak, even if few of its existing lead protagonists made the transition at the same time. The silent era moved animation from an initial period of technological experimentation and focus on novelty toward a production process predominantly—and profitably—led by a central character.

The only major development in the live-action model that these first-generation cartoon protagonists failed to emulate was the star scandal. The private lives of human performers were placed under increased scrutiny as the 1920s progressed, sometimes leading to damaging revelations. It is perhaps unsurprising that animation producers did not actively attempt to further negative publicity during this sensitive time. However, with the coming of sound, and the economic uncertainties caused by the Great Depression, representations of both live-action and animated stars went through significant renegotiation. Fan magazine discourse became emboldened in the early 1930s, and a number of Hollywood movies tested the boundaries of content regulation. During this period, animated characters finally showed that they were just as capable of transgressing as their live-action counterparts, as well as running the risk of being censured by fans when they appeared to go too far.

Chapter 2

Stars and Scandal
in the 1930s

I n the earliest years of the star system, publicity implied that everything about the star's personality could be found within his or her movies, but the rise of fan magazines in the latter half of the 1910s suggests that for a sizeable subset of viewers, the information provided in the films was no longer enough. As Richard deCordova argues: "All discourse about those who appeared in films emerged in a secretive context. The fascination over the players' identities was a fascination with a concealed truth, one that resided behind or beyond the surface of the film." DeCordova suggests that each of the stages of the discourse—the actor, the picture personality, and the star—"introduced a level of secrecy and truth beneath or beyond a previous one. . . . The private finally emerged as the ultimate or most ulterior truth" (*Picture Personalities* 140).

Magazine articles increasingly focused on actors' off-screen lives and not just on their cinematic releases, implying that readers could *finally* learn the "truth" about their favorite performers. Although such publications claimed to be acting in service to movie fans, the underlying business model was rather more complicated. As Anthony Slide suggests:

Fan magazines were never totally under the control of the studio heads, but they did provide a constant and reliable outlet for publicity stories. . . . The relationship was never spelled out to the reader, but it was an open secret within the industry . . . . One fed upon the other, but which was the predator and which was the prey was open to question. (7)

Because the magazines generally relied on industry cooperation to secure interviews and photo shoots with the stars, studios could exert a great deal of influence to ensure that content remained in line with "official" publicity. DeCordova's work shows that Hollywood attempted to present an underlying "moral healthiness" in its live-action star system, distancing film actors from the ill repute frequently attached to theatrical performers ("The Emergence of the Star System" 27–28). Focus was often placed upon the "domestic bliss" of the star's home life in terms of family, marriage, or (respectable and monogamous) courtships (*Picture Personalities* 106). Nonetheless, as Slide indicates above, the power relationship between the studios and fan magazines was not entirely one-sided, and some articles did begin to question this "idyllic" view by giving sporadic prominence to reports of actors' sufferings, divorces, and bad behavior. The early 1930s, in particular, saw a rise in journalists' efforts "to circumvent the studio publicity departments." Publications placed an even greater focus on "confessional" stories, with hyperbolic claims of unveiling the truth about a given celebrity—and, by extension, exposing the apparent falseness of earlier publicity (Barbas 131).

The treatment of animated characters again shows a remarkable consistency with these wider trends. Indeed, Slide notes that 1930s fan magazines gave more coverage to Mickey Mouse than to some live-action stars (131). Although Felix the Cat had received a degree of reportage that purported to give insight into his off-screen "existence," the writing on Mickey goes a lot further in separating the public and private images. *New Movie Magazine* claimed to have received the very first interview with the Mouse in its May 1930 edition, and the article divulges a lot of information about his life before the movies. Mickey reportedly has nine brothers and fourteen sisters, and it is inferred that his mother has passed away, with the interviewer noting that the Mouse's voice "broke a bit" and that "he sniffed" during this discussion (Hyland 37). The star's apparent vulnerability is also shown in his revelation of a failed relationship with a country girl called Sandie Titmouse. Mickey claims to have been a struggling actor on a Felix the Cat film and that he met Sandie during a period of disillusionment with his career. He states:

> I finally said that I was not going to leave her, that I would stay and marry her and live a life of freedom, there close to nature.
>
> But she said no. She loved me, yes; I must believe that. But she recalled to me my public, my art, my urge for the better things in life. Told me that she was but an interlude, and that I would forget her. She was wrong. I never have. . . .
>
> I left her and returned to the studio—to work and gain surcease. Soon after that they gave me the opportunity to play leads, and the future looked brighter. But for her I would still be just another unknown mouse. (Qtd. in Hyland 129).

The Sandie Titmouse affair draws attention to the star's romantic history, which, as Samantha Barbas notes, was extremely prevalent subject matter in fan magazines of this period: "Even the traditionally more conservative *Photoplay* printed articles with titles like 'Lupe [Velez] and Johnny [Weissmuller] were Lovers' and 'I Had to Leave John Gilbert'" (98). The headlines of many subsequent Mickey interviews were equally suggestive, including "My Love Life and Other Things" (Mouse and Belfrage); "Confessions of Mickey Mouse" (Franklin), with a teaser claiming, "Mickey tells all!"; and "The Love Life of Mickey Mouse" (McEvoy). Throughout these publications, the Mouse makes several surprising statements about his private life, reiterating that he has just as much potential for such behavior as any of his live-action counterparts: "You ask, can an animated cartoon have intimate moments? Naturally, I answer. Why not an animated cartoon just as well as any of the human cartoons who call themselves stars in Hollywood nowadays? Intimate is hardly the word for some of my moments—and, if you will excuse the vulgarism, how!" (Mouse and Belfrage 68).

Almost all the disclosures involve amorous trysts. In one article, for instance, Mickey reveals that he was a one-time "boy-friend" of the "It Girl" Clara Bow, "coming chronologically between [actor] Gilbert Roland and [director] Victor Fleming in the list." He also admits to having been engaged on seven occasions to "prominent [live-action] movie actresses," including Polly Moran and Mary Nolan (Mouse and Belfrage 69, 96).[1] In another piece, Mickey states that he has already been through five marriages: four ending in divorce and one, in a relatively uncommon reference to his species, due to his wife being eaten by a cat (Franklin, "Confessions" 53). Most articles suggest that Mickey has now settled down with Minnie Mouse—either engaged or married—but even in these instances, there is room for speculation and innuendo. In 1932, *New Movie Magazine* reported gossip that Mickey and Minnie were to separate and that Minnie "continued to shop in smoked glasses, and avoid all interviewers." The article ultimately dispels these rumors, but not before exposing another past relationship between Mickey and a Hollywood actress—in this case, Marie Dressler (McEvoy 46).[2]

Mickey was not the only cartoon star to attract such attention. A *Screenland* article, "The Love Life of Betty Boop," dubbed Betty the "most fascinating of all picture stars." The byline promises that she "reveals some intimate soul secrets in her first interview," again placing a focus on the private rather than the public. Betty is shown as being complicit in these revelations. After being prompted by the interviewer to discuss her "aesthetic ideas" and her "Art," she reportedly giggles and asks, "Would you mind if I skipped all that hooey and talked about my love life? Because I'm a woman as well as an artist, you know." She claims that her off-screen romances are legion: "If I were to write a book about *my* life and loves it would make Isadora Duncan's hectic autobiography look like a treatise on refrigeration." She remains coy about naming all her partners, although she identifies child star Bobby Coogan as her "first love," and the article mentions rumors that "Gable, Cagney, Barrymore and [George] Brent have all applied for the chance to play opposite her" (Franklin, "Love Life" 63).

The prevalence of writings about the romantic entanglements of Hollywood figures has often been posited as an almost inevitable outcome of the public's increasing desire for information about stars. DeCordova notes that "sexuality has become a particularly privileged site of truth." In the fan system, the "sexual scandal is the primal scene of all star discourse, the only scenario that offers the promise of a full and satisfying disclosure of the star's identity" (*Picture Personalities* 141). By the 1920s, there was ample precedent for a movie fan to be suspicious about a live-action idol's sexual activities and proclivities. One of the most discussed and controversial scandals was the trial of the slapstick comedian Roscoe "Fatty" Arbuckle, accused of the rape and manslaughter of actress Virginia Rappe in 1921. Although Arbuckle was ultimately exonerated, his career was severely damaged, and the case became a cause célèbre for moral campaigners attacking the cinema. The studios responded by introducing morality clauses into many performer contracts, which "permitted the dismissal of any actor whose conduct hurt the company or the actor's own marketability." The problem, however, was not easily solved, and other scandals emerged throughout the decade (133). Furthermore, Barbas even suggests that certain fans became skeptical of publicity that was entirely positive, dismissing accounts that made no reference to any murkier aspects of a star's image as mere "ballyhoo" (101–108). The reports of Mickey's and Betty's occasionally tumultuous private lives appears to be a response (albeit a playful and "knowing" one) to this desire for complication and revelation in fan magazine articles.

The notion of audiences challenging the official representations of stars, and emphasizing their status as sexual beings, was played with in another (unofficial and illegal) media text of this period: the Tijuana bible. Short comic books that generally portrayed well-known figures in pornographic scenarios, the bibles initially adapted characters from newspaper comic strips (including some who had shifted into cartoons, such as Mutt and Jeff and Popeye), but increasingly featured stars of both live-action and animated cinema as well (Raymond 25). The comic "William Powell and Myrna Loy in 'Nuts to Will Hays!'" (Ever), for instance, sees the recurrent co-stars engage in an off-screen affair, performing a vast range of sexual acts upon each other. "Joan's Calls For D-Urante" features Joan Crawford and Jimmy Durante in a secret rendezvous. In almost every instance, hand-drawn representations of famous idols are presented in graphic detail, from images of throbbing appendages to unconcealed views of penetration.

The same was true of the bibles featuring animated stars. Betty Boop was a frequent "performer" in these pamphlets: "Betty Boop in 'Hot Pants'" involves the character indulging in anal sex during a visit to the doctor, while "Betty Boop in 'Flesh'" (Crustycrotch) sees her with a casting director. Even Disney characters were featured on occasion: "Mickey Mouse and Donald Duck," for instance, involves both Mickey and Donald pleasuring Minnie Mouse with erect, anthropomorphic penises. "Mickey Mouse in 'Of Mice and Women'" (Pisney) features Mickey and Goofy having sex with a human woman, as well as another sequence of Mickey and Minnie copulating.

Many bibles attempted to authenticate their outrageous "exposés" by incorporating elements of the star's well-publicized persona. For instance, recalling one of his catchphrases, Durante is shown exclaiming "Am I mortified" during lovemaking ("Joan's Calls"), while Popeye's co-star Wimpy is distracted from his own passionate encounters by his love of hamburgers ("J. Wellington Wimpy"). It is also suggestive that several bibles allowed animated and live-action figures to interact as "equals," essentially making explicit the sort of couplings hinted at in the fan magazine articles. "Mae West and Popeye" sees both the sailor and Wimpy indulging in intercourse with the Paramount star. "The Love Guide" features a variety of characters, including Popeye, taking part in an orgy supposedly directed by Mae West (herself a regular subject of these publications).

Pornographic images of animated stars have circulated extensively, if often illicitly, throughout the twentieth century. The unlawful status of the Tijuana bibles means that surviving production records are by no means extensive, but it has been estimated that sales could well have exceeded 20 million copies during the Great Depression (Holt 197). In a 1934 article on Mickey Mouse, the novelist E. M. Forster even makes a covert reference to the existence of "'privately shown' Mickeys" (i.e., animated sex films featuring Disney's star), although he claims that he has no desire to see one (81). Other similar productions—unofficial pornographic artwork and cartoons featuring the likes of Bugs Bunny and Tom and Jerry, distributed through a variety of underground channels by anonymous illustrators and animators—have continued to be made throughout the decades (Capino). Perhaps the most notorious example is the work of an artistic collective known as the Air Pirates, whose explicit representations of various Disney characters prompted a lawsuit directly from the Disney Company and a lengthy battle in the courts (Levin). The Air Pirates' case focused on boundaries of free speech and parody, although the artwork—as with virtually all the above—clearly also had a baser intent. As José B. Capino suggests, of the numerous "overlapping transgressions" in animated pornography based on popular cartoon figures, "the triumphant infringement of copyright" is likely the "least serious" for all but the parent studios (55).

While some studies have suggested that the primary focus of the Tijuana bibles was to amuse—and there is certainly a streak of (very crude) comedy running through many of the titles—Phillip Smith and Ellen Wright argue that the comics nonetheless "seem to coherently engage with the erotic potential of their stars" (153). As R. C. Harvey suggests, the bibles (and other such productions) offered, if not documentary evidence, then at the very least a reassurance that "despite the 'public appearances' of these [figures] where they seemed pristine and sexless, offstage they had 'secret sex lives' just like everyone else did" (6). Even though the images of live-action performers were simply caricatures, several commentators have ventured that the books still had the potential to thrill with their promise of visualizing a seemingly suppressed (or, perhaps, tantalizingly concealed) secret about the chosen subject.[3] The texts focusing on cartoon stars such as Mickey Mouse and Betty Boop ultimately do a very similar thing: artists and readers are speculating on the private lives and intimate parts of these figures, just as they did with Mae West, Clark Gable, and so on. Although animated stars do not truly have physical bodies, Capino suggests that the bibles emphasize the extent to which these characters have, at the very least, a "discursive existence" (61). The variety of reactions to such material, he points out,

> indicates both our recognition of the corporeality of these bodies (i.e., acknowledging those bodies as being somewhat like our own) and our willingness to project upon them similar values that we assign to real bodies (i.e., bodies like our own). . . . [The] bodies in animated pornography possess a phantom status that is arguably substantial and real enough to become the subject of angry protests and serious lawsuits (55–56, 61).

The fact that studios have attempted to legally suppress the circulation of pornographic images featuring animated characters reiterates that these are clearly "unauthorized" representations. Nevertheless, these texts offer some insight into the phenomenon of stardom. Richard Dyer has emphasized that a film star's image is a collection of "complex and contradictory" meanings from a variety of different sources and that "the star is all of it taken together." As Dyer notes, "Jean-Paul Belmondo imitating Humphrey Bogart in *À bout de souffle* is part of Bogart's image, just as anyone saying, in a mid-European accent, 'I want to be alone' reproduces, extends and inflects Greta Garbo's image" (*Heavenly Bodies* 8, 3). The Tijuana bibles may be an extreme example of this, but no less valid in execution. As Smith and Wright suggest, such materials "offer the historian a glimpse of unofficial popular discourse, to see what audiences knew or guessed of the [stars'] private lives . . . [and to comprehend certain fans'] hunger for Hollywood scandal—the dirtier the better" (169). Seeing a character like Mickey Mouse engaging in such acts might seem rather startling to viewers familiar with only the Mouse's "official" persona, which is now heavily controlled by the Disney Studio and largely presented as a paragon of innocence. However, these "unofficial" works still form part of Mickey's overall image, reiterating the many, at times paradoxical, ways in which different consumers can engage with and interpret the star.

Were the creators of the cartoon stars entirely naïve about these potential readings? Animator Shamus Culhane alleges in his autobiography that, during the production of *Snow White and the Seven Dwarfs* (1937), "[t]here was a spontaneous avalanche of pornographic drawings from all over the [Disney] studio. Drawings of Snow White being gang raped by the dwarfs, and mass orgies among the dwarfs themselves. Even the old witch was involved." Culhane notes that some of the drawings, "were about comic sexual aberrations that Krafft-Ebing would never have dreamed of" (180). Leslie Cabarga similarly notes that the artists in the Fleischer studio contributed "a scene apiece to a special stag cartoon made when the studio moved to Florida. One scene had Betty [Boop] sexually assaulting Popeye!" (81). Most of these claims are ultimately rumors, and it is unclear whether such material still exists, or even if it was produced at all. At the very least, Cabarga (133–136) reproduces some pages from a copy of *Fleischer's Animated News*, an official studio newsletter produced by and intended exclusively for those in the industry. The front cover shows Betty Boop wearing a swimsuit at the beach and looking rather shocked, with other characters from the Fleischer stable standing behind her and laughing. A second drawing from the reverse angle reveals that the back of Betty's costume has ripped open, revealing her bare bottom.

Another surviving text is *Eveready Harton in Buried Treasure* (ca. 1928), a short pornographic cartoon reportedly produced as a collaborative effort by artists from a number of the silent era's major animation studios. This production provides a startling narrative of sexual debauchery. Although the film does not feature an existing animated protagonist, the main character, Eveready Harton, has a pun-based name, offering a ruder variation of cartoon figures such as Colonel Heeza Liar and Paul Terry's Farmer Al Falfa. He is presented as a fairly generic human male (perhaps with certain elements amalgamated from comic strip and animated stars Mutt and Jeff), but displays a pronounced and unsheathed erection. As with most mainstream cartoons from the period, the majority of gags in this film are based around the elasticity of both the animated body and otherwise inanimate objects, even though the extreme subject matter of these routines—including penetration, (accidental) homosexual sex, and bestiality—could never have been shown in a regular production. Eveready's penis is essentially

FIGURE 2.1. A crude take on mainstream animation aesthetics in *Eveready Harton in Buried Treasure* (ca. 1928).

analogous to Felix the Cat's tail, in that it can be detached and transformed at will to fulfill various functions (fig. 2.1): at one point, Eveready uses his appendage as a sword in a duel with a rival suitor for, disturbingly, the affections of a donkey.

Of course, like the Fleischer newsletter material, this film was never released to the public; most accounts suggest that *Buried Treasure* was made for a private event to honor the artist Winsor McCay (see, for instance, Cohen 12). Nonetheless, its insider-joke status offers a revealing meta-commentary by the animators themselves on the traditional boundaries of the animated body. The film is by no means an undiscovered "master-piece"—it is, like the Tijuana bibles, extremely juvenile and one-track in its presentation of a parade of sexual acts. Nevertheless, the infusing of this crude imagery with comedic and protagonist-led narrative formulas found in many animated star cartoons prompts a rereading of the mainstream studio releases of the period.

The "rubber-hose" animation style, which transitioned from the silent era into the first years of sound cartoons, presented a malleable world capable of being manipulated in potentially subversive ways (as explicitly shown in *Buried Treasure*). Sean Griffin defines the Disney Studios' output between 1924 and 1930—including Mickey Mouse's first three years of cartoons—as embodying a spirit of the "carnivalesque," suggesting that the films "revel in the possibilities of sexuality and the potentiality of the body" (6). Images of cow udders recur through several of the early Mickey films, with much of the humor emerging from their exaggerated, rubber-like movement, swinging from side-to-side between the creature's legs. *Plane Crazy* (1928), the first Mickey cartoon to be produced, features a sequence in which a runaway plane careens down a road with a cow running ahead, desperately trying to avoid its path. One shot, evoking a three-dimensional viewpoint, sees the plane's propeller making contact with the creature and throwing it in the air, briefly filling the frame with a close-up of its udder. The cow lands on the back of the plane and Mickey, who has been chasing the vehicle, tries unsuccessfully twice to hoist himself up by grabbing one of the cow's udders. On both attempts, he ends up showered in milk squirted directly from the grasped organ.

Variations of these two gags recur in a number of subsequent Mickey films, such as *Steamboat Willie* (1928) and *Mickey's Choo-Choo* (1929). J. P. Telotte reads even further into the representation of the cow udder in *The Shindig* (1930), wherein we see the Mouse's co-star, Clarabelle Cow, in her home (a barn):

> [She is] implicitly "naked" and reading the scandalous Elinor Glyn novel *Three Weeks* (1907). When her country suitor Horace Horsecollar rings her doorbell/cowbell, Clarabelle looks embarrassed, quickly hides the book within her bedding and then dashes behind a partition to don a covering for her udders before admitting him. While the cow rushing to cover her udders is in part just another of those barnyard gags, this scene clearly operates on a more sophisticated level as well. . . . [It] suggests a point of transition, an interest in or openness to modern sexuality that is still bound up with an older attitude and a tendency to keep that sexuality repressed or hidden, as most cartoons tried to do. ("Disney's Cows" 220–221)

Telotte indicates that barnyard gags had generally avoided scandal in the 1920s because they were linked to a seemingly innocent "natural" world. Clarabelle was a cow, and the presentation of a real cow's udders in a live-action film was considered acceptable during this period. Yet, at the same time, Clarabelle's response in the scene reflects her overriding anthropomorphic status: her "shame" and desire to cover up parts of her body are human attributes, which have parallels with deCordova's notion of an underlying "truth" relating to the star image.

The Shindig is an early example of animation creating public controversy, with a report in the *New York Times* indicating that the film was banned in Ohio because of the Clarabelle sequence. Mickey did not feature directly in the scene, but the article refers to him specifically in relation to the scandal: "Although there is no morality clause in the contract of Mickey Mouse, that vivacious rodent of the animated . . . cartoons must lead a model life on the screen to meet the approval of censorship boards all over the world. Mickey does not drink, smoke or cut any suggestive capers" ("The Censor!" X5). This pronouncement about Mickey's "good" behavior was not strictly true in 1930, although his on-screen actions—and his off-screen admissions in fan magazines—would certainly be curtailed over the course of the decade. The period was ultimately one of transition for the Hollywood system, with many performers' images (both live-action and animated) undergoing significant modification.

Hollywood and Content Regulation

Lea Jacobs and Richard Maltby have argued that changes in cinematic content and star behavior must be considered in relation to issues concerning wider industry reform (2). The 1910s had seen the growth of a number of integrated film studios, whose rigorous control of production, distribution, and, in several cases, exhibition was viewed by some as anti-competitive (see chapter 6). For the most part, attempts to instigate external regulation during this decade were either sidestepped or restricted to a limited range of territories (Geltzer 53). However, the emergent star scandals of the 1920s, including the Arbuckle trial, not only emboldened moral campaign groups, but also provided valuable leverage for those wishing to put other Hollywood business practices under scrutiny.

In 1922, the major studios voluntarily formed an organization called the Motion Picture Producers and Distributors of America (MPPDA), popularly known as the "Hays Office" in reference to its president Will Hays.[4]

The intention was to reassure critics that the industry could be trusted to self-police its product, a goal that was achieved in part by choosing its battles strategically. As Jacobs and Maltby note, the studios could sidestep allegations regarding antitrust activities by engaging directly with debates on censorship, which were "of greater public interest, and could also be resolved at less economic risk" (2). The decade saw the introduction of initiatives designed to take a proactive stance against problematic material. The Studio Relations Committee (SRC), for instance, was created in 1927 to liaise with the public and producers. That same year saw the publication of the "Don'ts and Be Carefuls" list. In 1929, and following the growth of sound filmmaking, the MPPDA discussed renewing and further clarifying its guidelines, which culminated in a new document, the Motion Picture Production Code. By 1930, the Code was theoretically in effect and contained a number of pronouncements about cinematic content, particularly in relation to sexuality and crime, drawing heavily from complaints and excisions made by local censor boards over the preceding decade (Maltby, "The Genesis" 11; Maltby, "Documents" 33; Vasey, "Beyond Sex and Violence" 66).

One of the problems with all these schemes, however, was the implementation. The boundaries of acceptability were still not entirely defined: the Code did allow some sensitive subject matter to be approached, and disagreements continued to arise over whether certain films treated these subjects in an appropriate or exploitative manner. Although the major studios agreed in 1930 not to release any works that did not meet the SRC's approval, Jacobs notes that the arbitration process was usually sympathetic to the filmmakers in the early years of the decade, and recommendations from the committee "were easily ignored" ("Industry Self-Regulation" 89–90). As the effects of the Great Depression worsened, a number of producers turned more explicitly to controversial, but often profitable, areas that skirted the edges of the Code's guidelines (Curry 66). Live-action movies such as *Three on a Match* (1932) and *Female* (1933) hinted at protagonists engaging in casual sexual liaisons, alcohol consumption, and substance abuse. The period therefore saw Hollywood outwardly proclaiming a standard of ethics, yet the product itself did not always fully conform.

The short animation of the early sound era was similarly capable of transgression. Mickey Mouse's fledgling screen appearances, for instance, presented the character as somewhat devious, with seemingly no qualms about committing questionable acts. *Steamboat Willie* sees the Mouse shirk

FIGURE 2.2. Mickey Mouse as an unrepentant convict in *The Chain Gang* (1930).

his duties and try to impress his love interest, Minnie. Mickey is caught by the ship's captain and forced to peel potatoes as punishment. He throws a potato at a parrot that is taunting him, causing the bird to fall into the sea. The film ends with the Mouse laughing merrily as gurgled cries for help can be heard in the background. *The Chain Gang* (1930) even presents Mickey as a convict serving time in jail. The protagonist shows little penitence for his (undisclosed) crimes: a parade of disheveled and miserable animals paying their debt to society at the beginning of the narrative is countered by the sight of Mickey happily sitting on a ball and chain that is being dragged by the rest of the inmates (fig. 2.2).

Mickey also initially proved rather boisterous in his flirtations with Minnie. He is cast as the "good" suitor in these films, regularly contrasted against more vicious antagonists such as Peg-Leg Pete (whose advances Minnie never wants to reciprocate). Nevertheless, he is by no means the inoffensive figure of later Disney products. Mickey shows a degree of sexual aggressiveness toward Minnie in *Plane Crazy* when he grabs her by force and tries to kiss her. When she refuses and slaps him in the face, he throws her out of his plane, forcing Minnie to use her bloomers as a parachute. Indeed, a repeated gag in many early shorts involves Minnie's underwear being revealed, grabbed, or even pulled down. As Mickey tries to use a crane to carry Minnie onto the boat in *Steamboat Willie*, for instance, the hook "comes to life," lifts up Minnie's skirt, and hoists her by her underwear, leaving her hanging and exposed in midair.

The Fleischers' cartoons featuring Betty Boop also indulged in humor based around the possibility of nudity. Betty first appeared as an unnamed prototype, seemingly originally intended as a one-off cameo, in the *Talkartoon* film *Dizzy Dishes* (1930). The plot revolves around the character Bimbo the Dog acting as a nightclub waiter and chef, eventually being distracted by one of the club's singers. In this original incarnation, Betty is presented as a canine love interest for Bimbo, and yet she is also anthropomorphized as a parody of human nightclub performers, wearing a low-cut dress that displays ample cleavage as well as her curvaceous figure and long legs. Betty's potential as a star seems to have been recognized almost immediately, and her visual appearance was, over subsequent installments, progressively streamlined to downplay the rather bizarre bestial quality found in her first outing. By early 1931, only a pair of drooping dog ears suggested her animal status, and *Mask-A-Raid* (1931) turned these into a pair of hooped earrings, completing the transformation.

Even while the character design was being reworked, Betty's body (if not face) was decidedly human, and the cartoons created humor in this being partially exposed. In *Mysterious Mose* (1930), for instance, Betty is so scared by the shadows in her bedroom that her nightdress literally flies off—not once, but twice. On both occasions, Betty's breasts are barely covered by the bed sheets. In *Silly Scandals* (1931), during Boop's brief appearance as one of a number of vaudeville acts, her dress falls down and reveals her bra—again on two separate occasions—as she sings a particular section of a song. The early Mickey Mouse films, as noted, occasionally featured reveals of Minnie's undergarments and somewhat suggestive representations of cow udders, but the gags involving Betty increasingly referred directly to human sexuality. Even though she wore a skirt and had some anthropomorphic attributes, Minnie could still be conveniently categorized as a mouse to diffuse potential criticisms. Betty Boop, by contrast, was never entirely canine in her appearance, and the eradication of those lingering elements brought her even closer in representation to a live-action screen siren. Once Betty was fully human, the "revealing" gags continued apace. Many cartoons saw her dress ride up in some way, displaying her underwear. Another frequent image, and perhaps the most iconic, involved Betty's suggestive garter belt, usually falling down or at the very least drawing attention to her exposed legs and short skirt. The garter became such a symbol of Betty's sexuality that certain gags drew attention to her displaying it in somewhat incongruous contexts: in *Betty Boop's Life Guard* (1934), for instance, she wears it with a swimming costume at the beach.

As the decade continued, a number of reform groups began to complain more vociferously about alleged transgressions of the Code. Most significantly, the National Legion of Decency, an organization established by the Catholic Church in 1933, started encouraging boycotts of features that were deemed immoral. The increasing numbers of local censorship cases, as well as the aggressive social policies that were being enacted by newly elected president Franklin D. Roosevelt under the New Deal, renewed studio concerns that a federal investigation into their affairs could be imminent. Vasey notes that, in March 1933, the MPPDA board of directors "issued a statement reaffirming their commitment to the Production Code. Hays recognized that this reaffirmation had to amount to more than an empty gesture if the industry was to escape governmental intervention" (*The World According to Hollywood* 128). This led to the creation of the Production Code Administration (PCA), headed by Joseph Breen, which began its operations in mid-1934. Unlike the Studio Relations Committee that it replaced, the new body was much stricter in its approach: producers risked a hefty fine if they ignored the declarations of the PCA, and films would be issued a certificate of approval specifically indicating to the public that they had been cleared according to the rules of the Code.[5]

The apparent officiousness of the PCA from 1934 onward has prompted a reading of the preceding years of the decade as ones of cinematic debauchery, only reluctantly tempered by this new regulator. The period from 1930 to 1934—in essence, *after* the Code was actually written, but *before* it was aggressively implemented by Breen—has been retrospectively termed "pre-Code." This period is often discussed as a unique moment of subversiveness, in which producers were frequently defying, and perhaps even thumbing their noses at, those wishing to "censor" the movies. In recent years, Richard Maltby has made a valuable qualification to such a perspective: he suggests that pre-Code has essentially become a latter-day "critic's genre, much like '*film noir*' or 'melodrama,' with no roots in industry practice" ("The Production Code" 242). Although on-screen examples of bad behavior are not uncommon in early-1930s American cinema, this was by no means a unified effort actively pursued by all Hollywood filmmakers, nor was it entirely self-contained within the so-called pre-Code years.

Kevin Brownlow's book *Behind the Mask of Innocence*, a survey of censorship and the presence of "sex, violence, prejudice, [and] crime" in silent live-action films, has a stated aim to "set the record straight" about this era of production. He suggests that the lack of distribution of the majority of these works in modern times has led to the misassumption of their relative purity compared to the first years of sound filmmaking (1). In the case of animation, a great deal of the supposed pre-Code work drew upon conventions from this earlier period. The impoverished and often rambunctious rural settings of Mickey's initial appearances have precedents in many silent comedy series, such as Hal Roach's live-action *Our Gang* series and cartoons such as Paul Terry's *Aesop's Fables*. Disney's own previous works, the *Alice Comedies* and *Oswald the Lucky Rabbit*, also frequently reveled in this arena. Indeed, Mickey's early characterization drew heavily from the persona of Oswald, and much of his aggressiveness can be traced to this preexisting, but perhaps less remembered, set of films.[6]

There is, however, little evidence to suggest that silent animation was subjected to the kinds of regulation subsequently faced by Mickey Mouse, despite the continuity in terms of content.[7] This may reflect the comparatively marginalized position of the short film—even following the rise of the PCA, features received more attention than the supporting works—but also the inconsistency and segregation of local censorship boards of the time. The increased fame of a number of animated stars by the early 1930s may also help to explain why scandal appears to have been more intense in the pre-Code era. Virtually all the examples of "censorship" of Mickey's films during this period were still isolated, regional decisions, and yet the character's notoriety meant that these stories were considered newsworthy in national publications. A strong focus was thus placed on the Mouse's meaning and influence as a star in a manner that had rarely been extended to previous cartoon protagonists. This was posited by several contemporary commentators, including Terry Ramsaye in a February 1931 article in the *Motion Picture Herald*:

Mickey Mouse, the artistic offspring of Walt Disney, has fallen afoul of the censors in a big way, largely just because of his amazing success. Papas and mamas, especially mamas, have spoken vigorously to censor boards and elsewhere about what a devilish, naughty little mouse Mickey turned out to be. Now we find that Mickey is not to drink, smoke or tease the stock in the barnyard. Mickey has been spanked.

It is the old, old story. If nobody knows you, you can do everything, and if everybody knows you, you can't do anything—except what [everyone] approves, which is very little of anything. It has happened often enough among the human stars of the screen and now it gets even the little fellow in black and white who is no thicker than a pencil mark and exists solely in a state of mind. ("Terry Ramsaye Records" 10)

Although emphasizing Mickey's status as a drawing, Ramsaye nonetheless highlights that the Mouse's censuring had parallels with existing live-action performers, including those working within the comedy genre. As Joe Adamson notes, "Charlie Chaplin, Harpo Marx, and W. C. Fields started life as devilish characters and softened their comic malevolence in the interest of greater audience sympathy" (*The Walter Lantz Story* 180). In each instance, the actor's on-screen bad behavior initially passed with little comment, but became the target of criticism from some quarters once the films were more widely seen and discussed, requiring a rapid alteration of his or her persona in a bid to avoid further scandal. The Chaplin example is particularly significant since it occurred during the Tramp's rise to prominence in the mid-1910s, well before the emergence of the more formalized structures of the Production Code Administration.

As Maltby suggests, any sense that the industry truly came to terms with content regulation only post-1934 is a fallacy, and one that fails to account for the overarching commercial goals of the Hollywood system. While some filmmakers undoubtedly experimented with edgier material in the hope of making a quick profit in the Depression-addled pre-Code era, there were both short- and long-term risks to such an approach. Making cuts to release prints could be expensive—especially with the comparatively inflexible sound-on-disc process used by a number of studios in the 1930s—and an outright ban by a local censor would mean the complete loss of revenue (Maltby, "The Genesis" 15). A scandalous work also had the potential to be damaging to the ongoing profitability of the studio, the star, and even the industry as a whole. Disney's decision to make refinements to Mickey's star image at a relatively early stage of the 1930s, much like Chaplin many years before, had arguably much more to do with economic self-interest than with an explicit act of external censorship.

Part of the financial incentive to deliver "reputable" animated product during this period was the increased targeting of young cinemagoers as a specific demographic. Although these cartoons were made primarily for exhibition ahead of a feature aimed at an adult or, at the very least, "general" audience, a second market began to emerge in the form of matinee screenings for children.[8] In 1929, Disney launched such an initiative called "The Mickey Mouse Club," which rapidly spread to cinemas throughout the United States and even internationally.[9] By January 1932, it was claimed that membership figures were close to "that of the Boy Scouts of America and the Girl Scouts . . . combined" ("Mickey Mouse's Fourth Birthday" 43). As deCordova notes, matinee clubs had actually been seen as a positive influence by reformers, and many of the Mickey Mouse events did emphasize community-minded activities in addition to screening movies and advertising merchandise ("Tracing the Child Audience" 218–221). Attendees also pledged to abide by the Club's creed:

I will be a square shooter in my home, in school, on the playground, wherever I may be. I will be truthful and honorable and strive always to make myself a better and more useful citizen. I will respect my elders and help the aged, the helpless and children smaller than myself. In short, I will be a good American. (Qtd. in deCordova, "Tracing the Child Audience" 221)

Furthermore, as Robert Heide and John Gilman note, "calling out in unison, the matinee boys and girls would declare: 'Mickey Mice do not swear, smoke, cheat, or lie!' Mickey Mouse also instructed kids on how to brush their teeth, wash behind their ears, and make their own beds" (*Disneyana* 33). Given this paratextual emphasis on Mickey as a beacon of good behavior, instances of the Mouse or his associates contravening this advice in the films had the potential to attract the ire of moral groups and thereby threaten the viability of the matinee screenings.

From 1931 onward, it is possible to identify a slow-building momentum toward "civilizing" the character of Mickey Mouse. An immediate casualty was the udder gag; later appearances of Clarabelle Cow featured her wearing a skirt. As Griffin notes, films based around characters throwing parties and "[shimmying] to ragtime music or [imitating] 'cooch' dancing"—acts frowned upon by the Code since they emphasized notions of sexuality and the body—took a little longer to disappear. However, even these raucous musical cartoons eventually morphed into Mickey simply "listening to [Minnie] play the piano in her living room" (14). The Mouse ultimately became a "respectable" boyfriend, arranging dates and turning up at Minnie's house with chocolates and flowers in true gentlemanly fashion. These actions are clearly a world away from his forcefulness in *Plane Crazy* and his song about stealing to the henhouse in the barnyard for some romantic time in the film *Minnie's Yoo-Hoo* (1930). In the later cartoons, Mickey and Minnie also become property owners, assuming the value systems of their new suburban surroundings and tending toward sentimentality rather than crude barnyard gags.

The shaping of Mickey's persona—as with many forms of stardom—arguably took place just as much outside the films as within them. The extent to which Mickey had changed by 1931 is indicated by Disney's legal action against rival animation producer Van Beuren for plagiarism of the Mouse in a number of cartoons. A *New York Times* headline stated that "'Mickey Mouse' Sues to 'Save Reputation'," and the article implies that Mickey *personally* "filed suit . . . through Walt Disney Productions, Ltd. . . . [because] his alleged double is doing all sorts of things which he would not think of doing" (26). *New Movie Magazine* also claimed that Mickey had telephoned one of its reporters to complain that "some bozo has gotten together a flock of mice and is imitating me, and Minnie, and all our pals. . . . They look something like us and I'm afraid people will think they are us" (qtd. in "The Hollywood Who's Who" 31, 93). One cited incident of misbehavior—in which "the alleged Mickey's [girlfriend] lost important garments" ("'Mickey Mouse' Sues" 26)—occurs in several of these knock-off films. For instance, Van Beuren's *A Close Call* (1929) sees the fake "Mickey" unhook "Minnie's" skirt so that, when she jumps in the air, it falls from her body. "Mickey" squeezes the garment and produces music as if it were an accordion, and "Minnie" dances happily until she discovers her state of undress (fig. 2.3). Yet, the sequence is largely in the spirit of many such underwear gags in early *official* Mickey films, such as *Steamboat Willie* (where Mickey also created an accordion from an unrelated object—in that case, a pig). The Disney Company's complaint appears to essentially deny Mickey's past, suggesting that the gags in Van Beuren's production were *entirely* out of character.

A 1934 article in *Photoplay* titled "Is Walt Disney a Menace to Our Children?" further highlights the shift in responses to Disney's mouse. The author initially flirts with controversy by suggesting that one of his

FIGURE 2.3. Fake Mickey and Minnie behaving badly in *A Close Call* (1929).

friends, a "father of six-year-old twins . . . has to reject for juvenile consumption about six out of eight Mickey Mouse films, for such reasons as the [drunken] horse and [a violent swarm of] wasps" in *The Steeple Chase* (1933) (McCord 30).[10] The rest of the article, however, semi-humorously charts the author's frustration at trying to find anyone else who will say anything bad about Disney's work. It concludes with a psychiatrist, Dr. Walter Beran Wolfe, stating, "I think Mickey Mouse is a civilizing influence [upon American childhood]," seemingly overriding the earlier objections raised by the author's friend (qtd. in McCord 103). An article written in the same year by Walt Disney himself reiterates the Mouse's newfound respectability, again presenting Mickey as a collaborator in the process:

> If Mickey were to say or do one thing to hurt the child audience in any way, he would die of shame. . . . But this will never happen . . . . If our gang ever put Mickey in a situation less wholesome than sunshine, Mickey would take Minnie by the hand and move to some other studio. . . . No, Mickey would never stand for it. He is never mean or ugly.

He never lies nor cheats nor steals. He is a clean, happy, little fellow who loves life and folk. . . . Sex is just another word to Mickey, and the story of the travelling salesman of no more interest than the ladies' lingerie department. . . . Now how could a fine, upstanding lad like Mickey ever do or say anything to hurt a child? ("The Cartoon's Contribution" 138)

By mid-1933, the fan magazine "confessional" pieces about Mickey had been phased out, and the studio's approach to publicity was considerably more careful. Note, for instance, a series of articles titled "Mickey Mouse's Movie-Go-Round," which ran in *New Movie Magazine* between August and December 1933. Billed as "the world's most popular actor," Mickey comments on the latest Hollywood news, often making comedic but abstemious remarks. For instance, on word that "Herbert Marshall will have the chief male role" in *Solitaire Man* (1933), the Mouse merely quips, "This should click! It's in the cards" (Mouse and Horne 55). There is still clearly a desire to evoke Mickey as an off-screen presence and the contemporary of many live-action stars, but there is no longer any attempt to court controversy with innuendo or salacious revelations. In a 1947 article in the *New York Times*, the author Frank S. Nugent claims to have asked Walt Disney if he could interview Mickey directly, only to be refused. Disney is reported as saying:

I dunno . . . . It's a little irregular. We've kinda frowned on direct interviews. The Mouse's private life isn't especially colorful. He's never been the type that would go in for swimming pools and night clubs; more the simple country boy at heart. Lives on a quiet residential street, has occasional dates with his girl friend Minnie, doesn't drink or smoke, likes the movies and band concerts, things like that. (Qtd. in Nugent, "That Million-Dollar Mouse" 22)

Although his "country boy" origins had been a part of the early pre-Code publicity, the notion that the Mouse never really transgressed is contradicted by the earlier interviews discussed at the beginning of this chapter. For instance, one 1930 article saw the Mouse detail an apparent off-screen escapade in which he suffered hallucinations as a result of drinking bootleg alcohol, an act that, he suggests, then inspired the plot of his 1929 cartoon *Haunted House* (Mouse and Belfrage 68).[11] These later claims of Mickey's sobriety and sedate home life explicitly ignore the manner in which the star had been publicized in the past. The shift in Mickey's persona in fan magazine discourse was certainly not uncommon within the Hollywood of that period: James Castonguay's study of Myrna Loy, for instance, offers a valuable insight into how Loy was initially evoked in the early 1930s as an "exotic siren," only to be rebranded both on- and off-screen in 1934 as the "perfect wife" (222). Barbas also argues that, in 1934, the film industry as a whole took a much more restrictive attitude to fan magazine content than in the previous few years, with many producers now ensuring that all articles were submitted to them and vigilantly "edited and checked . . . before publication" (99).

The cleaning up of Mickey Mouse predated the rise of the PCA and re-iterates that not all alterations of star behavior were entirely dictated by this organization. While there were undoubtedly some figures—such as Mae West and Betty Boop—whose films changed significantly (and seemingly reluctantly) only in 1934, Jacobs and Maltby have argued that the notion that "the Code was inoperative or ineffective between 1930 and 1934 is simply incorrect" (1). Reflecting the economic imperatives outlined above, few producers aimed to deliberately bait the censor. Some filmmakers certainly went further than others in the presentation of challenging material in the pre-Code era, but there was still often an attempt to justify this within the established framework of conduct—an act helped by the vagaries of some of the documented rules.[12]

The Code stated, for instance, that "undressing scenes should be avoided, and never used save where essential to the plot" (qtd. in Maltby, "Documents" 54). In the pre-1934 Betty Boop cartoons, the sequences of the starlet disrobing are thus generally tied to some narrative requirement: in *Stopping the Show* (1932), Boop is presented as a vaudeville impressionist who is sporadically required to undertake costume changes in order to mimic different famous personalities. She does this on stage, and although a vanity screen prevents a clear view for either the diegetic or cinematic audience, one instance shows her dangling a pair of underwear on top of the partition. *Is My Palm Read?* (1933) sees Betty shipwrecked and washed up on a remote island, requiring her to again seek privacy in order to remove her wet clothes. What she believes to be a rock is actually a giant tortoise, which walks away and leaves her standing in her underwear. If these excuses appear somewhat flimsy, they are arguably no less so than many live-action productions of the same period. *Night Nurse* (1931), for example, used the fact that the female staff would need to change in and out of uniform to dramatize several undressing scenes in the hospital and nurses' quarters. The looseness of the qualification "save where essential to the plot" permitted some opportunity to test the boundaries in the formative years of the Code, relying on plausible deniability as a means of containing and hopefully defusing any censor's objections (Vasey, *The World According to Hollywood* 112). As a further example, the Code noted that "dances which emphasize indecent movements are to be regarded as obscene" (qtd. in Maltby, "Documents" 54). *Boop-Oop-a-Doop* (1932) plays with this restriction by initially appearing to show Betty in a skimpy costume performing an exotic belly dance, only for the "camera" to pan back and reveal that it was simply her image on a flag, with the illusion of misbehavior created by the material shimmering in the wind. A topless hula dance in *Betty Boop's Bamboo Isle* (1932)—in which only a strategically placed lei covers her otherwise bare chest—was at least partially downplayed by Betty's reconfiguration in this installment as an island native, rather than a "civilized" American woman.

Betty's star image between 1930 and 1934 is ultimately full of contradictions, indicated by the disparity between the following two critics' retrospective readings: Michael Gould describes Betty as "the absurdist's sexpot," arguing that "beneath her naive face and quivering body is the heart of a slut" (137), while Charles Garvie takes the opposing view that "beneath her exaggerated, sluttish body is the heart of the eternal innocent. . . . [Betty is] only looking for love and affection [but is] cursed with a body and sexuality which attracts all the wrong kind of attention" (15). Garvie's view is generally more accurate, particularly in terms of the narratives contained within the films themselves. Despite her frequent disrobing, she is usually portrayed as ashamed and embarrassed when she realizes that other characters (or in some cases, breaking the fourth wall, the cinema viewer) can see her in this state. For instance, the "accidental" reveal of her underwear in *Is My Palm Read?* sees Betty blush and say "excuse me" to the audience for revealing too much. Although she is often positioned as a "flapper"—a trope prevalent in 1920s America, describing a young woman who "could go out into the world and have madcap, even sexy, adventures" (Basinger 413)—the films generally suggest that Betty is oblivious to the desire that her revealing dress sense provokes in the male characters. In *Boop-Oop-a-Doop*, her outfit draws the attention of the lecherous circus owner, who threatens her job if she does not yield to him. Heather Hendershot's insightful discussion of *Betty Boop's Big Boss* (1932) notes that

Betty is given employment as a secretary because she is attractive to the manager—a group of "plain" women also interviewing for the position are summarily dismissed—but she is then sexually harassed. Boop stands as both a symbol of modernity, but also a victim of it, providing a "moral" of sorts for those who would disapprove of her appearance ("Secretary" 127). In this regard, Betty seems to be slightly less audacious than some of the live-action performers working in what Jacobs has termed the "fallen woman" film, sometimes referred to at the time simply as the "sex picture" (*The Wages of Sin* x). Mae West, for instance, was frequently shown in her pre-Code films indulging in knowing double entendres, and Jean Harlow's character in *Red-Headed Woman* (1932) works her way up the social ladder by sleeping around, breaking up marriages, and even attempting murder. In contrast, Betty tends to be presented as the unwitting victim, rather than deliberately setting out to cause trouble.

This reading is complicated, however, by the title sequence used for many of the Betty Boop cartoons before the creation of the PCA. The version included in *Betty Boop's Penthouse* (1933) is indicative of the usual approach. A medium close-up of Betty strutting along is framed by a large credit "FEATURING / BETTY BOOP" (with a smaller note "ASSISTED BY / BIMBO AND KOKO"), highlighting her star status. A song, performed by a male singer, plays in conjunction with the scene:

> *Made of Pen and Ink,*
> *She can win you with a wink [Betty says "yoo-hoo," and winks directly at the "camera"],*
> *Ain't she cute? [Betty delivers her catchphrase "Boop-oop-a-doop" with a giggle]*
> *Sweet Betty!*

Eric Smoodin suggests that this sequence takes on an "extradiegetic status," with Betty appearing essentially as "herself" rather than the persona found in the main section of the cartoon. The song emphasizes Boop's apparent desirability to members of the cinema audience—"whom Betty beckons with her wink and 'yoo-hoo'"—dismissing her "pen and ink" origins as being a potential barrier to this attraction (31). Betty is shown to personally endorse this viewing position, despite her opposition to male wantonness within the narratives. A number of contemporary fan magazine correspondents also appear to have overlooked Betty's "innocence": an unnamed reviewer of the short *Minnie the Moocher* (1932) notes that she "seems to be getting more sexy and alluring each time" ("Reviews of Sound Shorts" 10), while another proclaims her appearance in *Betty Boop's Penthouse* to be "pert and appealing" ("Showmen's Reviews" 41). The pseudonymous columnist Phil M. Daly describes Betty as having a "doll-like face BUT also a mature figure with oo-la-la-curves and a boudoir languor in her walk if you get what we mean" and even suggests that the Fleischers have "a million dollars wrapped up in her com-hither [*sic*] eyes and sexy seductiveness" ("Along the Rialto [1932]" 3). Whether or not most viewers legitimately got a voyeuristic thrill from these animated antics, Boop's body was frequently discussed, and even promoted in advertising, in a similar manner to that of live-action "pin-up" stars.

It is perhaps curious, then, that Betty rarely seems to have been targeted for censorship in these pre-Code films. Indeed, the few criticisms reported during this period almost exclusively refer to areas other than sex. A Nebraskan exhibitor's commentary on *Is My Palm Read?* in the *Motion Picture Herald* complains not because of the unsuitability of several scenes depicting Betty's near nudity but rather because of the presence of "horror" elements in the form of ghosts and the characters dabbling in the occult ("What the Picture Did for Me" 56). *Variety*'s brief story on *Red Hot Mamma* (1934) being banned by the British Board of Film Censors notes that it was "unsuitable for public exhibition" primarily because of "the comic treatment of hell" ("Boop Pic Nix" 13). In the United States, however, the film seems to have drawn little comment.

Betty cartoons do appear to have been regularly screened as part of youth-focused events, and one can find examples of matinee clubs, like those devoted to Mickey, being formed specifically around her star image (Sargent 19). In 1933, it was noted that a Betty Boop "birthday picnic" hosted by a Texas exhibitor attracted more than twenty-five-hundred guests, while in the following year, a Detroit operator reported that six thousand kids attended a "Betty Boop party as a Saturday matinee" ("Betty Boop Picnic" 70; "Detroit News" 4).

The fact that Betty generated less controversy than Mickey Mouse—despite more frequently taking liberties with the interpretation of the Code—highlights once again that many subjective factors play into an audience response. As Ramona Curry argues in relation to Mae West, it was not that her apparent on- or off-screen indiscretions were entirely unique, or even necessarily the worst examples of the time, but for various "economic and ideological" reasons, it was *her* star image that rapidly congealed into "a dominant personification of transgressive female sexuality," often at the expense of a closer focus on her contemporaries. Betty would seem to have more in common with West, but it was Mickey's greater fame—and by extension, the prominence given to reports of his misdemeanors—that arguably led to him, rather than Boop, playing the most significant "iconographic role" in the discourse surrounding the regulation of animated stars (58, 67).

Betty's persona did not, however, entirely survive the changing landscape of movie morality following the rise of the PCA. As Hendershot argues, it would be inaccurate to call Betty's later movies "censored": in all likelihood, Paramount, the series distributor, "advised Fleischer to make Betty's cartoons less risqué," and the changes were enacted to circumvent the likelihood of *future* censorship ("Secretary" 118). In this regard, short films did face one additional challenge when it came to the process of regulation. Unlike features, which required the submission of a script to the PCA during preproduction and thus theoretically permitted the elimination and/or reworking of contentious material *before* undertaking the expense of filming, cartoons were generally scrutinized only once completed.[13] Given the cost of creating the high-quality animation displayed in many cartoons of the 1930s, producers had to be careful in this more sensitive era that their investment would not simply hit the cutting room floor after being submitted to the PCA.[14] Even more so than before, the inclusion of any problematic material was a financial gamble and not just an ideological or moral issue.

The post-1934 Fleischer films downplay Betty's sexuality considerably. *A Little Soap and Water* (1935) is fairly indicative of Boop's later roles, presenting her in a long dress that fully covers her chest and legs and placing her in a domestic environment. If these later Betty cartoons occasionally indulged in a moment of impropriety, that immodesty paled relative to earlier material. In *Judge for a Day* (1935), for instance, Betty gets soaked with water and raises her lengthy skirt just enough to provide the briefest glimpse of her (now usually hidden) garter belt; such an occurrence in a pre-Code film would almost certainly have been used as an excuse to make her change clothes and get completely undressed. Betty's new staid fashion sense has parallels with costume alterations in live-action films. The *Tarzan* series offers a useful point of comparison since the actors played the same characters before and after the stricter imposition of the Code. Whereas

FIGURE 2.4. Pre-Code and Code-approved variants of cinematic stars: Betty Boop in *Is My Palm Read?* (1933) and *A Little Soap and Water* (1935) and Maureen O'Sullivan as Jane in *Tarzan and his Mate* (1934) and *Tarzan Finds a Son!* (1939).

early installments featured Maureen O'Sullivan in a skimpy outfit and living in Tarzan's rugged jungle environment, post-Code films in the series saw the character in a much longer dress and approximating middle-class life in a treehouse with various household "appliances" fashioned out of natural objects (fig. 2.4).

Much has been written in recent decades about the supposed decline of the Mickey and Betty cartoons as the 1930s continued. This again appears to have been more of an internal problem for the studios: both Mickey and Betty continued to appear in films throughout the decade, and it is still possible to find positive reviews and exhibitor reports about these later works in contemporary trade and fan journals. Hendershot's study of Boop is particularly valuable in critiquing the dominant view subsequently espoused by Fleischer animators and historians that changes in Betty simply made her "boring, old, and fat"; Hendershot instead views these changes as a more complex process of redefining the star image

("Secretary" 118). Nevertheless, the increased prominence of supporting cast members in the *Betty Boop* and *Mickey Mouse* series is indicative of some of the new restrictions placed on the lead protagonists. Both Boop and the Mouse acquired pet dogs shortly after their respective redesigns: Pudgy replaced Bimbo the Dog, who had often performed an ambiguous role as Boop's love interest even after she became human, and Pluto was added to Mickey's cast. Griffin argues that this permitted the cartoons to retain some of the forcefulness of previous installments by displacing the transgressions onto "dumb animals" who "could be read as innocent of the havoc they are creating" (15). The more active roles taken by Mickey and, to an extent, Betty in their initial appearances tapered, with subsequent narratives usually presenting them attempting to quash chaos caused by other characters, rather than originating it themselves.

Henry Jenkins argues that many comedic personas, both live-action and animated, were fundamentally altered during this period, with protagonists increasingly involved in much more carefully outlined "romantic" or "goal-centered" narratives (*What Made Pistachio Nuts?* 240–241). The Marx Brothers, whose celebrated film *Duck Soup* (1933), as Jenkins notes, contained no romantic plot at all, were prime examples of this shift. A later production, *At the Circus* (1939), sees the trio trying to help a circus owner and his sweetheart retrieve their stolen money. The moments of lunacy enacted by the Brothers are not only significantly toned down from previous films, but also are specifically tied to the fate of the romantic plot: Groucho and Chico, in particular, are no longer ruthless con men out for themselves, but are unselfishly trying their best to help a young couple who have been wronged. The Brothers, just like Mickey Mouse and Betty Boop, were ultimately sidelined in their own starring films.

This is not to suggest, however, that all comedy characters were entirely well-behaved as the decade continued. The introduction of Donald Duck to the *Mickey Mouse* series in 1934 offers a valuable example of the quirks of content regulation because, as Walt Disney himself later noted, "the Duck's allowed to have a temper. Mickey isn't" (qtd. in Jamison SM27). Unlike Pluto or Pudgy, Donald was not safely contained as a "dumb animal" and theoretically should be judged in the same "humanized" terms as Mickey, yet he seems to have been capable of embodying forceful representations that were now out-of-bounds for the Mouse. Such an example reiterates that not all "censorship" was directly tied to the Production Code, but instead reveals more about Mickey and Donald's relative currency as stars.

As noted above, the Mouse's image became increasingly associated with innocence across the 1930s, with many of his earlier, morally ambiguous appearances expunged from surrounding discourse. Donald, by contrast, was much more carefully introduced as an anti-hero from the outset. This meant that once the Duck was established, it would be harder for anyone to retrospectively complain—as had occurred with Mickey—that moments of bad behavior were in any way incongruous with his public persona. Whereas the studio would often get letters if the Mouse appeared to have transgressed, an unnamed Disney writer succinctly summarized the Duck's privileged position in a 1949 interview: "Everyone knew he was bad and didn't give a damn" (qtd. in Wallace 21).

Popeye the Sailor is another cartoon star who, like Donald, had the benefit of emerging on-screen roughly at the same time as the rise of the PCA, and thus his "badness" was similarly contained within acceptable limits moving forward. Whereas the Fleischers' other main series featuring Betty Boop had frequently traded in representations of sexuality, the Popeye cartoons placed a greater focus on violence, which was not as intensively regulated. As Maltby notes, in this regard, the Code was mostly concerned with avoiding representations of crime that could be imitated, as well as overtly brutal or gruesome imagery (Maltby, "The Spectacle of Criminality" 120–121; see also Vasey, *The World According to Hollywood* 113–115). Although the characters' rubber-hose bodies still hinted at a carnivalesque world, the removal of sex from the equation—and the lack of blood or evidence of long-term injury in the stylized fights—allowed the series to pass with little to no criticism from censors at the time of release.

Popeye was occasionally even able to use the cloak of violence as a means of commenting on the pressures to neuter the animated star. *It's the Natural Thing to Do* (1939) begins with Popeye and Bluto already engaged in a fistfight, offering the audience a brief glimpse of the slapstick that had become a recurring—and popular—part of the series formula. (Indeed, the presence of such a scene at the start of the narrative is itself slightly disorientating, since the spectacle of the fight is usually saved for the cartoon's climax.) Olive Oyl, the object of their romantic rivalry, initially invites them to have fun with their roughhousing but then breaks up the altercation when she receives a telegram:

DEAR OLIVE, POPEYE AND BLUTO,
WE LIKE YOUR PICTURES BUT WISH YOU WOULD CUT OUT THE

ROUGH STUFF ONCE IN A WHILE AND ACT MORE REFINED. BE LADIES
AND GENTLEMEN. THAT'S THE NATURAL THING TO DO.
POPEYE FAN CLUB
P.S. NOW GO ON WITH THE PICTURE.

The wording satirizes the vociferous response of supposed fans who claim to enjoy the series yet want to change it beyond all recognition. The subsequent confusion expressed by Popeye and Bluto reflects the difficulty of reconciling these demands with their regular on-screen personas. Bluto comments, "Gentlemen, eh? Must be a character part." Popeye similarly notes, "I can act rough, but what's 'rough-ined' [refined]?" This exchange self-reflexively plays with the notion that Popeye and Bluto are movie stars, but it implies that they are being miscast in these new roles.

The characters nonetheless return to Olive's house, wearing formal attire and prancing around with exaggerated faux balletic movements. Bluto wears a severely ill-fitting jacket, and it is this divide between intention and execution that is explored in the main section of the film. Referring to the comment in the telegram, the characters frequently sing, "It's the natural thing to do," and yet their affectations appear increasingly outlandish and labored. The humor arises from their attempts to maintain the illusion of sophistication, despite their obvious discomfort. The sequence thus offers a tongue-in-cheek "warning" of what the *Popeye* series would be like if the reformers got their way. Instead of the fast-paced action of the previous cartoons, the protagonists sit around making "polite," but horribly stilted, conversation (fig. 2.5). A cutaway gag involving a clock further underscores the tedium: the hour hand has become so bored and lethargic that it gets stuck at seven o'clock. The minute hand literally has to drag time forward.

At the end of the film, Popeye begins to laugh at the ridiculousness of the situation, and the others join in, realizing the futility of attempting to be something they are not. Popeye and Bluto's jocular backslapping becomes increasingly aggressive, and eventually they start punching each other square on the jaw, descending into a full-on brawl. The characters appear absolutely delighted to be dishing out—and, even more bizarrely, to be on the receiving end of—ferocious acts of brutality. Bluto actually notices a can of spinach—Popeye's source of super-strength—and *deliberately* throws it in his direction, mumbling, "Oh, now we're really getting going! Here we go!" This contrasts with the fight scenes of most Popeye cartoons, where the action is usually tied to a narrative (however formulaic) and there are

FIGURE 2.5. A satirical "nightmare" scenario of a refined Popeye in *It's the Natural Thing to Do* (1939).

FIGURE 2.6. The brawling conclusion of *It's the Natural Thing to Do* (1939).

some stakes involved in the characters winning or losing, such as Popeye needing to rescue Olive from Bluto. In this instance, however, Olive gets a rare opportunity to be just as violent as the boys, even whacking Popeye's head with a crowbar several times. As the iris closes, all three characters are in a kinetic scrum, fists flying, with each pausing only momentarily to sing a section of the final line: "Can't you see? It's the natural thing to do!" The uncanny decadence of this final sequence appears to make a rather boisterous statement: rather than consenting to censor Popeye and make him more acceptable for "refined" audiences, the violence is made even more pronounced (fig. 2.6).

The release of *It's the Natural Thing to Do* in mid-1939 was concurrent with the Fleischers' decision to finally discontinue the *Betty Boop* series, and the film can potentially be read as indicative of the studio's frustration over Boop's demise. The notion of making a deliberately gratuitous work in the post-1934 era was not an impossible feat: as Vasey notes, the Breen-controlled PCA "never managed to receive 100 percent cooperation from the studios," and there was still vagueness in the Code that could be exploited. Producers nonetheless had to find even more ambiguous ways to "cloak" these difficult subjects to avoid overt offense (*The World According to Hollywood* 132, 136). The on-screen representation of the complainant as the "Popeye Fan Club," rather than the PCA or another moral reform group, sidesteps accusations that the film was a direct attack on a specific regulatory body, while still allowing the underlying points to be made by stealth. Jacobs suggests, furthermore, that it was possible in some PCA-approved live-action films to "interpret scenes or sequences in sexual terms, but this interpretation is not confirmed and is sometimes explicitly denied through action or dialogue" ("Industry Self-Regulation" 98). The celebratory fight at the end of *It's the Natural Thing to Do* is somewhat sadomasochistic—perhaps even orgiastic—and yet the film is again careful not to overtly define the characters' pleasure and liberation as sexual. As a result, the *Popeye* series was able to reflect on censorship—and play out an imagined victory over bluenose interference—in a way that the Betty Boop cartoons could not.

The tendency to ignore or even disavow animated stars within film theory—often on the basis of their obvious artificiality—is complicated when one considers just how much the threat of external regulation affected the representational strategies of *all* mainstream American cinema. As Vasey notes in relation to live-action productions of this period, "the Hollywood universe" under the watchful eye of the PCA "was established as a conventionalized arena with its own internal set of logical processes and outcomes. The palpable mismatch between this set of realities and the reality inhabited by audiences outside the cinema underlined the status of the movies as constructed objects of entertainment" (*The World According to Hollywood* 210). The mortal figures of the screen also frequently occupied a space that was coded and synthetic, where references to the baser elements of human existence could be suggested only obliquely, if at all. The impact of censorship and/or self-regulation created an "instability of meaning" within both the film text and the star image (Jacobs, "Industry Self-Regulation" 99). Producers often aimed to evoke controversial themes, while also at least partially disavowing them to avoid the censor's wrath. In the case of Mickey Mouse, the lingering memories of past entries in the series had the potential to undermine his newer, less aggressive persona. This was also true of a figure such as Mae West, whose provocative early screen appearances sometimes colored subsequent responses to her post-1934 works, despite these later films being made with the supervision (and ultimate approval) of the PCA (Curry 60–64). External figures—such as film journal authors and even regular viewers (as highlighted by the production of unauthorized Tijuana bibles)—were also capable of contributing to this multiplicity of signification.

Although the Production Code undoubtedly had a major impact on the content of films in the latter half of the 1930s, each star's individualized persona—and its circulation within wider popular discourse—clearly also played a significant role in determining what he or she could get away with. This chapter has indicated that notions of acceptability were not the same across the board: in the world of animation, Donald Duck and Popeye thrived during the same period in which Mickey Mouse and Betty Boop struggled.[15] Neither did these boundaries remain consistent over time. The Code offered little resistance to gags that were disparaging to ethnic minorities, and virtually every animated star has at least one text in his or her filmography that is no longer shown on television, or has to be heavily cut, because of such regrettable material.[16] Violent content similarly caused problems when theatrical cartoons were reissued on the small screen, despite being passed by the PCA upon original release.

As a result, entries in any given star's filmography that were seen as perfectly acceptable at the time have the potential to generate retrospective scandal at a later stage. This is particularly the case with animated stars, whose earliest work is now in some cases more than ninety years old.[17] Even in the 1930s, however, the perception of figures such as Mickey Mouse behaving badly and "out of character" highlights just how seriously cartoon protagonists were taken by certain members of the audience. Animated stars were quite capable of attracting controversy, and this often became part of discussions about their "personality," seemingly separate from a "performance" in any given film.

Chapter 3

The Second World War

I n the 1930s, American animation was an international phenomenon. Prints of cartoons were exported across the globe, and fan magazine articles frequently emphasized that characters such as Mickey Mouse and Betty Boop had been embraced by many different cultures.[1] In 1933, Walt Disney himself commented on the extent of this widespread success:

> The Mickey audience . . . has no racial, national, political, religious or social differences or affiliations. . . . Mr. Mussolini takes his family to see every Mickey picture. Mr. King George and Mrs. Queen Mary give him a right royal welcome; while Mr. President F. Roosevelt and family have lots of Mickey in them too. . . . Mickey is one matter upon which the Chinese and Japanese agree. ("The Cartoon's Contribution" 138)

Unbeknownst to Disney, by the end of the decade, these heads of state would be locked in a world conflict, the Mouse would be a sworn enemy of the Axis powers, and the "Mickey audience" would be split across political and national lines. Even at the time the article was written, the Nazi Party had already labeled Mickey an unwelcome icon for the German people (Leslie 80). Disney acknowledges this in his writing, but treats the matter with levity: "Mr. A. Hitler, the Nazi old thing, says that Mickey's silly. Imagine that! Well, Mickey is going to save Mr. A. Hitler from drowning or something one day. Just wait and see if he doesn't. Then won't Mr. A. Hitler be ashamed!" ("The Cartoon's Contribution" 138).

American wartime animation, by contrast, takes a much more partisan stance. Far from wanting to save Hitler from drowning, a cartoon such as *Blitz Wolf* (1942) revels in its depiction of a lupine caricature of the Führer being blown up by a bomb and finding himself in hell. This chapter therefore focuses on a specific period in which the animation industry was not aiming to satisfy a worldwide spectatorship and instead became more insular and direct in its mode of address. It evaluates the manner in which the animated star image was used during the war and how this compared with the promotion of live-action performers.

The Road to War

Disney's relatively light-hearted remarks about Hitler in 1933 were indicative of a broader effort in Hollywood not to alienate important foreign markets. As Clayton R. Koppes and Gregory D. Black note, most studios generated between 40 and 50 percent of their total revenue overseas during this period (21). One magazine "interview" with Mickey Mouse made this point particularly clear. The Mouse is reported to have "exclaimed hysterically":

> Why do I subscribe to the monthly reports of the League of Nations? Why do I spend sleepless nights reading Senator Borah's speeches in the *Congressional Record*? . . . Why do I follow the Hitler movement in Germany? Why do I bother with Stalin and the five-year plan? Simply because, my dear boy, the unrest prevailing in the world threatens my sales! . . . I work and live for humanity and when I open my eyes in the morning to find out that [a] European President has been shot or a bomb has been thrown into a group of Japanese generals in Shanghai, I know instantaneously that today there will be a terrific drop in the Chinese and French attendances of my films. (Qtd. in Fairbanks 45)

There was widespread concern about how such international incidents could affect American economic prospects. Nevertheless, Colin Shindler states, "the mood of the film industry throughout the 1930s, like the mood of the country in general and that of Congress in particular, was overwhelmingly isolationist" (2). The hope was that, if the United States did not allow itself to be drawn into the worsening situation in Europe and Asia, Hollywood could continue exporting movies to as many countries as possible. As a result, the majority of films produced during the decade avoided making any comment on these contemporary issues, and animation largely followed this trend.[2] Indeed, in 1937, during this period of political uncertainty within the global marketplace, Will Hays, the MPPDA president, singled out Mickey Mouse, rather than any live-action star, as embodying "that universal appeal for which the screen is continually striving, and for which it must continue to strive in order to be successful" ("Hays Discusses" 38). By 1939, however, with Hitler's army marching into new territories, anti-war propaganda began to appear with greater intensity in American films, both live-action and animated. In some cases, this took the form of pacifist sentiment—urging an end to all hostilities—while others focused explicitly upon nonintervention by the United States.

The cartoon *Peace on Earth* (1939) is an example of the former. Although it does not feature a recurring protagonist, it draws on the conventions of star-led films to add intensity to its message. The film begins with an idealized scene: an elderly squirrel walks through a snow-lined street on Christmas Eve as a group of young animals sing a carol to the tune of "Hark! The Herald Angels Sing." However, when the squirrel's grandchildren become confused by a lyric in the song, which wishes "good will to *men*," it transpires that the narrative is set at some point in the future, when humankind has been obliterated. The sentimental images of cute animals—common in many 1930s animated films—contrast with vivid flashbacks to a past war, which raged so persistently that every last soldier on earth was eventually killed. The grandfather explains that, after the hostilities ceased, the animals found a copy of the Bible and built a new society based on its teachings, including "thou shalt not kill." The film emphasizes the futility of war and so implicitly urges against American involvement, even if its moral is also applicable to the rest of the world.

The title of the Popeye cartoon *Leave Well Enough Alone* (1939) reaffirms the noninterventionist position. The film begins with Popeye feeling guilty as he walks past Olive Oyl's Pet Shop, which has a group of dogs staring longingly out of the window. He goes into the store and spends five hundred dollars to buy every animal, intending to set them free. The parrot, however, is reluctant to go, stating, "Why should I go out and take my chances against the world when I know I'm safe here? No sirree!" He then sings: "I've got my butter and bread and a roof over my head. . . . I know my stuff and I'm smart enough to leave well enough alone!" The bird is proven correct, as the other animals struggle to survive outside the store, and most are rounded up by the local dog catcher. Popeye realizes the error of his ways and pays to have all of the creatures returned to the shop. The cartoon closes with the sailor looking meek as the parrot reiterates the need to "leave well enough alone!" While the film does not explicitly mention the conflict in Europe, its allegorical message is hardly subtle. The implication is that although Popeye acted out of compassion for those seemingly in need, he ultimately caused a great deal of unnecessary expense and suffering. Popeye eventually supported the war effort fully in cartoons produced in 1941 and beyond, but in 1939, his star image was clearly activated in an (unsuccessful) attempt to protect the economic interests of Fleischer Studios.

By this stage, however, Japan had already "gradually banned [American and many other foreign films] from being shown in public" (Hu 66). The other Axis powers took a similar approach: Thomas Doherty notes a "progressive decline . . . of the German market for Hollywood product" across the latter half of the 1930s (*Projections of War* 39), which culminated on 17 August 1940, when the Nazi Party forbade all "American films from areas under its control . . . [and] Italy naturally followed suit" (Koppes and Black 34). The definitive closure of these foreign markets (including some Allied countries, such as France, which were occupied by Axis forces) had an enormous impact on Hollywood and the animation industry. Disney's ambitious and expensive feature films, *Pinocchio* (1940), *Fantasia* (1940), and *Bambi* (1942), which had begun production before the outbreak of war, each failed to turn a profit during their initial releases, bringing the studio dangerously close to bankruptcy (Barrier, *The Animated Man* 176, 180). Similarly, the losses incurred on the feature *Mr. Bug Goes to Town* (1942) contributed to the ousting of the Fleischer brothers from their own studio by Paramount (Cabarga 190). Animation producers once again relied heavily on the revenues generated by short cartoons, with several taking on commissions from the US government to create training and propaganda films. Having either ignored or opposed the possibility of war in films of the 1930s, animated stars took on many different roles between 1941 and 1945, some of which extended beyond the cinema screen.

The Star as Entertainer

The main function of animated stars during the war was simply to continue entertaining audiences, just like the live-action stars who did not go off to fight. Although the industry had lost crucial international business, cinema attendance in the United States was strengthened by local theaters performing a "community role" for those on the home front (Schatz, *Boom and Bust* 149). Koppes and Black state that "studios quickly grafted the war upon their traditional formula pictures: gangster stories, screwball comedies, frothy musicals. Even Tarzan, isolated in [the] jungle . . . enlisted for the allies" (61). Cartoon franchises also added war story lines, with several stars joining different branches of the armed forces on-screen. Donald Duck, for instance, became an army recruit in *Donald Gets Drafted* (1942), and a number of subsequent installments saw him undergo training and, eventually, deployment. Popeye, living up to his "sailor man" moniker, joined the navy and, beginning with *The Mighty Navy* (1941), swapped his previous costume for official navy whites.[3] Like Donald, Popeye featured in cartoons about life as a recruit, as well as in others where he was engaged in battle. Both Donald and Popeye also appeared in texts during the same period in which they were presented as civilians, sometimes not even referring to the war at all. The flexibility of the animated star image meant that the films could deal with many different aspects of contemporary life—the protagonist was never tied to a particular set of circumstances.

Doherty states that the live-action comedy genre offered "a safe haven to act out the impossible and utter the unspeakable" during wartime, and cartoon stars were similarly able to approach a large number of controversial issues (*Projections of War* 184). *Draftee Daffy* (1945), for instance, bases its humor around Daffy Duck's desperate attempts to avoid conscription into the army—a distinctly unpatriotic act, but one that is rendered palatable due to the exaggerated circumstances of the narrative. *Der Fuehrer's Face* (1943) even presents Donald Duck as a member, albeit an oppressed and alienated one, of the Nazi regime in Germany. A lengthy factory sequence sees Donald desperately trying to screw together munitions on a fast-moving conveyor belt, while being obliged to "heil" at a never-ending stream of images of Hitler. (At one point, a photo shoots past as Donald is bending over, and he is forced to use his tail and rear end to perform a somewhat less than respectful Nazi salute.) The task eventually drives him insane, and he spirals into a stream of abstract hallucinations. The story concludes with Donald waking up in his American bedroom, in his Stars and Stripes pajamas. He runs over to a miniature Statue of Liberty and embraces it, stating, "Oh boy! Am I glad to be a citizen of the United States of America!" Despite this coda, the presentation of the Disney Studio's biggest star of the 1940s in Nazi uniform for the majority of the film was still a bold move. It is difficult to imagine a noncomedic live-action star such as John Wayne or Errol Flynn being presented in such an ambiguous role during the war years.[4] Donald's appearance, however, was celebrated at the time as valuable anti-Nazi propaganda, and *Der Fuehrer's Face* even won the 1943 Academy Award for Best Animated Short Film.

The United States Office of War Information (OWI) nonetheless expressed concern about racial stereotyping in Hollywood's wartime output. While the OWI encouraged criticism of the enemy in terms of political ideology, it suggested that studios were instead often producing "hate pictures," particularly when directed at the Japanese (Koppes and Black 248). Animated stars were by no means immune from such prejudices. *Commando Duck* (1944) sees Donald Duck flood a Japanese air base, drowning all the soldiers stationed there. *You're a Sap, Mr. Jap!* (1942) and *Scrap the Japs* (1942) are two notorious examples within the *Popeye* series. *Bugs Bunny Nips the Nips* (1944) has been described by Susan Elizabeth Dalton as "the most sadistic and unsettling of all the war cartoons" (161). In one sequence, Bugs hands out ice creams (with hand grenades inside) to Japanese troops, referring to one as "monkey face" and another as "slant eyes." The next scene shows Bugs painting a series of Japanese naval symbols on a row of trees, with each seemingly counting for one "kill." Even the title of the film, as with the Popeye cartoons above, uses a derogatory term for Japanese people.

Despite OWI objections, and the criticism that such cartoons have received when rediscovered by later generations, most evidence indicates that audiences of the 1940s cheered the violent resistance displayed by the animated stars, celebrating these characters as "heroes" of the war effort. In a 1970 interview, Warner Bros. director Robert Clampett recalled:

Bugs Bunny has been loved for over a quarter of a century now, but he has never been loved the way he was during those war years. . . . [Bugs] was a symbol of America's resistance to Hitler and the fascist powers. . . . [We] were in a battle for our lives, and it is most difficult now to comprehend the tremendous emotional impact Bugs Bunny exerted on the audience then. You must try to recapture the mood of a people who had seen the enemy murder millions of innocent people in gas ovens, blitzkrieg defenseless civilians, sink our fleet in a sneak attack, and threaten our very existence. (Qtd. in Barrier and Gray 23)

Bugs Bunny cartoons surpassed Disney's output in 1943 and proved the highest-grossing American cartoon series for the remainder of the war. The rabbit's rise during this period reflects a broader trend toward stars with brash personalities, such as Popeye and Donald Duck ("Leading Short Subjects"). Mickey Mouse, the most popular character of the 1930s, had become too passive as a result of the changes to his personality, and, following *Symphony Hour* (1942), the series was effectively suspended until the end of the war.[5] A similar fate befell certain live-action performers: Shirley Temple, for instance, whose childlike innocence had been extremely successful during the previous decade, saw a significant box-office decline in the early 1940s. Jib Fowles hypothesizes that "with attention turning from the Depression and toward the menace of war, [a different type of star was] needed" (75). The animated entertainer during wartime was required to be versatile enough to appear in the usual knockabout comedy routines, but also in thrilling action sequences.

Although the short cartoons featuring these protagonists were produced primarily for domestic release, a sizeable number of prints were also distributed internationally for the consumption of Allied forces (Gaines, "The Showgirl" 58). Again, contemporary reports suggest that the mixture of war themes and humorous content was appreciated there just as much as it was on the home front. Joe Adamson notes: "During World War II, the [Warner Bros.] Studio received countless requests for drawings [of Bugs Bunny] and letters attesting to The Rabbit's popularity among servicemen. [Sgt. Chaitt of Cochran Field in Macon, Georgia, stated that] 'even outranking Betty Grable in popularity was your character Bugs Bunny, who receives far more whistles, cheers, and applause than anyone else'" (*Bugs Bunny* 65). A report for *Photoplay* by a Pvt. Waschman of Gardner Field, California, makes a similar assertion:

I know of some ten rugged GIs in my barracks who sweated out the line a second time so they could whistle at Rita Hayworth again in [*You Were Never Lovelier* (1942)]. That happens with Betty Grable, Gene Tierney and Veronica Lake, too. . . . But there are three who are top with the GIs, at least at Gardner. You guessed it. They are Donald Duck, Porky Pig and [Bugs Bunny]! (Qtd. in York, "Inside Stuff" 15)[6]

Such statements clearly highlight the degree to which animated characters appear to have been accepted as stars by military personnel. These cartoon personalities were frequently discussed, with no self-consciousness, in the same category as live-action performers, and their films were at times even seemingly chosen ahead of those featuring some of Hollywood's most famous—and desired—players.

Many stars also moved beyond the movie screen in their efforts to entertain the troops. United Service Organizations (USO) reportedly produced more than four hundred thousand live shows during the war (Hoopes 193), with Hollywood personnel flown all over the world to perform. Adamson quotes another letter sent to Warner Bros. by "two sailors on board the U.S.S. McNair," which indicates a demand for the studio's top *animated* comedian to take part in the USO events: "Dear Bugs Bunny: How come we don't see more of you in the far-flung Pacific? I think it is only natural for you as an aspiring star to be out here with us. This request comes on behalf of many thousands of servicemen who hold your inimitable countenance in high esteem" (qtd. in *Bugs Bunny* 65).

Cartoon stars could not, of course, actually participate in live performances, but they made up for this in part through appearances in other media texts created for military personnel. A particularly notable example is the radio series *Command Performance* (1942–1949), broadcast on the Armed Forces Radio Service (AFRS), which transmitted programming exclusively to US troops serving across the globe. *Command Performance* was a weekly variety show with a twist. As Patrick Morley explains, "the thought was that the forces should be able to 'command' their favorite performers to appear on the program," with the introduction to each episode promising "the greatest entertainers in America, as requested by you—the men and women of the United States Armed Forces" (69, 71). The series aimed to empower its listener base—providing an opportunity to influence content—while simultaneously authenticating the popularity of the chosen performer by virtue of the fact that he or she had been specifically demanded by the audience. The appearance of a number of cartoon characters on several installments further indicates the fluidity between live-action and animated stardom during this period.

Although a couple of episodes briefly credit the artist who provides the voice of the character (such as Mel Blanc as Bugs Bunny and Arthur Q. Bryan as Elmer Fudd), it is made clear that the animated star is the requested guest. In the 21 August 1943 episode, for instance, the host Ginger Rogers states that "hundreds of you wrote in . . . and said 'let's have more of Bugs Bunny!'" Bugs appears entirely as "himself" in the 8 May 1943 installment, explaining that he has been given the day off from his job at Warner Bros. He even flirts with the actress Martha Raye and makes a few gags about the reproductive cycles of rabbits. It is implied that the relaxed attitude toward risqué content on the AFRS (relative to domestic networks) allows him to reveal a slightly more lecherous side to his off-screen personality. The 3 May 1945 episode is significant because it features animated stars from both Disney and Warner Bros.: Donald Duck, Goofy, and Clara Cluck from the former, and Bugs Bunny, Elmer Fudd, and Porky Pig from the latter. Although the two groups do not directly interact, it marks the first time that they officially appear together in the same text—more than forty years before *Who Framed Roger Rabbit* (1988) featured character cameos from a range of studios.

The above examples demonstrate just how widely the animated star image was mobilized to entertain both domestic and armed forces audiences during the war. Although the cinematic texts remained the most consistent source of engagement with the viewer, cartoon stars were able to move beyond this medium and boost morale in several ways.

The Star as Government Spokesperson

The divide between entertainment and propaganda was at times difficult to distinguish during the war years. The OWI continued to advise film producers on their choice of subjects, asking that they consider questions such as "will this picture help win the war?" (Koppes and Black 66). Nonetheless, many actors also donated their time—and their popular star images—to support the war effort outside their regular film roles. One popular endeavor was the selling of war bonds to the public to raise money for vital wartime needs both at home and abroad. This usually involved stars touring the United States and performing in person at local fund-raising drives (Hoopes 112). As with the USO shows, animated stars could not literally travel around the country, but they could appear in other texts, separate from their entertainment releases, in order to deliver important messages. For example, *Leon Schlesinger Presents "Bugs Bunny"* (1942), now popularly known as *Any Bonds Today?* due to Bugs's performance of Irving Berlin's song of the same name, sees the rabbit extolling the benefits of purchasing bonds. The cartoon begins with a theatrical curtain parting and, except for a single use of close-up, it is presented in a long shot, equating to the view from a front-row theater seat. The vaudevillian theme continues as Bugs slips into an Al Jolson impression, and Porky Pig and Elmer Fudd appear in cameo roles as backing singers. Throughout the film, Bugs stares consistently at the "camera," thus appealing directly to the cinematic audience. There is a resolute sense that Bugs is, again, appearing "as himself." Although he is still clearly operating in a performative context—just like the human stars taking part in live fund-raising shows—Bugs is freed from the narrative constraints of his usual cinematic roles. The ultimate message, therefore, is not just to buy war bonds, but also that *Bugs Bunny* wants people to buy them.

Star power was often used to make a personal connection with audiences in films of this nature. For instance, the live-action short *Winning Your Wings* (1942)—a brief return to the screen for James Stewart, who had put his Hollywood career on hold for military service—similarly emphasizes direct address in its attempt to convince viewers to enlist in the Air Force (fig. 3.1). Stewart is first introduced walking into the shot and doing a surprised double take, implying that what follows is entirely spontaneous. The actor maintains eye contact with the camera throughout his on-screen sequences and provides folksy comments during voice-over sections. Despite the fact that the movie is an official government product, Stewart's "performance" is designed to make the discussion appear as informal as possible. As with Bugs's appearance in *Any Bonds Today?*, the film trades heavily on an engagement with the star that appears to be somehow more personal (more "real"?) than his usual acted roles. *Winning Your Wings* was considered extremely effective upon its release, with some reports suggesting that enrollment in the Air Force doubled as a result of Stewart's appearance ("Films Swell Enlistments" 1).

Disney's short *The New Spirit* (1942), completed for the US Treasury, builds on such an approach. The cartoon implies that it is delving even deeper into the private life of its star, Donald Duck, in an attempt to encourage Americans to complete their tax returns accurately and efficiently. The film presents Donald at home, away from the Disney Studio, and sees him filling in his own tax form. He lists his occupation as "actor" (although his pen springs to life and cheekily adds a question

FIGURE 3.1. The star using direct address in war propaganda: Bugs Bunny in *Leon Schlesinger Presents "Bugs Bunny"* (1942) and James Stewart in *Winning Your Wings* (1942).

mark at the end of this statement) and declares his annual income. Over the course of the film, the usually grumpy Donald comes to realize the "privilege" of contributing to the war effort, using "taxes to beat the Axis." As Richard Shale notes, however, Treasury Secretary Henry Morgenthau envisioned "a Disney-created Mr. Average Taxpayer, and he opposed Walt's humor-oriented plan to use Donald Duck as the Star. Disney argued somewhat testily that loaning Donald to the Treasury Department was like MGM loaning out Clark Gable because Donald was the Disney Studio's biggest attraction" (27).

Morgenthau's concerns had some validity, as "Mr. Average Taxpayer" is not a role that most live-action stars would have been able to play convincingly, regardless of the prestige that they might have brought to the film. The average annual salary for an American employee in 1942 was $1,778 (Edelstein 360). By contrast, as Thomas Schatz states: "A $25,000 salary ceiling decreed by the director of economic stabilization in October 1942 . . . sent shock waves through the movie industry, whose top talent earned well over that maximum on individual pictures. . . . According to the Internal Revenue Service, eighty individuals at MGM alone earned over $75,000 in 1942" (*Boom and Bust* 144). The reluctance to cast Donald in *The New Spirit* appears to have been based on his perceived status *as* a movie star. Nonetheless, as an animated creation, Donald's star image was more flexible than that of his human counterparts—in reality, he had no exorbitant salary that would undermine the credibility of the film. The Duck lists his income as "$2,501.00"—a little above the national average, but a figure that had some relevance for ordinary cinemagoers trying to work out their own tax obligations (fig. 3.2). A review in *Time* offers a suggestive commentary on Donald's earnings, compared to live-action performers:

> *The New Spirit* . . . reveals the astonishing fact that one of the world's most beloved cinema actors earns less than $50 a week. That miserable retainer not only has to support himself in the extravagant lifestyle to which Hollywood is accustomed, but also has to feed, clothe and house his three adopted nephews. This underpaid box-office paragon: Donald Duck.
>
> Bachelor Duck has complained about a lot of things, but his salary . . . is not one of them. Its revelation is pure patriotism on his part. ("The New Pictures" 36)

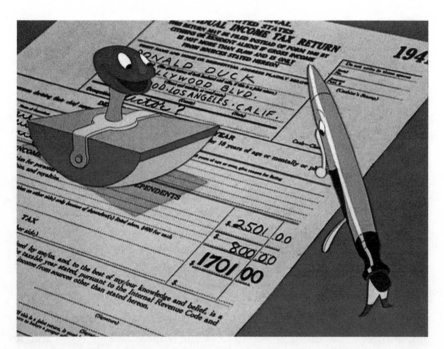

FIGURE 3.2. Donald Duck's tax form and salary deduction in *The New Spirit* (1942).

The film was widely considered a success. It is estimated that 26 million people saw *The New Spirit* during the war and, like *Winning Your Wings*, it was perceived to have made a tangible change in attitudes: "[P]olls showed that one in three said it influenced their willingness to pay taxes" (Editors of *Look* Magazine 194). Cartoons such as *The New Spirit* and *Any Bonds Today?* reflect studios working directly with the government, using animated characters to promote a particular cause, with the added side effect of simultaneously raising the profiles of the stars. Indeed, Shale notes that Walt Disney "ordered a full scale publicity campaign just as if *The New Spirit* were a feature film. . . . Louella Parsons had leaked word of Walt's patriotic mission early in January, and publicity breaks were set for [magazines such as] *Life*, *Look*, and *Liberty*" (29). As with the *Time* piece above, many of these articles treated Donald's "personal" involvement, separated from the efforts of the Walt Disney Studio, with just as much, if not more, reverence than that shown toward live-action performers. The *New York Times*, for instance, stated that "Donald Duck this month joined the ranks of Hollywood players who are fighting the battle of the Home

Front . . . . Pluto and Mickey Mouse, fellow actors at the Walt Disney studios in California already have put their shoulders to the wheel in Canada and elsewhere" ("D. Duck Joins Up" SM20). *Film Daily* was just as congratulatory: "After this short don't be surprised if Donald Duck turns up on a dollar bill. He deserves it" ("Shorts" 7).

The New Spirit did, however, manage to generate controversy. It was produced using full animation for Donald Duck's scenes, essentially matching the quality of a regular entertainment release. Although Disney still made the film at a loss, the Treasury agreed to contribute $40,000 for its production and a further $40,000 for print costs (Shale 28–30). This caused debate in the US Congress, with some members questioning such expenditure on a film designed to show the value of each tax dollar received. Donald, in addition to Walt Disney and the Treasury, became embroiled in the scandal, although many commentators jumped to the Duck's defense.[7] The film critic Bosley Crowther, for instance, wrote an article disapproving of the decision to withhold funds for an "excellent morale film" featuring "our old friend, Donald" and chiding a "Congressional wag" for delivering the "witless slogan . . . 'Not a buck for Donald Duck'" ("Up and at Them" X5). A *New York Post* column jokingly suggested that Congress was "jumping up and down like Donald Duck *on* Donald Duck," referring to the spectacular—and often misguided—tantrums that Donald frequently enacted in his own cartoons (qtd. in United States Congress 88.1: 1344, emphasis added). Senator Sheridan Downey even spoke up for the Duck in Congress:

> The Treasury Department was thinking of the morale, not of our soldiers and sailors but of the taxpayers, when it sought the influence of Donald Duck to stimulate and encourage tax payments. Poor Donald, too, is now in the doghouse, placed there by a slim majority in the House of Representatives. He had blithely and happily donated his services in the interest of national defense. . . . For only a portion of the out-of-the-pocket money a film of incalculable propaganda value was given our government. . . . Advertising experts and newspapers and the American people generally are, I think, almost a unit in declaring that it was one of the soundest investments the government has yet made. (Qtd. in United States Congress 88.1: 1128, 1345)

The treatment of Donald as if he were a real person extends even to the index for the *Congressional Record*, which lists "Duck, Donald" separately from "Disney, Walt" (United States Congress 88.11: 151, 160). It is revealing, too, that *The New Spirit* was debated alongside ambiguous expenses and/or salary that the live-action star Melvyn Douglas was claiming as head of the arts council for the Office of Civilian Defense (United States Congress 88.1: 1149; "House Forbids OCD Funds"). The issue of celebrities receiving compensation for their government work continued to be a point of contention throughout the war, and Donald's inclusion in these discussions vindicates his star status.

The desire to produce propaganda cartoons of the quality to which the public had become accustomed nonetheless indicates one problematic area in terms of the versatility of the animated star. A live-action performer in Hollywood could potentially donate his or her services to films supporting the war effort. Although there would still be expenses incurred in making and distributing the film, the basic presence of the star—and the performance enacted for the camera—did not necessarily have to cost anything. As noted, however, simply animating and scoring Donald's appearance in *The New Spirit* cost in excess of $40,000. Studios had the option of using limited animation techniques to reduce the amount of work, but this risked undermining the on-screen vitality of the star and, in turn, the propaganda message of the film. Such productions, therefore, decreased in number as the war continued. *Out of the Frying Pan into the Firing Line*, which featured Minnie Mouse and Pluto, marked one of the last government-sponsored cartoons produced by Disney (or indeed any other producer) to involve any well-known stars: "Pressing budgets and time schedules were making elaborate character animation a luxury the studio could no longer afford" (Shale 34). The decline of the cartoon star as spokesperson in the final years of the war should not lead us to underestimate the impact that many of these early films reportedly had upon the public. Animated characters had the potential to command significant influence, just like live-action performers, but this did come at an economic premium.

The Star as Educator

Animation was used extensively in training films during the war. The medium was capable of presenting complex instructions in a relatively straightforward manner. A film such as *Four Methods of Flush Riveting* (1942), produced by the Walt Disney Studio, shows close-up, cross-sectional views of each of the different flush riveting processes being enacted. Sergeant Franklin Thomas, a Disney animator assigned to the First Motion Picture Unit during the war, noted that "through drawing we can portray fields the regular camera cannot reach" (135). Most of these films were put together relatively cheaply, with a basic voice-over and on-screen text to provide context for the moving images. Animated characters were not usually included because of prohibitive costs, but there was also debate as to whether the star—either in live-action or animated form—was suitable for films intended to educate.

The "star-as-spokesperson" campaigns were generally effective because the underlying message was a simple one—"buy war bonds" or "join the Air Force," for instance—and the endorsement of a trusted celebrity helped to reinforce this. Despite Morgenthau's initial objections about using Donald Duck, Shale suggests that *The New Spirit* was successful "because it was designed not so much to explain how to fill out the tax forms but to show the need for payment and how simple the process was" (27). Audiences saw Donald go through an emotional change—from being against taxation to happily paying his fair share—and, hopefully, were convinced to view the situation in the same way. These films used personality to sell a single idea. Would Donald, or Bugs Bunny, or even James Stewart have been as useful in a step-by-step guide to filling out a more complex and intricate document or in a film about the intricacies of flush riveting?

This question was relevant to the production of a series of films by Disney for the Office of the Coordinator of Inter-American Affairs. The series, designed to spread education and propaganda in various Latin American countries, includes *The Winged Scourge* (1943), which uses Disney's Seven Dwarfs to inform audiences about the threat of malaria. However, as J. B. Kaufman states:

> Walt, mindful of his mission, was determined not to let the Dwarfs' scenes overwhelm the film's message. "The only reason to bring in the dwarfs," he warned the story crew, "is to add a little interest; when you begin to get into gags and impossible things, you're not accomplishing the job we're supposed to do—show in a simple way how to get rid of mosquitoes." (*South of the Border* 132)

The finished film still contains a large number of "impossible" gags co-inciding with important information. In a variation of the house-cleaning sequence from *Snow White and the Seven Dwarfs* (1937), the characters fix up their property and its surroundings to protect against mosquitoes, all set to the tune of "Whistle While You Work." Birds cover the beds with netting, and a woodpecker is shown sealing up the floorboards. It could be argued that the humor in these scenes helps make the film's lessons memorable, but there is also a risk that the Dwarfs' antics take the place of more practical demonstrations of techniques to safeguard the home. Disney subsequently canceled a suggested sequence featuring Donald Duck in the film *Tuberculosis* (1945), "telling his team that they should use the footage to convey the film's message straight away" (146). The animated star was, ultimately, used sparingly in educational films produced for civilian audiences during wartime.

It is revealing, then, that a number of recurring animated stars were developed specifically for soldiers.[8] The most famous, and prolific, of these characters was Private Snafu, who appeared in alternate installments of the biweekly *Army-Navy Screen Magazine*. The *Magazine* was a "20-minute collection of newsreels and special features . . . screened at United States military bases around the world, usually accompanying a Hollywood feature film," essentially mimicking the schedule of a cinema screening back home (Smoodin 71). The majority of the Snafu films were produced by Warner Bros. animators, and the cartoons frequently draw upon the conventions of the *Looney Tunes* series. Mel Blanc's voice characterization for Snafu is similar to Bugs Bunny, and a number of gags involve stuttering and mis-pronunciations of words in a manner reminiscent of Porky Pig and Daffy Duck. Indeed, Bugs even makes a brief appearance in the film *Gas* (1944), uttering his famous "What's up, Doc?" catchphrase after being pulled out of Snafu's equipment pack. The cartoons also use a great deal of the broader filmic vocabulary already established for the short film animated star. Each installment features a title card in which Private Snafu's face and name fill the screen, underscored by a short musical phrase operating as the character's "theme tune" (fig. 3.3). Snafu is presented as a recurring comic figure with a consistent persona. However, while his position in the armed forces remained appropriate to his rank (except in imagined and/ or dream sequences), his particular duties and location served the needs of the story in any individual installment rather than offering a continuing narrative arc.

As Bugs Bunny's innuendo-laden appearance on *Command Performance* suggested, media texts produced solely for the troops did not have the

FIGURE 3.3. Private Snafu's star image evoked in the title card for *Spies* (1943).

same content restrictions as mainstream domestic releases. Snafu's name was itself a veiled reference to an acronym originated by American soldiers during the war. Situation Normal: All Fucked Up reflected an underlying discontent toward the army system. While the introductory film of the series, *Coming! Snafu!* (1943), tames the acronym to "All *Fouled* Up," the *F* visibly shakes on screen before "Fouled" is revealed, clearly signaling another meaning to the audience. The films also contain numerous sexual references, images of pin-up girls in posters around Snafu's bed, and even moments of barely concealed (and, in a couple of instances, actual) female nudity. Snafu also appears naked in a number of films, in sequences played for laughs. The racy comedy in these cartoons distinguished them from the formal nature of most training sessions. As Sergeant Thomas states:

> Situations normally termed "corny" by the men are not only convincing but entertaining in animation. There is an immediate response to the entrance of a cartoon character—an interest and sympathy which is in sharp contrast to the reaction caused by the entrance on the screen of

the cultured sergeant who usually explains the material in the film. No matter how much he tries to be a good Joe and speak man to man, privates are still conditioned against sergeants and the fellow on the screen is licked before he starts. The addition of a cartoon character . . . would obviously add immeasurable interest to the picture. (135)

Eric Smoodin notes that the Snafu films (and indeed the *Army-Navy Screen Magazine* as a whole) "addressed an audience that was overwhelmingly male, primarily Christian, predominantly white, and significantly disgruntled" (79). Snafu was thus intended as an "everyman" character, someone whose status and experiences broadly mirrored those of his military audience. As with the portrayal of Donald Duck's initially sour response to the idea of taxation in *The New Spirit*, the Snafu films do not attempt to paint an idealized image of life in the armed forces. They acknowledge that poor morale and low motivation do exist (although this attitude is often challenged comedically in the narrative). For instance, in *The Infantry Blues* (1943), Snafu bemoans his menial "dogface grunt work" as a member of the infantry, believing it to be harsher than the duties undertaken by others. After being visited by Technical Fairy, First Class (a recurring character in the series), Snafu is magically transported to the Tank Service, the Navy Fleet, and the Air Corps, with disaster ensuing in each instance. At the end of the cartoon, Snafu enthusiastically returns to his own infantry position, secure in the knowledge that "all the roads are pretty rough . . . and all the services are tough." A number of other basic morals recur throughout the series run: films such as *Spies* (1943) and *Censored* (1944) warn about the dangers of sensitive information falling into the wrong hands, while others such as *The Goldbrick* (1943) and *Fighting Tools* (1943) see Snafu shirking his duties in some way—including failing to attend training or not maintaining his weapons and equipment—only to find himself lacking in the heat of battle.

If viewers were invited to identify with Snafu as a peer, they were also given stern warnings against emulating his actions. His comedic buffoonery, with parallels to other "regular" animated stars, was reiterated throughout the series as ultimately dangerous. The character had a surprisingly high mortality rate, actually being killed off at the end of at least six cartoons, as well as a number of lucky escapes in several others by waking from a dream or emerging from some other imagined scenario. Snafu had the luxury of returning unscathed in each new installment, but the immediate repercussions of slapstick violence were made clearer than was usual for most animated stars. By encouraging the soldiers to laugh *at* Snafu and his mistakes, the films also implicitly taught them to be vigilant in their own conduct. As Michael Birdwell suggests, "Snafu died—again, and again and again—so that many GIs might live. . . . Through the use of humor and the outrageous situations afforded by animation, the misadventures of Private Snafu made a lasting impression on the average soldier" (203–204).

Another animated star, Trigger Joe, was not quite as disaster-prone as Snafu, but the educational content of the films was delivered in a similar manner.[9] As Alex Greenberg and Malvin Wald state:

> [Trigger Joe] could make side-splitting mistakes in learning the theory and practice of a new gunsight. He could fly on a magic carpet, ask that his target's speed be slowed, even stopped, to help him (and our audience, of course) understand what he was doing, and he could take the usual pratt falls [*sic*]. "Trigger Joe" was conceited one moment, astounded at his ignorance the next. . . . However, by the end of the film Joe understood the new gunsight perfectly and so did most of the students who saw him.
>
> Joe's instantaneous appeal to his audience was no accident. . . . Each gunnery student found a little bit of himself in Joe. Really, when laughing at Joe the student was laughing at himself, his own foibles, stubbornness, and difficulties. That was Joe's big appeal, the self-identification by the audience. (413–415)

Greenberg and Wald imply that the maximized "ordinariness" of Snafu and Trigger Joe encouraged an affinity with the viewing audience.[10] These characters had personality and were fallible, attributes that formed part of their "rhetoric of authenticity" as stars (to return to Richard Dyer's term). Smoodin notes that the Snafu films "posit *each recruit* as a body politic just as important in deciding the outcome of the war as all of the force, technology, and authority of the state" (95, emphasis added)—a notable contrast to American cartoons that caricatured the enemy, particularly Nazi forces, as rows of identical soldiers marching robotically in unison. There is a degree of irony in that the *Snafu* and *Trigger Joe* series ultimately promoted "a consensus military culture, a culture in which difference must be dangerous and unity the greater good," but the mode of address in these works helped to make these arguments more palatable (Smoodin 76). The personality of the star was designed to go beyond the macro-concerns of most training films and to inspire the individual soldier's response at a micro-level.

The apparent effectiveness of such films has been reiterated by many in the production crews who worked on them. John Hubley and Zachary Schwartz claim that "the Signal Corps found that the reaction to the animated 'Snafu series' was greater than the reaction to any of the live-action films" (361). Greenberg and Wald similarly note that "anyone who could teach as convincingly and clearly, and yet interestingly, as [Trigger Joe] was bound to be a hit" (415). Nonetheless, some commentators indicate concerns similar to those raised about the Disney civilian education films. Carl I. Hovland, Arthur A. Lumsdaine, and Fred D. Sheffield suggest that "an animated cartoon might be much more interesting and entertaining as a film vehicle than a serious documentary presentation, but the cartoon might have little educational effects because it was *too entertaining*—the audience might be 'set' to be amused rather than learn and the message of the animated cartoon might be lost completely" (81). They summarize an experiment in which five films from the *Army-Navy Screen Magazine* were shown to soldiers, including the Snafu cartoon *Gripes* (1943) alongside four live-action shorts. During the screening, the subjects were given buttons to press whenever they liked or disliked what they saw. Of all the films, *Gripes* received the highest number of "like" presses and the lowest number of "dislike" presses. However, a subsequent questionnaire, in which the same subjects were asked to rank the films from "best" to "worst," put the Snafu film in third place. Hovland, Lumsdaine, and Sheffield use this data, along with selected quotations from individual soldiers, to suggest that the comedy of the film distracted from its educational value (109–112). This remains, however, a controversial study: David H. Culbert argues that this analysis is misleading and does not show the full range of positive responses to the film (96n30).[11] Furthermore, Charles F. Hoban and Edward B. Van Ormer point out that the experiment does not compare "two film treatments of the same topic" and therefore does not provide reliable evidence "on the value of cartooning as a presentation variable" (8–17).

It is suggestive that Snafu, of all of the stars developed for the forces, had the broadest "range" as a screen "actor." Indeed, the frequency of Snafu releases—with new installments appearing, on average, on a monthly basis—almost necessitated a degree of variety to his adventures. Trigger Joe, by contrast, reportedly did not move far beyond his specific role as a "waist gunner" (Solomon, *Enchanted Drawings* 114). Another character called "Mr. Hook," a navy recruit who appeared in four films produced by the Lantz and Warner Bros. studios, was entirely focused on encouraging sailors not to spend their wages recklessly and to invest in war bonds. A few Snafu cartoons, such as *Pay Day* (1944), also covered the issue of saving for a postwar life, but, as indicated, many other subjects were addressed in the series as well. The final Snafu films are also notable because they drop the pretense of educating soldiers. *Operation Snafu* (1945) and *No Buddy Atoll* (1945), in particular, play as straightforward comic adventures, full of humorous "business" rather than moralistic tales. In these two entries, Snafu is more competent and successful in his role as a soldier (if still clearly a slapstick comedian). He manages to infiltrate a Japanese military base in the former film and successfully fight and kill a Japanese soldier after they are both washed up on a desert island in the latter.

Even Snafu's persona was, ultimately, so closely tied up with army life that the conclusion of the war marked the end of his "career." There was no attempt to transfer the star power of Snafu (or Trigger Joe or Mr. Hook) into civilian life, returning home at the same time as his previously enlisted audience. This is perhaps a reflection of complicated rights issues: although the majority of Snafu and Hook films, for instance, were helmed by Warner Bros. directors, both characters had appeared in films produced by other units (such as Lantz and MGM), and the films had been commissioned by government and military sources. However, these ephemeral stars did have some influence on postwar production. Figures such as Donald Duck appeared in later instructional films, including *Donald in Mathmagic Land* (1959), which outlined various aspects of mathematics, and educational content was included in a number of series as animated stars began to appear on television. The focus on human characters such as Snafu, Mr. Hook, and Trigger Joe also inspired the postwar development of the United Productions of America (UPA) studio (see chapter 5).

The lack of definitive data makes it difficult to reach a conclusion about the instructional value of the *Snafu* and *Trigger Joe* films. However, these texts reflect a further application of the animated star in wartime, regardless of whether Snafu and others were propagandist educators or merely entertainers—and there is still room to question whether the two must be seen as mutually exclusive.

The Star as Icon

The symbolic value of the animated star was well understood during wartime. Images of characters such as Mickey Mouse routinely appeared on posters promoting various causes, such as volunteering in the Home Guard (Rawls 12–13). The Mouse even featured on packaging for children's gas masks, as it was felt that his presence would prove calming during air raids (Heide and Gilman, *Mickey Mouse* 80). Animated stars were also adopted as mascots for a variety of armed forces and squadrons. As Walton Rawls notes, of the Disney characters, "Donald Duck was by far the most frequent . . . draftee for military service on insignia. He made at least 216 appearances" (39). Other studios followed suit. Images of Universal's Woody Woodpecker, Andy Panda, and Oswald the Lucky Rabbit were all featured on military uniforms and vehicles (Solomon, *Enchanted Drawings* 123). Adamson notes that Bugs Bunny was the most popular of the Warner Bros. cartoon stars, his likeness appearing "on the equipment of the 385th Air Service Squadron, on the first Liberator Bomber that struck at Davao in the Southern Philippines, on every vessel and piece of equipment of the Motor Torpedo boat command, and as a morale builder on the country's biggest hospital ship, the U.S.S. *Comfort*" (*Bugs Bunny* 64).

The representation of figures such as Donald Duck and Bugs Bunny as insignia could potentially be seen as reducing them to mere logos, rather than engaging with the wider ramifications of the star image. In attempting to complicate this assertion, however, a suggestive parallel would be live-action female stars, whose pin-up images were widely circulated to American troops. The most famous was probably Betty Grable, who was photographed from behind, looking seductively over her shoulder and wearing a bathing suit. Roy Hoopes cites a letter that one soldier wrote to Grable: "We would be exhausted, frightened, confused and sometimes hopeless about our situation, when suddenly someone would pull your picture out of his wallet. Or we'd see a decal of you on a plane and then we'd *know* what we were fighting for" (qtd. in Hoopes 94). As this quotation indicates, stars were considered to be extremely powerful morale boosters, even if they were just presented as still photographic images or painted onto the sides of planes. Hoopes, in fact, collapses this iconography even further, stating that "Jane Russell's breasts, Veronica Lake's hair, and Betty Grable's [rear end] went to war" (96). One can identify several other accounts that reduce the iconic value of the star to a specific body part (see, for instance, Woll xi; Shindler 76).

Although it does not appear that cartoon characters were fetishized in the same way as female pin-ups during the war, evidence suggests that the animated star-as-logo was similarly capable of inspiring troops and encompassing a wide range of complex, ideological meanings. As noted earlier in the chapter, Warner Bros. received many requests from soldiers for drawings of Bugs Bunny, and, like popular female stars, cartoon characters were often praised for their contributions to life in the armed forces. Marcia Blitz states that the image of Donald Duck "was there throughout every battle and every dark moment of the war, serving as a symbol of American determination" (124). Both animated *and* live-action star images thus displayed a significant degree of transportability as icons to support the war effort.

The hand-drawn status of animated characters nonetheless made it easier for them to be evoked anywhere in the world, including by the enemy. While it was certainly possible to caricature live-action stars—which, as with the Grable decal, could still be effective—it would be difficult to convincingly incorporate actual footage of, for example, John Wayne or James Stewart in an anti-American film. By contrast, cartoon stars could be easily mimicked, which offered the possibility of producing work that bore a close resemblance to their "official" texts. The international fame of the characters during the 1930s had occasionally inspired foreign producers to "borrow" stars to support their own productions. For instance, *Mabo no Daikyoso* (*Mabo's Big Race*, 1936), part of a series of Japanese cartoons featuring the original character Mabo, intercuts a shot of Mickey and Minnie Mouse, Betty Boop, and Felix the Cat cheering on the protagonist. The sequence implies that these American figures considered Mabo as an equal and that this was a valuable endorsement. During the war years, however, appropriations of these same figures by the Axis powers were done for a different purpose. On the surface at least, they were presented as dangerous symbols of the American enemy.

The Japanese animation *Momotarō no Umiwashi* (*Momotaro's Sea Eagle*, 1943) dramatizes a Japanese air attack on a naval port of "Demon Island," somewhat akin to Pearl Harbor. During the battle, Bluto from the *Popeye* series is prominently featured and subjected to a series of humiliating defeats. *Nimbus Libéré* (1944), produced in Nazi-occupied Vichy France, brought together protagonists from a number of different studios. The film features a French family, headed by the popular French comic character Professor Nimbus, picking up a radio broadcast from London (Delporte

372–374). The radio announcer (drawn as an exaggerated Jewish stereotype) promises that British intervention will be imminent. The family chatter excitedly about the prospect of British food, drink, and cigarettes, unaware that an American bomber squadron is flying overhead. The planes—piloted by a host of American stars, including Mickey Mouse, Goofy, Donald Duck, Popeye, and even Felix the Cat—indiscriminately unleash their bombs and destroy the house. The film ends with an image of the Grim Reaper hovering over the rubble, as the radio continues to make its optimistic claims.

The underlying intent of these appropriations remains ambiguous, however. *Nimbus Libéré* begins with a drawing of Professor Nimbus alongside a number of the American characters, appearing to trade upon their collective star value, rather than making an ideological judgment or attempting to separate the two cultures. The film's director, Raymond Jeannin, even claimed after the war that "he had attempted to sabotage his own work by depicting the American pilots as symbolic, funny, friendly characters such as Mickey Mouse or Donald Duck, with whom the public would be familiar," disregarding their actions later in the narrative (Delporte 371). *Momotarō no Umiwashi* is similarly curious in that it associates the Japanese air force with the "hero" role usually occupied by Popeye, showing them defeating the villain Bluto, rather than attempting to demonize any of the Fleischers' more likeable protagonists. The film also goes to significant lengths to achieve accuracy in its representation of the character. Bluto's visual appearance and voice are closely mimicked, and there are numerous gags—such as a character riding a torpedo missile like a horse and Bluto continuing to climb into midair even after the ladder on the ship has sunk into the ocean—that are particularly influenced by American cartoon aesthetics. Although the publicity for *Momotarō no Umiwashi* called Popeye an "American gangster" and argued for the superiority of Japanese animation, the prominent use of images of the sailor and Betty Boop (who do not actually appear in the film) in printed advertisements highlights the contradiction at play in many of these appropriations ("*Momotaro's Sea Eagle* Ad Gallery"). Since few American films received distribution in Axis power countries during the war, there were no new installments of the official animated series to entertain audiences. Cartoons such as *Nimbus Libéré* and *Momotarō no Umiwashi* consciously traded on the ongoing appeal of the characters, even if the ultimate message was outwardly proclaimed to be anti-American propaganda.

Whether or not the vilification of these characters actually worked on citizens of Axis countries is debatable. Rawls notes that, despite the Nazi Party's disdain for Mickey, the Mouse appeared on military insignia for the Luftwaffe during the Spanish Civil War and even on a number of German planes throughout the Second World War (14). In 1938, the Italian government even briefly considered making a special exception to permit the continued publication of Mickey Mouse, Donald Duck, and Popeye comics at a time when most other American works were being banned within the country ("Italy Grants Stay" 14; "Protests and Benefits" 17). After the war was over, and Hollywood was once again free to export its product around the globe, consumption of American animated films resumed in Germany, Italy, and Japan. There is now even an official Disneyland resort in Tokyo, reflecting the ongoing popularity of the Disney characters. Ruth Vasey notes that, across several decades in the early 1900s, it had been standard practice for American producers to encourage "the idea that Hollywood belonged to the world, rather than to the United States alone" (*The World According to Hollywood* 69). For the Axis powers, these associations proved difficult to counteract. The complex, and often contradictory, evocation of cartoon characters during wartime ultimately indicates the strong emotional effect that their star images were believed to inspire among residents of many different nations.

The Star as Soldier

While most actors' contributions to the war were based primarily on their fame and performance skills, some stars—such as Douglas Fairbanks Jr., Clark Gable, Henry Fonda, and James Stewart—did actually halt their screen careers in order to enlist with the armed forces (Hoopes 138–163; Doherty, *Projections of War* 14–15). Those who remained at home were, at times, subjected to comparative criticism. As Doherty states, "the apparently fit crooner [Frank] Sinatra—certainly fit enough to ignite the not-so-subliminal passions of hordes of swooning young females—was far and away the privileged object of [home front] desire most heartily despised by frontline fighters" (*Projections of War* 194). By contrast, there were no such expectations placed upon animated characters: nothing that cartoon stars did to boost morale was tainted by the suggestion that they could instead be supporting the forces by enlisting alongside them.

Adamson nonetheless claims that, despite his lack of corporeality, Bugs

Bunny "was considered an unofficial member of both the Seventeenth Weather Squadron and the Fourth Parachute Battalion" (*Bugs Bunny* 64), while Tom Shales notes that "the U.S. Navy and Marine Corps" similarly regarded Donald Duck (H5). Perhaps even more surprising, though, is the apparent *official* recognition for these stars. In 1942, the *Washington Post* revealed that "Bugs Bunny received a warrant as an honorary sergeant in the Marine Corps" ("Creator of Looney Tunes" 18); in 1947, *Film Daily* noted that Bugs had been "promoted to master sergeant for his services to the Marine Corps recruiting campaign" (Daly, "Along the Rialto [1947]" 3). The Marines reportedly even created a service record book for the rabbit (Adamson, *Bugs Bunny* 64). Theoretically, Bugs appears to have a more extensive documentation of wartime duty than many human actors. Similarly, the *Washington Post* relayed that, as part of Donald Duck's fiftieth "birthday" celebrations in 1984, "Gen. Arthur Brown, director of Army staff, issued Donald his official discharge papers, with a rank of Sgt. E-5," in recognition of the Duck's "morale-boosting" service, which had begun in the 1942 short *Donald Gets Drafted* (Shales H5). While this was, ultimately, a publicity stunt, it once again highlights the importance of these animated creations to the armed forces, and the tangible input they are perceived to have made. Indeed, such examples also indicate the extent to which the animated star was presented—through media texts and then corroborating reportage *about* those media texts—as truly *existing* during the war. Richard Shale's scholarly account of the Disney Studios war films sustains this notion of the animated star as a real person: "When Donald Duck joined up to aid his country's wartime needs, he could scarcely have predicted that the length and scope of his service would make him one of World War II's most important volunteers" (112). These characters were able to keep pace with, and in some cases exceed, the contributions of live-action performers toward many diverse areas of the war effort.

Richard Dyer suggests that "stars articulate what it is to be a human being in contemporary society . . . [and] represent typical ways of behaving, feeling and thinking" (*Heavenly Bodies* 8, 17). In chapters 1, 2, and 3, I have argued that animated characters frequently offered significant insights into the human experience throughout the first half of the twentieth century. The silent and early sound era saw these figures respond to the growing phenomenon of stardom, most notably the boundaries of a performer's on- and off-screen presence. The Second World War required cartoon protagonists to engage with even more fundamental aspects of contemporary life, speaking to audiences on emotive subjects such as patriotism, duty, death, and sacrifice. Dyer notes that stars can also register "doubts and anxieties" about personhood (*Heavenly Bodies* 10), and animated characters have again proven capable of such acts. As I indicated in chapter 2, the lack of a physical body did not prevent figures such as Mickey Mouse and Betty Boop from raising concerns about human sexuality. Wartime productions similarly drew objections—which have generally only intensified in subsequent decades—about the prevalence of racism and hatred, with both live-action and animated works sometimes *dehumanizing* the enemy in an attempt to justify the activities of war.

The first section of this book offered evidence of the numerous ways in which cartoon characters truly function as stars. While there are many valuable areas of crossover with the live-action model, there are also notable points of divergence. The following section considers in more detail how animated stardom can fit within existing star theory and suggests that there are problematic assumptions that can be productively challenged by adding the animated medium to the discussion.

SECTION II

Conceptualizing Theatrical Animated Stardom

Chapter 4

The Comedian Comedy

I n *Felix in Hollywood* (1923), Felix the Cat travels to California and manages to talk his way into an audition with a studio mogul. After demonstrating his ability to emote in close-up performances of "sorrow" and "joy," the Cat exclaims, "Now here's something original." He removes his tail, transforms it into a cane, and enacts a version of the walk made famous by Charlie Chaplin's Tramp character. Felix inadvertently continues to perform the routine in front of Chaplin himself (rendered in animation), who angrily exclaims, "Stealing my stuff, eh?" and chases the Cat from the building. Outside, Felix looks directly at the "camera" and notes, "That ruins my chance in the movies!" Although Felix's impersonation of the Tramp is presented as a quick throwaway gag, the animated star system was undoubtedly influenced by the meteoric rise of slapstick performers such as Roscoe "Fatty" Arbuckle, Mabel Normand, and, particularly, Charlie Chaplin in the 1910s. Almost every series of short animated films featuring a recurring star produced during the silent and studio eras was principally comedic in nature.[1] The increasing deviation of early animated newspaper adaptations from the narrative worlds and characterizations of the parent strip (such as *Krazy Kat*, as identified in chapter 1) can be seen in part as an attempt to mimic the popular forms of live-action comedy. Comic strip devices such as speech balloons and elaborate wordplay gags were slowly phased out in favor of faster-paced chase narratives more akin to the latest Keystone Studio offering.

Animated characters created specifically for the cinema took this inspiration even further: both Felix the Cat and Mickey Mouse have been identified in numerous sources as direct spiritual successors of Charlie Chaplin (see, for instance, Gehring 53–54; Jackson, "Mickey and the Tramp"). Likewise, Henry Jenkins argues, "the whole vocabulary of anarchistic comedy [adopted by various sound film comedians of the early 1930s] was inherited by the character cartoons of the 1940s, with Bugs Bunny's humiliation of the stodgy Elmer Fudd a pleasurable reworking of the earlier confrontations between Groucho Marx and Margaret Dumont" (*What Made Pistachio Nuts?* 281). Caricatures of famous live-action comedians also appeared frequently in animated shorts (almost certainly without authorization from the performers themselves). *Mickey's Polo Team* (1934) is an especially star-packed example. Mickey, Goofy, Donald Duck, and the Big Bad Wolf engage in a celebrity polo match against Harpo Marx, Laurel and Hardy, and Chaplin. Many other Hollywood celebrities are seen interacting with Disney stars in the crowd, and all behave exactly like their screen personas, even though they are supposedly enjoying their off-screen leisure time.

Was, then, the relationship between the comedian and the cartoon star one of mutual respect and friendly rivalry, as imagined in *Mickey's Polo Team?* Or was it a more parasitic dependency, prompting the comedian's justifiable indignation, as imagined in *Felix in Hollywood?* At the very least, most slapstick stars generally praised animation in public. For instance, Chaplin was, in reality, on good terms with the makers of Felix the Cat, having previously cooperated with them in the production of a short series of cartoons featuring the Tramp (Canemaker, *Felix* 38). Chaplin was also friendly with Walt Disney and selected a Mickey cartoon to support screenings of his 1931 film *City Lights* (Inge 63).

It is important to note, however, that the major live-action slapstick performers, such as Chaplin and Buster Keaton, were already making the transition to full-length features even as Felix the Cat was growing in popularity. For comedians remaining in short subjects, animation proved a much greater threat. Most cinemas aimed for variety in their selection of supporting films, and the two genres clearly overlapped a great deal. A 1933 article in the *Los Angeles Times* ran with the striking headline, "Mickey Mouse Charged with Death of 'Live' Comedians," contrasting the rise of Disney's star with the "rapid decline" of his human counterparts in the early sound era (Scheuer A1). Similarly, a 1935 *New York Times* piece saw slapstick director Al Christie accuse Mickey of "grand larceny": "That's what's happened to all our old gags: they've been swiped by Mickey Mouse. Don't let [anyone] tell you that Mickey's popularity is based on some elfin appeal, or because he represents any universal quality. Mickey and the cartoons are slapstick and that's why they're good" (qtd. in Nugent, "The Slapstick Professor" X3).

It is, ultimately, unfair to characterize the animated star as a mere carbon copy of the cinematic comedian. Both are considered to have links to earlier forms of comedic theater. Critic Morton Eustis suggests that Disney's Mickey Mouse and the live-action Keystone comedians "are direct descendants of . . . the Commedia dell'Arte players or the comic actors of the ancient Greek festivals" (680). Vaudeville and music hall traditions of the nineteenth and early twentieth centuries had a momentous influence as well. Nonetheless, the type of fame conferred by the mass medium of cinema united the animated star and film comedian in a particularly meaningful way. As André Bazin states, "[I]t is Felix the Cat or Mickey Mouse rather than Molière's Misanthrope or Tartuffe who can throw light on the existence of Charlie [Chaplin]" (104) and vice versa.

The roots of a star system in both animation and early slapstick comedies developed a little later than in most of the film industry, which is one of many reasons why existing star theory may not adequately address either form. Although comedic filmmaking was ubiquitous in the early "cinema of attractions" era, Eileen Bowser notes that the number of comedies actually declined significantly from 1907, when most other forms of American cinema began to integrate more narrative elements, and only slowly regained momentum from 1911 onward (179–180). A few comedians, such as John Bunny, were recognized relatively early on as burgeoning picture personalities, but the promotion of comic performers remained inconsistent for a number of years. Indeed, Keystone Studios, arguably the most influential producer of comedic film series during the 1910s, downplayed the value of any individual star well into the middle of the decade. Until this point, the studio's advertisements kept the players largely anonymous or identified them only as part of a group, instead emphasizing the quality of the producers, directors, and the Keystone "brand" as a whole (Riblet 187; R. King 83). Animation studios took even longer to begin routinely promoting films on the basis of a recurring central protagonist. As I state in chapter 1, hand-drawn cartoons were produced mostly as sporadic one-offs into the 1910s, with a tentative star system gaining traction only during the second half of the decade.

Comedy as a cinematic genre is, of course, a wide-reaching, and thus potentially unproductive, category that includes a multitude of conflicting practices and styles. In this chapter, I focus on a comparison between the animated star and a specific live-action subgenre identified by Steve Seidman as the "comedian comedy," which he characterizes as operating in a manner different from that of most other areas of the Hollywood system.[2] His work is one of the few full-length studies to discuss how live-action comedians function as media personalities. Although there is rarely any suggestion that they do not qualify as stars (unlike cartoon figures), there is also little consideration of how the articulation and deviation of a comedic performer—especially one working in short films rather than in features—may deviate from that of a dramatic actor. Seidman argues that comedian comedy texts are overtly led by the personality of the comedian, potentially at the expense of a coherent narrative. Furthermore, the comic figure often draws attention to the artificialities of the filmmaking process and acknowledges the cinematic audience. Although most of Seidman's examples are drawn from slapstick and early sound comedies, he suggests that some performers have continued to manifest the same "stylistic and thematic preoccupations" to the present day (2).

There is a danger, as Henry Jenkins and Kristine Brunovska Karnick suggest, that Seidman's model is "limited by its ahistoricism" ("Introduction" 3). The same issue arises with animation: one can identify several differences between the comic styles of, for instance, Felix the Cat and Bugs Bunny, just as there are obvious disparities between Charlie Chaplin and Groucho Marx. As I indicated in chapter 2, one can even chart major alterations *within*, for instance, Mickey Mouse's star image from the late 1920s to the mid-1930s. However, by wishing to separate these different eras of production, Jenkins and Karnick conversely risk downplaying the remarkable consistencies apparent in many incarnations of this particular type of comic star. I do not intend to provide a diachronic reading of the changes to the cartoon "comedian" over the course of the twentieth century, but rather to indicate more general trends that can be identified across this period.[3] The films cited to support this approach will therefore be drawn from a wide chronological range. It should nonetheless be reiterated that some animated stars fit certain aspects of the comedian comedy model better than others and that a star may not necessarily reflect exactly the same attributes throughout the entirety of his or her cinematic "career."

Before analyzing the specific approaches taken by the comedian comedy and animated cartoon, it must be acknowledged that all film stardom, by its very nature, creates a degree of instability within the cinematic text. As Jenkins and Karnick note, Richard Dyer's work has highlighted that "the star always brings to a given role much more semiotic significance than can be successfully contained within the individual film narrative" ("Acting Funny" 151). Indeed, Richard deCordova's model for the emergence of stardom explicitly involves audiences making intertextual links between all of a particular performer's films, regardless of the many disparate roles he or she may have played (*Picture Personalities* 90–92). Knowledge of a performer's private life, especially moments of scandal, also threatens to overpower the relatively "solid and integral diegetic world" assumed by the classical Hollywood system (Bordwell, Staiger, and Thompson 30).

However, as Peter Krämer argues, star vehicles typically "resolve this tension by matching image and role, rather than playing out the contradictions between the two" (102).[4] The comedian comedy and animated star film models often break from the majority of Hollywood productions by *deliberately* mismatching the star's persona with the scenario of the film for the sake of humor. The incorporation of the comedic protagonist within another established genre accentuates this. As Frank Krutnik suggests:

> The comic effect in these films, then, derives in large measure from the comedian's deviance in terms of the generic functioning of the hero: [Bob] Hope [in the comedic western *The Paleface* (1948)], for example, is in most ways the inverse of the typical western hero and the comedy elaborates his "aberrant" characteristics—he is a show-off, a coward, useless at shooting, and continually fails to consummate his marriage to Jane Russell. ("The Clown-Prints" 53)

In animation, the gangly frame and clumsy personality of Disney's Goofy, for instance, regularly impedes his integration into the scenario of a given cartoon. In *How to Be a Detective* (1952), he is cast as a private eye somewhat akin to Sam Spade, but never quite achieves this aspired hard-boiled tone. After pausing to consider where he has seen a suspicious-looking character before, he ends up falling down an empty elevator shaft. He also fails to understand any of the colloquialisms common to the genre: when an apparent hoodlum instructs him to hand over his "heater" (slang for gun), Goofy instead throws an electric heat lamp.

Some cartoons offer variations on this approach. Tex Avery's Droopy, for example, appears ineffectual and slovenly in both appearance and characterization, but actually proves to be remarkably (and somewhat inexplicably) capable. In *Dumb-Hounded* (1943), his first-ever appearance, bloodhounds are released to track down an escaped criminal. In an extended shot, a group of these powerful animals run purposefully in pursuit of their foe. Droopy is eventually seen walking wearily behind them, clearly much smaller and weaker than the other dogs. As if to highlight the incredibility of his position, he actually turns to the audience directly and meekly notes, "You know what? I'm the hero," before continuing to plod down the street. The end of the film finds Droopy victorious, having captured the crook and earned a huge cash reward (the sight of which causes him to scream and dance in celebration, only to suddenly revert back to his usual demeanor, stating "I'm happy" with a completely deadpan expression). Even *What's Opera, Doc?* (1957), which actually treats its source material with a degree of reverence for the most part, cannot resist finally allowing Bugs Bunny to spoil the illusion. Toward the end of the cartoon, Elmer Fudd (playing the role of a demigod) commands a lightning storm, which kills Bugs. This section of the film dwells upon the melodrama of the situation, rather than appealing for laughs, as Elmer immediately regrets his actions and tearfully carries Bugs's lifeless body toward a presumed heaven. Richard Wagner's music begins to swell and the "camera" zooms back to reveal a long shot of the wider landscape—both generic signifiers that the film is about to end. Suddenly, however, the sequence cuts to a close-up over Elmer's shoulder, and Bugs immediately springs up to ask, "Well, what did ya expect in an opera—a happy ending?!" He then resumes his death pose as the iris closes, undercutting the tragedy of the operatic form by explicitly signaling to the audience that he is simply putting on an act.

These examples, which could potentially be seen as failed attempts at drama in noncomedic genres, work in comedy because the momentary loss of sincerity in the star's performance is heightened and presented as intentional. Seidman suggests that narrative in the comedian comedy can be read using the theoretical term "*discours*" (28). As Brian Henderson elaborates: "*Histoire* suppresses or hides all traces of its telling. It refers neither to speaker [n]or to listener but only to the events it relates. . . . *Histoire* in general is used to make the events related seem more real, vivid, present, whereas . . . *discours* modes continually break such illusions, or at least may do so" (20). The *histoire* model broadly corresponds to the dominant practice of American filmmaking, described by Bordwell, Staiger, and Thompson as the "classical Hollywood cinema," which "strives to conceal its artifice through techniques of continuity and 'invisible' storytelling" (3). Seidman suggests that most Hollywood genres are hermetic, establishing an essentially closed narrative universe. He argues that comedian comedies are, by contrast, non-hermetic, and "comprised of a more open and expansive narrative structure which acknowledges the spectator, narrative exposition that is 'spoiled' by actors who 'step out' of character, a foregrounding of its marks of production, essential artificiality, and a destruction of its signifying practice" (55).

As with the discussions of the "semiotic significance" of stars above, it must be acknowledged that not all supposedly classical films adhere obediently to the *histoire* model: it is inevitable that some "traces of telling" (as Henderson puts it) remain in all filmmaking, however much a particular text attempts to deny it.[5] Conversely, there is a danger in overemphasizing the presence of *discours* in comedy films. In relation to anarchistic live-action comedies of the 1930s, Jenkins notes that "although they contain elements that transgress classical expectations about how stories should be told and how characters should be constructed," one should not let these moments overpower a balanced reading of the text.

> These films were, after all, produced within the mainstream commercial cinema and were answerable to the same institutional constraints as any other Hollywood movie. If these films are transgressive, it is because the Hollywood studios that financed, produced, and released them allowed and even encouraged these transgressions. For the most part, even these films conform to classical Hollywood norms. They are narratives. They have goal-centered protagonists. They [generally] maintain spatial and temporal coherence. They provide at least a minimal degree of causal integration. (*What Made Pistachio Nuts?* 24–25)

While my subsequent analysis in this chapter privileges selected moments of disruption in comedian comedies and animated cartoons, placing them in opposition to most forms of Hollywood filmmaking, these films were not overtly attempting to be avant-garde, selective in their appeal, or incomprehensible to audiences.[6] As Steve Neale suggests, different genres foster their own notions of realism or generic "verisimilitude." For instance, the musical (another frequently non-hermetic form) can justify its characters breaking into song for no apparent reason, while a similar occurrence would look out of place in a crime film (31). Audiences also accept that musicals generally revert to a more obviously classical dramatic mode between the song-and-dance numbers, just as a comedian comedy or a cartoon can return to an ongoing plot even though it might create diversions and suspend "reality" for the sake of gags. Thus, as Krämer concludes, the supposed digressions in comedian comedies generally "do not disturb the spectators' relation to the film because they are part of their generic expectations from the start" (105). Animation has the potential to disrupt classical values even more than the comedian comedy because it is not limited by the live-action photographic medium, but this potential for excess is again largely naturalized as part of the generic expectation.

The Comedian As Enunciator

Several cartoons already cited in this chapter, such as *Felix in Hollywood* and *What's Opera, Doc?*, have seen the animated stars break the "fourth wall" of cinema and talk to the audience. As André Bazin suggests, most classical Hollywood cinema operates on the assumption of the viewer "alone, hidden in a dark room, [watching] . . . a spectacle that is *unaware of our existence*" (qtd. in Seidman 4). Both the comedian comedy and the animated star cartoon, however, often assume the presence of a spectator. Seidman describes this as taking an "enunciative" stance—an essential element of the comedian comedy's use of *discours*—and suggests that this was inspired by the performance of comedy in live contexts such as music halls. He argues that most of the devices are broadly theatrical—for instance, film comedians frequently bow as if taking a curtain call and give knowing looks to the camera ("the functional equivalent of the vaudeville 'aside'") (4, 19–22).

It is important to note that many of the earliest experiments with cinema in the 1890s and 1900s had already borrowed heavily from theatrical traditions, not just by recruiting music hall players to present extracts of their routines, but also by establishing a relationship between the (on-camera) performance and the (cinema) audience. As Tom Gunning argues:

From comedians smirking at the camera, to the constant bowing and gesturing of the conjurors in magic films, [the cinema of attractions] displays its visibility, willing to rupture a self-enclosed fictional world for a chance to solicit the attention of the spectator. . . . Fictional situations tend to be restricted to gags, vaudeville numbers or recreations of shocking or curious incidents (executions, current events). It is the direct address of the audience, in which attraction is offered to the spectator by a cinema showman, that defines this approach to filmmaking. Theatrical display dominates over narrative absorption. ("The Cinema of Attractions" 57, 59)

For the most part, therefore, subjects of these texts consciously displayed an awareness of being filmed. Cinema did, of course, separate the moment of performance and the moment of consumption, which would normally have occurred simultaneously in a theatrical event. Nonetheless, acknowledging the camera created the illusion of a direct (if only one-way) interaction with the audience, akin to a live performance.[7] However, as Gunning states, the development of the classical Hollywood cinema mode eradicated this direct address from most genres:

The period from 1907 to about 1913 represents the true *narrativization* of the cinema, culminating in the appearance of feature films which radically revised the variety format. . . . The transformation of filmic discourse that D. W. Griffith typifies bound cinematic signifiers to the narration of stories and the creation of a self-enclosed diegetic universe. The look at the camera becomes taboo and the devices of cinema are transformed from playful "tricks" . . . to elements of dramatic expression, entries into the psychology of character and the world of fiction. ("The Cinema of Attractions" 60)

Traditionally, film criticism often implied that early slapstick comedy simply failed to keep up with the times and continued with "primitive" methods before "artists" such as Chaplin embraced a more classical approach (see, for instance, Kerr 62–63). However, Bowser has subsequently argued that "slapstick films *challenged* new narrative systems by *returning* to some of the forms of pre-1909 cinema" (183, emphasis added). The fact that comedy had been somewhat absent from the screen during the "narrativization" period—as Bowser's research has shown—suggests that the "theatrical display" of the emergent Keystone films was a conscious choice, rather than an unheeding continuation of "outdated" techniques. Furthermore, one can identify a shift in the enunciative device from the cinema of attractions era to later films featuring comedians and animated stars. While early motion pictures may have presented humorous figures participating in direct address, viewers were generally directed to engage with the novelty or spectacle of the film rather than with the input of a specific performer (see deCordova, "The Emergence of the Star System" 23–24). By contrast, the communication initiated by later comedians often displayed much more self-awareness about their status as cinematic personalities and the continuation of these personas across various films.

Animation followed a similar trajectory as the concept of the cartoon star began to develop. The first instances of hand-drawn animation in cinema were found in films that reproduced, and then extended, the vaudeville "lightning cartoonist" routine. The live-action performer initially controlled direct address; for instance, J. Stuart Blackton's *The Enchanted Drawing* (1900) sees the artist frantically creating an image on his drawing board, sporadically turning to smile at the "audience," and later explicitly gesturing at the camera while demonstrating a trick—a precursor to the full frame-by-frame animation technique—in which he appears to turn a sketch of a wine bottle into a real-life object. However, as the animator slowly retreated behind the scenes, in favor of presenting drawings that appeared to move under their own volition, the animated protagonists began to assume their own direct address.

The cartoon *Colonel Heeza Liar at the Bat* (1915) contains at least a dozen instances in which the eponymous hero acknowledges the audience. The film begins with the Colonel in his car, and when it fails to start, he directs a puzzled expression toward the "camera." Heeza eventually arrives at a baseball field and takes the position of pitcher. Although the batter laughs at the sight of the diminutive and aged figure, the Colonel turns to the viewer and winks to indicate that he has a trick up his sleeve. He throws a pitch that defies the laws of gravity, spinning in random circles and eluding the batter's swing. Reflecting the limited budgets of early studio animation, the winking gesture is used again to indicate the character's success and twice more when the Colonel plans a similar ploy for his second pitch. Donald Crafton argues that a by-product of recycling the same drawings was that these early shorts "implied film-to-film consistency and encouraged the spectator to place the character in his fictive universe"

(*Before Mickey* 272). In the case of this footage, however, the repetition also emphasizes Heeza Liar's ability to break out—at least temporarily—from the diegesis and interact with the cinema audience in a manner similar to the live-action film comedian.

One aspect of Seidman's model that complicates a direct comparison with animation, however, is the importance attributed to the comedian's career *before* his or her appearance in films. This directly challenges one of the central tenets of star studies theory. DeCordova argues that the picture personality (and subsequently the star) emerged as a result of cinema producers downplaying the performer's previous theatrical experience, instead creating an intertextual link between their appearances in films and the publicity generated by those films (*Picture Personalities* 50–51). I have already applied the same logic to the development of the animated star, highlighting a similar intertextual shift from cartoons based upon preexisting comic strip characters toward series based around new protagonists developed specifically for the screen. Indeed, many of the major *noncomedic* live-action film stars of the classical Hollywood era, as Seidman acknowledges, "worked in legitimate theater (though few of them enjoyed success in it), but all of them were basically 'created' by the movies and were recognizable to audiences as such. They can be seen as filmically generated icons" (17–18).

However, Seidman ultimately claims that, unlike the dramatic star, "the iconicity of [the comedian] was generated prefilmically" (18). Krutnik elaborates:

> The comedian has not only a previously-defined extra-fictional image [the character or persona that he or she performs in the films] but an image which is established in extra-cinematic terms. Most of the comedians had successful careers in other media [including vaudeville, television, and radio] before their first films . . . . The comedian's [persona] was initially established in a direct performance situation, where the comedian relied upon interaction with an audience (even in radio, where there would generally be an in-studio audience). A key expectation the spectator brings to a comedian comedy is to witness/participate in the performance—the "act" of the comedian, and this necessitates a compromise between the performance mode and the institutional requirements of the individual film. ("The Clown-Prints" 52)

The Marx Brothers, for instance, began their feature-film career with adaptations of two of their successful Broadway shows, which had already largely established their iconic characterizations. Charlie Chaplin was hired by Keystone Studios as a result of being seen on stage as part of the Fred Karno Music Hall troupe. Animated stars, by contrast, lacked any performance history before their emergence on screen.[8] However, it should be noted that Chaplin's initial film appearances were not explicitly publicized with an intertextual link to his career in vaudeville. (Indeed, Chaplin joined Keystone at a time when, as indicated above, the studio was still largely resisting publicizing individual actors at all.) Chaplin's cinematic fame was thus created almost exclusively by the cinema itself. Seidman also admits that Harold Lloyd "did not become a well-known comedian until after several years of working in film comedy shorts," but concludes that since his films "respond to those of his contemporaries, Chaplin and Keaton, his work clearly falls into [the comedian comedy] grouping" (2–3). As such, it can be suggested that an earlier career in another medium was not necessarily a prerequisite for the filmic comedian. Seidman does (somewhat contradictorily) acknowledge that there was "a widespread familiarity with the performing conventions of vaudeville. Since the fledgling film industry sought the largest possible audience for its product, there was an attempt to duplicate the already popular conventions and performing styles of vaudeville" (25). The Harold Lloyd example highlights that a performer without a significant level of prefilmic experience could nonetheless create a viable cinematic "comedian" persona. This approach was mimicked in animation, and it is possible to identify many stars, such as Bugs Bunny and Mickey Mouse, explicitly "performing" on-screen in a manner that consciously draws upon the conventions of vaudeville.

Numerous animated films feature the stars directly on a music hall or theater stage—a tactic that Seidman notes helped live-action comedians cement their relationship to this earlier tradition (26; see also Krutnik, "A Spanner in the Works?" 24n21). A number of Mickey Mouse cartoons, such as *Orphan's Benefit* (1934), are based around theatrical shows, with Mickey and supporting characters performing musical numbers and skits. *Puttin' on the Act* (1940) sees Popeye and Olive Oyl resurrect an old vaudeville routine, which, as the film implies, they had performed regularly years earlier. Segments include impersonations of famous film stars, including Groucho Marx and Jimmy Durante, and various song-and-dance numbers. Perhaps most notable is *What's Up, Doc?* (1950), a cartoon in which Bugs Bunny recounts his life in show business to the "Disassociated Press."

A young Bugs is seen studying ballet and performing as a chorus boy on the Broadway stage and then hitting a rough patch in his career before being hired as Elmer Fudd's stooge in a traveling vaudeville show. However, the rabbit grows increasingly frustrated with his role and decides to turn the tables, making Elmer the victim of the pranks. The new dynamic receives an enthusiastic response, and Bugs and Elmer transfer to Hollywood, recreating their stage act for the big screen. Bugs, then, is explicitly presented as having had a successful prefilmic career that directly influenced his cinematic persona. Although this was clearly not the case in reality—Bugs, of course, originated entirely on-screen, and the early films worked through several potential avenues for his persona before settling on the established formulas of later entries—the cartoon is a particularly revealing example of the animated star being mythologized in relation to the traditions of music hall.[9]

During Elmer's vaudeville show, Bugs ad-libs the line "What's up, Doc?" and elicits a huge cheer from the assembled crowd. For a viewer watching the film, the sequence provides a secondary moment of humor, as it presents itself as the "origin story" for a catchphrase that had become extremely popular within Bugs's cartoons. Often associated with live-action vaudeville stars, catchphrases gained even greater cultural currency when performers moved into other media such as radio, film, and television because they could reach a mass audience in a short period of time, and comedians could regularly repeat the phrase across a number of different texts. Many animated stars had their own popular catchphrases: for instance, Daffy Duck is known for "you're despicable," Donald Duck for "aww, phooey," and Sylvester the Cat for "sufferin' succotash." Cartoons also frequently parodied—and at times simply stole—catchphrases made famous by popular performers: Al Jolson's "Mammy" is a regular allusion made in cartoons from the 1930s and early 1940s, for instance. Catchphrases became important identifiers for both comedians and animated stars, but, as Brett Mills suggests, the repetition of phrases "puts quotation marks around them, and stops them appearing to be genuine utterances" (78). As Krutnik notes, while "comedian-centered films seek to maintain the sense of witnessing or participating in the performer's act, . . . this inevitably requires some form of compromise between the interactive performance mode and the structuring processes of narrative, resulting in the instability of the comedian's character identity" ("A Spanner in the Works?" 24). One may potentially expect Oliver Hardy to utter a variant of

"Well, here's another nice mess you've gotten me into!" to Stan Laurel, or Bugs Bunny to deliver the line "What's up, Doc?," regardless of the specific scenario of any given film. The catchphrase is another vaudevillian device used to separate the audience from a coherent narrative world and instead place a focus on the comedian explicitly engaged in the act of performance.

Although Seidman identifies theatrical precedents for many of these devices, comedians also regularly emphasized that they were appearing in a cinematic medium. In addition to the theater-set narratives, it is also possible to identify a number of comedies set in a film studio. Chaplin's *Behind the Screen* (1916), for instance, sees the Tramp as a stagehand who eventually gets to appear in front of the camera. *The Dumb Bell* (1922) presents "Snub" Pollard as an actor clashing with a temperamental film director, only to become just as difficult when he is promoted into the job. Buster Keaton's *Sherlock Jr.* (1924) is particularly renowned for a sequence in which Keaton literally enters the screen in a cinema and gets caught in a rapid montage of scenes. Animated stars were also frequently presented in filmmaking contexts—figures such as Bugs Bunny and Daffy Duck were specifically coded as Warner Bros. stars and appear at the studio in a number of cartoons. Several films also parodied aspects of the technology itself. In the aforementioned short *Dumb-Hounded*, a wolf fleeing from Droopy runs so quickly that he actually "breaks away" from the frame, past the sprocket holes of the projected film, and into a white void. Some cartoons see the stars manipulating the iris—a black circle used to reveal or conceal sections of the frame in live-action filmmaking. Most commonly, as the iris closes to suggest the end of the film, the star will squeeze through it or briefly hold it open to deliver a final gag (see, for instance, Felix the Cat in *Comicalamities* [1928] or Foghorn Leghorn at the end of *Crowing Pains* [1947]).[10]

There nonetheless remains an inconsistency in terms of the level of enunciative control that the protagonists of these films are able to muster. Some cartoon stars may be granted more "powers" than others. When Wile E. Coyote paints a picture of a tunnel onto a rock face in, for example, *Fast and Furry-ous* (1949), the Road Runner can somehow pass through it as if it were a real tunnel. When the Coyote tries, he ends up simply running into a wall. Krutnik thus challenges Seidman's assertion by arguing that comedians are only "allowed, at specific and regulated moments, to *masquerade* as enunciator," rather than possessing the ability at all times ("A Spanner in the Works?" 24, emphasis added). Sometimes the protagonists find themselves bound to the demands of the narrative: Chaplin's Tramp cannot, for instance, magically produce the coin he needs to pay for dinner in *The Immigrant* (1917) or merely excuse himself from the scene. Even Bugs Bunny, a protagonist who regularly—and self-consciously—manipulates the film narrative to ensure that he emerges victorious, occasionally loses control. In *The Unmentionables* (1963), for instance, he is forced to serve a prison sentence alongside two gangsters he apprehended because he loses the keys to the handcuffs.

Both comedian comedies and animated star cartoons therefore fluctuate between moments where the performer is permitted to break out of the diegesis and others where they are essentially "trapped" within the character. There is usually no signal as to when the "rules" of the world that the comedian inhabits have changed, nor any clear explanation as to *why* they have changed (other than, more broadly, for the purposes of creating humor or developing the plot). That audiences do not find the films completely incomprehensible indicates that these texts still operate to some extent within recognizable cinematic conventions, however unsteadily these may be articulated.

Star vs. Character

Most Hollywood stars, from the silent era to the present day, portray different characters with each new film. Rudolph Valentino, for instance, played Sheik Ahmed Ben Hassan in *The Sheik* (1921), Lord Hector Bracondale in *Beyond the Rocks* (1922), and Juan Gallardo in *Blood and Sand* (1922). Although one can find similarities among the roles—reflecting a tendency to cast Valentino as a certain character type within a limited range of genres—each protagonist has a separate backstory and the narratives are self-contained.[11] In contrast, serials were designed from the outset as multi-chapter texts released to the cinema at regular intervals. This form came to prominence in the early 1910s and continued to be produced for theatrical exhibition into the 1950s. The serial establishes an explicit link between installments, usually through the use of cliff-hanger endings. Each new film generally revolves around the protagonist extricating him- or herself from the peril of the previous entry, only to be placed in yet another precarious situation by the end, with resolution again deferred to the next installment. Moviegoers were enticed to return to see the star portraying a recurring protagonist in an ongoing narrative, rather than displaying a range of characterizations in successive productions.

Broadly speaking, the comedian comedy short and the animated star cartoon fall within the definition of a third model: series filmmaking. Unlike the, for instance, one-off Valentino features, a series is expected to display some consistency in terms of character and location. Unlike the serial, however, each installment in a series has a complete narrative and the entries do not necessarily need to be seen in order (Blandford, Grant, and Hillier 210). Writing about the television sitcom, a later form of series comedy, Steve Neale and Frank Krutnik argue that it "relies upon a trammeled play between continuity and 'forgetting'" (235). The first episode generally introduces a fixed scenario, with each subsequent installment providing a variation of the formula. As such, viewers are occasionally required to ignore continuity lapses and logical flaws if these are necessary to preserve the underlying situation and character relationships, allowing the repeatable "pleasures" of the series to continue in new episodes (Bowes 132).

The comedian comedy and the animated star cartoon nonetheless complicate these definitions. Although there is still a reliance on continuity in some areas, both require significantly more forgetting between installments than the sitcom and most other series formats. Rather than attempting to preserve the situation from film to film, the comedian comedy and star cartoon frequently alter settings and characterizations. For instance, three Chaplin shorts released in sequence saw the Tramp character (or potentially a variant of the Tramp) as a fireman in *The Fireman* (1916), a violinist in *The Vagabond* (1916), and an inebriated homeowner in *One A.M.* (1916), all without a clear explanation of the link between the films. Although coded primarily as a sailor, Popeye has appeared in one-off films in various professions including a chef in a diner in *We Aim to Please* (1934), a professional dancer in *Morning, Noon and Nightclub* (1937), and a lead actor in *Shakespearian Spinach* (1940). Protagonists can even be transported through history: Mickey and Minnie Mouse are living at the close of the nineteenth century in *The Nifty Nineties* (1941), Popeye inexplicably appears in Middle Ages Europe in *Popeye Meets William Tell* (1940), Daffy Duck is a futuristic superhero in *Duck Dodgers in the 24½th Century* (1953), and so on. There is often no attempt to justify their presence in this new environment (such as explaining that these are ancestors or descendants of the regular characters).[12]

Romantic relationships are also inconsistent. In comedian comedies, the protagonist was regularly smitten with a female character portrayed by a recurring performer. Many Chaplin shorts, for instance, featured Edna

Purviance, and Virginia Fox appeared in various Keaton films. However, the success or failure of these dalliances is never continued from one film to the next. Similarly, numerous Popeye cartoons feature Popeye and Bluto vying for the affections of Olive. Although Popeye usually succeeds at the end of the film, the situation is reset by the next installment. Popeye and Olive sometimes begin a film as a couple, but this relationship is not linked to the closure of a previous cartoon. Occasionally, Olive will reject Popeye—in *Shape Ahoy* (1945), for instance, she sails away with a caricature of Frank Sinatra—and vice versa, as when Popeye turns down her suggestion of marriage in *Beware of Barnacle Bill* (1935). In some Mickey Mouse cartoons, Mickey and Minnie are dating; in others, they display a degree of animosity toward each other; and, on more than one occasion, they appear to meet for the first time. Once again, the lead character attempting to woo a belle can be seen as one of the repeatable pleasures of the genre. The resolution has to be undone in order to allow for more variations.

Returning to Krämer's point, one assumes that the audience would be familiar enough with the conventions of the genre to accept this. Nonetheless, it is revealing that Walt Disney felt obliged to make the following qualification in 1933:

> In private life, Mickey is married to Minnie. A lot of people have written to him asking this question, because sometimes he appears to be married to her in his films and other times still courting her. What it really amounts to is that Minnie is, for screen purposes, his leading lady. If the story calls for a romantic courtship, then Minnie is the girl; but when the story requires a married couple, then they appear as man and wife. ("Mickey Mouse is 5 Years Old" 36)[13]

Disney's explanation relies upon Mickey's star status as a means of explaining the inconsistencies between films. It implies that Mickey, the "actor," is altering his persona to fit the requirements of a particular narrative.

Given the various discrepancies between installments of these series, certain scholars of comedian comedies have attempted to define where viewers *can* locate consistency, and these approaches have relevance for understanding the animated star. Charles Musser argues:

> [Chaplin's] pictures are essentially parts of a longer, larger metafilm. The tramp falls out of one situation and into another, always entering the

new one on the bottom rung. This circularity is most evident in films . . .
where Charlie starts on the road and ends up there. In between he has
entered society, played with its values and foibles, found the comfort
attractive but its long-term costs too high. A new film may catch Charlie
when his circumstances have improved slightly and the costume is not
quite so shoddy, but the character is the same. (53)

Musser's implication, therefore, is that Chaplin's films collectively offer
a cohesive, if episodic and disjointed, account of the Tramp's life. Such
a reading is undoubtedly appealing, but still relies to an extent on the
audience forgetting certain details. The character does frequently fail to integrate himself into society, but not all the installments display the explicit
"circularity" that Musser finds in films such as *The Tramp* (1915), in which
"Charlie" conclusively leaves behind his current situation. Indeed, Musser
is forced to explain away texts that deviate too much from the usual down-
beat endings. *The Fireman*, for instance, which sees the Tramp rescue and
seemingly win the heart of the girl, is dismissed as "a low point in Chaplin's
creative output." Musser also suggests that the romantic union in a film
such as *The Pawnshop* (1916) can be read as "implausible and unlikely to
be sustained." Further, by intellectualizing Chaplin "underscoring the
affinities and parallels between artist and tramp" in *The Immigrant*, Musser
excuses the happy ending as "a special case" (53–54). His model—by his
own admission—also fails to offer a wider, universally convincing account
for the narrative complexities of other comedian comedies. Stars such as
Buster Keaton, whose characters tended to be "reintegrated back into
society" and ultimately successful with their love interests, resisted the
open-ended narratives that give credence to arguments for a Chaplin
metafilm (53).

Writing about 1930s two-reel comedy series in general (but with specific
reference to Laurel and Hardy), Mick Eaton states that "what remains
stable from film to film is the character of the two main protagonists—the
situation itself is continually shifting and continually being annihilated"
(24). Douglas Riblet, by contrast, defines "character" as containing elements "unique to a specific film's diegesis, such as a job or marital status," implying that the character is itself annihilated (in Eaton's terms)
with the changing situation of every new film. By not assuming that, for
instance, Harold Lloyd is portraying the same character every time, Riblet suggests that "we are not confused by his having different relatives,

different hometown, different job, etc. in each film" (182n48). Instead, he argues that a more generalized continuity exists in the "screen persona—a recognizable screen presence based upon continuities of performance style, comic business, character traits and external appearance created by costuming and makeup" (182).

There are undoubtedly examples of animated series that could easily accommodate a metafilm reading. Chuck Jones's *Road Runner* cartoons offer a particularly clear through-line in terms of the Coyote's continual failure to catch his prey. Indeed, one could argue that most of the individual shorts are essentially a collection of vignettes, with the Coyote finding himself at multiple points back, in Musser's terms, "on the bottom rung." Furthermore, the films actually *have* been edited together and released as a longer text—for instance, as part of *The Bugs Bunny/Road Runner Movie* (1979), which contains excerpts from more than fifteen different Road Runner shorts. The majority of animated stars have had existing works compiled into another version at some point—including many whose cartoons lack the relatively open-ended structure of the Road Runner (or, indeed, Chaplin) series. It is possible to identify two predominant strategies for joining (at least partially) disparate texts: one that stresses continuity in terms of character and another that suggests that we are watching a film star performing as his or her "screen persona."

The first approach explicitly presents the films as the experiences of a consistent character, usually in the form of flashbacks. In *Big Bad Sindbad* (1952), for instance, Popeye and his nephews visit a museum, and a statue of Sindbad leads Popeye to reminisce about the time the two crossed paths. This prompts a lengthy segment of *Popeye the Sailor Meets Sindbad the Sailor* (1936). Another cartoon, *Assault and Flattery* (1956), sees Bluto take Popeye to court on the grounds that he has been "brutally beaten on several occasions" by the sailor, and the evidence from both parties includes scenes from previous adventures. Various Tom and Jerry cartoons also frame the characters' recollections of "past" events in different ways: *Jerry's Diary* (1949) involves Tom reading entries in the mouse's journal, *Life With Tom* (1953) sees Jerry publish a supposed novel that Tom recognizes as a thinly veiled account of their countless scrapes, and *Smarty Cat* (1954) purports to be a collection of "home movies" of Tom's encounters with his canine nemesis, Spike. The newly produced linking scenes serve to downplay inconsistencies in the excerpted segments, although not always with complete success. The house in which Tom and Jerry reside in

Jerry's Diary and the homes in each of the clips from earlier shorts vary in design for no apparent reason. *Assault and Flattery* includes excerpts from a cartoon where Bluto is a swami with hypnotic powers—attributes that he does not appear to retain in the courtroom scenes. Rather than offering a viable backstory that unites the entire cinematic canon, the continuity of characterization stressed in these compilation cartoons frequently works only as a result of omitting sections from the original films and indeed by overlooking certain elements that remain. Nonetheless, the prevalence of such entries within many animated stars' filmographies does serve to perpetuate the notion (or, perhaps, illusion) that one is essentially watching the same character throughout the series, even if this does require a lot of forgetting.

The second approach embraces the inconsistencies between films by recontextualizing them as a collection of works created by a film actor. *Betty Boop's Rise to Fame* (1934) sees the star interviewed by a newspaper reporter, and she "recreates" past roles for him. One excerpted sequence is from *Betty Boop's Bamboo Isle* (1932), a film that presents the protagonist as a tropical island native with much darker skin than usual. While this change in ethnicity went unexplained in the original short, *Rise to Fame* sees Betty applying ink to her face and body before entering the scene. The lack of continuity between Betty's visual appearance in *Bamboo Isle* and other installments of the series is clarified with the suggestion that each film is a performance by Betty rather than a coherent chronicle of a single character. Similarly, *Adventures of Popeye* (1935) contains a live-action wraparound sequence in which a bullied young boy purchases a piece of Popeye movie merchandise—a storybook—and the sailor comes to life to coach the child into standing up for himself. This is achieved through illustrations of Popeye's own fighting technique, while the sailor's introductions—"Here's what I did in the rodeo picture," and "Now I'll show you what I did in another of me pictures"—explicitly establish reused footage as clips from old Popeye-starring cartoons. Indeed, despite some exceptions noted above, the majority of Popeye compilation films use a similar explanation involving Popeye having a movie career.[14] The very title of *Popeye's 20th Anniversary* (1954) indicates that the sailor has been a film star since the 1930s and sees him at a testimonial dinner with the likes of Bob Hope and Jimmy Durante, introducing several "movies what made me famousk [*sic*]." *Popeye Makes a Movie* (1950) even begins with a shot of the Paramount Pictures studio and reveals that Popeye has a production facility on the lot. The sailor's nephews arrive to see him shoot a film, allowing reuse of footage from *Popeye the Sailor Meets Ali Baba's Forty Thieves* (1937) interspersed with new material in which the nephews break into the action to offer assistance to Popeye (causing the director to cut the scene and shout "get those brats off the set!").

The fact that many cartoon series use *both* the character and star persona models to offer continuity complicates any definitive conclusion. As the date ranges of the Popeye cartoons indicate, the two approaches were used interchangeably—one did not necessarily supersede the other. Dyer's work implies that the star reading overrules any other explanation because it authenticates its own apparent "truth" by exposing the character as a constructed entity, explicitly performed by the actor ("*A Star is Born*" 136). Although this necessarily creates a disjunction between the "fictional" characters in the regular films and appearances as "themselves" in the "behind-the-scenes" or "star-as-host" segments, the vast majority of cartoons ultimately try to have it both ways: separating the text and subtext (as discussed in the introduction to this volume), while, to some extent, implying that there are still continuities between the two. Popeye, for instance, retains his crude speech patterns outside of his character performances, and he still bests Bluto in a fight after eating spinach in the "off-screen" sections of films such as *Popeye's 20th Anniversary*. Bugs Bunny, too, generally keeps his wisecracking persona in his extratextual appearances, Daffy Duck remains jealous of Bugs's successes, Mickey and Minnie continue to have romantic feelings for each other, and so on. The dividing lines between character, screen persona, and (implied) private life of the animated figure are difficult to define and frequently blur together to such an extent that it may seem almost impossible to isolate them in any meaningful way.

Theories of live-action stardom are, of course, often built around such ambiguities, and yet the (comparatively little) scholarly research that has been undertaken on actors working exclusively within series or serial forms has usually posited that a somewhat different approach may be required. In his analysis of series produced for television, for instance, John Langer makes the following distinction:

One speaks of a "John Wayne film" or a "film with John Wayne in it," rarely remembering the name of the character that John Wayne actually played. The star absorbs the identity of the film character, taking it over as his/her own, so that finally it vanishes completely. The process seems to operate in reverse in relation to television personalities. Who, for example, recalls that Archie Bunker is really the actor Carroll O'Connor, or Starsky is played by Michael Glaser[?] In television fiction it is the characters themselves that maintain a high public profile and are retained as memorable identities. The actors who "play" them are virtually invisible and anonymous. What is remembered in television is not the name of the performer, but the name of the recurrent character or personality in the series. (359)

Langer does acknowledge certain exceptions to this argument, particularly series based around a star's existing name and persona, including sitcoms such as *The Jimmy Stewart Show* (1971–1972) and *The Doris Day Show* (1968–1973). However, he notes that successful and long-running examples have had a transformative effect upon the star's identity: "over time, the distant and inaccessible Lucille Ball becomes familiar and predictable 'Lucy'" (359–360). Jennifer M. Bean's research into female-led adventure serials of the 1910s and 1920s offers a similar discussion of the "semantic slip between the 'she' of the character and the 'she' of the star" in both surrounding materials and the films themselves. The recurring characters played by Pearl White were invariably also named Pearl, while *The Hazards of Helen*, which ran between 1914 and 1917, was initially built around the star Helen Holmes. Bean notes, however, that when the latter series was forced to recast its lead following Holmes's departure, the succeeding actress Rose Gibson was rebranded as "Helen Gibson," highlighting the fluidity of the power relationship between star and character ("Technologies of Early Stardom" 21–22).

Seidman notes that live-action comic performers would often appear in movies as "characters who maintain the real names [or at least the stage names] of the comedians, such as Laurel and Hardy; Larry, Moe and Curly (of The Three Stooges); Harry Langdon; and Harold Lloyd, the latter two usually named 'Harry' and 'Harold' in their films though their last names are fictional" (27). Chaplin's Tramp character was popularly known by the same name as his creator, "Charlie," and a great deal of publicity from the period conflated the two. Amy Sargeant notes that, according to Jean Epstein, audiences in France frequently confused Chaplin (the artist) with "Charlot" (the French name for the Tramp character), using the two names interchangeably (200). Since animated stars were specifically created for the purpose of appearances in films, it is even more common for the name to remain the same in all cinematic and extratextual appearances. Mickey Mouse, then, is almost always referred to as "Mickey Mouse" both on- and off-screen. The opportunity for the performer to overpower the protagonist is thus more complicated in these instances: whereas viewers might choose to label a collection of works as "John Wayne" movies, even though the actor may portray a figure called, for instance, "Sean Thornton" in one text and "Ethan Edwards" in another, a reference to a "Charlie Chaplin" or "Bugs Bunny" film generally evokes both the star and the textual character simultaneously, with neither being unequivocally dominant.

Such "slippage" is also apparent in the visual appearances of both comedic and animated stars. While this is possible with any performer—Roy Rogers, for instance, reportedly dressed (and acted) like a cowboy in his private life as well as on-screen (Gaines, *Contested Culture* 167)—slapstick and cartoon characters frequently became known for an image that challenged the standards of glamor associated with Hollywood stardom and at times exceeded the usual cinematic representations—and limitations—of the human body. The practice fits within particular traditions of comedic acting in which performers literally donned a mask with heightened features to perform character types—perhaps most famously in Commedia dell'Arte (Madden 4).

This technique, especially when combined with the mass medium of cinema, helped to make the biggest comic creations instantly recognizable to audiences, even when reduced to one or two simple characteristics. For instance, Buster Keaton became known for his emotionless facial expressions, Groucho Marx for his greasepaint moustache, Harold Lloyd for his horn-rimmed glasses, and Stan Laurel for his gangly frame, which contrasted against comedy partner Oliver Hardy's stockier build. Once established, comedians tended to keep these traits consistent in all screen appearances, which not only strengthened the notion of an ongoing and cohesive persona, but also usually spilled off-screen and became shorthand for visualizing the performer in any context. For instance, a 1915 *Photoplay* article (Chaplin and Carr 28–30) purporting to be Chaplin's recollections of his early life and rise to fame is illustrated with drawings of him as a child already sporting the Tramp's iconic hat, cane, and toothbrush moustache— even at school and at home (fig. 4.1). Although clearly tongue-in-cheek, the article is indicative of a widespread tendency for the image of a comedy performer's most popular creation to overshadow his or her "real-life"

FIGURE 4.1. Imagining Charlie Chaplin's childhood through the lens of his screen persona, *Photoplay* (July 1915).

status. The ability to cultivate a separate, and potentially more "normal," private appearance does differentiate these figures from their animated counterparts—since the latter have no definitive existence—but this does not appear to have been a significant function of their stardom during the studio era. Photographs of Chaplin without his Tramp costume, or Groucho Marx without the applied moustache, were simply not circulated to the same extent, and were therefore not as universally recognizable, as their cinematic characterizations.[15]

The exaggerated visual manifestation and destructive screen personas of many comedians often presented them as being at odds with—and somehow unfit for—society's norms. In his study of early-1930s sound comedies, Henry Jenkins draws upon Mikhail Bakhtin's conception of the "grotesque body" and its contrast "with a more classical conception of the body, one which emphasizes limits and boundaries rather than apertures and orifices, closure rather than openness and individuality rather than commonality." Although Jenkins demonstrates this conflict playing out *within* Marx Brothers movies—comparing Groucho's grotesqueness with the "more carefully controlled and tightly closed body" of Margaret Dumont—wider parallels can be drawn between comedian comedy stars and the types of players generally found in other genre films (*What Made Pistachio Nuts?* 223). "Regular" stars were routinely scrutinized using increasingly unforgiving standards of beauty—particularly by the burgeoning fan magazine market—and were encouraged to fix or downplay supposed "imperfections." By contrast, comedian Ben Turpin turned his crossed eyes into a selling point, and Jimmy Durante drew attention to his oversized nose, embracing the nickname "The Schnozz." The comedian comedy frequently showcases a body that accentuates elements of Bakhtin's "grotesque": a body that is potentially seen as "inhuman" by the repressed standards of classical Hollywood cinema.

On the surface level, most animated stars are distinguished from live-action comedians by their status as animals.[16] However, Seidman provides a large selection of examples from live-action comedies where the comedian actually assumes animalistic behavior. For instance, in *Behind the Screen*, "when a stagehand catches Chaplin stealing parts of his lunch, Chaplin barks, pants, and begs like a dog" (66). Equally, the sexual aggressiveness of Harpo Marx's screen performances appears more animal-like than human, driven purely by lust rather than the sentiment regularly articulated by Hollywood's romantic leads. The characters dip in and out of this behavior—losing and regaining a sense of their humanity—with little warning and often without any logical reason.

Conversely, the majority of animal cartoon characters display broad anthropomorphic qualities and possess lifestyles that have more in common with the human experience than with those of their designated species. Mickey Mouse—particularly in cartoons from the mid-1930s onward—seemingly owns a suburban house, performs a variety of jobs (including mechanic and band conductor), and even has a pet, Pluto (whose animalistic canine traits serve to emphasize Mickey's essential "humanity"). Bugs Bunny, similarly, is bipedal, can talk, and displays more intelligence and cunning than many of his human foes. Wile E. Coyote approaches the task of catching the Road Runner like an engineer, relying upon elaborate (if always flawed) technological inventions. However, slippages still occur in these star personas, too: Bugs usually lives in a hole in the ground and is the target of hunters during rabbit season, while the Coyote is still at heart a ravenous animal hunting his prey. The animated star's persona, akin to that of the live-action comedian, is presented as unpredictable, inconsistent, and not always synchronized to the visual representation of his or her body. This juxtaposition between human(-like) attributes and a sense of "otherness" unites both of these forms in opposition against "typical" Hollywood stars.

Physical Performance and Special Effects

As I note in the introduction to this book, Stanley Cavell denies that cartoons can be categorized as movies because, supposedly unlike live-action cinema, they leave us "uncertain when or to what extent our [real-world physical] laws and [metaphysical] limits do and do not apply" (168). Live-action comedian comedies offer a suggestive rebuke to this statement as they—just like cartoons—frequently revel in the malleability of the world represented on-screen, usually directly in relation to the star as protagonist. Seidman describes the potential for "magic" within the comedian comedy, which "permits various kinds of instantaneous transformation and allows bodies incredible properties, including immortality and invulnerability" (124). A recurring feature of the early Keystone shorts, for instance, was exaggerated outbursts, such as fights involving thrown bricks, yet Riblet notes that "characters almost never died or suffered permanent, serious injury" (173).

The ability of slapstick comedians to transgress the usual limitations of the human body undoubtedly proved an influence upon similar experiments with the cartoon form. The development of the cel system over the latter half of the 1910s led to the popularization of "rubber-hose" animation, which offered new possibilities for gags that challenged the physical world. Characters created in this style could be reduced, in their most basic form, to a collection of circles (his or her face, ears, stomach, and so on) and "rubber-tube" limbs. Each of these constituent shapes is configured as elastic, therefore allowing the body to be temporarily manipulated in various ways without the character feeling any pain (except, potentially, in the immediate moment) or lasting disfigurement. Felix the Cat's tail, for instance, could transform into all sorts of different objects, but it would still ultimately revert to functioning as a tail and conform to the ongoing character design. Many of Mickey Mouse's early films also allowed for significant manipulation and distortion, while retaining a consistent point of return—a recognizable, stable body image that could be exploited in the same way as that of live-action stars. In a famous example from *Steamboat Willie* (1928), Mickey's stomach is grabbed by the villainous Pete and stretched onto the ground. Caught whistling and dancing while he is supposed to be working, Mickey shows an element of surprise, but no enduring distress. He simply pulls his stretched torso back into his shorts and his stomach returns to its original shape (fig. 4.2). The lack of consequences undermines the usual "cause-and-effect" logic central to most classical Hollywood narratives.[17]

Despite these suggestive parallels between slapstick and animated comedy shorts, particularly in opposition to other genres, academic work still often separates the two. For instance, in his study of live-action comedy, Alex Clayton makes a distinction between the original Laurel and Hardy films and a cartoon version made for television in the late 1960s. His preference for the former evokes Cavell in emphasizing the importance of the "vividness of the bodies involved, inhabiting spaces with a real-world weight and possessing physical attributes that were generally rooted in an everyday experience of one's own and others' bodies" (Clayton 1–2). Although animation is only briefly discussed elsewhere in his text, it is referenced primarily to highlight what the medium *lacks* compared to live-action performance: the latter is praised because of how "the body is *presented*, rather than created or constructed" (11). Clayton uses the example of a sequence from *Bringing Up Baby* (1938), in which Cary Grant's character slips on an olive:

FIGURE 4.2. An example of "rubber-hose" animation in *Steamboat Willie* (1928).

The force with which he hits the ground is undeniably the force of a real grown man, of precisely Grant's size and shape, falling with a thwump to the floor. It *is* Cary Grant who has fallen. . . . [The] brutal force of the slapstick pratfall has the capacity to reawaken us to the fundamental physicality of the world, and hence to its detail: to its textures and rhythms, to relationships elemental and vivid, to the momentary triumphs and failures of human endeavor, to the physical laws and properties that restrict and permit human activity. . . . To acknowledge that the body that falls is that of a real human being is to recognize the fact that characters on film are embodied. This is a feature that cartoon representations of human beings cannot truly be said to possess. (11–12)

There is certainly little reason to doubt the veracity of the fall in the "olive scene." It is filmed as a single take and the framing of the shot clearly presents Cary Grant's face and body while the stunt is being performed (fig. 4.3).

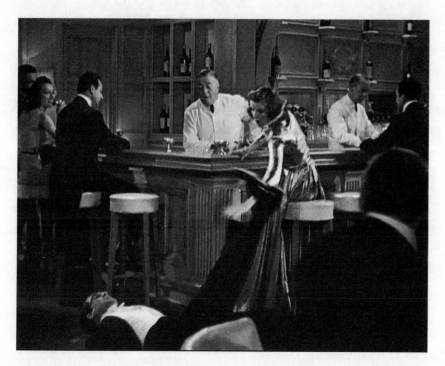

FIGURE 4.3. The physical body of Cary Grant performing a stunt in *Bringing Up Baby* (1938).

However, there is still arguably a danger in placing too much trust in the "truth" of the photographed body. *Sherlock Jr.*, for instance, contains a number of examples that complicate such a definitive pronouncement about the performer's contribution. One celebrated sequence involves Buster Keaton's character getting a ride on a motorcycle by sitting on the handlebars. Gillette, the driver, falls off the back after hitting a pothole, and Buster is left unknowingly piloting the machine. Keaton reportedly doubled for the actor playing Gillette at the moment where he falls from the bike, meaning that there is, for the duration of that particular shot, a different actor embodying "Buster Keaton" on the handlebars (Brownlow, "Buster Keaton" 201–202). While Keaton did physically perform most of the stunts in the overall sequence—including his brief, anonymous contribution as Gillette—some were achieved only by using the cinematic technology to temper or manipulate the on-screen representation. Certain shots were sped up in the finished version, while others were carefully framed to obscure filming aids such as a tow rope and a stabilizing third wheel on the motorbike. What appears to be one of the most dangerous feats—the motorcycle careens toward a hole in a bridge just as two conveniently sized trucks drive underneath to fill the gap—was in actuality achieved with relative safety. The filmmakers captured the trucks moving into the space and took a separate shot of Keaton driving along a fully assembled bridge. The two takes were composited together to create the *illusion* that the events occurred simultaneously within the same space ("Movie Magic & Mysteries"). Although, as Henry Jenkins notes, there are moments in the film where Keaton explicitly "wants us to be aware of the camera manipulation" ("This Fellow Keaton" 47), this particular trick is *not* clearly signaled to viewers, creating the potential for confusion about the "reality" of the diegetic world (fig. 4.4).

Comedian comedies have at times also indulged in "impossible" gags, which overtly push the limitations of the performer's body. In the Laurel and Hardy short *Liberty* (1929), a police officer is squashed by an elevator. Rather than enduring a horrific injury, his body remains perfectly functional and is simply compacted—a gag that evokes the rubber-hose animation of contemporary cartoon shorts and was achieved in this instance by substituting a shorter actor for the original performer at the appropriate moment. In *Way Out West* (1937), Stan Laurel surprises himself by flicking his thumb and creating a flame at the tip like a cigarette lighter, and Oliver Hardy's neck is stretched temporarily beyond human limits—in a similar

FIGURE 4.4. An "invisible" special effect. Unacknowledged composite photography in *Sherlock Jr.* (1924).

manner to Mickey's torso in *Steamboat Willie*—as Laurel attempts to free him from a trap door.

While live-action slapstick is regularly celebrated for its "fundamental physicality," to use Clayton's term, it should be emphasized that comedians have sometimes been *hindered* by the "real-world" conditions in which they film. Chaplin reportedly "once said he envied the perfect timing of gags in animated cartoons, attributing it to the fact that cartoons never had to take the time to breathe" (Canemaker, *Felix* 102). The neck-stretching sequence in *Way Out West* required the construction of a prop that resembled Hardy's features, and the final scene was intercut with shots of his actual head in an attempt to blur the boundaries between the real body and the special effect (fig. 4.5). A gag in *The Patsy* (1964) in which Jerry Lewis's character falls off a hotel balcony, lands on the diving board of the swimming pool below, and bounces straight back into the room was similarly achieved by using a succession of still photographs of Lewis and editing techniques to recontextualize snippets of live-action footage. Where comedians do

FIGURE 4.5. Cutting between the real and faked body in *Way Out West* (1937).

engage in "impossible" humor, it is usually necessary to interrupt their performance—the immediate pro-filmic event, which is so central to Cavell's concept of cinema.

The live-action body has to subject itself to cinematic manipulation and at times even literally become *animated*. This revelation indicates that existing models of stardom fail to fully account for all types of live-action performance and exposes a degree of inconsistency in the implicit denial of star status for the cartoon protagonist. It is suggestive that the comedian's body within film theory has been characterized variously as "robotized," "mechanical," and even as a "sideshow marionette" (Stewart 297, Alderman 154, Walter Benjamin qtd. in MacKay 310). Frank D. McConnell reads Chaplin's Tramp as embodying "the struggle of the human to show itself *within* the mechanical" (176). He argues that these impulses exist in all film personalities, but are rarely articulated at the level of performance. Certainly, to return to Bordwell, Staiger, and Thompson's work, such a contradiction would challenge the "invisible" classical style that is often assumed in star theory.

Live-action comedy may not be automatically obliged to acknowledge its own artifice, given that it has the potential to appear photo-realistic (unlike hand-drawn animation), but it still frequently *chooses* to manipulate this "reality" for the purposes of humor. Clayton is undoubtedly correct in highlighting the centrality of the physical body in slapstick. There are clearly moments in these films when the thrill comes from watching a real person putting him- or herself in a legitimately dangerous situation, performing an action that few others could achieve or even dare to attempt. However, while Clayton does briefly reference the possible use of prosthetics, costume, camera tricks, and so on, this does not prevent him from emphasizing that live-action comedy "bypasses the human hand in the creation of its forms" (11).

By contrast, scholarly discussions of animation seem unable to *avoid* the inferred presence of the artist's hand. Despite acknowledging (but downplaying) the existence of some live-action comedies that "[call] into question their actors' ontological status," Nicholas Sammond suggests that cartoons differ because they primarily exist in, and relate to, "a world that was clearly *drawn* by *somebody*" (99). He concludes that the uneasy boundaries between the individual character, the wider persona, and the personal life of the comedian cannot be effectively applied to the animated protagonist because of its more overtly manufactured nature. Instead, he posits the fundamental relationship for a cartoon star as the "triad of animator(s), plasmatic substance, and character" (297).

While there is a logic and legitimacy to both these positions, Clayton's and Sammond's arguments come at the expense of closing down alternative reading positions. Although figures such as Chaplin and Keaton had primary control of their own bodies, there are still moments when their vitality on-screen owes just as much to the director, or the prop master, or even sometimes an animator, and yet this is rarely explored in detail within slapstick theory. Conversely, regardless of the artificial nature of the animated star, there is still the potential that his or her "performance" could encourage the viewer to look beyond, or even ignore, the behind-the-scenes personnel (and the underlying technology) that worked to construct it.

The basis of the comedian comedy in live-action has served to distance it from animation, even though both forms also possess (less discussed) properties that may productively challenge certain assumptions surrounding Hollywood stardom. In particular, the recurring evocation of a character within a series or serial, and its impact upon the star's image, remains an area worthy of further study. From the perspective of animation studies, the focus on a "creator," inherently separated from that of the "creation," has provided a similar barrier to a closer union with the comedian comedy. Nonetheless, studio-era cartoon stars are presented with a textual (and often extratextual) persona that—regardless of its origin—largely emulates the complexities of the public versus the private, and the persona versus the character, played out by many human comic performers.

Chapter 5

Authorship

uthorship theory has traditionally been rooted in the concept of individual expression, and yet animation, like all other forms of mainstream American filmmaking, is almost exclusively a collaborative medium (Sellors 11, 19). Admittedly, the very earliest animated films *were* largely the work of single artists—such as J. Stuart Blackton and Winsor McCay—and usually featured them on-screen in some capacity, reiterating the seemingly straightforward relationship between creator and creation. However, as noted in chapter 1, the intensive labor required to complete such films, coupled with the desire of several producers to release cartoons on a regular basis, quickly led to a shift in the way animation was made. By the mid-1910s, Bray Studios had developed a system that echoed Fordist and Taylorist production and efficiency principles—that is, a workforce specializing in specific areas of manufacture, with each employee contributing part of the finished product rather than completing an entire film individually (Crafton, *Before Mickey* 162–167). This rapidly became the standard in theatrical short cartoon series production, with

Disney Studios, in particular, establishing very clear divisions of labor among different departments.

Tom Sito notes that, even when a crew consisted of "dozens, often hundreds of artists, writers, technicians and support staff," the intention was almost always "to create a film that *looks like* it was made by one hand" (*Drawing the Line* 7, emphasis added). As this quotation indicates, the singular author (the "one hand" that supposedly created the entire film) is a fallacy in commercial animation production, but a pervasive construct nonetheless. Although the process of collaboration was frequently acknowledged, almost every short film animation released during the silent and studio eras privileged one individual above all others in its credits and/or surrounding publicity.

Authorship claims have proven problematic throughout animation history, initially due to the falseness of the claims linked to a specific figure and in more recent years due to the commendable—but at times perhaps overzealous—attempts to redress the balance in favor of previously neglected artists. Beyond this, however, the characters themselves were presented with a sense of vitality that complicates notions of off-screen authorial control. The profitability of these recurring protagonists often came at the expense of greater variety and experimentation in cartoon production. The ambitions of artists, such as Walt Disney, and United Productions of America (UPA) were disrupted by the need to serve an animated star. Indeed, it will be argued that these cartoon figures could perhaps be seen as virtual "auteurs" in their own right, imposing formulaic requirements that the creative artists were compelled to obey, rather than permitted to react against.

The History (and Limitations) of Authorship Claims

In the 1910s, at the beginnings of the cartoon industry, many early comic strip adaptations not only drew upon the existing fame of the protagonists, but also repeated the authorship credits of the original text. Although the French artist Émile Cohl was the lead animator on *The Newlyweds* cartoon series, released between 1913 and 1914, his name never appeared in advertising. "Instead, all the credit for the series went to [the comic strip artist, George] McManus, whose popularity, it was hoped, would attract the public" (Crafton, *Emile Cohl* 164). The *Mutt and Jeff* adaptations operated in a similar manner. A great deal of the publicity for the cartoon versions (particularly in the 1910s) suggested that Bud Fisher supplied all the stories

FIGURE 5.1. Fred Quimby's signature credit in *Mouse Trouble* (1944).

and animation.[1] However, in a retrospective interview conducted in the late 1960s, Dick Huemer, one of the animators on the series, stated that Fisher financed the production "but had nothing whatever to do with the pictures" and rarely visited the studio (qtd. in Adamson, "A Talk with Dick Huemer" 32).

As animation units grew larger and began generating original stars for the screen, a new figurehead generally took precedence: the producer and/or head of studio. Nicholas Sammond notes that many of the on-screen "battles" enacted between the artist and his/her creation during the 1920s involved the "producer performing *as* animator," usually failing to communicate to the viewer that this was not the person responsible for making the cartoon characters move in the finished film (40). Although this trope had largely diminished by the sound era, the managerial figure could still indulge in self-promotion by other means. For instance, the boss of the MGM animation unit, Fred Quimby, frequently received a full-screen credit on each cartoon, more prominent than any other contributor. His name was also the only on-screen signature, further implying that his was the foremost authorial "voice" on the project (fig. 5.1). With a couple of exceptions,

Quimby's status as producer entitled him to be the sole recipient of any Academy Award nominations, and he reportedly collected and personally kept the statues when the cartoons won. However, subsequent research has claimed that he had no direct input into the animation or storytelling, "knew little about the field he found himself in," and even "had no sense of humor" (Sito, *Drawing the Line* 42; Maltin, *Of Mice and Magic* 283).[2]

Such examples highlight the problematic nature of authorship claims: audiences could be led to believe that the cartoons—and the animated stars contained within them—are the authentic vision of certain individuals, such as Fisher or Quimby, and yet in actuality these individuals made a minimal contribution to the actual *creative* work on the screen.[3] Even Walt Disney, who in the 1930s (and beyond) publicly acknowledged that he had personally long since retired from the day-to-day work of actually drawing the films, still encouraged a reading in which he, as producer, could be seen as the "maker of the magic of animation," as a force "in control of"—but crucially "distinct from"—his employees (Sammond 118). The animator was often presented as a skilled, but largely interchangeable, craftsman. This perspective remained dominant throughout the studio era, as the artists themselves were rarely quoted directly in fan magazines or trade journals.[4]

The most influential challenge to the producer-as-author model emerged externally from the industry. In the 1950s, a group of French critics, many writing in the pages of the journal *Cahiers du Cinéma*, proposed a reading of film history that privileged the role of the director as the primary creative figure, the "auteur." As Andrew Dix suggests, "auteurism played a significant part . . . in the establishment and consolidation of film studies itself, providing this new discipline with its core authors and texts" (138). One can identify similar attempts to legitimize animation studies as an academic pursuit by the early 1970s. A new generation of fans and scholars challenged the limited, and mostly Disney-centric, attention that had been paid to cartoons in the past, even seeking out surviving industry veterans for interviews and, in many cases, giving them a platform to speak about their contributions for the first time.[5] Although this brought valuable credibility during a period in which television cartoons were viewed as tarnishing the medium's wider reputation (see chapter 7), such an approach undoubtedly had its own agenda.

One example can be found in the retrospective criticism surrounding Felix the Cat. During the 1920s, it was widely circulated that Pat Sullivan, the head of the studio that issued the films, had created Felix. Subsequent research in the 1970s and 1980s revealed that Otto Messmer, one of Sullivan's animators, actually designed the character and was heavily involved with the entirety of the series run. He earned a basic studio salary, had no official share in ownership of the character, and received none of the profits or plaudits that Sullivan enjoyed. Animation historians have undoubtedly done an admirable job in finally recognizing Messmer's input into one of the world's most iconic cartoon figures. However, in an attempt to redress the injustice of the producer taking too much personal credit, much of this analysis overtly stressed a connection between the previously "faceless" animator-director and the cartoon star within his/her films as a means of identifying the supposedly *genuine* author of the work. For instance, in his pioneering book, *Before Mickey*, Donald Crafton suggests that Felix was, in fact, the "index of a real personality," that of Messmer himself (338). John Canemaker similarly asserts that "the films and their star were essentially extensions of Messmer's personality and a manifestation of his unique creative mind" (*Felix* 59). Such accounts have suggestive parallels with star theory by rooting the "proof" of Felix's creation within Messmer's existence as a person. As with Richard Dyer's concept of the rhetoric that suggests that "what is behind or below the surface is unquestionably and virtually by definition, the truth" (*"A Star is Born"* 136), this claim is seemingly verified in part by exposing the falsehood of the previous discourse surrounding Sullivan. Indeed, Timothy Corrigan suggests that auteur theory has, at times, uncritically promoted the director to quasi-star status (105–108). Messmer undoubtedly had more creative input than Sullivan, but he still did not draw every single frame or conceive every gag in the series. The direct conflation with Messmer and Felix not only continues to diminish the role played by many other personnel at the Sullivan studio, but also downplays the on-screen vitality of the Cat himself (who had been enjoyed for numerous decades by audiences with no knowledge of Messmer's contribution).

The inefficiencies of auteurism are similarly visible in attempts to determine the origins of Bugs Bunny. All the major *Looney Tunes* directors created films featuring Bugs, making it difficult to determine conclusively who can lay claim to specific elements of his body image and persona.[6] From this perspective, the rabbit does not seem to be the unequivocal index of any specific director's personality. A 1970 interview with director Robert Clampett sparked controversy when he appeared to take most of the credit for the creation of the character (Barrier and Gray 19, 21). After similar declarations in the documentary *Bugs Bunny Superstar* (1975), Chuck Jones wrote a detailed letter (with annotations from Tex Avery) refuting this version of events (Cohen 199n37). In *The Bugs Bunny/Road Runner Movie* (1979), directed by Jones, Bugs Bunny states that he has several "fathers," and the scene cuts between caricatures of a number of *Looney Tunes* directors and scriptwriters (and Mel Blanc, the voice of Bugs). Clampett is notably absent from this sequence. In 1980, Patrick McGilligan suggested that "the situation is further muddied by the clamorous cult of devotees who gather in each animator's circle" and identified publications that appeared to side with either Jones or Clampett ("Robert Clampett" 152). The pursuit of an "auteur" again risked creating a binary approach in which celebrating the achievements of one artist involved denying the contributions of others. The focus on the apparent uniqueness of a specific director's "vision" may also come at the expense of a wider understanding of collaboration—as well as appropriation—that often occurred in short cartoon production.

Stars and Originality

In his seminal essay, "The Death of the Author," Roland Barthes highlights the futility of trying to find a point of "origin" for the production of textual meaning, arguing that all texts are "made of multiple writings, drawn from many cultures and entering into mutual relations of dialogue, parody, contestation" (148). Although Barthes arguably overstates the need for complete denial of authorial intention, his thesis is valuable in encouraging scholars not to isolate the work in question (or, for the purposes of this volume, the star) from a wider culture of textual production. During the silent era, for instance, staff turned over frequently among the various New York studios, and animators would regularly emulate competitors' films (Sammond 104). A popular aspect of the Felix the Cat series, the rubber-hose animation style had antecedents in earlier works by artists such as Bill Nolan, and many other producers made cartoons with similar aesthetics throughout the peak years of the Cat's success. Technical issues with early monochrome photography also encouraged a relative uniformity in terms of character design, with most animal stars of the period having black fur and white faces—an approach, Sammond convincingly argues, that also draws from traditions of theatrical blackface minstrelsy, even if this has not generally been acknowledged by the industry (257). As previous chapters indicated, short animation was also influenced by a variety of other media forms, including comic strips, vaudeville, and even live-action cinema.

The development of Mickey Mouse by Disney Studios offers another suggestive example of this tendency to mythologize, and sometimes strategically forget, aspects of the creative process. Although Mickey is now considered one of the most iconic and recognizable characters in the world, several aspects of his visual appearance and behavior can be traced to other preexisting sources. As Russell Merritt and J. B. Kaufman note, the Mouse "was not [originated] in a vacuum" (*Walt in Wonderland* 11), regardless of accounts that present Mickey as an unequivocal expression of Walt Disney's own personality, or even, in some cases, as a seemingly biological offspring.[7] In early 1928, Disney Studios was continuing work on its *Oswald the Lucky Rabbit* cartoons, which had debuted the previous year. Buoyed by its rapid success, Disney planned to request an increased advance payment per film from his distributor Charles Mintz, but was countered with the threat of a pay *cut* and other terms that would reduce Disney's control of the studio (Korkis, "Secrets" 57). Disney did not own the character of Oswald and discovered that Mintz had brokered separate deals with the majority of his animators to continue producing the series without him if an agreement could not be reached. Discussions ultimately broke down, but Disney remained obliged to fulfill his existing contract before his lucrative creation and production staff were taken away from him.

During this period, he assembled a small team to work secretly on developing a film featuring a hastily conceived new character: Mickey Mouse. As Neal Gabler suggests, "Mickey was the product of desperation and calculation—the desperation born of Walt Disney's need to [save his studio] and the calculation of what the market would accept" in terms of a new product (114). The character was a basic, rounded design without any "frills that would slow down [production]," using the prevalent rubber-hose method of animation (Walt Disney qtd. in Schickel 117). Rubber-hose characters were arguably most distinguishable from each other by the manner in which simple shapes were assembled, rather than by particularly complex or detailed visual attributes. In this regard, Mickey's circular mouse ears, as opposed to Felix's triangular cat ears or Oswald's longer rabbit ears, mark perhaps the most distinctive aspect of the character's visual profile.

The fluid nature of the animation style, which allowed characters' bodies to be stretched and manipulated at will, coupled with a trend toward anthropomorphism meant that animal cartoon stars of the period quickly

FIGURE 5.2. A precursor to Mickey Mouse in Paul Terry's *The Fable of the Traveling Salesman* (also known as *Smart Salesman*, 1923).

transcended the "limitations" of their designated type. Just as Mintz had instructed Disney to create Oswald as a rabbit, due to the perception that there were "too many cats on the market," Mickey's species was generally of little importance beyond the need for product differentiation (Gabler 102). As Disney later remarked, "we canvassed all the animal characters we thought suitable [but] . . . all the good ones . . . seemed to have been preempted" by other cartoonists (qtd. in Griffiths 67). Mice were by no means original in animated cinema at this point, but had been used mostly in minor roles with little characterization underpinning their appearances (fig. 5.2). Mickey's alliterative name and the basic graphic markers that established his "mouse-ness" helped to avoid accusations of overt plagiarism, but he still essentially conformed to the overriding tradition of rubber-hose animal stars that were proving so popular with audiences.

The Disney Studios creation was not intended to revolutionize the animation industry and originated as a fairly derivative character. A seemingly safe bet based on existing trends, Mickey was meant to replace the departing star, Oswald, with as little disruption as possible. Indeed, several of the initial Mickey films even borrowed routines and plots from Disney productions: for instance, the Mouse's transformation of a goat into a gramophone in *Steamboat Willie* (1928) had been enacted by Oswald earlier that same year in *Rival Romeos* (fig. 5.3).[8] Mickey's rising status eventually served to render a generic mouse design synonymous with the public perception of his star image. Crucially, though, this occurred only in hindsight. At the point of his creation, Mickey was little more than the refinement of an existing prototype, drawing heavily on the star images of existing characters.

Early media appearances by celebrities are often a source of (retrospective) fascination and amusement for fans because they show a now-famous figure before his or her screen persona had been fully consolidated. Jib Fowles notes that many young performers initially modeled themselves on other stars before enjoying peak success: "The lass Clara Bow idolized Mary Pickford. The lad Elvis Presley styled his hair and mannerisms after . . . Tony Curtis [whom] he had viewed on a Memphis movie screen; a year or two later, he was thinking of himself as a Rudolph Valentino successor" (43–44).

This was also true on an industrial level: as Martin Barker states (summarizing the research of Cathy Klaprat), studios such as Warner Bros. "took a number of years and experimented in various ways before hitting a winning formula" for many of their top performers (19). Some actors even garnered fame on the very basis of their apparently derivative status. For instance, Jayne Mansfield was frequently labeled in reviews—and at times actually promoted by 20th Century–Fox—as "Marilyn Monroe, king size," or as a "Super-Monroe," essentially reducing her to a hyperbolic echo of (but also potential replacement for) Monroe's already highly sexualized body (Faris 5). Such examples reaffirm that star images are never merely a reflection of the performer's natural personality—or even, in the case of animation, the personality of the identified creative artist—but are instead a negotiation between various aesthetic and market forces.

The moment at which a star becomes widely accepted as individualized and unique is rather ambiguous. With Mickey Mouse, Disney's decision to create yet another recurring series based on a central animal protagonist unexpectedly served to expose the oversaturation of the animated star system by 1928. The studio originally produced two Mickey films—*Plane Crazy* (1928) and *The Gallopin' Gaucho* (1928)—as silent cartoons, but failed to attract any interest from a distributor. Mickey's implicit promise of

FIGURE 5.3. Recycling of gags in pre- and post-sound Disney cartoons: Oswald the Lucky Rabbit in *Rival Romeos* (1928) and Mickey Mouse in *Steamboat Willie* (1928).

"more of the same" had turned from a selling point to a liability. It was only with the addition of sound to the third entry, *Steamboat Willie*, that Disney finally received a distribution deal. Contrary to claims in some historical accounts, *Steamboat Willie* was not the first sound cartoon, but Crafton notes that "of all the producers Disney had the strongest desire to master sound technology for its own sake" (*Before Mickey* 212). The quality of the synchronization in Disney's films (particularly when contrasted against the desultory application of sound in his competitors' cartoons, such as *Mutt and Jeff* and *Felix the Cat*) does appear to have shifted focus away from the imitative aspects of Mickey's star image and posited him as a symbol of cutting-edge filmmaking. As Kaufman suggests, even gags that Disney was recycling from earlier silent cartoons were at least partially altered and "enhanced by sound" ("The Shadow" 71).

It is nonetheless surprising that some animation historians have specifically dismissed so many of the new animated series developed by competing studios in the early 1930s as second-rate derivations of Mickey Mouse. These include Bosko (the first star of the *Looney Tunes* series), Cubby Bear (produced by Van Beuren Studios), and Flip the Frog (produced by Mickey Mouse co-creator Ub Iwerks after he left Disney Studios in 1930).[9] Given the arguments surrounding Mickey's own unoriginality, is it accurate to suggest that other animated characters of the period were directly imitating Disney's star? For instance, Leonard Maltin states that Cubby Bear "was just another in the long line of Mickey Mouse descendants who populated movie screens of the 1930s" (*Of Mice and Magic* 203). Charles Solomon, in contrast, counters that Cubby was "another black-and-white character in the Felix the Cat tradition" (*Enchanted Drawings* 93). Although Solomon's account offers a bit more historical nuance, both critics offer very little analysis of the character beyond suggesting that he was cribbed from something else. The focus on Cubby's similarities to Mickey and/or Felix, rather than on the points of divergence, implicitly denies the character any sense of autonomy: his existence is seen as entirely dependent on another, more popular star, seemingly lacking any value on its own terms. Maltin's *Of Mice and Magic* and Solomon's *Enchanted Drawings* were two of the earliest and most influential attempts to offer a comprehensive studio-by-studio overview of American animated production (rather than just focusing on Disney), and so there is a risk that their respective dismissals of Cubby could rapidly congeal into an unreflective consensus and deter additional research.[10]

A fruitful comparison can be made with Charlie Chaplin, whose on-screen persona is perceived to have inspired competing screen comedians—such as Billie Ritchie and Billy West—who supposedly copied aspects of the Tramp's appearance and characterization (see, for example, McCabe 89; Sobel and Francis 143–144). These accounts again tend to be limited to brief discussions of plagiarism, often without citing any specific films or surrounding publicity. With this in mind, Steve Massa and Jon Burrows have each argued for a reevaluation of Ritchie. Their respective work offers valuable insight into how claims of imitation can potentially distort academic histories in favor of a dominant subject. Both suggest (to varying degrees) that similarities between Chaplin and Ritchie could reflect broader influences from earlier music hall and comedic filmmaking traditions, rather than ideas originated by Chaplin and "stolen" by others. Returning to Mickey Mouse, then, it should be argued that the majority of the early 1930s animated stars were (consciously or not) still drawing upon an older tradition, which Mickey may have served to repopularize (and to an extent recontextualize), but Disney's Mouse was in many ways just as complicit in the act of imitation as the others.[11]

It is important to reiterate that Disney *did* take legal action against Van Beuren Studios in 1931 for the alleged evocation of the Mouse in several *Aesop's Fables* cartoons, such as *A Close Call* (1929), *Western Whoopee* (1930), and *The Office Boy* (1930), but received some criticism due to the indefinite provenance of certain aspects of Mickey himself. In this regard, the history of another Chaplin imitator is revealing:

[A] Mexican actor, Charles Amador . . . brazenly changed his name professionally to Charlie Aplin and copied outright prize Chaplin routines. Chaplin sued. Amazingly, Amador's lawyers made some detailed and verifiable points surrounding their client's "right" to the Chaplin costume and walk. They proved through expert testimony that Chaplin's costume and make-up were not singular. The brush [moustache] had been worn by a Chicago actor named George Beban in 1890; . . . at the turn of the century an act called the Nibble Brothers did much stage business with a flexible cane [and so on]. (McCabe 89–90)

Both Chaplin's and Disney's cases raised the question of where the line can be drawn between integrating preexisting sources into (supposedly) original work and the murkier practices of plagiarism. In his study of early stardom, Richard deCordova identifies the performer's name as a key component of his or her "unique" image (*Picture Personalities* 20).[12] The transparency of Amador's screen moniker, Charlie Aplin, undoubtedly contextualized his other appropriations and weakened his case. (Chaplin did not, after all, sue either West or Ritchie.) The "theft" of a name occurred in the two foremost cases of plagiarism in silent animation. Around 1915, J. R. Bray released an unauthorized remake of Winsor McCay's *Gertie the Dinosaur* (1914) under the same title as the original (and sometimes also known as *Diplodocus*), and Paul Terry's use of a feline character called "Felix" reportedly led to an intervention from Pat Sullivan (Crafton, *Before Mickey* 212; Canemaker, *Felix* 90). Seemingly reflecting the increased tendency toward litigation in the movie industry by the 1930s, no American producers launched a competitive series specifically containing a recurring character called "Mickey Mouse." Indeed, Van Beuren Studios took great pains during the aforementioned legal proceedings with Disney to suggest that the mice identified as plagiarisms were actually Milton and Mary Mouse, characters who had appeared under those names in a number of *Aesop's Fables* cartoons during the silent era, several years before Mickey's creation (United States Court of Appeals 94).

Body image is also an area of (relative) legal certainty for both live-action and animated stars. Jane M. Gaines makes a distinction between the "ephemeral literary character—who is constructed with word portraits too abstract and vague to be visualized (and hence protected)—and cartoon characters, whose concrete existence as artistic renderings makes uniqueness (or imitative proclivities) easier to verify in court" (*Contested Culture* 212). Like Chaplin, however, Disney was challenged over certain aspects of Mickey's appearance and costume that could be traced back to earlier on-screen figures. In a similar manner to Amador's lawyers, Van Beuren's defense noted films such as *The Romantic Mouse* (1922), and its surrounding publicity, in which Milton had already appeared wearing items such as gloves and shoes well before Mickey's first cartoon (United States Circuit Court of Appeals 97). Furthermore, it was argued that "the idea of the creation of a character drawn in the form of a mouse and of dressing the character in various costumes in motion pictures" did not even originate with Van Beuren Studios and could be found in animated precedents by Bray in the 1910s (Harry D. Bailey qtd. in United States Circuit Court of Appeals 112).

Chaplin ultimately won his court battle, arguing that "nobody ever wore the combination that I adopted until I put them on" (qtd. in Bean, "The Art of Imitation" 252). Such a statement appears to presage Barthes's suggestion in "The Death of the Author" that a creator's "only power is to mix writings" that already exist into new variants (146). Disney's case succeeded by making a similar contention. The affidavit of one of the studio's animators, William Norman Ferguson (previously an employee of Van Beuren), offers a point-by-point account of how the mouse character in the *Aesop's Fables* films changed significantly after Mickey's rise to fame. Although Ferguson suggests that, in his opinion, there was as much difference between Mickey and the 1920s version of Milton "as exists between different races of human beings," he concludes that the latter evocation of Milton was "substantially identical" to Mickey, and thus, in a sense, that Van Beuren had mimicked the specific "combination" that Disney's studio had adopted (qtd. in United States Circuit Court of Appeals 60–64).[13]

The boundaries of acceptability remained ill-defined, however. In 1932, the live-action star Helen Kane accused Fleischer Studios of caricaturing her to create Betty Boop, making particular reference to Betty's frequent use of the phrase "Boop-oop-a-doop." Kane was popularly known as the "Boop-Boop-a-Doop Girl," reflecting her "baby talk" style of singing, and some publications had openly hypothesized about Kane's influence on Betty before legal action began (see, for instance, York 108). Nonetheless, once the case finally reached court, the defense countered that another performer, Baby Esther, had "interpolated words like 'boo-boo-boo' and 'doo-doo-doo' in songs at a cabaret" that Kane and her manager had attended prior to her own successful performances in the late 1920s. Fleischer Studios prevailed, not because Betty was deemed wholly original, but because Kane could not conclusively prove that she originated these aspects of her persona.[14] Ironically, around the time that Kane initially criticized the Fleischers, several competing animation studios appeared to be incorporating variants of Betty in their own productions.[15] This prompted Max Fleischer to take out an advertisement accusing others of capitalizing on the fact that Betty had "reached stardom," while asserting his ownership of the character with warnings of litigation for any subsequent appropriations (fig. 5.4).[16]

Cathy Klaprat notes that, during the studio era, producers often based their "product differentiation" on the basis of the apparent "uniqueness of a star," whose services would be under an exclusive contract (369). Simply

FIGURE 5.4.
Max Fleischer's
attempt to protect
Betty Boop's star
image from imi-
tators, *Film Daily*
(10 June 1932).

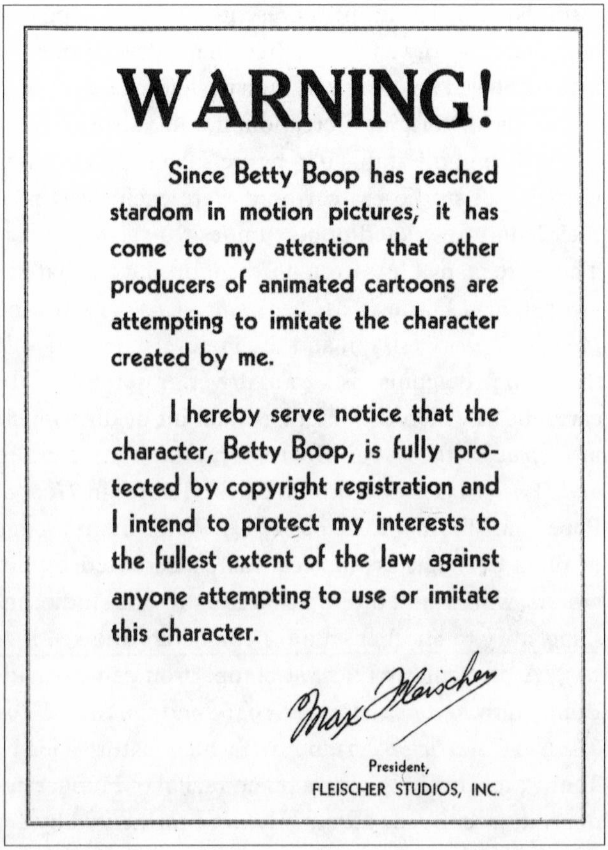

WARNING!

Since Betty Boop has reached stardom in motion pictures, it has come to my attention that other producers of animated cartoons are attempting to imitate the character created by me.

I hereby serve notice that the character, Betty Boop, is fully protected by copyright registration and I intend to protect my interests to the fullest extent of the law against anyone attempting to use or imitate this character.

Max Fleischer

President,
FLEISCHER STUDIOS, INC.

put, any studio could make a comedy or a musical, but in theory only one could make a Clark Gable or a Bette Davis film.[17] The anxieties of Chaplin, Disney, Kane, and Fleischer indicate that imitation proved a threat to the "product differentiation" aims of both live-action and animated stars. Indeed, the action taken in each case was much more concerned with protecting the "uniqueness" (or unique combination) of the subject as a profit-generating entity than as a biological one. Roy O. Disney (Walt's brother and co-founder of the studio) later noted that no financial damages were ultimately claimed from Van Beuren: the importance of the injunction was to establish the copyright surrounding Mickey in order to dissuade further unauthorized emulation (B. Thomas 68). Much of the publicity surrounding this battle was framed in terms of Mickey's *personal* displeasure at being misrepresented by an "impostor." Although Disney had clearly borrowed from others in the development of the character, such actions played an important role in shaping a contemporary reading of the Mouse as an "original" creation, not least from a legal standpoint.

Protecting the status of a figure such as Mickey was important because virtually all studio-era cartoons were exclusively rooted in comedy, and their length restricted opportunities for sustained narrative development. There are many films from different producers that have a similar premise: for instance, Disney's *Mickey's Choo-Choo* (1929), the Porky Pig-starring *Porky's Railroad* (1937), and the Popeye short *Onion Pacific* (1940) all cast the main protagonist as a train driver. A number of stars have appeared in cartoons in which they run a restaurant or diner, including Mutt and Jeff in *Flapjacks* (1917), Van Beuren's human characters Tom and Jerry in *Pots and Pans* (1932), Oswald the Lucky Rabbit in *Ham and Eggs* (1933), and Popeye in *We Aim to Please* (1934). Walter Lantz suggested that repetition of plots between producers was exacerbated by hiring freelance story writers, who would often "sell a story to one studio, and then . . . adapt the same story to another studio's characters and sell it again" (qtd. in Peary 195). A particularly relevant comparison can be made between the Bugs Bunny film *Rhapsody Rabbit* (1946) and the MGM Tom and Jerry cartoon *The Cat Concerto* (1947), both of which feature a lead character (Bugs and Tom, respectively) giving a piano recital of Hungarian Rhapsody No. 2 by the composer Franz Liszt, only to be tormented by a mouse (an unnamed rodent and Jerry, respectively). The two works were produced at roughly the same time (although *The Cat Concerto* was released later) and both studios accused the other of stealing the basic idea (Mallory). However, the Tom and Jerry cartoon is much more rooted in the ongoing battle between the cat and mouse duo. Tom, as a relatively serious character, is also more concerned than Bugs with completing the piece professionally. *Rhapsody Rabbit* contains lots of gags in which Bugs just messes around, jumping on the piano and playing with his feet or treating the instrument like a typewriter that needs to be reset after a specific number of key presses (fig. 5.5). Although the differences between the films were ultimately the result of the distinct personnel working behind the scenes, the above quotation from Lantz is apt in highlighting that the presence of the star—and his or her singular on-screen personality—became the most important means of distinguishing films from different studios at the point of release.

FIGURE 5.5. Different star personas in similar scenarios: Tom in *The Cat Concerto* (1947) and Bugs Bunny in *Rhapsody Rabbit* (1946).

The Star as Auteur? Creator vs. Creation

In his study of James Cagney, McGilligan attempts to generate a model for reading the *star* as auteur: "[U]nder certain circumstances, an actor may influence a production as much as a writer, director or producers. . . . There are certain rare performers whose acting capabilities and screen personas are so powerful that they embody and define the very essence of their films" (*Cagney* 199). Every short cartoon series based around a recurring character contains what were essentially "star vehicles" for the main protagonist. Richard Dyer describes live-action vehicles as films that are "built around star images," but the most suggestive detail here is that, although the text was entirely designed to showcase the star and *appeared* to be an expression of his or her personality, the actor's input could, in fact, be relatively passive (*Stars* 62). As Barry King indicates, the star is publicly viewed as "the possessor of the image . . . . The fact that such an image may be a studio fabrication, and hence may be technically an icon not an index of its bearer, qualifies but does not refute this fundamental relationship" ("Stardom as an Occupation" 168).

A character such as Bugs Bunny is frequently *presented*, both off-screen and on, as being in control of his screen persona and thus seemingly capable of undertaking an authorial role. The majority of his cartoons begin with a credit sequence featuring either a close-up of Bugs's face or a wider shot of him atop the Warner Bros. logo. A second card shows the rabbit above the text "BUGS BUNNY in," preceding the reveal of the title of the cartoon (fig. 5.6). Although this segues into a list of other creative personnel—and the director is given particularly prominent billing—Bugs is offered as the main focus of the audience's attention.[18] Chuck Jones recalls two stories that reaffirm the *public* perception of Bugs's personal agency. One involves Bill Scott, a writer on the series: "He wrote a letter to his grandmother in Denver and told her he was writing scripts for Bugs Bunny. And she wrote back a rather peckish letter that indicated she wasn't very happy about that. She said, 'I don't see why you have to write scripts for Bugs Bunny. He's funny enough just the way he is'" (Jones qtd. in Academy of Achievement 165–166). In the other story, Jones describes being personally introduced to a "six-year-old-boy . . . as a man who drew Bugs Bunny." The boy "looked at me, and was furious. He said, 'He does not draw Bugs Bunny; he draws pictures of Bugs Bunny!' Which is exactly the way I felt about Tom Sawyer. It never occurred to me that [Mark Twain] was *writing* Tom Sawyer. He was *reporting* Tom Sawyer; he's writing *of* Tom Sawyer" (qtd. in Solomon, "Live

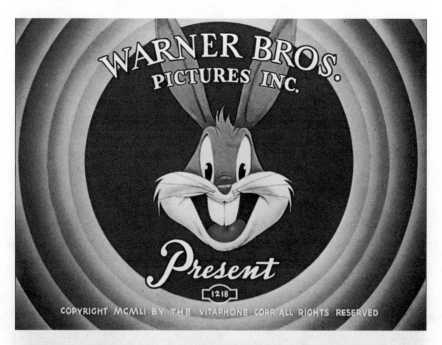

FIGURE 5.6. Bugs Bunny's prominent credits in *Rabbit Seasoning* (1948).

From Trumps" 134). Hugh Kenner concludes that, for the *Looney Tunes* and *Merrie Melodies* directors, "it was important—hence meaningful—to think of a Bugs whose autonomy they were obliged to respect" (80).

The cartoon *Duck Amuck* (1953) is revealing in this regard. The film opens with Daffy Duck as a musketeer in the middle of an action sequence. He continues to perform in character, but eventually notices that the background has disappeared and that he is standing in empty white space. Daffy converses with the off-screen animator and asks for some scenery. A paintbrush appears and fills in a barnyard setting, forcing the Duck to change into a farmer's costume. When he returns, the location abruptly changes to a barren, snow-filled environment. The cartoon continues in this vein, with Daffy desperately trying to adapt his performance to fit whatever has been imposed upon him, only to be thwarted again by the animator. At one point, Daffy tries to speak and finds his vocal chords have been replaced by sound effects; at another, the animator uses the eraser at the end of a pencil to eradicate Daffy's body and redraw him as a bizarre creature.

Duck Amuck would appear to reaffirm the primacy of the animator as author. Although Daffy is seen as autonomous on a basic level—highlighted by his increasing frustration at what is being done to him—he is powerless to prevent the artist's control over any aspect of his being. It is only in the coda of the film that this reading is subverted. Daffy eventually demands to know who is responsible and the "camera" tracks back to show Bugs Bunny at the drawing board. He turns to the audience and proclaims, "Ain't I a stinker?" As discussed in the previous chapter, certain characters were permitted more enunciative powers than others. Daffy seems the ideal target for abuse in *Duck Amuck* because his star image, by this point, had developed into that of a frustrated loser, who believes he is entitled to success and who throws tantrums when this does not materialize. Bugs, by contrast, almost always achieved victory effortlessly (and had already outwitted Daffy in a number of cartoons). As Richard Corliss asserts, Bugs "is his own auteur . . . . He knows what's going to happen, in the next frame or three scenes away, and he knows how to control it. He's the boss" (18).[19] The decision to reveal Bugs at the end of *Duck Amuck* indicates the importance and agency of his star status.[20] That the film did not go for the insider joke of featuring director Chuck Jones, or another member of his unit, is significant. To the viewing audience in 1953, Bugs simply meant more than Jones.

Very few "behind-the-scenes" animation personnel could expect to be known or recognized during the studio era and, as noted earlier, credit was generally limited to heads of studio and dominant producers rather than to directors. Walt Disney emerged as arguably the most personally famous figure of the time, although even he struggled against the notoriety of his screen protagonists. At the point of Mickey's creation, Disney was not entirely unknown, having been credited in his earlier *Alice Comedies* and *Oswald the Lucky Rabbit* series. However, his was hardly a household name, and while the quality of his studio's output was respected within the industry, the initial difficulties in finding a distributor for the Mickey films showed that it did not command any great influence. As the *Mickey Mouse* series geared up in late 1928 and 1929, Disney began to receive some press attention as Mickey's "creator," but his role at this stage largely involved providing contextual information about his star, not about himself. For the most part, it was Mickey, rather than Walt, who was the outward face and name of Disney Studios—everything had to be related back to the Mouse in order to ensure the public's attention. The title cards for the early films display Mickey's name much more prominently than Disney's and feature portraits of Mickey and Minnie as the stars of the series. The merchandising enterprise, which began in 1929, similarly served to extend the Mouse's image as the most recognizable (and profitable) asset to the studio. A 1931 article about European intellectuals embracing animated films noted that "they seem to ignore the very name of Walt Disney, the young cartoonist who created *Mickey Mouse*, since they give full credit to *Mickey* himself" ("Europe's Highbrows" 19).

Disney later commented that he felt "trapped with the mouse" during this period. Mickey "was a big hit, so I was stuck with the character." His solution, therefore, was to pursue "diversification" (qtd. in J. McDonald 201). In 1929, the studio launched a second, more experimental cartoon series titled the *Silly Symphonies*. Given Disney's increasing desire for personal recognition over the course of the next decade, it is telling that these films went against the prevailing status quo of the industry and avoided recurring stars. Each installment was to be self-contained, and the intention was to instead exploit the studio's perceived superiority in the use of synchronized sound. The decision was a bold one, and not universally supported: Disney's distributor at the time, Pat Powers, initially rejected the pilot *Symphony* film, *The Skeleton Dance* (1929), reportedly "telling Disney to stick to mice" (Schickel 132–133). Disney pressed on, however, and through a series of previews, eventually managed to secure national distribution (via Powers) by Columbia Pictures (Merritt and Kaufman, *Walt Disney's Silly Symphonies* 33).

Mickey Mouse nonetheless loomed heavily over the *Symphonies* series, even though he never starred in any of its films. Walt Disney noted in another retrospective interview that, in the early 1930s, "all the exhibitors wanted was Mickey. Okay, I gave them Mickey, but they had to take my *Silly Symphonies* too. Mickey was the club I used over their heads" (qtd. in Jamison SM27). The character was used in many aspects of publicity and merchandising, which clearly attempted to link the Mouse's marketing power to a series that began as a tougher sell to audiences. By the time the studio's output was distributed by United Artists, the wording "Mickey Mouse presents a Walt Disney Silly Symphony" had become a permanent fixture on the films' title cards. At least one advertisement for the series (qtd. in Tieman 7) omitted Disney's name altogether, while treating Mickey's own "endorsement" of the series as a valuable commodity:

> On the main title, Mickey Mouse is proud to link his name with Silly
> Symphonies and will announce:
> MICKEY MOUSE
> presents
> SILLY SYMPHONIES

The *Silly Symphonies* were slowly distinguished by virtue of their aesthetic experimentations. Although *Steamboat Willie* had showcased Disney's first attempts at synchronized sound, the *Mickey Mouse* series would never again debut any of the studio's major technological innovations. The *Symphonies* adopted Technicolor beginning with *Flowers and Trees* (1932), whereas the Mouse did not make the switch from monochrome until 1935. Increasingly seen as the "prestige" series, the *Symphonies* began to make a serious claim to being animation art, separate from Mickey's populism. The Academy Award for Best Animated Short Film was introduced in 1932. Although a number of studios received nominations—and several Mickey films (as well as a Donald Duck cartoon in 1938) from Disney were also shortlisted—it was a *Silly Symphony* cartoon that won on each occasion across the entirety of the decade.[21] Slowly, focus began to shift away from Mickey as the pseudo-author of the *Silly Symphonies*: later installments even featured title cards that mention only Disney's name, now in a more pronounced position, with no attempt to evoke the Mouse.

Gabler argues that Walt had achieved personal "stardom" by the mid-1930s and that press interviews with him increasingly dwelled on his private life and childhood, rather than only on his roster of characters (203–205). This recognition was further enhanced by the release of his first animated feature, *Snow White and the Seven Dwarfs* (1937). *Snow White* was made in the mold of the *Symphonies*, with no preexisting animated stars. By the late 1930s, the power balance between Mickey Mouse and Walt Disney had clearly changed. At the beginning of the decade, virtually every studio production had to be filtered through Mickey; at the end of the 1930s, Disney's name was used to advertise new projects. However, it is important to emphasize that, throughout this period, the Mickey Mouse films, and the ancillary revenues generated by the character, subsidized the studio's more ambitious output. Disney later admitted that even the external funding for *Snow White* was raised "solely on the strength of Mickey's popularity" (qtd. in Jamison SM27). The studio had achieved diversification, but only with the continued assistance of the Mouse.

Mickey's appearance in "The Sorcerer's Apprentice" within the feature *Fantasia* (1940) marked the only star-led sequence in a film otherwise dominated by one-off characters and more abstract combinations of animation and music. The Mouse's presence lends itself to an allegorical reading of this still-ambiguous relationship. As Gabler notes, the animator Bill Tytla drew the sorcerer "with Walt's own famously cocked eyebrow and . . . named him Yen Sid, 'Disney' backward, to make the connection between the sorcerer's magic omnipotence and Walt's [omnipotence at the studio]" (295). At the beginning of the film, Yen Sid is shown using his powers to summon the vivid image of a butterfly, the sort of Technicolor marvel one might expect to find in a *Silly Symphonies* cartoon. In what might be a reflection on the formulaic nature of the cartoon star films, Mickey, the apprentice, is stuck doing repetitive but necessary chores. Yen Sid leaves the room, and Mickey steals his magic hat, masquerading as the figure in charge. Matters quickly get out of hand, and the sorcerer returns to clean up the mess. Mickey submissively bows to his master and resumes his previous task. Although Yen Sid appears to display a wry smile at the Mouse's actions, he reaffirms his dominance by spanking Mickey's backside with a broom. On the surface, then, the apprentice is clearly put in his place.

There is a certain irony here in that *Fantasia* can potentially be read as Disney overindulging his own artistic pretensions. As Robert Heide and John Gilman state, "critics lauded 'The Sorcerer's Apprentice' as Mickey's greatest performance. But *Fantasia,* as a whole, opened to mixed reviews and lukewarm business" (*Mickey Mouse* 16–17).[22] Faced with a domestic flop, and the inaccessibility of many overseas markets due to the outbreak of the Second World War, the studio was forced to retreat from full-length narrative features for the remainder of the decade.[23] Cultivating an image as "the kindly 'uncle Walt,'" Disney remained well-known for the rest of his life, hosting the ABC television series *Disneyland* (1954–1958) and *Walt Disney Presents* (1958–1961) and the NBC show *Walt Disney's Wonderful World of Color* (1961–1969) until his death in 1966 (Bell, Haas, and Sells 2). However, Disney also relied heavily on his short film characters for the remainder of the studio era, and this continued on television as well as in other expansions, such as the company's theme parks. Walt Disney may have risen to fame on the back of Mickey, but the "author" never *quite* managed to fully eclipse the star.

Disney's attempt to eradicate recurring characters in the *Silly Symphonies* shorts, and the rising artistic reputation that he enjoyed during this period, was undoubtedly appealing to his fellow producers. Indeed, the response to the *Silly Symphonies* from several competitors was arguably even more pronounced than the perceived wave of imitators following Mickey's success. The often alliterative naming conventions of these subsequent series clearly reflect an attempt to evoke the Disney strand. Examples include *Merrie Melodies* (Leon Schlesinger/Warner Bros.), *Happy Harmonies* (MGM), *Color Classics* (Fleischer), *Swing Symphonies* (Lantz), *Comicolor Cartoons* (Ub Iwerks), and *Toddle Tales* (Van Beuren). Each series began with the intention of producing one-off, unrelated films (or quickly shifted to such an approach shortly after launch). Yet, it is notable that many eventually added stars toward the end of their respective cycles, seemingly in an attempt to revive audience interest. For instance, after the positive response, including an Academy Award nomination, to the *Color Classics* cartoon *Hunky and Spunky* (1938), the eponymous protagonists returned in six more cartoons (including the final four installments released under the *Color Classics* brand). Similarly, the *Merrie Melodies* series eschewed recurring personalities for much of the latter half of the 1930s. However, once the likes of Bugs Bunny and Daffy Duck gained prominence in the early 1940s, *Merrie Melodies* became essentially interchangeable with the studio's other series, *Looney Tunes.*

Even Disney was not entirely immune from the value of popular characters appearing *within* the *Symphony* cartoons. The series provided two starring roles for Pluto, without Mickey, in *Just Dogs* (1932) and *Mother Pluto* (1936) and bowed to the immense popularity of *The Three Little Pigs* (1933) by producing three direct follow-ups. As Merritt and Kaufman state, the *Pigs* cartoons "paved the way for more of the same: the stars of *The Tortoise and the Hare* (1935) and *Three Orphan Kittens* (1935) made return appearances in later pictures, and one of these, *Toby Tortoise Returns* (1936), featured characters from several other *Symphonies* as well" (*Walt Disney's Silly Symphonies* 42). In 1966, Disney voiced his personal dislike of the later *Pigs* films: "I could not see how we could possibly top pigs with pigs. But we tried, and I doubt any one of you reading this can name the other cartoons in which the pigs appeared" (qtd. in Schickel 156). Ultimately, for many producers, animated stars proved too tempting to resist as they provided a stable and recognizable method of selling the films to exhibitors and audiences, even if this forced artists to work within a set formula with each new entry.

The most contentious relationship between a studio and recurring characters arguably existed within United Productions of America (UPA). Formed in 1943 and initially known as Industrial Film and Poster Service, the studio attempted to challenge the foundations of American cartoon production. In 1948, UPA signed a four-picture trial with Columbia, re-placing the studio's in-house Screen Gems animation unit. This partner-ship brought UPA to national attention and, for a few years, enabled its employees to pursue a variety of independent projects. However, like the numerous examples highlighted above, the popularity of certain animated creations eventually began to weaken the studio's commitment to original productions. UPA lobbied to produce one-off cartoons featuring human characters. Their first attempt—*Ragtime Bear* (1949), itself a compromise due to the presence of a feral co-star—introduced Mr. Magoo, a cantan-kerous old man whose bad eyesight led to comedic misunderstandings and occasional peril. The film was a success, but had the unintended consequence of convincing Columbia of Magoo's viability as an *ongoing* presence. As Michael Barrier notes, "Magoo was the first continuing character to emerge from UPA, a studio that had for five years disdained [other] studios that enjoyed great success with such characters" (*Hollywood Cartoons* 522). On the release of Magoo's third short, the character was up-graded to his own starring series, with the rest of UPA's output distributed by Columbia under the series title *Jolly Frolics*.

The studio's release structure paralleled that of the Disney studio of the early 1930s, with production split between the profitable star (Mickey/ Magoo) and more avant-garde material (*Symphonies/Frolics*). The *Frolics* cartoon *Gerald McBoing Boing* (1950) remains one of UPA's most celebrated and successful works and is representative of the studio's modern, minimalist approach: the backgrounds are sparse and expressionistic, and the characters are simple, flat designs, far removed from the weight and naturalism found in Disney. *Gerald* won UPA its first Academy Award for Best Animated Short and cemented the studio's reputation as being innovative with the aesthetics of animation. Based on a story by children's author Dr. Seuss, the film features a young boy named Gerald McClory, who is capable of "speaking" only through sound effects, rather than through the use of words. His classmates mock him with the nickname "Gerald McBoing Boing," and he eventually decides to run away. The narrative ends with Gerald being hired to produce radio sound effects, finally achieving acceptance and fame *because* of his uniqueness. As Adam Abraham suggests:

> It is hard not to imagine that *Gerald* is also the story of the artist—[Theodor] Geisel, [Robert] Cannon [the film's director]—or even UPA itself: the sensitive outsider, who can never truly conform, finds his métier and reaches an apotheosis. . . . Thus, it is appropriate that by producing *Gerald McBoing Boing*, UPA distinguished itself from its cartoon-making competitors and perfected the art of the "modern" animated film. (89–90)

Gerald's success was a double-edged sword, however, and in many ways the film is UPA's equivalent of Disney's *The Three Little Pigs*. Both reached a level of popularity that inadvertently separated the texts from their respective containing series (the *Frolics* and the *Symphonies*), with a great deal of public interest seemingly focused directly on the protagonist(s) rather than on the technical or aesthetic achievements. Unlike some of UPA's more abstract experiments, *Gerald McBoing Boing* features a sympathetic and engaging central character, who managed to appeal to a wide demographic. As Bosley Crowther notes: "Significantly, this popularity does not appear to be confined to adults. Children are falling as much in love with Gerald . . . as their delighted . . . parents" ("McBoing Boing" SM14–15). The audience response again prompted Columbia to insist on Gerald's return to the screen. Three direct follow-ups were eventually made, overturning UPA's initial intent to keep the *Frolics* cartoons as one-offs.

The situation was further complicated by the mixed reactions to some of the studio's other experimental *Frolics* shorts, most notably *The Tell-Tale Heart* (1953), which was based on the short story of the same name by Edgar Allan Poe. The film received enthusiastic write-ups in the press and even an Academy Award nomination. As Leonard Maltin concludes, it was "not just another cartoon, to be treated in the same way as the new *Heckle and Jeckle* release" (*Of Mice and Magic* 336). However, for better or worse, cinema owners and audiences knew what to expect from Heckle and Jeckle, while the chilling and serious tone of Poe's narrative lacked the comedic appeal associated with most theatrical short cartoons. *The Tell-Tale Heart* was a box-office flop, and UPA was forced to borrow money from Columbia, which came with certain content stipulations (Abraham 93). Magoo featured more heavily than ever in the studio's output, and the number of original *Frolics* productions swiftly declined.

Such an outcome highlights the difficulty in trying to be different while also working within the Hollywood system. UPA had tried a number of new approaches, which did not always connect with audiences, and these commercial failures gave Columbia cause to place restrictions on subsequent works. Ironically, the same was true of their apparent triumphs: it could be suggested that characters like Magoo or Gerald were, in a sense, *too successful* in that they prompted the profit-minded distributor to simply demand more of the same. The vast range of subject matter and art styles that characterized UPA's earliest cartoons was slowly eroded into a pattern of bankable formulas and popular characters.

Steve Schneider makes a valid point in his assertion that "animation is probably the ultimate 'auteurist' cinema, as its directors can control every element of their films' content with a precision that extends down to the individual frame" (30). While true in theory, such potential was rarely achieved within the "Taylorized" mass production practices of most studio systems, with the UPA example in particular highlighting how the auteurist goals of many creative figures were secondary to Columbia's interest in a character such as Mr. Magoo. Sianne Ngai has suggested that, under such conditions, "the nonliving entity that is animated [the star] comes to automatize its animator" (113). There were undoubtedly attempts to fight this process: Sammond argues that the "industrial alienation" and "severe social dislocation" felt by these unacknowledged workers affected their creative choices, and the "disobedient, willful, and playful" character types can be viewed as "an expression of the tensions surrounding the laboring body" (83, 85).

At the same time, however, the extent to which the average viewer would recognize this—especially in relation to a specific "auteur" personality—before the rise of animation studies is open to question. Sammond notes, for instance, Chuck Jones's claim that the lisping voices given to Daffy Duck and Sylvester the Cat were a sly dig at the series producer Leon Schlesinger, who reportedly had a similar speech impediment. The animating team felt underpaid and underappreciated, and one of their few means of protest was to sneak gags at the boss's expense into films for which Schlesinger often took credit, despite his delegation of the work to others (Sammond 104). Schlesinger was not, however, truly famous in his own right: his only noteworthy media appearance was playing himself in the *Looney Tunes* short *You Ought to Be in Pictures* (1940). The narrative ultimately treats him fairly sympathetically, and there is no hint of his lisp in the line readings included in the finished film. Whatever subversive enjoyment the artists gleaned from seeing Schlesinger and the spluttering Daffy Duck share the frame was seemingly not accessible to the regular 1940 cinemagoer. (Indeed, the very act also relied upon Schlesinger's continued ignorance: if he had discovered the intent, those responsible may very well have been fired for insubordination.)

Crafton, perhaps inadvertently, summarizes one of the major problems with retrospective auteurist readings when noting that, "for those of us fortunate enough to have met some animation legends, we know that Jones, when he was the lead animator of Bugs Bunny, *was* Bugs, that Friz Freleng *was* Yosemite Sam, and that Messmer *was* Felix the Cat" (*Shadow of a Mouse* 54). Putting aside the issue of whether it is accurate to make such a singular link between a specific artist and a character, this quotation reiterates that only a privileged few have had a personal audience with these individuals in order to verify such claims.

I noted in the introduction that Crafton has criticized film and star studies for "clinging to the primacy of the physical body" as an essential truth, rather than recognizing that "this very attitude is an acculturated anthropocentric practice" (*Shadow of a Mouse* 56). One could argue that animation studies—again, largely taking its cue from film scholarship—has historically neglected to interrogate its own relatively uncritical foregrounding of auteur theory. There is a danger, then, that such readings fail to account for the manner in which the texts were generally presented (and, arguably, consumed) at the time of release—that is, on the basis of the recurring character. This is clearly "an acculturated anthropocentric practice" itself, but one that was undoubtedly widespread and worthy of further critical attention. Michael Saler emphasizes that, despite academia's traditional privileging of auteurism, there has, in fact, been a lengthy history of read-ers—engaging with everything from classical literature to motion pictures to video games—who choose "to downplay or ignore the original author, whose [comparatively] mundane existence could be seen as an impediment to their belief in the autonomous existence of the fantasy worlds" contained within the text (26). Indeed, despite devoting a large section of his book on Felix the Cat to the contested authorship claims surrounding the star, John Canemaker briefly acknowledges that "the general public . . . [did not] care" who made the films (*Felix* 59). Alan Cholodenko, in his article "(The) Death (of) the Animator," suggests that as "to the perennial ques-tion bedeviling animation scholars—who animated, authored, originated Felix?—Pat Sullivan or Otto Messmer?—for us, Felix is the very answer to the question" (14).

Crafton offers a valuable compromise by proposing a triangular re-lationship among the toon stars, the animators, and the viewer, and the possibility of each having a flexible status when it comes to determining meaning. His writing acknowledges that he—or indeed anyone—is free to "reflect on the filmmakers, on their lives as workers, as people, and as lived bodies" when watching an animated cartoon, but also that this is a reflection of each person's own "inferences," rather than being an absolute truth. This can include an individual's acceptance of readings that are de-monstrably false: Crafton notes, for instance, that "we grasp why it pleases [some] fans to believe that 'Uncle Walt' animated Mickey Mouse," despite evidence to the contrary (*Shadow of a Mouse* 49, 53, 72). Such a model also opens the door to legitimizing scholarly interpretations based almost exclusively around the agency of the animated protagonist—including one that considers the complexities of his/her character, star persona, and (textually generated) private life—with little to no consideration of the underlying animation process and human effort that occurred in order to permit this illusion.

It is true, as Sammond argues, that characters such as Felix and Mickey Mouse rose above their conditions only "through the subjection of others" (244), and auteur-focused historians should certainly be applauded for helping to rescue such figures from obscurity.[24] At the same time, however, the star's propensity to dominate is a phenomenon worthy of study in its own right, especially as this was by no means unique to the cartoon medium. During the studio era, it was also rare for *live-action* directors or producers—and especially screenwriters or cinematographers—to enjoy personal fame, with corporeal actors similarly enjoying their privileged position through the frequent diminishment of these comparatively "invisible" or "below-the-line" contributors (Caldwell 9). John Thornton Caldwell's influential book *Production Culture* highlights that, while it is important to finally recognize the work of marginalized figures, there is also value in questioning how and why the media chooses to "self-theorize" its practices—often in ways that serve to obfuscate the underlying reality (15). The following chapter therefore discusses Hollywood's tendency to avoid the acknowledgement of tensions between creative personnel. Stars of both the live-action and animated varieties were instead regularly presented in the films and publicity as being in control of their own personal labor. The conflicts that did spill out into public consumption were generally those between performers and the studio system itself, displacing the issues between director and star—or creator and creation—onto a broader canvas.

Chapter 6

The Studio System

In the 1930s and early 1940s, the major Hollywood studios exerted such an exceptional level of control over live-action performers that their status as living human beings appears to have been considered negligible, and even somewhat inconvenient. Alexander Walker, for instance, describes the star system of this period using such extreme terms as "slavery" and "serfdom," even comparing the average Hollywood studio to a "concentration camp" (228, 240, 251). Other academic work has labeled stars as "commodities," as "property," as being "owned" (Maltby, *Hollywood Cinema* 89; P. McDonald, *The Star System* 66; Fowles 150). As Danae Clark indicates, a self-governing (or rebellious) actor risked "disrupting the coherent [star] images that studios wanted to present to the public," undermining carefully orchestrated publicity campaigns and damaging the box-office potential of his or her own films (25). The studios gained power through restrictive, long-term employment contracts to (surreptitiously) dictate virtually every aspect of a live-action performer's life and career, ranging from the choice of film projects to social engagements and even, in some cases, romantic partners (R. Davis 109). However, by the mid-1940s, the studio hierarchy had begun to weaken. The rise of trade unions, together with certain legal victories obtained by individual stars, contributed to the eventual decline of the system.

Animated stars thus clearly differ from their live-action counterparts in one crucial aspect: a lack of free will to resist or contest the regulation imposed upon them. From the studio's perspective, one could argue that characters such as Bugs Bunny and Mickey Mouse were the *ultimate* expression of the star system during this era: they could be wholly commodified and exploited in any manner that the moguls wished. This chapter examines instances in which the use of animated stars allowed studios to sidestep disputes with live-action personnel. However, this account is complicated by examples where the "coherent images" (to use Clark's term) of the animated star were also disrupted, both purposely by a specific studio and, at times, against its wishes.

The term "studio system" generally refers to a specific grouping of major studios. This "cartel," to borrow Barry King's description, began with the formation of the Motion Picture Producers and Distributors of America (MPPDA) in 1922, and eventually consolidated as a "'mature' oligopoly" in the early 1930s ("The Hollywood Star System" 153, 156). It should be noted that film studios existed, in one form or another, from the beginnings of cinema as a commercial medium. The relationship between the employer (the studio owner or producer) and the employee (for the purposes of this chapter, the star) underwent significant changes in the first few decades of the twentieth century. In the early 1910s, the extent of the public's developing interest in the screen actor, and the emergence of picture personalities, took the film industry somewhat by surprise. Many producers initially attempted to suppress the performer's name and posit them solely in "terms of the firm's trademark"—Florence Turner, for instance, "was known only as the 'Vitagraph Girl.'" However, this proved insufficient for audiences, who craved further information about the figures on the screen (Klaprat 353). The studios relented and began to publicize the names of actors, a strategy that often proved extremely lucrative. At the same time, it also weakened their level of control, facilitating "talent raiding" (the poaching of established stars by another producer), which reached its height during the middle of the decade. This intense competition meant that the industry's most popular performers could insist upon vast increases in salary. Charlie Chaplin, for instance, reportedly began his career at Keystone in 1914, earning a weekly wage of $150; signed with Essanay Studios a year later for $1,250 per week; and then, in 1916, joined Mutual Film Corporation, where he received $10,000 each week plus a $150,000 signing bonus (Huettig 26). In 1919, Chaplin joined with actors Douglas Fairbanks Sr. and Mary Pickford and director D. W. Griffith to form United Artists, an independent production and distribution company intended to bypass the existing studio structure. Tino Balio argues that "the founding of United Artists marked the apex of the star system," giving movie actors something at least approaching "complete autonomy over their work" for the first time ("Stars in Business" 159).

Cartoon stars could not, of course, evade such controls. Despite outward expressions of agency, their stardom depends on being owned and exploited by an external force. One can nonetheless trace a change in the manner of this ownership over the course of the silent era, running parallel to the increasing status of the live-action star. This change is especially notable in the shift from cartoons based on comic strips—the majority of animated series with recurring protagonists in the 1910s—toward characters developed entirely for the cinema by the 1920s. For instance, Mutt and Jeff were the most prolific stars during the silent era, appearing in at least three hundred cartoons, but the power to exploit this franchise rested primarily with the creator of the newspaper strip, Bud Fisher, not with the film producers or distributors (Bendazzi 58). Although adapting an existing property for the screen was initially seen as a safer option because audiences were already interested in the "brand," animation studios had no long-term investment in the star. During the earliest years of cartoon production, this may not have seemed such an important issue, as relatively few series lasted more than a year. However, the unexpected cinematic longevity of characters such as Mutt and Jeff highlighted that ownership of animated stars could, in some cases, be extremely lucrative over an extended period.

The increased emphasis upon developing original cartoon characters for the screen by the end of the 1910s theoretically served to remove much of the uncertainty—and profit sharing—that had surrounded the adaptation of someone else's work. However, when personnel began to move to different studios, and studios switched distributors, it became necessary to clearly identify who could claim the rights to these new stars. In most early instances, the characters tended to follow individual artists. For instance, Paul Terry left Bray Studios in 1917 and took his creation Farmer Al Falfa with him. Similarly, when Max and Dave Fleischer quit Bray to form their own company in 1921, they continued the adventures of their *Out of the Inkwell* clown. As units became increasingly industrialized, however, and cartoons were produced collaboratively by large groups in a production line process, the hierarchy of the studio also became more structured. Animators were frequently defined as workers, not artists with claims to authorship. For instance, as the previous chapter noted, Pat Sullivan's studio kept its lead animator Otto Messmer, who created Felix the Cat, as an anonymous salaried employee for the lifespan of the series, with no direct financial stake in the character.

Sullivan did, however, still face various battles over Felix. Initially created for a one-off cartoon in the *Paramount Screen Magazine* newsreel, the Cat began making regular appearances and was increasing in popularity. John Canemaker suggests that it was only when *Screen Magazine* was canceled in 1921 that Sullivan realized that "the copyright to Felix belonged, not to him, but to Famous Players-Lasky," the larger incorporated company that included Paramount. Drawing on the testimony of animator Hal Walker, Canemaker describes Sullivan's reaction:

> It seems the distraught cartoonist went to [the office of Adolph Zukor, president of Players-Lasky] in a drunken "stupor" and urinated on the desk. In disgust, Zukor asked Sullivan what he wanted.
>
> Zukor took the bread and butter out of his mouth, cried Sullivan, who demanded the copyright to Felix. To avert any further unorthodox negotiations, Zukor quickly phoned the company attorney and told him to honor Sullivan's request. (*Felix* 59)

Whether or not the more colorful aspects of this narrative are true, it is likely that Sullivan was reassigned copyright largely because Felix the Cat appeared to be of negligible ongoing value to Famous Players-Lasky or any of its subsidiaries. Although Paramount had begun to single out and promote the character's appearances in its newsreels, the studio still made comparatively little profit from the films and withdrew from animation completely in 1921 (Barrier, *Hollywood Cartoons* 21). Felix's subsequent success was an important turning point in realizing the commercial potential of animation. Sullivan's partnership with Margaret J. Winkler, formed after he had reclaimed the character from Paramount, marked an upsurge in the Cat's fortunes. Winkler secured widespread releases of the films, but

FIGURE 6.1. Felix in protest against his previous distributors in an advertisement in *Kinematograph Weekly* (13 August 1925).

also began an extensive merchandising regime involving Felix. The ability to generate revenue not only from the cartoons, but also from a variety of spin-off products, further underscored the importance of establishing ownership of the star.

Tensions arose, however, over the control of Felix. Sullivan ultimately split with Winkler and signed with new distributors, prompting a protracted legal battle. He eventually won, but the litigation kept Felix out of cinemas for a number of months. In this regard, Sullivan's broader copyright ownership of the character proved beneficial. He was able to authorize publicity pieces in which Felix, as a film star, commented directly on the dispute. One advertisement, part of a lengthy campaign in the British journal *Kinematograph Weekly*, displayed the Cat locked up in jail as a visual metaphor for the delay until the cartoon releases could resume (fig. 6.1).[1] Felix (and, by implication, Sullivan) was portrayed as an innocent victim, cruelly prevented from entertaining the public. Similarly, a full-page article in *The Picturegoer* saw Felix, credited as the author of the piece, pronounce his displeasure with the previous British distributor, Pathé:

When I was quite young Pat [Sullivan] and I used to work for Pathe's [*sic*], but I tell you I had a grouch against these folk. . . . I said to Pat at last, "It is no good, boss," I said, "you'll have to make other arrangements for me if I'm to stay in the industry." Pat's a good sport, so he said to me, "That's all right, Felix me lad. I'll fix things so that you'll be more comfortable in future." (Felix the Cat 18)

In reality, of course, Felix was just being used as a mouthpiece for Sullivan's own grievances with Pathé. However, the Cat is presented here not as an owned commodity, but as an autonomous and creative figure (with an accommodating boss).

Moving forward, such representations frequently became part of the discourse surrounding the animated star. Furthermore, the use of Felix to publicly criticize a major distribution company was comparable to the bravado displayed by certain live-action performers in the early to mid-1920s. The relatively high number of studios and independent production companies in operation during this period meant that top stars could burn bridges with any that did not agree to their requests, safe in the knowledge that they were in demand elsewhere (Walker 108, 230). Indeed, Murray Ross suggests that many actors, upon receiving a lucrative offer from another studio, would be purposefully "temperamental" with their current employers to break their existing contract, or at least renegotiate its terms (91). In 1925, Pat Sullivan could be equally bold. Felix was a proven box-office draw and quickly attracted interest from other companies when the deal with Winkler fell apart. Within just a few years, however, the situation was dramatically altered. Between 1927 and 1930, Felix the Cat moved among three different distributors in the United States largely due to Sullivan's initial reluctance to add, and the subsequent half-hearted inclusion of, sound into the cartoons. With each new distributor, the film releases declined in status, and Felix's popularity was severely damaged.[2]

As Walker suggests, "stars were never again to be so rewarded, and at the same time so free from restraint, as in the early years of the 1920s." During the decade, the exorbitant salaries that leading actors were demanding began to reach a "saturation point" (107, 110). Securing the biggest names increasingly required so much upfront expenditure that, although a large box-office yield was *almost* guaranteed due to their presence, the unexpected failure of a film could potentially bankrupt a studio (while not impairing the income of the star). Devoting resources toward the development of an actor's career was also a liability, due to the prevalence of talent raiding. Producers thus began to insist upon performers agreeing to long-term contracts, giving the studio a degree of protection over its investment. Although, as noted above, many stars initially circumvented these restrictions, the power relationship had changed by the end of the decade. Most significantly, the Depression reduced the number of producers in the industry. Walker notes that, in 1924, "there were still nineteen studios listed in the Hollywood directory," but by 1935, "there were only eight" major players (108). Stars simply had fewer options available, and the surviving studios were much less willing (or, in some cases, able) to indulge their demands. The top performers of the 1920s had valued independence, but in the uncertain times of the early 1930s, signing longer-term contracts and becoming exclusively affiliated with a specific studio appeared to be an increasingly safe option.

A comparable situation can again be found in the animation industry during this period. While Felix the Cat had moved among various distributors in the 1920s, cartoon stars (and the animation producers who created them) tended to be more closely linked with a single studio in the following decade. The eight surviving major studios came to be known as the "Big Five" (Warner Bros., 20th Century–Fox, Paramount, Metro-Goldwyn-Mayer, and RKO) and the "Little Three" (Columbia, United Artists, and Universal). Other smaller producers did exist, but generally either had to rely on one of the majors for national distribution or had to sell their product on a much less lucrative "states-rights" basis, making individual deals by territory with local distributors.[3] Douglas Gomery estimates that, although the relative share for each studio may have changed over time, the combined total for the Big Five and Little Three accounted for roughly "95 per cent of the US box-office takings" every year throughout the height of the studio era (*Hollywood Studio System* 12).

The major studios achieved this dominance in part by exploiting a system known as "block-booking." A group of feature films were sold to exhibitors as a single package, often leading to "lesser" titles being bundled alongside a desirable new release. Star power was an important determinant in this process. Eric Smoodin notes, for instance, that a cinema owner "may have had to program an entire season's worth of MGM films in order to show one Clark Gable movie" (49). A stable, ongoing market for cartoons was established by the regular inclusion of short films as part of these deals. This is not to suggest, of course, that animation was perceived simply as pre-sold filler with no value on its own terms. Indeed, popular cartoon stars such as Betty Boop and Mickey Mouse were sometimes used, like Gable, as the *enticement* to purchase a much larger selection of the studio's output (Smoodin 49). Even when the films were being sold as part of a bulk package, an unsuccessful animated star—much like a failing live-action performer—would not be tolerated indefinitely.

The 1930s saw a period of experimentation as studios attempted to find cartoon producers whose work complemented their live-action output. By the early 1940s, several of the majors moved animation in-house and took full control of the lucrative characters. For instance, Tom and Jerry were directly linked to (and owned by) the MGM Cartoon Studio, while the likes of Bugs Bunny and Porky Pig were frequently identified as Warner Bros. stars (even when the films were made on behalf of Leon Schlesinger before he sold his ownership to Warner in 1944). Cultivating a long-term relationship with one of the "Big Five" or "Little Three" and trading upon their branding proved beneficial for independent animation producers. Even Walt Disney Studios, which remained fiercely protective of the rights to Mickey Mouse and its other properties, was exclusively distributed by RKO for the majority of the studio era (following a short period with both Columbia and United Artists).[4]

It is revealing that many animated stars—closely associated with major studios—were represented as actually having studio contracts of their own. For instance, *Popeye the Sailor* (1933), the character's first cartoon outing, begins with a shot of a newspaper proclaiming "POPEYE A MOVIE STAR: The Sailor with the 'Sock' accepts Movie Contract." In *Duck Soup to Nuts* (1944), Daffy Duck proclaims to Porky Pig that he is no ordinary mallard, but a singer, dancer, and dramatic actor, flashing his "contract with Warner Brothers" to prove it. Although not rendered in any specific detail, Daffy's contract is clearly a multi-page document that contains a lot of text, a signature at the bottom, and some form of affixed seal, emphasizing its authenticity (fig. 6.2). For live-action actors, Jane M. Gaines argues, "the contract has a truth status because it bears the notarized signature of the actor, divulges his or her legal name, and contains confidential infor-mation about the real conditions under which the star works—including information about his or her salary" (*Contested Culture* 146–147). One can argue that there remains a degree of "truth status" in representations of the "contract" for the animated star, as it stands in for the studio's actual legal documents that establish ownership of the character and the right to make

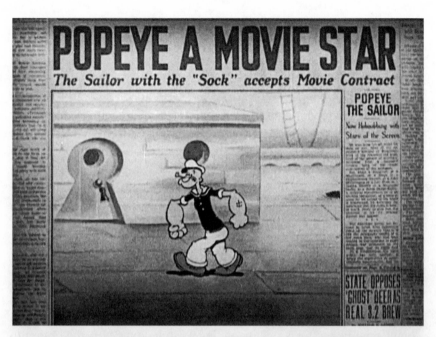

FIGURE 6.2. Cartoon star contracts: Popeye in *Popeye the Sailor* (1933) and Daffy Duck in *Duck Soup to Nuts* (1944).

cartoons featuring him or her. By simplifying these issues on-screen into a more straightforward relationship between star and studio, the films sustain the notion of animated characters as self-governing beings, in possession of a private existence.

There is an underlying irony that most live-action stars in the 1930s actually *forfeited* direct control over many aspects of their life and career when they signed studio agreements. The standard contract during this period required artists to pledge their services for seven years. The studio reserved the right to review the agreement at regular intervals (usually every six to twelve months) and either renew the option or terminate the actor's employment. Performers not only had no guarantee of a long-term career with any given studio, but they also lacked the power to break the contract themselves. If a studio continued to request their services, they were obliged to fulfill the full seven years, irrespective of any growth in their star status. Vacations and suspension periods were often deducted from the time served, meaning that a seven-year contract could, in fact, last well beyond a decade. The studio generally chose all the film roles and commercial tie-ins for an actor, at times withholding even the option to reject any that he or she considered unacceptable (Powdermaker 34, 84, 213–214; Gaines, *Contested Culture* 152; Clark 49; P. McDonald, *The Star System* 59). One could suggest that, on paper at least, both live-action and animated stars were comparably subordinate to the studios.

Star Disobedience

Ronald Davis suggests that, given the restrictive nature of the employment terms, "arguments between studios and their [live-action] contract personnel were endless" (109). As much as possible, reports of a star's discontent were suppressed, kept "inside the studio gates" in an attempt to avoid negative press (Walker 240). However, even when these disagreements did spill out into the gossip columns, studios were usually able to spin the story in their favor. For instance, in 1936, Bette Davis refused to honor her contract at Warner Bros., arguing that the bosses were assigning poor-quality scripts that would damage her career. The matter eventually went to court, and Davis later claimed that, during the hearing, the studio represented her as "a spoiled brat, an intractable infant who needed a good spanking" (159). As Clark notes, such disputes were generally presented as a "doghouse cycle . . . an irritating, but harmless game in which actors who cannot control their temperamental natures force benevolent producers to either discipline them or make special arrangements to accommodate them" (75). In this instance, Davis lost the case and was forced to resume her duties at Warner.

In his analysis of the live-action Hollywood star system, Barry King makes a distinction between "high autonomy" and "low autonomy" stars. The former (such as Bette Davis) aim to take control over their careers and frequently engage in battles with the studio, whereas the latter generally remain subordinate and fulfill every contractual obligation ("The Hollywood Star System" 327). Animated characters are, of course, low (or zero) autonomy stars as a result of their constructed nature, and publicity often drew attention to the comparative lack of trouble that cartoon figures created (while still emphasizing their apparent vitality). A reference to Betty Boop in a 1931 *Screenland* gossip column contrasted with reports of most corporeal performers in the same article, noting that Betty is "always on time at the set, isn't a bit upstage . . . [and] never misbehaves off the screen" ("Screen News" 87). Similar comments were made about Mickey Mouse the following year: "Walt Disney is the envy and despair of his fellow producers in Hollywood. . . . He does not have to supply ornate dressing rooms and personal press agents for his stars. . . . They [do not] . . . sulk over story situations, or become jealous if some other player is given too many close-ups" (Pringle 28). Even the *New York Times* indulged in such fancifulness in an article about Paul Terry's studio roster of protagonists: "[T]hey never quarrel over the assignment of a role, never demand more salary or the star's bungalow dressing room. They are, in short, an impresario's dream of what actors should be" (Strauss X3).

For the most part, cartoon characters were presented as loyal to, and thriving under, the constraints of the studio system. However, some accounts also chose to hint at potential problems: the *New York Times* article makes brief reference to Terry's actors occasionally becoming "temperamental" (Strauss X3), while another piece notes that even Mickey Mouse was prone to difficult moments:

> Disney may admit that he is sitting pretty, but he . . . insists solemnly, it is
> not at all true that Mickey is devoid of temperament. There are frequent
> days when he will not dance as he is supposed to dance. Hours are spent
> in the sound-proof recording room during which no progress is made.
> Mickey can be elusive and obstinate. And sometimes he muffs a role or a

dramatic moment. . . . Then everyone blames it on Mickey, an obnoxious little beast. (Pringle 28)

Although these issues were actually technical problems or failings on behalf of the production team, it is revealing that the Mouse was presented (albeit humorously) as the source of the problem as a troublesome actor. Such examples highlight that animated characters were at times permitted to *masquerade* as "high autonomy" performers, indicating that the addition of some complications to the "perfect" image of the star was not always undesirable in certain contexts.

This trope was most prevalent in the early-1930s fan journal reports of Mickey Mouse (see chapter 2). In addition to a focus on the Mouse's sexuality, several pieces also flirted with the notion that he may have become "spoiled" by his fame. One "interviewer" describes an encounter with Mickey off-screen in which he is wearing an elaborate outfit: "a morning coat, striped trousers, a gleaming white vest, . . . pearl-grey spats . . . [and] a be-ribboned pair of nose-glasses." He asks to be addressed as "Michael," rather than Mickey, and drops random phrases of French into his conversation (Franklin, "The Art" 27, 96). Another article claims that the Mouse was affecting an "Oxford accent" while talking "pompously" about his work (Franklin, "Confessions" 52). This would appear counterintuitive to the usual perception that the studio system aimed for undisrupted images of its performers and—as noted previously—Disney did admittedly tread more carefully as the decade continued. However, Clark also argues that star personas are ultimately a "construction that results precisely from the struggle over image-labor relation," a combination of the living "person" (with free will) and the artificial "image" that studios wished to impose upon them (22). These instances of constructed rebellion undoubtedly contributed to the complexity of the animated star persona, implying again that his or her "private life" could be as rich as any human performer.

Even in the pre-Code era, the articles on Mickey Mouse were still careful to reverse any particularly damaging claims. In one piece, the star becomes his usual happy-go-lucky self again when Minnie interrupts the interview and invites him to a party (Franklin, "The Art" 27, 96). In another, after Mickey's secretary leaves the room, he winks at the journalist and explains that "since a couple of highbrow critics discovered that my stuff was Art I've had to live up to it and be a doggoned artist" (qtd. in Franklin, "Confessions" 52). Although it is initially implied that the Mouse has been "revealed" as an ostentatious celebrity, these writings are able to claim the best of both worlds. They create some intrigue about uncovering his "true" character, only to reauthenticate the notion that, below the surface, Mickey is (in his "own" words) just a "plain, honest, fun-loving mouse" after all (qtd. in Franklin, "Confessions" 52).

Richard Maltby argues that "one of Hollywood's most telling characteristics is that, while appearing to draw attention to the mechanisms of its industrial processes, it masks one level of its operations by selectively highlighting another" (*Hollywood Cinema* 93–94). In addition to external publicity, Maltby also focuses on Hollywood-produced movies that directly represented the business of filmmaking. The (live-action) release *A Star is Born* (1937), for instance, sold itself in part as an exposé of Hollywood, and it does offer *some* insight into how stardom is explicitly constructed. The heroine, Esther Blodgett, is given a new name (Vicki Lester) and a falsified life story once the studio signs her up for a career as an actress. Yet, as Maltby indicates, the film carefully shifts blame for the more problematic aspects of the story. The cynical and vicious press agent, Matt Libby, is seen as working "in a subsidiary industry, and his motives are contrasted with those of the industry proper. Set against his parasitical malevolence is the paternalist figure of Niles, head of the studio, whose only concern is the best interest of his stars" (*Hollywood Cinema* 98–101).

The *Looney Tunes* short *You Ought to Be in Pictures* (1940) provides a similar balancing act in the realm of animated stardom. The film sees the ambitious Daffy Duck vying to become the studio's top cartoon star. He convinces Porky Pig to quit the studio for a career in live-action features as "Bette Davis' leading man." Spurred on by Daffy's taunts, Porky goes to the office of Leon Schlesinger (the actual producer of the cartoons at the time, appearing in live-action footage as himself). After explaining that he has languished in cartoons for long enough—"What's Errol Flynn got that I haven't?"—Porky requests to have his "cartoon contract" canceled. Schlesinger responds by ripping up the document and wishing him luck. Porky's attempt at breaking into features is a failure, and he returns to beg for his old job. Schlesinger happily reveals that he had swapped the contract for some different papers, meaning that Porky's employment had not actually been terminated. The cartoon ends with Daffy again trying to tempt Porky—this time with a supposed role alongside Greta Garbo. However, the Pig, now fully content with his position at the studio, simply pelts Daffy with a tomato.

As with *A Star is Born*, the film appears to reaffirm certain inconvenient "truths" about the downsides of the Hollywood system. Daffy is presented as a jealous star, willing to ruin Porky's career for his own advancement. Schlesinger—faced with Porky's apparent resignation—chuckles to himself and notes that the Pig will be back, highlighting his awareness of the disruptive "game" that must be played with highly strung actors. However, the cartoon also mythologizes many of these same attributes. The actual process of animation production is not shown, with Porky simply coming to life on an artist's drawing board. Schlesinger, in particular, is presented as the "benevolent" or "paternal" studio boss, willing to grant Porky the opportunity to explore options elsewhere, but also pleased to welcome him back without holding a grudge or imposing any sanctions. In reality, even this illusion of freedom was rarely granted to stars: for instance, James Cagney's offer in 1932 to act in three Warner Bros. films for free in an attempt to get out of his longer-term contract with the studio was summarily rejected by those in charge (McGilligan, *Cagney* 45). The studio's usual response to an actor's belligerence would be a period of suspension without pay (Balio, *Grand Design* 143, 160).

Films and publicity pieces in which the animated characters appear to rebel are ultimately indicative of the complete control held by producers. This should not suggest, of course, that live-action performers were immune from fictionalized accounts of their own apparent dissent. One can find numerous examples of contemporary publications that, like the early Mickey Mouse interviews, speculate in a potentially alarmist manner about whether certain stars have lost touch with the common people, only to safely conclude—for the most part—that they have not (see, for instance, Albert). However, the fact remains that corporeal performers could also *truly* misbehave in ways not carefully concocted by the studios and fan magazines. Animated stardom could thus offer further benefits to the moguls in helping to guide audience responses to these actions—in some cases, diffusing them with humor, but also at times encouraging censure. It is perhaps unsurprising that the *Looney Tunes* and *Merrie Melodies* series, which used the studio backlot as a setting for more cartoons than any other producer, were released by Warner Bros. This studio is considered to have been one of the most restrictive and exploitative of the majors during this period, and some notable public eruptions relating to contractual issues came from its stars, such as Davis and Cagney (Hagopian 16). While the cartoons were certainly not studio-mandated propaganda, one can still read them as products of the Warner system. The plotlines may appear to revel in the transgressions of the animated star, but there is often a more conservative moral at the conclusion that reaffirms the status quo. In *You Ought to Be in Pictures*, for instance, Porky learns an important lesson about over-estimating his reputation within the industry, and Daffy is punished for his deception. By satirizing the apparent foibles of live-action performers using animated ciphers, these characters contribute to a larger discourse that presents disobedient studio-era stars as ungrateful and volatile, failing to realize just how privileged they are to be working in the movies and adored by millions.[5]

Salary

Whereas a figure such as Charlie Chaplin managed to jump from studio to studio on a frequent basis in the silent era, multiplying his existing salary many times over with each new deal, the long-term contracts of the 1930s and 1940s generally had very rigid payment clauses. If an actor suddenly increased in popularity (and box-office earning power) while under contract, the studio could theoretically continue to pay the rates agreed at the beginning of the seven-year term (Klaprat 375). Indeed, Walker notes that Clark Gable "stayed on a salary basis at [MGM] from the day he came in 1930 to the day he left in 1954" (242). Although some major stars did manage to fight for a more lucrative deal, these increases would still inevitably be well below the true market value that the performer could command if he or she was able to negotiate with other producers. A studio's unwillingness to share profits with popular stars thus became a recurrent source of dispute.

In the 1920s, extravagant wages had been heavily publicized as evidence of the star's high status (essentially as vindication that the performer was better than, and should be worshipped by, the public). However, Clark notes that, as the Depression took its toll in the following decade, fan magazines began to run articles criticizing stars' excessive consumption (70–75). The issue became so divisive that star salaries were almost placed under direct government regulation, with strict caps on top-level earning, as part of President Roosevelt's National Recovery Administration Code in 1933 (Ross 50–52). Studios could take advantage of (and at times even incite) public indignation to justify significantly lower wages and exert further control over their personnel. During Bette Davis's battles with

Warner Bros. in the mid-1930s over the quality of her assigned roles, she claimed that the studio publicly announced "that I was dissatisfied with my salary of five thousand a week, a fictional figure that was plucked out of the air. I was made to seem greedy and high-handed; the quality of my screenplays and directors was never mentioned. My lack of artistic freedom was brushed aside in a publicized story of a hold-up for more money" (158). Even when the disputes were at least partly financial, the studios could still prevail. James Cagney, for instance, claimed that he was made to appear churlish for pursuing a pay increase of several thousand dollars, with Warner obfuscating the fact that they were actually making "millions from his work" (Warren and Cagney 88).

Publicity for the animated star was able to sidestep such debate. Even in the early 1930s, when articles occasionally joked about Mickey Mouse's possible transformation by the studio system, there was still usually a tendency to construct a narrative of struggle to justify his subsequent good fortune. One author even claimed that:

Mickey is entitled to be [a screen star] and ride in Scootmobiles, live in a penthouse, and have his own private golf course. Because, with all his great success, Mickey Mouse has remained kind and simple. . . . [He] was not always rich and famous. He has known what it means to be right down to the last rind. He has actually lived in tenements where they did not have as much as a piece of bacon, even on Christmas.

And believe me, this great public idol, this mouse whose name has been billed over almost every other star in the business, has not forgotten it. (Hyland 36)

In this context, Mickey's rags-to-riches tale was presented as inspirational, a symbol of optimism in harsh times. As criticisms of star salaries intensified across the decade, it is revealing that a number of articles shifted the evocation of Mickey to now specifically mention his *lack* of monetary demands. A piece titled "The Only Unpaid Movie Star" notes that the Mouse "has become one of the greatest 'box office' actors in the world—though he is the only one who doesn't receive a salary" (Carr 55). In another article, written on the anniversary of the star's fifth "birthday" in 1933, Walt Disney comments that "Mickey is a very busy young star—and the only one in Hollywood who isn't paid! I often regret that it is impossible to reward him in some way for all the fun he has given to the world" ("Mickey Mouse

Is 5 Years Old" 36). Unlike many live-action performers, whose claims of financial exploitation by the studios (however valid) sat uneasily against the widespread unemployment affecting the nation, the Mouse was presented as a screen figure who gave significantly more than he took.

Some later cartoons did very occasionally present the illusion of animated characters earning an excessive salary, but this was almost always for the purposes of humor. Returning to *You Ought to Be in Pictures*, for instance, Daffy tries to lure Porky into feature film roles by initially promising a $3,000-per-week salary (with a running gag being that it increases by another $3,000 every time it is subsequently mentioned). Again, one can read this as a satire of the perceived excesses of the live-action system, rather than an indictment of Porky's greed. For animation studios, the full ownership of animated characters meant never having to negotiate salary, or share profits, with the star.

Publicity and Image Rights

The extensive product licensing of animated characters such as Felix the Cat and, particularly, Mickey Mouse, has often been retrospectively analyzed by scholars in isolation from consideration of a more general process of exploiting *all* star images in the studio era. Charles Eckert's influential essay "The Carole Lombard in Macy's Window" highlights the extent to which Hollywood did actually incorporate product "tie-ins" into live-action movies during the 1930s. As Richard deCordova notes (tellingly in an essay titled "The Mickey in Macy's Window"), "the period Eckert discusses coincides with the period of Mickey Mouse's ascendance as a commodified cultural icon" (204). Ultimately, both animated and live-action star images adorned a variety of product ranges and tie-ins.

Gaines indicates that the standard live-action star contract of the period gave studios the right to use the actor's image in both direct advertising (such as "trailers, posters, magazine, and newspaper copy referring to the film") and indirect advertising ("any opportunistic consumer good tie-up or even to the most tangential and offhand use of the actor's name, voice, and likeness"). As Gaines notes:

> More often than not, stars were stuck with unwanted advertising associations simply because the studio authorized them. In the early contracts, term players, with very few exceptions, had no right to withhold the use of

their images from these *indirect* commercial arrangements—especially if the motion picture was mentioned in the advertisement. An actress might be shocked to see her image reproduced in conjunction with products as diverse as Auto-Lite car batteries or Serta mattresses and box springs, but there was little she could do about it. (*Contested Culture* 157, 160)

The studios generally received all the income from such product licensing, and stars simply had to be content with the additional exposure generated by the advertising. As Penny Stalling and Howard Mandelbaum suggest, "the spreads were gorgeous and the copy flattering" for the most part (43).

By the 1940s, some actors did manage to establish a degree of personal control over tie-ins—albeit usually only to veto unwanted associations, rather than to choose between or profit from them. Gaines notes that "the star who successfully reserved the right to negotiate such matters was the exception during this period." Citing Bette Davis's 1943 contract with Warner Bros. as a representative example, she argues that the document "is worded in such a way that the studio can claim 'Bette Davis' as its own corporate trademark for seven years" (*Contested Culture* 161). As such, it is important to emphasize here that animated *and* live-action stardom was heavily commodified and, crucially, that this was almost exclusively controlled by the studio rather than by the subject.

As noted in earlier chapters, numerous media texts were supposedly dictated or endorsed by characters such as Felix the Cat and Betty Boop. While these were, of course, ghost-written by studio publicists and journalists, the same was frequently true of live-action stars: Bette Davis personally contributed just as many words (zero, according to Gaines, *Contested Culture* 161) to a regular *Photoplay* advice column bearing her name as Minnie Mouse did to her gossip column, "Hollywood Chatter."[6] Furthermore, as indicated above, contract players were often unaware of the brands with which the studios had associated them, risking scandal if it was ultimately discovered that the celebrity did not actually use the products that he or she "endorsed" (Marchand 97–98). Animated stars seemed to avoid such controversy because, at a base level, everyone knew that they were fictional (even though the material regularly emphasized the characters' authenticity and kept tongue-in-cheek references about their constructed status to a minimum).

What seemed duplicitous in fabricated representations of a live-action star could be explained away as a fanciful gag, a bit of fun, with the animated equivalent. Indeed, unlike later concerns voiced during the television era (see chapter 7), the process of marketing cartoon stars appears to have been discussed during this earlier period with relative openness, and largely celebrated as a public relations success. One publication, for instance, hailed Mickey Mouse as "the world's super salesman [who] finds work for jobless folk and . . . lifts corporations out of bankruptcy." The article notes that one company, which had been in receivership, added "2700 workers to its payroll" as a result of winning the contract to manufacture Mickey Mouse watches, and that a knitting mill tasked with "making sweatshirts with [Mickey's] portrait" on them was able to hire a third of the local town's population, keeping them "assured of three meals a day from the overtime work alone" (Robbins SM8). The author occasionally hints at his amazement (or bemusement) at the sheer number of Mickey-branded items that one could buy, but expresses little of the cynicism or criticism that factors into many recent academic studies of commercialism.

In terms of direct merchandising, Gaines suggests that products associated with live-action stars tended to focus on "inanimate props . . . [rather] than actors' faces and bodies" (*Contested Culture* 158). These included copies of items owned by a star's character within the diegesis, such as clothing, "furniture, dinner settings, chocolates, shaving brushes, watches, clocks, and so forth" (Eckert 113). A photograph of the star might be featured in store displays or on the item's packaging, but rarely on the actual product. Animated character merchandise, by contrast, tended not to recreate on-screen objects, but instead to directly reproduce the personal iconography of the star. One could not, then, purchase a watch "worn" by Mickey Mouse in a given cartoon, but could buy a watch that had Mickey's face on it.

With these products, patrons were not simply imitating a live-action star's on-screen consumption, but were engaging specifically with the cartoon character's image. This is particularly true in the case of dolls, since these were three-dimensional representations of the animated protagonist's face and body. Almost no figurines bearing the likeness of a human performer were produced during this period. Those that were tended to be linked specifically to a character from a film, rather than to a more general representation of the actor.[7] As such, while animation missed out on some of the more lucrative "luxury" merchandising that could be tied in with live-action features, manufactured goods featuring cartoon characters allowed for a much closer symbiosis of product and star. Because the protagonist was actually visible on the item itself, a child carrying around a Mickey Mouse doll (for example) was essentially advertising Disney's films to the wider public and helping to establish brand loyalty for the studio's output, in addition to providing extra revenue. It could be argued, therefore, that animated stardom offers a more hyperbolical realization of the star system than was traditionally inhabited by live-action performers during this period.[8] The transferability of the cartoon character image offered an even more flexible range of options for producing branded, tradable products that could supplement the studio's overall income.

Loan-outs

Contracts generally gave the employer the right to loan an actor to another studio, again usually without any consultation with the star before the deal was made. Such "loan-outs" often produced clear economic benefits. Hortense Powdermaker cites an example in which a star was "loaned out for eight weeks, [with] his studio receiving four fifths of his annual salary" (84, 213). Furthermore, if the film was a hit, the parent studio's subsequent in-house productions would benefit from an increased audience interest in the star. For instance, Tino Balio notes that "Clark Gable and Claudette Colbert were in lulls when MGM and Paramount, respectively, [dispatched] them to Columbia to star in *It Happened One Night* [1934]. Because of the film's success, their careers took off" (*Grand Design* 158). Although animated characters could not literally be sent over to work at a different studio's backlot like a flesh-and-blood actor, it is possible to identify instances in which an animation producer allowed a cartoon star to move beyond his or her regular series and appear in an entirely unrelated film.

Warner Bros. star Bugs Bunny makes an appearance in *Jasper Goes Hunting* (1944), part of the stop-motion *Puppetoons* series released by Paramount. As the title implies, the lead *Puppetoons* protagonist Jasper is on a hunting expedition along with other series regulars, Scarecrow and Blackbird. At one point, they come across a rabbit hole, and Bugs (rendered using hand-drawn animation) jumps out. He rests his arm on Scarecrow's gun and utters his famous catchphrase, "What's up, Doc?" Scarecrow looks at the camera and exclaims: "Well, what do you know—Bugs Bunny!" A fanfare begins to play and Bugs initially basks in the attention, but then has a moment of realization: "Hey, I'm in the wrong picture!" He waves

FIGURE 6.3. Guest Mickey with Jimmy Durante in *Hollywood Party* (1934).

sheepishly at the characters, jumps back into his hole, and Jasper continues his adventure. Even before the release of the film, Bugs's appearance was considered newsworthy: a 1943 publication ran a story stating that "for the first time in screen history a cartoon star is being loaned to a rival studio" (qtd. in Sampson 37). Although revealing in its use of "loaned," since the term was usually linked to the live-action star, this assertion is, however, not quite true, as there are at least a couple of precedents. While his cartoons were still being distributed by Columbia, Walt Disney produced a short sequence featuring Mickey Mouse for the comedic travelogue *Around the World with Douglas Fairbanks* (1931), released by United Artists (wherein the Mouse is introduced as "Hollywood's most famous star"). The MGM feature *Hollywood Party* (1934)—produced while Disney was contracted to United Artists—includes a scene in which Mickey Mouse interacts with other live-action stars, such as Jimmy Durante (fig. 6.3).

As these examples indicate, the cartoon character's appearances were relatively short and tended to temporarily disrupt, rather than radically shape, the wider narrative. Henry Jenkins suggests that, after the Disney sequence in *Hollywood Party*, "the plot resumes, more or less, where it had been abandoned" before Mickey appeared (*What Made Pistachio Nuts?* 308). No animated star was cast as a lead character in a rival studio's film, unlike Gable and Colbert in *It Happened One Night*. However, the general principle behind the loan was essentially the same: the animation studio was able to charge a fee and/or raise the prestige of its star. Mickey's presence in *Hollywood Party* was treated with just as much credibility and deference as that of any other performer. He even receives an on-screen credit in the film's opening sequence, formatted in exactly the same way as his live-action counterparts.

By loaning Mickey to this production, Disney and United Artists were able to present the Mouse as a peer of many famous feature-film actors. Furthermore, the spectacle and novelty of an animated star's scenes often attracted a great deal of critical attention, despite the relative brevity of the appearance. *Hollywood Reporter* specifically mentions Mickey Mouse's contribution to *Hollywood Party* (as well as a cameo by Laurel and Hardy) as "a standout sequence . . . in an otherwise dull musical" ("Laurel and Hardy" 3). Similarly, the magazine *Boxoffice* states that, in *Jasper Goes Hunting*, the "novel introduction of Bugs Bunny, way off limits from his own stomping grounds, is the highlight of the reel" (qtd. in Sampson 37). While such deals with rival film studios occurred much less frequently with animated stars than with live-action ones, the outcomes appear to have been just as beneficial to the parent studio on most occasions, reaffirming the value of ownership of the characters.

Studios also regularly loaned film stars to radio. Although these media forms were essentially in competition—staying home to listen to a broadcast would, of course, mean foregoing a trip to the cinema—the two industries often collaborated in mutually beneficial ways. By loaning out a star to a radio program, the particular episode would be likely to receive high ratings, and the studio would receive extensive publicity for its current release, which listeners would be encouraged to seek out at their local theater as soon as possible. As Christine Becker emphasizes, "most of the [Hollywood stars appearing on radio] were under contract to studios and were thus following studio orders" (27). In addition to the Armed Forces Radio examples discussed in chapter 3, animated stars also made guest "appearances" on domestic commercial radio at various points throughout the studio era. For instance, the 18 November 1943 episode of *The Abbott and Costello Show* (1942–1947) features Bugs Bunny in a number of scenes. The plot involves Abbott's character attempting to win a woman's affections by purchasing a pair of nylon stockings—a task that proves very difficult due to wartime shortages. Bugs appears as himself, first working as an elevator attendant at a department store and then in the women's clothing section, where he comments on the many patrons sprinting to get to the counter (to claim the one remaining pair of stockings) as if they were participating in a horse race. Only in the opening announcements—where regular *Looney Tunes* voice artist Mel Blanc is briefly credited as playing "the famous Leon Schlesinger cartoon character Bugs Bunny"—is the character not treated as an autonomous entity. Within the context of the main narrative, Bugs is presented as no less real than the episode's other guest, Lucille Ball, also appearing "as herself."

Some animated characters were also given *starring* roles in ongoing radio series. None of these shows were particularly successful in the longer term, but they are yet another revealing indicator of the extent to which Hollywood studios drew upon a live-action model in promoting animated stars. *Betty Boop Fables* (1932–1933) was a fifteen-minute weekly show developed around the Fleischer Studios starlet (Terrace 36).[9] Woody Woodpecker also reportedly had a radio series in the late 1940s, produced by the Mutual Network (Korkis and Cawley 75). Even Walt Disney loaned his studio stars for the NBC series *The Mickey Mouse Theater of the Air* (1937–1938), initially as a cross-promotional exercise for his upcoming film *Snow White and the Seven Dwarfs* (1937). As with Bugs's appearance on *Abbott and Costello*, animated stars such as Mickey Mouse, Donald Duck, and Goofy were presented in the show as fully living beings, not as characters impersonated by an actor. Walt Disney (Mickey's primary voice artist in the films during this period) did appear in some episodes, but only as himself, clearly separated from the Mouse. Jim Korkis claims that an actor named Donald Wilson was hired to play Mickey on the radio and that the show's announcer, John Hiestand, actually pretended to be Walt on a number of broadcasts when the studio head was too busy to attend the recording personally (*The Vault of Walt* 377, 380). Such a revelation highlights the problematic nature of authenticity in media production, which is, of course, one of the major concerns of this volume. Although listeners were essentially being asked to associate a disembodied voice on the radio with Mickey Mouse's fictitious body, the truth claims relating to the appearances of Walt Disney in this series were also rooted in fabrication.

That the voices on these broadcasts can be identified as somehow "belonging" to Mickey Mouse or Bugs Bunny—despite the lack of a visual cue—highlights the pervasive nature of the animated star's persona, but also the importance of branding. Virtually all the surviving episodes of these shows contain overt reminders that the protagonists are also cartoon stars from a particular studio, encouraging listeners to link the audio to images of the characters who had appeared on the cinema screen. However, a similar observation can be made about programs featuring live-action stars: for instance, Michelle Hilmes's analysis of the *Lux Radio Theater* series indicates that segments were structured to contextualize the guest star in relation to his or her wider film career, as well as to prompt discussion of "recent and upcoming films and small plugs for other studio-related material" (102). These loan-outs were usually carefully monitored by the parent studio to ensure that the star was used in an appropriate fashion and that listeners were frequently reminded of his or her status as a cinematic icon.

If animation did not necessarily offer any substantial benefits to loaning out an actor compared with live-action, this section has nonetheless highlighted that cartoon stars could be exploited by studios in many of the same ways as their human counterparts. Indeed, while the silent and early sound eras were rife with animation producers simply drawing plagiarized versions of a rival's popular characters, the fact that official loan-out deals were made during the studio era reflects an increased respect for (and protection of) the animated star as a legal entity.

Workload

In the 1930s and 1940s, regular cinema attendance was common among American movie fans, even during some of the harshest moments of the Depression and the Second World War. There was consequently a high audience demand for rapid turnover of new releases.[10] In his autobiography, James Cagney notes: "[I]n my early movie days . . . it seemed as if the Warner boys were confusing their actors with race horses. The pace was incredible. I think I did about six pictures in the first forty weeks" (43). Similarly, Walker states that "at its height [MGM] was turning out one picture every nine days. But this was possible only because the [actor] had surrendered all freedom of choice" (240). Both quotations posit studio labor as exploitative and even inhumane, certainly far removed from the images of the star's work as "play" that were perpetuated in contemporary Hollywood discourse (see, for instance, Rosten 53). The number of films in which a given performer was expected to appear became a frequent contractual dispute. Studios generally wanted to maximize output, not least because films featuring a popular star were essentially pre-sold (and could help to sell others in a package) under the block-booking system. Actors, by contrast, usually wanted to reduce their workload. The mid- to late 1930s saw the rise of unions, such as the Screen Actors Guild, which campaigned for better conditions for performers across the industry.[11] Some popular stars were also able to individually negotiate particularly favorable deals for themselves in the midst of these wider threats of industrial action. For instance, in his 1939 contract with Warner Bros., Cagney reached an agreement that limited his acting commitments to a maximum of just three films per year (Hagopian 20). Over the course of the decade, the heads of the major studios were forced to make concessions that reduced the amount of labor that they could expect from their personnel, especially the top stars.

Once again, the animated protagonist offered no such opposition: if a cartoon star became popular, the number of films would generally increase to meet audience demand, rather than decline because the actor's bargaining position had strengthened. In 1932, Mickey Mouse starred in fourteen cartoons; in 1940, Popeye appeared in fifteen. Because these characters were not flesh-and-blood entities, this "labor" could be extended further. Even the most committed live-action performer still needed to eat and sleep, and if an actor was on the set of one movie, he or she could not be filming another project at the same time. By contrast, the number of cartoons featuring an animated star that could be created simultaneously was, in theory, essentially limitless. At Warner Bros., for instance, several different directors produced Bugs Bunny cartoons over the course of any given year, and it is inevitable that work on two or more of these films overlapped on a relatively frequent basis. Bugs's lack of a physical body, along with the easy reproducibility of his image, meant that the studio never had to worry about organizing the star's shooting schedule, providing lunch or rest breaks, honoring contractual obligations, and so on.

However, the notion that there is no upper limit to the animated star's potential output does not fully account for the human labor still necessary to produce the films. The "golden age" era was full of clashes between animators and studios over employment issues, including salary and excessive working hours. Such conflicts culminated in various strikes and even the formation of medium-specific unions such as the Screen Cartoonists Guild.[12] These disputes are significant because they marked rare instances in which animators did manage to voice their "subjection" via the cartoon star (as discussed in the previous chapter), especially when these workers actually used the iconography of famous characters when protesting against management. Images of the particular studio's protagonists often adorned placards carried by aggrieved employees: for instance, Tom Sito reproduces a photograph from the Disney strike of 1941 in which a picture of Pluto appeared next to the slogan "I'd Rather Be a Dog Than Be a Scab!" A board from the 1947 Paul Terry Studio strike portrays the character Katnip as a greedy boss, hoarding riches and literally paying peanuts to his on-screen partner Herman, the worker surrogate, who is standing on a collection of unpaid bills. Flyers and pamphlets promoting strike action also frequently incorporated cartoon stars: one anti-Disney leaflet features an angry Mickey Mouse wearing an American Federation of Labor badge and holding a placard proclaiming "Disney UNFAIR" (Sito, *Drawing the Line* 122, 132, 206). Another, from the 1937 Fleischer Studio industrial action, shows Betty Boop, Popeye, and Olive Oyl surrounding the heading "THE ARTISTS WHO DRAW US ARE ON STRIKE!" (Deneroff 11).

Such acts did, of course, flout the copyright ownership of the star held by the studio, and so (unlike Pat Sullivan's use of Felix the Cat as spokesperson, mentioned above) these controversial images could not be widely circulated in the mainstream media. Nonetheless, the approach still ensured that stars were name-checked in press reports. Covering the Fleischer Studio strike, which occurred alongside action by a number of different unions, a *New York Daily Times* article stated that "two more famous stars joined the motion picture . . . walkout last night—Popeye and Betty Boop" (qtd. in Deneroff 9). A *Daily Worker* headline proclaimed "Betty Boop And Popeye Pickets [*sic*] For Cartoonists" (10), again crediting the characters with a sense of personal agency and belief in the cause.

Live-action performers rarely became involved in labor issues solely relating to technical crew, and so the "easy reproducibility" of the animated star actually worked against the studio's wishes in this instance. The animated star technically offered unlimited, free output, but producers still needed to employ human workers to take advantage of this. That these staff members sometimes felt exploited by the studio system does not, however, necessarily undermine the advantages that animated stars offered over live-action performers in terms of volume of work.

Typecasting

Once an actor proved popular in a particular type of role, studios would often attempt to re-create this success in further cinematic vehicles, projecting the characterization as an essential part of the performer's off-screen persona. Surveying the industry in the late 1940s, Powdermaker noted wryly that "most stars are so typed that it would be possible to exchange close-ups from one film to another without noticing the difference" (248). This is parodied in the cartoon *The Big Snooze* (1946), which opens with the familiar scenario of Elmer Fudd chasing, and then being outwitted by, Bugs Bunny.[13] Rather than plot another scheme, however, Fudd shouts, "I quit! I'm thwough! I get the worst of it from that wabbit in every one of these cartoons!" Bugs becomes distraught at the possibility of Elmer leaving and starts begging: "You can't do this, I tell you. You don't want to break up the act, do you? . . . Think of your career. [He looks to the "camera" in sudden realization.] And for that matter, think of *my* career!" The cartoon endows Elmer with a sense of free will that can be separated from the motivations of his character—even if, by the end of the cartoon, he is browbeaten by Bugs and resumes the same formulaic chase. His anger is not due to his failure as a hunter in the specific narrative of *The Big Snooze*, but rather to the metanarrative running through his "career" as a result of typecasting, which requires him to be humiliated and injured in each new installment.

The Big Snooze highlights that, although virtually all of a studio's filmmaking resources in any given production—from the construction of the narrative to the use of cinematography—appear to be directed toward serving the star's persona, this "persona" is likely to be a construct of the studio, imposed upon the actor (Klaprat 370). Live-action stars often argued that they were reduced to one-dimensional clichés, constantly playing the same character type.[14] For example, James Cagney frequently emphasized his training as a dancer and a comedian (as well as a dramatic actor) in vaudeville and theater before his career in movies. However, the success of *The Public Enemy* (1931) cemented his cinematic image as a "tough guy," and, against his wishes, Warner Bros. assigned him to a plethora of gangster films. In Cagney's view, studio typecasting saddled him with a persona that failed to capitalize upon his varied talents (McGilligan, *Cagney* 63).

The Scarlet Pumpernickel (1949) is another cartoon that plays upon this frustration. It opens with a distant shot of a film studio, a screaming voice echoing across the lot: "You're killing me! I'm being murdered! I can't stand this torture anymore! I'm dying! You're killing me!" Any potential tension generated by this dialogue is immediately diffused as the film cuts to Daffy Duck—the source of the voice—standing unharmed in a producer's office. He continues: "I'm telling you J. L., you're typecasting me to death. Comedy, all this comedy! . . . Honest, J. L., you've just gotta give me a dramatic part!" (The unseen J. L. is another in-joke, alluding to Jack Leonard Warner, the president of Warner Bros.) Daffy's over-the-top protestations—comparing the studio's casting choices to the inflicting of physical pain—serve to perpetuate the image of the hysterical and demanding star. This is further compounded by the character's outfit—a pretentious beret and scarf—and the vanity project script that he pitches, presenting himself as "Daffy Dumas Duck" in an attempt to gain some literary credibility.

The proposed film steals liberally from Baroness Orczy's play and novel *The Scarlet Pimpernel*, although the script title ignorantly refers to a type of bread, pumpernickel, rather than to the iconic flower used by the original hero. The viewer is shown extracts of Daffy's vision for the cartoon. He is clearly miscast and inadvertently reverts to comedic business: as the Pumpernickel, Daffy jumps off a building, intending to land directly on his horse's saddle, but instead hits the hard pavement a couple of feet away from his steed. Battered and bruised, he turns to the "camera" and notes with confusion: "That's funny—that never happens to Errol Flynn!" Daffy's failures as a hero in the narrative are directly tied to his inability as an actor and would have been recognizable to contemporary audiences as a satire of live-action stars who overestimated their own talent and dramatic range. Indeed, the release date of *The Scarlet Pumpernickel* may have had additional significance, since it coincided with James Cagney's return to Warner Bros., after his second failed attempt at going independent in an effort to diversify his screen roles. The "homecoming" film—*White Heat* (1949), another gangster role—proved successful and appeared to reaffirm the value of typecasting in maintaining Cagney's career (Hagopian 20–30).

Despite Daffy's and Elmer's on-screen complaints, animated stars, of course, had no means of resistance against casting decisions. Certainly, cartoon characters (most frequently appearing in the sub-genre "comedian comedy") often flourished as a result of being typed, with recurring plotlines and running gags being an important part of an ongoing series. However, one can also find examples of stars, such as Van Beuren/RKO's Cubby Bear and Ub Iwerks/MGM's Flip the Frog, that failed, at least in part, due to the cartoons slavishly repeating set formulas. Even Porky Pig, once the top cartoon star of the *Looney Tunes* series, was mostly reduced to a supporting player by the late 1940s and 1950s—ironically enough, given the plot of *You Ought to Be in Pictures*, sometimes appearing as Daffy Duck's sidekick. In cases where a studio dropped a character entirely, his or her cinematic "career" was essentially over.[15] As Kim Newman (32) has noted, "unlike live-action stars with torn-up contracts, [animated stars] couldn't even make Poverty Row Westerns" (referring to the small collection of Hollywood producers operating with much less influence—and much lower budgets—than the Big Five and Little Three). One downside of a studio having full control, then, was that the studio was perfectly capable of mismanaging a star's career. On the whole, animated stars such as Bugs Bunny and Donald Duck were "looked after" because the films were profitable and popular, but as the system went into decline, full ownership of the stars became less of a priority.

The Collapse of the Studio System

The studio system of the 1950s was no longer as powerful, particularly in its control of stars. In 1943, the actress Olivia de Havilland filed a lawsuit against Warner Bros., challenging the studio claim that she still owed twenty-five weeks of work at the end of her seven-year contract (Powdermaker 211). According to J. L. Yeck, de Havilland felt that Warner Bros. was purposely offering her undesirable roles to force her into taking further periods of voluntary suspension, potentially stretching her contract commitment "into additional months or years." The studio lost the case, and the "de Havilland Decision" determined that no studio in California could enforce a contract beyond "seven calendar years" (Yeck 35–36). By the early 1950s, many of the biggest stars had become freelance labor, available to studios only on a per-picture basis. This led to a rise in talent agents, who took over the management of the star's career and who were able to parlay significant pay packages (and lucrative profit participation deals) for the most in-demand performers (P. McDonald, *The Star System* 75, 79; Kindem 88).

The animated character continued to be, in theory, the ultimate studio star. There were no legal battles, no agents, and no attempts at independence. The irony is that during this same period, the market for cartoons declined substantially. The primary factor was the outcome of the 1948 case *United States v. Paramount Pictures, Inc.*, which outlawed the process of block-booking. Of particular relevance to the cartoon star was the provision that no short films would be "forced on exhibitors as a condition of receiving features" (Whitney 170).[16]

Although the writing was on the wall, the timetable for the effects of the Paramount case ultimately varied greatly with each producer. A number of studios appealed the decision, meaning that individual decrees were signed at different times, often delayed well into the 1950s (Lafferty 238). Most studios continued releasing new cartoon material theatrically throughout the late 1950s and even the 1960s. Indeed, Walter Lantz was still producing Woody Woodpecker and other assorted character shorts for the cinema in the early 1970s. Shamus Culhane's assessment that the theatrical era for cartoons ended "not with a bang, not even a whimper, just a click as the lock snapped shut on the [Lantz] studio in 1972" highlights that it was a lengthy and drawn-out procedure, a slow fade into obscurity with a barely noticeable moment of finality (429).

Many cinemas continued booking cartoons even after they were no longer obliged to do so—highlighting the continued appeal of the animated star—but producers were increasingly forced to drop the rental price.[17] Sito indicates that, whereas in 1947, "a good quality Hollywood short cartoon . . . [cost] around $50,000 to $90,000, . . . [some] budgets [were] slashed to just $6,500 by 1961" (*Drawing the Line* 215). Studios such as MGM and Warner Bros. began outsourcing work on cartoons to independent companies in an attempt to save money, reversing the trend of the 1930s and 1940s that had moved animation in-house. The lack of direct studio supervision—and the lower budgets—meant that the star images were no longer as carefully managed. With reference to the *Tom and Jerry* cartoons outsourced to Rembrandt Films in Prague in the early 1960s, T. R. Adams states that "although they managed to retain the basic look of the characters—if you bumped into them in the street you'd probably recognize them—they didn't *act* like Tom and Jerry" (94, emphasis added). The *Looney Tunes* films produced by DePatie-Freleng Enterprises in the mid-1960s grouped together characters who had never (or only rarely) previously shared screen time, in an attempt to boost the overall "star power." *It's Nice to Have a Mouse Around the House* (1965), for instance, mixes Daffy Duck, Speedy Gonzales, Sylvester the Cat, and Granny. *The Wild Chase* (1965) places Sylvester and Speedy alongside Wile E. Coyote and the Road Runner. As Leonard Maltin notes, these previously unseen star partnerships were usually made to disguise the reuse of animation from old films, rather than for any clear narrative purpose (*Of Mice and Magic* 274, 276).[18] Nonetheless, the stars continued to be presented on-screen as willing performers, never complaining about the reduced quality and suitability of their assigned roles.

As the marketplace continued to shrink, animated characters were slowly retired from the screen, often without any fanfare. Although most studios still had full ownership of these stars, unlike their live-action counterparts, they were generally no longer seen as valuable cinematic commodities. A number of studios sold their pre-1948 back catalogues of theatrical cartoons to television syndication companies, believing that they were generating "significant profits on what—but for television—would have been obsolete, useless properties" (Hilmes 165). Warner Bros. relinquished its monochrome *Looney Tunes* films to Sunset Productions, Inc. in 1955 and the color films to Associated Artists Productions (A.A.P.) in 1956. Also in 1956, A.A.P. acquired all Popeye cartoons produced between 1933 and 1951 "for a reported $2,250,000 payment to Paramount and King Features Syndicate" (Pierce 153, 156). Although the new rights holders were generally respectful of the characters, the dispersal of control meant that there was greater potential for the "coherent images" of the star to be disrupted (to return to Clark's term). Television served to recontextualize animated stars and their films, usually by positing them almost exclusively as children's entertainment.

The studios also underwent substantial transformation over the second half of the twentieth century. RKO was dissolved in the early 1960s, United Artists became part of MGM, and MGM subsequently changed owners several times, even falling into bankruptcy in 2010. All the remaining major studios are now part of wider conglomerate groupings: Columbia Pictures is owned by Sony, Universal by Comcast, and so on (Schatz, "The Studio System" 14). Even Disney—which left RKO in the mid-1950s to form its own distribution unit, Buena Vista—is now a much larger media entity that, at the time of writing, is also attempting to acquire 20th Century–Fox. Only Disney, Warner, and Universal still retain (or have regained) the rights to the animated stars (and most, if not all, the films) that the studios produced during the classical Hollywood era.[19]

Many other animated characters have endured rather more complicated trajectories. Warner, for instance, now has the rights to the Fleischer and Famous Studios Popeye cartoons. King Features Syndicate still owns

Popeye, but he has been licensed to quite a few animation units, such as Hanna-Barbera for two television series in the late 1970s and early 1980s and to Lionsgate Entertainment for a computer-generated television movie in 2004. To some extent, the subsequent "careers" of these characters is similar to that of certain human stars who, as noted above, began to make films for a variety of different production companies from the 1950s onward. However, the ongoing existence of cartoon figures still revolves around them being traded as a commodity, with a figure such as Popeye continuing to have no input into the choice of his film roles.

The apparent "liberation" of the live-action star in the latter half of the twentieth century is nonetheless in need of qualification. As McDonald notes, while some enjoyed newfound creative freedom and increased financial compensation working on picture-by-picture deals, there were many other actors who suffered due to the decline in overall production. It is fair to suggest that the independence of Burt Lancaster and James Stewart proved more empowering than, say, that of Mickey Rooney, who later lamented the loss of "protections," such as the studio (generally) having a vested interest in suppressing negative publicity about its contracted stars (P. McDonald, *The Star System* 101–102; Becker 23–24). The final section of this book emphasizes that even for these seemingly less successful performers, the end of consistent involvement in cinematic productions did not necessarily mean the end of a career, and this is true of cartoon stars as well.

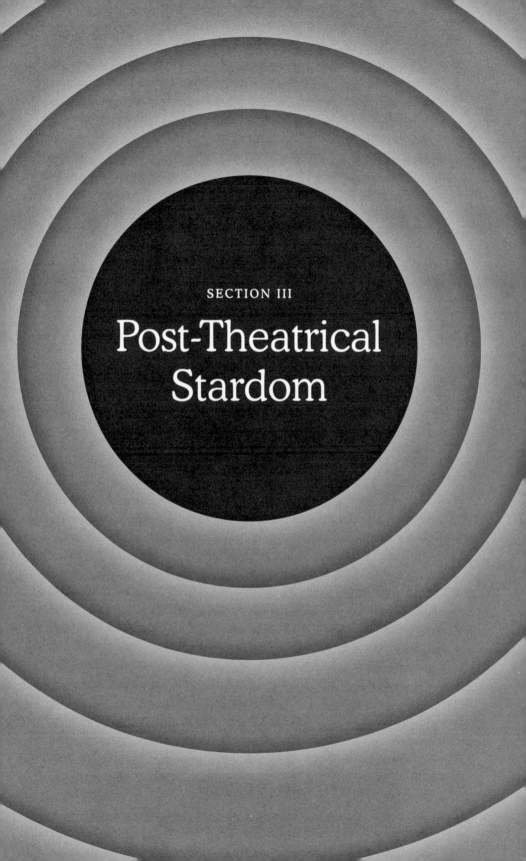

SECTION III

Post-Theatrical Stardom

Chapter 7

The Animated
Television Star

Steve Schneider states that "if television killed the cartoon stars, it just as certainly brought about their resurrection" (133). Although historians have subsequently refuted a simple cause-and-effect relationship—emphasizing that television was just one of many factors in the decline of the traditional studio system—the new broadcasting medium undoubtedly enjoyed rapid expansion at a time when cinema exhibition was struggling.[1] William Lafferty notes that "between 1946, the year of Hollywood's peak revenue, and 1953, motion picture audiences declined by 50 percent, while between 1946 and 1952, the presence of television sets in American homes rose from 0.2 percent of all households to over 34 percent" (237). According to Tino Balio, "by the end of the fifties, nearly 90 percent of the homes in the United States had television sets. . . . Television had grown to replace the movies as the dominant leisure-time activity of the American people" ("Retrenchment" 401).

Gorham Kindem notes that Hollywood "turned to the production of fewer, but higher budgeted, epics" in an attempt to entice audiences back to the cinema. As a result of this decline in overall production, "fewer actors were actively employed" by the major studios, and the number of performers on long-term studio contracts "fell from 806 in 1944 to just 216 by 1954" (Kindem 88–89; Stuart 220).[2] For all but the most consistently successful leading men and women, television became an increasingly valuable supplement to, or outright substitute for, work in the movies (Becker 32). While cartoon characters generally did not *personally* contribute to ongoing expenditures in the same way as an underused contract player, their series fell victim to the same cost-cutting measures that killed off virtually all studio-led short filmmaking (including live-action comedies and serials), rendering all these different stars (and their crews) surplus to requirements for ongoing cinematic production. By the same token, animated characters had no direct agency to seek out televisual work—unlike their human counterparts—and yet, as this chapter suggests, their star images were used in very similar ways.

Television has traditionally been given less critical attention than its cinematic equivalent. Biographies of famous film actors often gloss over appearances on the small screen and focus almost exclusively on movie roles.[3] In academic work, too, there has been a tendency to imply that television offers a diminished or inferior form of stardom relative to cinema.[4] Indeed, even animation studies—also marginalized within film scholarship—frequently makes sweeping value judgments about the relative quality of the two mediums. Susan Murray suggests that, in most critical accounts, "it would appear as though, while the cinema's star system was delineated by a complicated aesthetic, industrial and economic history, the television star is simply a fall from grace" (qtd. in Becker 4–5). Although many actors did turn to television in the 1950s because of difficulties in procuring film roles, this does not mean that their subsequent screen images should automatically be tainted with failure. Numerous figures—both live-action and animated—enjoyed a level of exposure on television that reworked, and potentially even exceeded, their previous status on the silver screen.

Theatrical cartoons tended to be defined as a supporting text within the context of cinema exhibition and, even though this volume has noted instances where the notoriety of a particular star challenged this subservient position, the television era made it even more explicit that certain characters were an attraction in their own right. As Jason Mittell states, "instead of working as an amusing break before or between features, cartoons became the feature themselves, attracting audiences who found cartoons enough of a draw for their viewing time" (*Genre and Television* 63). Like live-action sitcoms, such as *The Dick Van Dyke Show* (1961–1966), many cartoon series—such as *The Mickey Mouse Club* (1955–1959) and *The Bugs Bunny Show* (1960–1968)—were named after the star, emphasizing the value attached to specific personalities.[5] Many also secured strong ratings: *Mighty Mouse Playhouse* (1955–1966), for instance, reportedly averaged a "45.8 percent audience share" over its nearly twelve-year run (Erickson 2:547). This televisual success generated, at times, a *different* type of stardom, requiring adjustments to existing personas and the targeting of new audience demographics, which has sadly not always been given a great deal of consideration in academic or popular writing, even in volumes that focus explicitly on the trajectory of a specific animated character.

Whereas live-action television stardom has been dismissed as an immediate "fall from grace," animation is often perceived to have fallen even further as its presence on the small screen continued. The theatrical cartoon was usually marketed toward a general audience and—as contemporary evidence in previous chapters has indicated—heavily consumed by adults. The first television screenings of these films (as well as the earliest attempts to make new animated programming specifically for the medium) tended to occur in timeslots more accessible to children, but broadcasters regularly found that a significant adult audience was tuning in as well (Mittell, "The Great Saturday" 42). The early 1960s thus saw a boom in animation produced for primetime, historically defined as between eight and ten o'clock in the evening Eastern Standard Time. This broadcast slot is the most coveted because of its potential to "draw large, mixed-age-group audiences together in front of the television" (Farley 148–149). Hanna-Barbera's *The Flintstones* (1960–1966) explicitly targeted older viewers (as well as the wider family) and proved popular in the ratings, but this success rapidly spawned a large number of imitators that saturated the marketplace, and few of these other shows survived more than a single season. With the conclusion of *The Flintstones* in 1966, no animated works—beyond the occasional one-off special or limited-run series—enjoyed any form of prolonged success on primetime until the launch of *The Simpsons* (1989–). Instead, cartoons were "exiled" to areas of the schedule, most notably Saturday morning, that were almost exclusively aimed at children and became "culturally defined . . . [as *not* being] legitimate entertainment for adults as part of a mass audience" (Mittell, "The Great Saturday" 34). The reduced budgets for new programming, concerns over violence and other controversial content, as well as the potential exploitation of child viewers as "consumers" have all served to create a prevailing critical attitude that either derides or simply ignores most American television animation produced in the latter half of the twentieth century.

There are, undoubtedly, challenges to researching television, particularly when compared to cinema. The sheer quantity of material can be daunting, prompting suggestions that both live-action and animated star personalities were stretched thin during this period and thus lacked the "rarity value" of their big-screen counterparts (Ellis 314). Claims of overwork during the studio era, however valid, regularly paled in comparison to what was expected for the broadcast networks. William Hanna noted that, whereas his animation unit produced about fifty minutes of film per year when making the cinematic *Tom and Jerry* cartoons, the Hanna-Barbera television studio was, by the mid-1970s, "turning out eight half-hour shows per week. One person [produces] more footage per day than all of us combined used to" (qtd. in Slafer 257). Similarly, when King Features Syndicate acquired the rights to make a new direct-to-television *Popeye* series, it commissioned 206 episodes to be produced at a breakneck pace between 1960 and 1961, which, as Cawley and Korkis point out, almost matched the total number of Fleischer/Famous Studio theatrical cartoons made over the course of nearly thirty years (151). David Perlmutter notes that, despite frequent (but still ephemeral) reruns, many animated shows continue "to be shown in daytime and weekend timeslots, which traditionally have been given less critical attention than [those broadcast in primetime, and . . . much of this work remains unavailable [in full] for closer scrutiny on DVD" (3).

Stardom can therefore be a lot *messier* on television than in the studio era, with the same cartoons (as well as new ones) appearing on different networks at different times, in different contexts, and aligned with different sponsors and advertisers. Although a comprehensive series-by-series account is beyond the scope of this volume, this chapter attempts to outline some of the recurring traits in repositioning the animated star for the small screen, as well as challenge some of the prejudices about television often repeated in academic work.

The Recycled Film Star

Part of the bad reputation that television has acquired in relation to stardom is in response to its treatment of the performers' existing cinematic texts. As briefly indicated in the previous chapter, the mid-1950s saw virtually all of the major studios make their pre-1948 archives available for broadcasting.[6] This cut-off date was set largely because the (future) rise of television had not been adequately accounted for in previous decades of studio contracts, leading to heated debate about whether stars—and other key personnel—should be paid royalties when the films were given a new life on the small screen. The demands of older performers were essentially quashed when the Screen Actors Guild relinquished "monetary claims" on all works made before 1948 as part of its ongoing negotiations with studios for favorable terms on more recent productions (Segrave 3). As such, many actors with prolific filmographies—particularly those who had appeared in short films, which, like animation, were largely repurposed as children's entertainment—found themselves frequently appearing on the small screen without any creative consultation or financial compensation. Stars including Stan Laurel, Gene Autry, and Roy Rogers vociferously complained about both the treatment of their films on television and their association with advertising (Grossman 33, 37). The situation with the animated protagonist is, of course, different because there was no actual ill-feeling "expressed" by the star, regardless of what was done to his or her cartoons. Still, the animated star was treated as a malleable commodity in the early television era, and most live-action performers were equally powerless in practice. Autry and Rogers, for instance, separately tried to sue Republic to prevent the studio from selling their films to television, with little success in either case (Segrave 15).

Derek Kompare nonetheless emphasizes that many "Old Hollywood" stars and characters, including Bela Lugosi, the Three Stooges, and Bugs Bunny, "became staples of rerun television overnight, and would remain so for decades" (46). Conversely, Laurence Maslon and Michael Kantor suggest that Harold Lloyd (who, unlike most of his contemporaries, had managed to retain direct ownership of his cinematic texts) "never allowed his films to be shown on television, and it cost him a new generation of comedy fans" (202). Older stars' exposure on this new medium (even if unauthorized by them) at times offered new career opportunities. Surviving performers from the *Our Gang* theatrical shorts profited in other ways from the rebroadcast of their films, which resulted in public and even screen appearances for the actors (Kompare 46). Despite concerns about competing with their older films, both Rogers and Autry enjoyed lucrative and long-running original television series. In terms of animation, the success of the syndicated theatrical cartoons saw most studios reconsider the value of its stars. In some cases, even characters that had remained dormant for many years, such as Koko the Clown and Felix the Cat, were rediscovered on the small screen and given new shows. Television clearly had the power to endow stars with a renewed vitality and appeal.

During the 1950s, several animation studios went against the trend of clearing out their pre-1948 archives. Instead, these units retained ownership of their cartoons and made licensing deals directly with the networks. Following some experiments with one-off television specials, Disney Studios launched *Disneyland* (1954–1958), an anthology series, and *The Mickey Mouse Club*. The Walter Lantz studio similarly brought its most famous star to television in *The Woody Woodpecker Show* (1957–1958). Unlike studios that sold films outright to syndication companies, these two producers continued to profit when episodes were repeated, and because they retained control of the content of their shows, they could carefully cross-promote their studio brands, including individual products and stars (see, for instance, Telotte, *Disney TV* 5, 10). As a result, when the Screen Actors Guild finally agreed to the release of post-1948 films, most studios followed the approach of Disney and Lantz in their subsequent dealings with television (Lafferty 245). Warner Bros., for instance, launched its own network series, *The Bugs Bunny Show*, featuring newer *Looney Tunes* and *Merrie Melodies* cartoons. Although this series to some extent competed with syndication shows featuring a pre-1948 Bugs Bunny, the official studio production was able to supplement the existing films with new material featuring the popular star. Indeed, each of the previously mentioned shows—and many others—presented animated characters in ways that helped align the recycled theatrical shorts (which still made up the bulk of each episode) closer toward the televisual.

The Film Star as Television Personality

The prevailing critical view of the 1950s posited the capacity for live broadcasting as one of the defining qualities of television (Boddy 1–2, 72, 80–85). Susan Murray argues that, as a result, "the boundaries between what is perceived to be authentic or constructed [in early broadcasting] were quite different" from concepts of cinematic stardom: "Television's claim to intimacy and immediacy both with regard to its overall presentation and the personality of its performers leads into the way in which television stars were constructed and received. . . . Whereas film encourages spectators to pursue the 'real' in the movie star, the discourse of television aesthetics appears to thrust the authentic on its audience" (129). Murray suggests that, "more than any other type of performer, comedians were the ones that most fully embodied the [fledgling television] industry's commercial and entertainment aims and ambitions" (xiii). Many of the first successful stars of the small screen, such as Milton Berle and Jack Benny, had already established themselves as popular live performers on stage and on radio. The comedian's apparent spontaneity and use of direct address was perceived to make him or her more accessible to the home viewing audience, compared to the carefully edited, self-enclosed narrative worlds of classical Hollywood cinema.

Although the screening of old theatrical films on television in the 1950s seemingly went against the spirit of "liveness," the recycled animated shorts frequently operated as comedian comedies, which (as discussed in chapter 4) were often at odds with most other genres of filmmaking. These cartoons were clearly not live broadcasts (or even created specifically for television), but a protagonist like Bugs Bunny regularly implied an interaction with the viewer, through instances of direct address already present in his films. Such moments undoubtedly eased the tensions between cinematic and broadcast aesthetics, but the comedian comedy approach was still not entirely analogous with the methods used by the first wave of television personalities. In discussing Groucho Marx's transition to the small screen (via radio) in the successful quiz show, *You Bet Your Life* (1950–1961), Becker states that, "even though his asides to the camera recalled his direct-address tendencies from his features, Marx adopted a more nuanced performance style for the show" (74). As such, it is in the newly produced framing sequences for many animated series that the cartoon characters most clearly demonstrated their suitability for television stardom.

The Mickey Mouse Club and *The Bugs Bunny Show* are two prominent examples that approximate the mode of variety programming that had proven so successful for live-action comedians. The title sequences of both series feature song-and-dance numbers involving a wide menagerie of stars from the respective studios, often maintaining eye contact with the "camera" throughout. Bugs and Mickey similarly talk directly, and consistently, to the audience in their capacity as hosts. The Mouse tended to feature prominently only at the beginning and end of each episode, but he performed tasks such as greeting the viewers and reminding them what would be on the following installment. Bugs Bunny appears on a theatrical stage during most of his segments and, like Mickey, was presented "as himself." Indeed, the opening voice-over regularly refers to him as "that Oscar-winning rabbit," emphasizing his status as a celebrated actor and personality, rather than a mere "character." There was, then, generally a divide between the moments when the star was hosting the show, with an explicitly presentational mode of address, and moments, such as the recycled theatrical shorts, that were somewhat more narratively focused.[7]

Although variety shows of the period rarely screened film segments, Becker nonetheless indicates that, during the 1950s, many comedians

> developed hybrid shows that bridged the variety and sitcom formats, with separate proscenium and stage spaces serving different comedic forms and functions. These comedians also developed vivid personalities that could operate both in the presentational space as well as in the representational context, albeit in different ways. For example, [Jack] Benny's monologue was driven by jokes about his stinginess and vanity, and the comedy sketches he acted in were specifically developed around those aspects, as well. (151)

The Bugs Bunny Show often presented the theatrical cartoons within the episode as performances from Bugs's film career that he was sharing with the audience, with this transition operating in a manner similar to the variety comedians shifting from monologue to sketch. As Murray suggests, variety shows (and by extension, these hosted cartoon series) did risk destabilizing the star's identity with the different sections and performance styles, but this was carefully managed to reassert "the relatively consistent personality that existed beneath the performances" (74). For instance, like Jack Benny, Bugs would generally engage in activities during his hosting segments that tied in to the plot of the films (or sketches). The episode "Do or Diet" (transmitted 16 January 1962) features the cartoon *Bedeviled Rabbit* (1957), in which Bugs faces off against the Tasmanian Devil. The new material surrounding the cartoon short sees a similar interplay between the two characters—with Bugs again getting the upper hand—but these sections are explicitly played out on the show's proscenium, and Bugs continues to talk directly with the viewer throughout (fig. 7.1).

In terms of live-action stardom, Denise Mann has argued that some television shows still had difficulty integrating the already well-known

FIGURE 7.1. Bugs Bunny addressing the audience in *The Bugs Bunny Show* (episode "Do or Diet," transmitted 16 January 1962).

image of the Hollywood performer, which was generally associated with opulence and distance (62). Becker, similarly, notes that "if ordinariness was quintessential for television talent," this raised questions about how "a crossover film star's prior elevated status [could] be recuperated by the upstart medium" (71). A number of popular series formats of this period thus attempted to mesh preexisting star power "with the unique aura of liveness and intimacy that the medium was fostering as a strategy of distinction and took strategic advantage of these altered images to lend prominence and prestige to the programs and their stars" (Becker 8). Most of these shows did not try to deny the actor's status as a film star; instead, they were frequently placed in situations where this could be celebrated, while also giving the impression that more of the actual "person" was being revealed and shared to the viewer. One such example was *This Is Your Life* (1952–1961, following an earlier run on radio), in which an unaware subject was approached live on air by host Ralph Edwards and brought to the studio, where their biography would be relayed from the show's signature red book. As Mary Desjardins elaborates:

> *This is Your Life* . . . combined aspects of talk, game, inspirational and variety shows to present stars in settings or situations that emphasized their private lives or feelings. . . . [While] it did trade on the glamor of Hollywood film stardom [with] Edwards often surprising the program's star subjects at award ceremonies or premieres . . . , the primary focus was the ordinary human behind the star—the star as "authentic" individual. (119–120)

It is revealing that the *Walt Disney Presents* television series (1958–1961), which succeeded *Disneyland*, adopted the format for "This Is Your Life, Donald Duck" (transmitted 11 March 1960). As the title implies, the episode features Donald as the subject of *This Is Your Life*. It begins with Donald sitting down in his own living room to watch the program and laughing heartily when the host, Jiminy Cricket, sheepishly announces that the intended guest has not shown up—a reference not only to the live, "anything can happen" format of the source program, but also to the sense of immediacy within the episode itself.[8] Donald's nephews kidnap him and whisk him to the television studio, where he is amazed to discover that *he* is the subject of the episode. Again, this reveal takes advantage of the properties of the broadcast medium to covertly restructure the performer's image:

> When stars surprised by Edwards were caught off-guard, they seemed as vulnerable and ordinary as anyone discovering they are on national television (some, like Nat King Cole, looked more than momentarily horrified). . . . [The] celebrity's surprise, because indicative of his or her non-involvement in the planning or production of the show, "naturalizes" the association between star aura and product. (Desjardins 121)

Donald, similarly, appears shocked *and* concerned—positing him as someone with a private life (some of which he may not want revealed), as well as suggesting a moment of candidness not typically associated with earlier forms of Hollywood stardom (fig. 7.2).[9] Although Donald gets grumpy at certain information being presented during the episode—such as the revelation that he was kicked out of college—he slowly relaxes into the proceedings, noting midway through that "I'm beginning to like this."

FIGURE 7.2. The moment of surprise: Boris Karloff in *This Is Your Life* (transmitted 20 November 1957) and Donald Duck in *Walt Disney Presents* (episode "This Is Your Life, Donald Duck," transmitted 11 March 1960).

FIGURE 7.3. A celebration among friends: Boris Karloff in *This Is Your Life* and Donald Duck in *Walt Disney Presents* (episode "This Is Your Life, Donald Duck").

As Desjardins suggests, this was part of the show's structure: a broadly chronological journey through the guest's life, "which usually demonstrated the subject overcoming obstacles, helping others on the way and ultimately reaching goals of happiness" (120–121). The end of the episode sees a large cluster of Disney stars—including Mickey Mouse, Goofy, and even characters such as Snow White and Captain Hook—walking on stage singing Donald's theme song and then launching into a chorus of "For He's a Jolly Good Fellow." Throughout this, Donald is shown weeping and insisting, "I don't deserve it. I don't deserve it!" At the end of the song, he laughs modestly and gratefully, surrounded by all of his friends (fig. 7.3). The episode presents Donald going through a notable change, one that leaves him humbled and emotionally expressive—qualities that were highly valued by the aesthetics of early broadcasting.

The pastiche of *This Is Your Life* nonetheless indicates the producers' awareness of the underlying formulas at play in representing all forms of television stardom. As Becker acknowledges: "This personality ideal was not created simply by placing dynamic entertainers in front of a camera and having them act as they would naturally. A convincing expression of unpretentiousness essentially qualified within early television as a systematic mode of performance, yet it still required the calculated construction of a star image in order to resonate with audiences" (70–71). Finding its own profitability and claims to authenticity under threat from television, cinema attempted to fight back by revealing these "secrets behind the screen" at several points in the 1950s. Films such as *It's Always Fair Weather* (1955) and *A Face in the Crowd* (1957) presented small-screen personalities as conceited and false, using the pretense of intimacy to hoodwink loyal viewers.[10]

In terms of animation, the *Merrie Melodies* theatrical short *This Is a Life?* (1959) is particularly suggestive in its scathing take on the aforementioned *This Is Your Life*. In this version, Bugs Bunny is chosen as the program's subject, and his feigned surprise (including alternating between laughing and crying hysterically) is heightened to the point of dishonesty. Bugs also overplays his meekness with exclamations such as "oh, no, not little old me!" and "oh, ha-ha-ha, I'm so unimportant!" The film parodies and challenges the outward expressions of sincerity that Donald Duck would present with relative earnestness in the *Walt Disney Presents* episode. However, Bugs received his own "official" studio-produced television series a year after the release of *This Is a Life?* and *The Bugs Bunny Show* subsequently also tended to reproduce, rather than denounce, many of the medium's markers of authenticity.

This is not to suggest, though, that television animation did not show any self-awareness. For example, an earlier *Disneyland* episode, "The Goofy Success Story" (transmitted 7 December 1955) offers a surprisingly wide-reaching deconstruction of authenticity in stardom. There are, of course, jabs at the cinematic system: the young, almost penniless Dippy Dawg is discovered by Hollywood; tied to an ironclad, long-term contract, which is immediately padlocked as soon as he signs; and renamed "Goofy" on the whim of a producer.[11] The claims of "ordinariness" affected by rich celebrities are also subjected to ridicule. A voice-over flatly states (with implicit irony) that "Hollywood hasn't spoiled Goofy. He believes in the simple life, and only has one pool for each day of the week, with a special one for Friday and—of course—Saturday." Although the subject is a film star, this episode—which involves, in part, footage of Goofy's personal life being captured for television—also implicates the role of the smaller screen in creating these inherently contradictory representations.

The sequence recalls the successful series *Person to Person* (1953–1961), in which the journalist Edward R. Murrow, sitting in a studio in New York, interviewed prominent people live from their homes, using a complex relay of footage and a large number of strategically positioned cameras. As Ted Schwarz suggests, despite the enormous technical feat that this required (usually involving several days of on-site preparation for the crew, as well as a mass of carefully concealed cabling), "there was an [aesthetic of] intimacy to the show, as though Murrow had just shown up; the lens would, in effect, be another guest. As the celebrity showed Murrow different rooms . . . , the viewer would be made to feel he or she were also present, unseen but all-seeing" (491–492). The series did, perhaps problematically, dwell to some extent on the glamor of the stars' luxury surroundings but, like *This Is Your Life,* the main focus was on normalizing their private lives and presenting them as "real" people with many of the same concerns as the "common man." Family members—spouses, children, parents—made fleeting appearances, the subjects discussed their off-screen hobbies and interests, and episodes generally began in the living room, mirroring the location from which most viewers would be watching in their own homes. Erik Barnouw notes that "the series was seldom controversial" in terms of Murrow's questioning but that, in being an even more heightened and direct version of the "star-at-home" articles often found in fan magazines, it also had an underlying "voyeuristic element" (178).

"The Goofy Success Story" makes this voyeuristic element explicit. During one sequence, the voice-over states:

No longer could this unassuming star keep his private life hidden from his adoring fans. And so, through the magic of television, we take an intimate peek inside the modest home of that well-known star of the entertainment world: Goofy. Amidst these humble surroundings, silently, quietly, our TV cameras move in to show his simple . . . personality. His most intimate life is revealed by the all-seeing eye of the TV camera.

The images serve to expose the underlying rhetoric of the dialog, with claims of Goofy's modesty being juxtaposed with shots of his palatial estate

FIGURE 7.4. The intrusiveness of television in *Disneyland* (episode "The Goofy Success Story," transmitted 7 December 1955).

and an excessively large and ornate bed.[12] At the same time, however, we see a television camera slowly creep in through the bedroom window and then cut to see more than a dozen cameras also planted inside the room. Goofy is wakened and appears startled at the level of intrusion before composing himself and greeting the viewing audience (fig. 7.4). The cameras continue to pursue the star with an almost prurient level of interest, even following him behind his dressing screen and later joining him in the bath. Of course, *Person to Person* was not permitted such a level of access—if anything, the interviews were reportedly much less free-form than the finished broadcast implied (Schwarz 492). Nonetheless, the format of several other shows, including *This Is Your Life* and *Candid Camera* (1948–1967), did involve the host thrusting a camera in a subject's face and essentially forcing them to gamely play along—an invasive tactic that did attract some contemporary criticism, but usually high ratings as well (Desjardins 127–128; Clissold 39). Although softened by its comedic exaggeration, "The Goofy Success Story" floats the possibility that the intimacy of television—often posited as one of the medium's greatest strengths—might be requiring the star to reveal *too much*.

In instances where animated protagonists appeared alongside live-action figures—as in both *Disneyland* and *The Woody Woodpecker Show*, which featured Walt Disney and Walter Lantz, respectively—there was a tendency to undermine the host's authority and thus emphasize the cartoon star's own agency. In the *Disneyland* episode "The Plausible Impossible" (transmitted 31 October 1956), for instance, Donald Duck refuses to be shot from a cannon. When Walt notes that the viewers are waiting, Donald looks angrily at the "camera" and announces, "Let them wait!" Woody Woodpecker was even more frequently presented as a comedic foil, making wisecracks at Lantz's expense as he attempted to link between the different cartoons. In one installment (episode nine, transmitted 26 November 1957), Lantz comments that Woody was "just another woodpecker, before we made him what he is today." Woody retorts, "Who made who? . . . If it weren't for me, you'd be *selling* pencils instead of drawing with them." Most of these newly filmed sequences deconstruct the business of animation production, with episodes covering subjects such as story creation, photographing cels, and the use of sound effects. Yet, Woody's very presence implicitly contradicts this technical information. In episode fourteen (transmitted 31 December 1957), following the statement that a cartoon is "a series of drawings that have to be brought to life," the fully animated Woody appears on-screen and nonchalantly states, much to Lantz's chagrin, "Oh, that shouldn't be hard."

As in the studio era, animation appears to have been given latitude to lampoon the broadcast industry and its constructions of stardom while also operating within it. However, such an approach was less rare in 1950s television than in the earlier years of cinema. In this new realm, many hosts of the small screen were encouraged to be playful—if never overtly "transgressive"—about the underlying business practices and would often "acknowledge certain artificialities" of their own star images as a means of (seemingly) revealing themselves "as 'real' folks with a sense of humor" (Becker 36). The continuing reflexivity of animation was ultimately just another instance of the star giving him- or herself over to the formulas of early television. The performance style constructed for these stars adopted signifiers of liveness and intimacy and aimed to create a greater link with the viewer. Walter Lantz was one of several producers to comment that fan mail sent directly to the studio's cartoon stars intensified after they appeared on television: "I get letters from kids living all over the country. They want to know where Woody sleeps, what he eats, and whether he's just as fresh at home as he is [on screen]" (qtd. in Peary 200). This direct approach—stressing naturalness above all else—was also a necessity for commercial reasons.

The Star as Salesperson

Unlike cinema, network television shows are free to view and require an alternative source of revenue. For most American broadcasters, this has primarily been achieved through advertising. Until the 1960s, television networks generally followed the sponsorship model developed on radio, whereby a single company "paid all of the production costs of a show and was the only product or [brand] associated with it." In contrast to the "magazine format," which featured "advertisements for many different products" in a designated commercial break or between shows and would come to dominate the medium, these sponsor messages were part of the program text itself, meaning that external corporations often exerted an exceptional level of influence over a show's content and the molding of a star's image (Lotz 156–157). As Murray suggests:

> The selling and merchandising of one's own persona had become an absolutely essential component of a television star's career. . . . Instead of conforming to the more unified aims of a single [film] studio, which only sold movies and related merchandise, the television star was required to advertise a product while also representing the [sometimes competing] textual and industrial strategies of a television network. . . . [As such,] the commercialism of a performer's persona in television was much more overt and the system in which it functioned was more diffuse than it had been in Hollywood. (ix, xi)

Stars were, on the one hand, required to entertain the viewer and deliver the main content of the show, but also had to appear authentic and "sincere" in selling a sponsor's products (Murray 72). The need to transition smoothly from diegesis to sales pitch, so as not to negatively affect viewer engagement with either mode of address, required a very delicate balance of performance, and, as Becker indicated above, involved a significant amount of construction in order to create the appropriate veneer of naturalness.

Variety stars on radio had proven to be adept at juggling these dual roles, and thus many moved successfully into early network television for reasons that went beyond mere comedic talent. By contrast, as more Hollywood performers began to appear on the small screen by the mid-1950s, several complained about the difficulty of playing "themselves"—particularly in the sponsored segments. Becker notes that the film stars who prospered tended to be those with an "ample background in vaudeville entertainment and musical theater" (72, 105, 109).

The animated star's preexisting tendency toward the comedian comedy, and subsequent emulation of variety show aesthetics on television, undoubtedly aided the process of fulfilling the obligation to the sponsor. As with live-action comedians, cartoon characters were able to be quite flexible about incorporating elements of comedic narrative and personal address. Most of the commercials within *The Bugs Bunny Show*, for instance, saw Bugs indulge in familiar routines with antagonists such as Elmer Fudd and Yosemite Sam, as well as the jealous Daffy Duck, but these were also retooled toward the sponsor's brand. For instance, the comedic chase plotline in one of the advertisements involves Bugs ignoring his usual taste for carrots and attempting to steal Elmer's Post Alpha-Bits cereal. Throughout the sequence, Bugs frequently turns to the audience and extols the virtue of the product—noting that it is "made from oats. . . power-packed with energy"—while continuing to participate in the story. Even at the end of the commercial, Bugs is dodging Elmer's gunfire, clutching his box of Alpha-Bits, and still managing to sing the closing section of the sponsor's song: "They're A-B-C-Delicious." Mr. Magoo, who promoted products such as General Electric lightbulbs and Stag Beer, similarly repeated much of the short-sighted bumbling found in his regular cartoons.[13] One television spot for Stag sees the character loudly trying to order a beverage in a library, which he mistakenly believes to be a tavern. The one thing Magoo *is* capable of seeing, however, is the "camera," so that he can address the viewer directly with the tagline: "The next time you look for complete refreshment, look for Stag Beer."

These commercials usually emphasized that the cartoon stars *personally* recommended and enjoyed the products they were endorsing. Bugs Bunny, for instance, stresses that "I'm crazy about Post Alpha-Bits," and in a spot for Tang, he is seen finishing a glassful of the flavored drink and proclaiming "I like it!" Similarly, an advertisement for Colgate sees Mighty Mouse state that it is not only "the world's favorite toothpaste" but, crucially, his

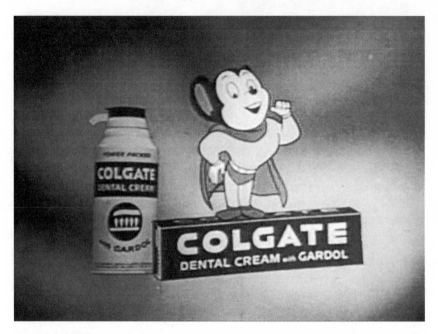

FIGURE 7.5. Mighty Mouse giving a personal endorsement in a Colgate commercial (ca. 1960).

as well (fig. 7.5). Such productions further extended notions of these characters having their own agency and opinions, on par with any live-action actor. Indeed, certain broadcasts even mixed the two types of performer together. Bugs Bunny starred in, among others, a 1969 Kool-Aid spot with the band the Monkees, as well as a 1970 Yellow Pages advertisement with fellow small-screen personalities Rose Marie and Johnny Brown. The latter sees the trio participating on a supposed television talk show—"The Yellow Pages Show"—which name-checks its sponsor when Rose Marie spills lasagna on Bugs and he needs to find a dry cleaner. As with many media texts from the studio era, this commercial presents Bugs as just as viable a participant in the proceedings as either of his two human co-stars.

These commercial endeavors can be seen as yet another instance where cartoon characters kept pace with live-action stars, but the influence ran the other way, too: Hollywood stars appearing on television (and new performers who gained fame on the medium) often had to adapt to a level of commodification already broached by animation. As noted, cartoon characters had been much more widely exploited for merchandising purposes than were film actors during the earlier decades of cinematic production. Although Hollywood studios generally had as much direct ownership and control over the images of its live-action performers as networks and sponsors would later have on television, the former usually chose to emphasize the "glamor" of the star when engaging in product tie-ins (Murray 146). Fans could buy luxury items to be *like* the stars in their films, but could rarely buy artifacts *of* the stars themselves (beyond, for instance, the carefully managed photographs in fan magazines). By contrast, the inclusion of a Woody Woodpecker–themed prize in a cereal box or even the creation of an actual Pink Panther–branded cereal in the early 1970s (which turned the milk pink!) were little more than extensions of the "star-*as*-product" merchandising that had involved Felix the Cat (and many others) from as early as the 1920s (Bruce 123; Cawley and Korkis 147). In the television era, live-action stars had to be equally adaptable. As Murray suggests, more than ever before, these performers "were replicated through consumer products bearing their names and images" (175). For instance, the phenomenally successful sitcom *I Love Lucy* (1951–1957) was spun off not just into items such as furniture, clothes, and jewelry (mimicking some of the approaches taken during the live-action studio era), but also in comic books and even figurines. Eighty-five thousand Lucy dolls, modeled directly on the actress Lucille Ball, were reportedly sold in just thirty days in 1952 (Murray 173), evoking the success of Mickey Mouse toys in the 1930s. Performers were thus frequently being collapsed into drawn images and figurative icons to satisfy the new commercial needs of television.

The presence of animation in television commercials went beyond using preexisting stars. Many companies developed new cartoon mascots as a means of promoting their brands. As Warren Dotz suggests, the value of these "spokes-characters" was that they could be developed as the complete embodiment of the product: for instance, "the buff Jolly Green Giant is the personification of the link between vegetables and good health" (Dotz and Husain 8, 35). Whereas it might be revealed that, in his private life, Jack Benny did not really like Jell-O or that Lucille Ball preferred a brand of cigarettes other than those produced by Philip Morris, an animated spokesperson like Tony the Tiger would never proclaim Frosted Flakes to be anything other than "grrrrreat!" in official representations (which were essentially his only representations).[14] Yet, characters such as Bugs Bunny differed significantly from ones like Tony the Tiger. Theatrical cartoon stars had a preexisting fame that could make them more appealing to advertisers than a newly formed, untested product mascot; at the same time (and very much like a live-action performer), those mascots also came with a tangible *past*—a diverse nexus of associations and meanings that could, for all of the star's appeal, negatively affect the sponsor's brand in unpredictable ways.

The repackaging of older theatrical films—created outside the sponsor's control—had the potential to cause controversy. Even the implementation of the Production Code in the mid-1930s, which aimed to reduce offensive content in American films, was generally less censorial when it came to certain elements such as cartoon violence. The rise of television, however, led to a number of socio-psychological studies that expressed concern about the effect of fictionalized acts of aggression, particularly upon children (see Crawford). Broadcasters became increasingly cautious and scrutinized the films extensively. Indeed, as Heather Hendershot indicates, a lot of programming was self-censored by networks, producers, and other intermediary bodies as a preemptive gesture to avoid any issues for either themselves or the advertisers (*Saturday Morning Censors* 36). David Pierce notes that Columbia's theatrical Scrappy and Krazy Kat cartoons were sold to television in 1954 on a film-by-film basis, with the syndication company's contract permitting them to veto (and thus not pay for) any title that was "unsuitable for exhibition to children or . . . politically offensive or objectionable" (154). When the Walter Lantz studio brought Woody Woodpecker to television in 1957, all the films were reviewed by Lantz personally, as well as by Leo Burnett Company, an agency representing Kellogg's, the sponsor of the eventual series. More than twenty-five cuts were reportedly made from the initial fifty-two cartoons chosen to air. These edits included instances of drinking, violence, implied sexuality and kissing, jokes about disabilities, and even a sequence from the end of Woody's first-ever appearance, *Knock Knock* (1940), where the bird is taken away to a psychiatric hospital. Later, Lantz noted that such edits sometimes caused continuity issues, potentially leaving viewers confused about what had happened ("Censorship Invades" 13–15). However, the representative from the advertising agency countered: "[I]f there was a question at all on a scene, our feeling was why do it? It might cause some group or other to bring pressure, and [Kellogg's] doesn't want to make any enemies" (qtd. in "Censorship Invades" 14–15). The animated star's ongoing success on television was dependent upon financial support from sponsors, and so changes to his or her image for reasons of decency were often deemed necessary.

The previous quotation indicates that television producers were especially concerned about advocacy groups, whose collective power could be harmful to a sponsor's brand. By the mid-1950s, the increasing status of the National Association for the Advancement of Colored People (NAACP) and other civil rights organizations led to racial humor being excised from repeats of theatrical cartoons.[15] Although most directors have claimed that they never intended to be racist or promote violence, the removal of certain works from circulation on television has undoubtedly served to retrospectively mark them as transgressive texts. Lantz, for instance, lamented that several of his films featuring African American characters were vetoed by sponsors before there was even an opportunity to discover whether viewers would actually find them offensive (Peary 196).[16] Even the biggest animation protagonists, such as Bugs Bunny and Mickey Mouse, had films "banned" on television due to problematic content. For instance, *Mickey's Mellerdrammer* (1933) involves the Mouse donning blackface to play the titular role in a stage production of *Uncle Tom's Cabin*, and *All This and Rabbit Stew* (1941) sees Bugs terrorizing a slow-witted, heavily stereotyped African American hunter. This is another instance in which cartoon star images have acquired a level of contradiction over time. As Paul Wells suggests, animated shorts were often associated with nostalgia during the television era, but there was a growing realization that these celebrated texts could also contain challenging, outdated content (*Animation and America* 85). Sponsors and networks frequently sought to resolve this contradiction by simply preventing any of this material from reaching the airwaves, an act considerably easier to achieve in the pre-Internet age.

The levels of censorship also changed over time, usually becoming more severe. Concerns over violence in a wave of superhero-themed Saturday morning cartoons in the late 1960s, coupled with the national headlines caused by real-life violence (including the assassinations of John F. Kennedy and Martin Luther King Jr.) during the same period, led to the formation of Action for Children's Television (ACT), another pressure group that intensively lobbied for reform. As Hal Erickson notes, the early 1970s saw another round of cuts to older cartoons (1:24, 27). The production of new made-for-television series featuring theatrical stars also involved a negotiation between their preexisting personas and what was considered acceptable under the tightened restrictions. When Hanna-Barbera brought Tom and Jerry to the small screen in 1975, these newly created installments repurposed the duo as friends rather than the deadly enemies they had been during the theatrical era. John Cawley and Jim Korkis state:

> Tom and Jerry would often stare at each other, puzzled, as talking characters babbled on around them. No doubt old Tom and Jerry fans were equally puzzled, if not a little disappointed. Even [co-creator] Joe Barbera commented that he yearned for a return to the old days so that "when a cat chases a mouse, he doesn't have to stop and teach him how to blow glass or weave a basket." (202)

A subsequent revival of the stars by the cartoon studio Filmation in 1980 did return the characters to their mutual antagonism, but this was still dampened by censorship. As Hal Erickson states, "Tom and Jerry were re-channeled into 'safe' rivalry: athletic events, competition at the workplace, and the like" (2:860–861).

Such an approach was regularly taken when adapting star personas that had previously been associated with violence. Erickson makes similar observations about Hanna-Barbera's series *The All-New Popeye Hour* (1978–1981):

> Now Bluto was more concerned with outwitting Popeye than beating him up, and more preoccupied with winning races and coming out ahead financially than in seducing Olive Oyl. Likewise, Popeye never resorted to punching out Bluto; instead he used his spinach-sparked strength to outperform his opponent rather than outfight him. And at fade-out time, a chastened Bluto would usually admit that his reliance on cheating . . . was wrong and Popeye's straight-arrow approach was right. The boys did everything but kiss and make up. (2:637)

In an attempt to counteract any contentious elements still remaining, producers increasingly added "pro-social" morals to the end of episodes—"avoid overloading electrical outlets, stay away from strange automobiles, eat a balanced breakfast, protect the environment, and so on"—delivered by the stars themselves (Erickson 1:28). Characters previously celebrated for their anarchic tendencies were rendered increasingly safe during the heights of Saturday morning television and, as the tones of the above quotations indicate, this has been viewed negatively by critics as a dilution of the star image. The reasons behind these changes are extremely complex, involving negotiations among a number of different organizations with many intersecting (and conflicting) interests, but the economics of television undoubtedly played a key role. Although, by this stage, the sponsored program had largely been phased out, networks still needed brands to buy commercial space in the breaks between and during the programs. Controversy—in children's television especially—threatened to drive away advertisers, undermining the profitability of the program and, by extension, the viability of broadcast television as a whole.

The commercial imperative of children's television was itself subjected to increased scrutiny during this same period. The phenomenal success of Mattel's Burp Gun toy—one of the sponsored products featured during the first broadcast run of *The Mickey Mouse Club*—is often cited as a turning point for television advertising. Children were increasingly seen as a discrete consumer unit to be targeted directly, using programs that would appeal to young audiences (Kline 166–167). The block scheduling of cartoons on Saturday mornings by each of the major networks from the early 1960s onward was largely driven by the realization that these timeslots could attract a high percentage of viewers from this specific demographic. Indeed, as Mittell notes, the slot was also valued because the broadcasts "could actually reach *fewer adults*, thus raising the percentage of children per rating point and advertising dollar" (*Genre and Television* 77). Stephen Kline has indicated that shows and advertisements became increasingly sophisticated at targeting specific age and gender ranges *within* this wider grouping. This, in turn, generated parental concerns about whether children could or could not "be assumed to have the knowledge, experience and emotional background to act as rational consumers" (Kline 216, 284). The issue has ultimately had a convoluted history, which has permitted different freedoms and restrictions to advertisers at different periods, affecting the way different series—and the constituent stars—have been represented.

Following the rise of parental pressure groups in the late 1960s, the National Association of Broadcasters (NAB) delivered the following decree in 1973: "Children's program hosts or primary cartoon characters shall not be utilized to deliver commercial messages within or adjacent to the programs which feature such hosts or cartoon characters. The provisions shall also apply to lead-ins to commercials when such lead-ins contain sell copy or employ endorsement of the product by the program host or primary cartoon characters" (qtd. in Hollis 21). This ruling banned the sponsored segments that figures such as Bugs Bunny had delivered on earlier shows, implying that these stars were essentially abusing the trust and power that their appearances commanded. However, the networks were generally permitted to self-monitor these operations, and external criticism of such programming continued (with little impact) throughout the 1970s. Despite rumors that the Federal Communications Commission (FCC) was preparing to set restrictions for commercials in children's programming in the early 1980s, the Commission ultimately enacted a *deregulation* of the industry following the election of Ronald Reagan. As Hal Erickson states, "if toy manufacturers, videogame firms, movie producers and cereal companies [now] wanted to transform their licensed characters into cartoons, so be it, as long as the public wanted it" (1:28–29).[17]

Throughout the 1980s, cartoons were frequently based on existing properties, especially toys. Companies like Mattel developed action figure lines and then subsidized the production of animated series, such as *He-Man and the Masters of the Universe* (1983–1985), to create demand for these products. Kline suggests that these cartoons associated the characters with tangible personalities and histories, as well as promoting successes and "battles between good and evil" that offered clear (and, it was hoped, appealing) opportunities for children to translate these values into play using the action figures (195, 218–219). Although such shows have often been dismissed as "half-hour commercials," lacking in artistic merit, this marketing imperative nonetheless dictated a close attention to characterization and shaping of narrative. Cy Schneider, an advertising executive involved in many such campaigns during his career, elaborated on the process:

> The character must be—or become—an essential part of the American popular mainstream. While the character can relate to or be reminiscent of characters which have come before, he or she must be unique in some important way. Uniqueness is usually achieved by a difference in personality, design, graphic execution, story line, or identity. . . . The characters are usually larger than life . . . [but] the character or the environment in which the character lives must [also] have an instant ring of familiarity. (112, 124–125)

While he does not address this directly, Schneider's description actually has parallels with the underlying principles of star theory: historians of classical Hollywood cinema have cited the value of uniqueness as a strategy of product differentiation and the importance of balancing a star's "transcendent" qualities with a sense of "social normativeness" (Klaprat 369; Dyer, *Stars* 99). The notion of television stardom—and, more recently, the "product personality," to use a term coined in Schneider (57)—operating as a maximized, but still related, variant of the cinematic star system is one that Hollywood has tended to deny or downplay. Indeed, filmic discourse has frequently derided broadcast stars but, as Murray suggests, there is an irony that "the very feature that defines their so-called inferior status—their overt commercialism—was the thing that made their images so culturally prolific and influential" (21). Most Hollywood stars are, like He-Man, personas "created" for the purposes of capitalist production. Their ongoing viability resides in box-office success (just as network television stars must generate viewership of commercials), but the rhetoric surrounding them has traditionally been different. For much of the studio era, in particular, the commercial realities underlying a star's prominence were overshadowed by a focus on glamor and the aura of his or her persona, whereas product personalities have been more direct in their appeal to children (and this practice has been "exposed" more readily by dissenting groups).

Although the more extreme and controversial examples of such exploitation featured newly created characters, theatrical cartoon stars also contributed to these practices and/or have been tainted by a general association with Saturday morning television. Given the apparent origins of the televisual child consumer in *The Mickey Mouse Club*, and reflecting the ongoing corporate expansion of Disney Studios, Mickey has often been presented negatively as an icon of consumerism in satire and countercultural literature from the 1960s onward. While the merchandising of Mickey had largely been celebrated during the studio era, the comments of children's author Maurice Sendak are evocative of a sizeable shift in opinion once the star moved to the small screen: "I think Mickey sold out. . . . Sure, Mickey was *always* commercial, but now he *looked* commercial" (qtd. in Merritt and Merritt 59). From the very beginnings of presenting theatrical cartoon stars on television, broadcasters and studios undoubtedly capitalized upon merchandising and advertising opportunities with renewed vigor (see, for instance, "Prolific Profits" 64). Nonetheless, Kline suggests that networks generally considered theatrical stars such as Tom and Jerry, Mickey Mouse, or Woody Woodpecker more "universal" than characters like He-Man that were *created* to sell action figures. The older stars tended to be aimed at general child audiences, rather than used to target a very specific range of young consumers, and largely avoided the saturation and "burnout" associated with the more aggressively marketed product personality fads (225, 284). As Cy Schneider notes, a star like Bugs Bunny was featured in one of "the top Saturday morning shows in 1975," which was "still among the top shows in 1985" (183), whereas many new characters had come and gone in the interim. Similarly, a 1980s Disney advertisement for its new syndicated weekday offerings emphasized that "He-Men were yesterday . . . robots were today . . . ghosts may be tomorrow, but . . . Disney is Forever" (qtd. in Erickson 1: 30).[18]

Ultimately, the transition to television and the embracing of its commercial needs has led to a significant shift in most animated personas. Even though this has sometimes involved less of an outright revision and more of an accentuation of certain existing tendencies than cinematic star theory has generally acknowledged, the controversies and prejudices associated with the broadcast medium have often negatively affected the stars' images, as well as the shows in which they appeared.

The Fall and Rise of Animation?

Although it was well understood that the time and budget constraints of the broadcast medium meant that compromises—including lower frame rates, a greater reliance on dialog, and simpler character designs—had to be made, it is important to emphasize that the possibility of finding artistic qualities within television animation was not *immediately* dismissed in critical discourse of the 1950s and 1960s. Indeed, it was often noted that, freed from the constraints of having to repackage preexisting theatrical shorts, producers could tailor the shows more closely to the demands of the broadcast medium. Some of the earliest experiments with made-for-television animated series, such as *Crusader Rabbit* (ca. 1950) and *Clutch Cargo* (1959), contained serialized narratives, rather than the self-contained plotlines of theatrical cartoons. Like many soap operas that featured prominently on 1950s daytime schedules, the cartoon episodes featured cliffhanger endings and were shown five days per week, with the intention of fostering repeat viewership at the same time and on the same channel. Hanna-Barbera's *The Flintstones* adapted the sitcom format to animation, with human characters and a single narrative (rather than several shorts edited together) constituting the entire episode. The Stone Age setting—filled with wacky takes on domestic life, such as a television set carved out of a boulder and a car powered by Fred's feet—offered a fantastical, but still recognizable, take on the same issues covered by contemporary live-action family and workplace comedies.

Television sets during this period produced quite a low-resolution image, and so it was suggested that the uncluttered backgrounds and thick outlines of the Hanna-Barbera characters actually read better on the small screen than the lavish detail found in recycled theatrical shorts (Grossman 346; Klein 233). Most television animation from the late 1950s onward was produced in color, providing another advantage over older monochrome theatrical films when color broadcasting expanded in the 1960s. Producers also claimed that the wittiness of the scripts—a prized commodity in radio and television comedy—offered ample compensation in lieu of detailed visuals (Patten 29; Mittell, "The Great Saturday" 42–43). Finally, shows made directly for television had the benefit of simply being new, a premiere rather than another rerun (even though, as noted, the repeats of theatrical cartoons still proved very popular).

Such a rhetoric was similarly used in trying to reposition theatrical characters as television stars in new productions. As the syndication company Associated Artists Productions was the direct beneficiary from the continuing circulation of the older Popeye films on television, the official publicity for King Features' newly produced *Popeye* series frequently emphasized that their cartoons were entirely in color (unlike the first decade of Fleischer/Famous productions). They also attempted to imply that, by the early 1960s, "the theatrical *Popeyes* had been run to death on TV, and that kids were beginning to tire of them" (Erickson 2:632).[19] A new series featuring Felix the Cat (1958–1961) similarly stressed that, unlike the silent and monochrome shorts that had been rebroadcast in the early to mid-1950s, the character would now speak, appear in full color, and feature in serialized adventures. A prominently run advertisement for the series noted that these were "NEW stories . . . designed specifically for television" (as well as predicting that Felix would be "1959's Brightest Television Star").[20]

By the end of the 1960s, however, this discourse was challenged by an almost universal rejection of television animation by critics and historians. Despite the contemporary ratings success of the initial Popeye and Felix the Cat television cartoons, later accounts regularly claim that the shows regurgitated formulaic and uneven plots and contained unappealing limited animation. Leonard Maltin famously labeled most small-screen works as "the Muzak of animation," before qualifying that "whereas Muzak is intentionally bland, the cartoons produced by Hanna-Barbera and their legion of imitators are consciously bad: assembly-line shorts grudgingly executed by cartoon veterans who hate what they're doing" ("TV Animation" 77). These "veterans" often concurred: the former *Looney Tunes* director Robert McKimson stated that "there is not much pride" in making *Pink Panther* television cartoons (qtd. in Nardone 149). Shamus Culhane claims "that the creative urge has been beaten into submission . . . . The artist has become a robot, a controllable part of a vast moneymaking machine" (431). Indeed, the heads of Hanna-Barbera also increasingly acknowledged in interviews that the quality of their small-screen productions had progressively declined (Slafer 260; Grossman 358). Several commentators even suggested that television had regressed the art form back to the limited animation found in the early silent era, removing all the apparent advancements that had been made in theatrical animation during the interim (Klein 244; Smith 11).

Such comments contributed to further accusations that television generated a diminished form of stardom. Wells, for instance, suggests that Hanna-Barbera and others

> sought to embrace the established narrative codes of radio and television story-telling. . . . The enhanced sense of performance by predictable and consistent characters, who exchange personality for "celebrity" in acting as a cipher for a simple and accessible ideological, ethical or moral archetype becomes the staple of what may be viewed as a highly conservative representative of American values and aspiration. Huckleberry Hound did not possess the moral ambivalence of Bugs Bunny; Yogi Bear does not engage in the social disruption on the scale of the not infrequently "insane" Daffy Duck. (*Animation and America* 88)

Indeed, even the television performances of Bugs Bunny and Daffy Duck were sometimes perceived to be lacking the qualities identified in their previous big screen incarnations.[21] Such accusations were, admittedly, not unique to animation. Live-action comedic and dramatic genres were similarly targeted on the small screen, particularly after the rise of the telefilm over the course of the 1960s, which, unlike the live broadcasts of the previous decade, made its aesthetic link to cinema more explicit (Boddy 196).

Historians have emphasized the role played by (often a relatively small number of) critics in establishing canons that can have much wider repercussions on the perceptions of an art form—including determining which texts continue to be revered and discussed and which are dismissed and/or forgotten (see, for instance, Wollen). Mark Langer has argued that the early 1970s saw the rise of the animatophile—"a taste group characterized by a high degree of knowledge about animation"—which foregrounded the establishment of animation studies as an academic pursuit. This discourse regularly juxtaposed a constructed "hagiography of great [theatrical] cartoon artists" against claims of the apparent bankruptcy of contemporary small-screen animation, emphasizing the cultural legitimacy of the former by highlighting just how far the medium had been permitted to decline ("Animatophilia" 146, 148). Although this critical bias was arguably reductive, it had a direct impact upon the subsequent trajectory of cartoon stardom. Slowly, the notion of an adult consumer of animation was revitalized as an acceptable cultural and commercial prospect, in conjunction with—and sometimes in competition against—the predominantly child-based viewership of Saturday morning television.

Much of this initial recontextualization was done by independent fans and scholars, writing in newly formed journals such as *Funnyworld* and *Mindrot* and even exploiting the fact that certain studios had sold (at least portions of) their animation libraries to external companies. Audiences rediscovered Betty Boop's salacious past through screenings of her old films at Led Zeppelin concerts, as well as through feature film compilations, including one with the provocative title *Betty Boop Cocaine Follies* (ca. 1974) (Klein 250; Sito, *Drawing the Line* 98). Several pre-1948 *Looney Tunes* cartoons were edited together for the feature *Bugs Bunny Superstar* (1975). Although the constituent films had been circulating on television for the past couple of decades, William A. Mikulak indicates that this theatrical repackaging was considered an event, with many newspaper reviewers "mentioning the chance it offered for adults to enjoy these classic cartoons on the big screen" (21).

Over the course of the decade, Warner Bros. animation took advantage of this critical rejuvenation, permitting museum exhibitions of theatrical cartoon artwork and even commissioning a handful of *Looney Tunes* specials destined for prime time, rather than Saturday morning, television (S. Schneider 136). The 1980s saw similar changes at Disney Studios. *Mickey's Christmas Carol* (1983)—a short presented in cinemas alongside a rerelease of *The Rescuers* (1977)—was the first new theatrical cartoon starring Mickey Mouse in thirty years. Disney also began production for first-run television syndication later in the decade and made further efforts to distance its new series from the product personalities that were drawing so much criticism. The studio's success prompted Warner Bros. to join the same marketplace, and the two rapidly engaged in direct competition, with each spending significantly more per episode than the average syndicated series. As Erickson suggests, "the fact that the early-morning, late-afternoon local market could stir up so heated a battle was proof that television cartoons of the 1990s would be treated with more industry respect than past seasons" (1:34).

Although still airing in timeslots primarily focused on children, several of the shows actively sought to attract adult audiences (and specifically animatophiles) as well. *Animaniacs* (1993–1998), for instance, is full of references to *Looney Tunes* cartoons, and, like the original theatrical shorts, contains allusions to diverse areas of popular culture, past and present. Many of these series feature Warner Bros. and Disney theatrical stars either as main or supporting protagonists and were often prominently identified as being driven by a single or small group of creators, thus aligning them closer to the celebrated "auteur-led" theatrical era than to the "tainted" corporate-led approach of earlier television. This supposed return to form in the late 1980s and early 1990s has even been posited by critics as a "second golden age of cartoons" (see, for instance, Simensky 290; Dobbs 57).[22]

While the above indicates that this "renaissance" was slowly gaining pace over several decades, numerous accounts have identified the critical and box-office success of *Who Framed Roger Rabbit* (1988) as a milestone for the renewed mainstream, adult interest in animation (see, for instance, Furniss 145; Mittell 80). The film has been deemed the "ultimate crossover movie," as it incorporates cameos of famous characters from different studios, including Fleischer, MGM, Universal/Walter Lantz, and Terrytoons (Cholodenko, "*Who Framed Roger Rabbit*" 218). Most notably, Disney and Warner Bros. permitted their two biggest animated properties—Mickey Mouse and Bugs Bunny, respectively—to officially share a scene together for the first time, reportedly requiring a great deal of negotiation between the two studios to ensure that neither star received more screen time than the other (Cawley and Korkis 28). The story is set in 1947, the peak of theatrical short cartoon filmmaking, just before the Paramount case and a wider box-office downturn weakened the studio system. As Alan Cholodenko suggests, for animation fans, *Roger Rabbit* both anticipates and recalls the decline of cartooning in the 1950s, acting as "a love letter and Last Will and Testament" ("*Who Framed Roger Rabbit*" 217). However, it also implicitly denies this fate, with the film's happy ending offering no textual inclination of the real-life turmoil that would engulf the industry shortly after the narrative's closure. *Who Framed Roger Rabbit* thus offered a convenient coda for this period of animation history—mythologizing the end of one "golden age" from the perspective of the late 1980s, where a second "golden age" was seemingly beginning to flourish, and preferring to forget the events between the two.

By automatically downplaying the value of animated star television appearances from the 1950s to the 1980s—despite acknowledging (usually with exasperation) that these programs regularly achieved strong ratings among younger viewers—many existing accounts have served to perpetuate received hierarchies. As Hendershot has noted, these critical evaluations are often based "on adult notions of aesthetic and narrative quality [that ultimately offer] little understanding of *what* millions of children viewed and, presumably, for innumerable reasons took pleasure in." Her work discusses seminars undertaken with now-adult students, who "have a lot to say about the stories and characters on shows [from their childhoods] that adults in the eighties claimed had no meaningful stories or characters" (*Saturday Morning Censors* 96, 134). Such a response indicates the danger of critics or biographers making value judgments about the relative unimportance of any section of a star's career. Fred M. Grandinetti's *Popeye: An Illustrated Cultural History* is one of the few volumes to give an almost equal focus to an animated character's cinematic *and* televisual appearances. Although Grandinetti admits that his opinion of the television cartoons has diminished over time, he acknowledges that his engagement with Popeye's star image as a child emerged just as much (if not more so) from the television version than the recycled cinematic shorts. He concludes that "these TV Popeyes, despite how one may feel about their quality, had a long broadcast life in the United States, airing on independent stations well into the mid-1990s and continuing to air internationally" (88). The *Felix the Cat* television series also enjoyed several decades of syndication (Erickson 1:326), and Cawley and Korkis, writing in the early 1990s, suggest that "his redesigned [late-1950s] TV persona is better known today than was his silent visage" in the 1920s (91).

Seemingly, then, there is a disconnect between the way that television animation and its stars have been portrayed in most academic and fan literature and the actual consumption of the same texts by other, perhaps critically marginalized, viewers (including children, the frequent target audience). What would be viewed in many other contexts as a comeback—a prominent cultural reinvention of the star for a new demographic—tends to be dismissed in conjunction with early television as a weakening of his or her image, as a selling-out. Even if the broadcast works made before the widely accepted late-1980s animation "renaissance" cannot be considered as artistically successful (by whatever criteria one wishes to impose) as the theatrical cartoons, they nonetheless form a valid portion of the star's overall textual history, and an area that remains in significant need of further research.

Chapter 8

The Death of the Animated Star?

The *Looney Tunes* cartoon *The Old Grey Hare* (1944) begins with Elmer Fudd crying about his repeated failure to capture Bugs Bunny. From the heavens, the voice of "God" urges Elmer to "try, try again" and invites him to take a glimpse into the future: "Come past the years 1950, 1960. . . past 1970, '80, '90 . . . . When you hear the sound of the gong, it will be exactly 2000 A.D." Elmer awakens as a bespectacled elderly man, with a white moustache and wrinkles. Bugs, similarly, appears with a wispy beard, a rather sagging neck, and a gummy smile in place of his usual buckteeth (fig. 8.1). The couple play out their regular back-and-forth routine, but Bugs's escape is hindered by his elderly, bent frame. Hobbling along with his walking stick, he bemoans the limitations caused by his lumbago. Unable to move quickly enough out of the line of fire, Bugs is zapped by Elmer's "futuristic" ray gun and appears to be on his deathbed.

Although mostly played for laughs, the cartoon hints at the melancholy of elderly movie stars, desperately attempting to recreate the image of themselves in their prime. The impact of age upon live-action slapstick

FIGURE 8.1. An aged Bugs Bunny and Elmer Fudd in the imagined year 2000 in *The Old Grey Hare* (1944).

performers, whose films continued to rely on variations of physical comedy, is particularly revealing. For instance, Robert Kurson notes the failing health of *Three Stooges* star Curly Howard:

> [W]atch Curly in *If a Body Meets a Body* (1945). His timing is a hair-breadth off-kilter, there are ribbons of deliberation in his usually instinctive and graceful movements, and his high-pitched voice warbles instead of rings. . . . [As] 1945 turned into 1946, Curly was never to be the same. He struggled through the next ten films but seemed unable to make his body do what had come so naturally before. (8–9)

Curly's retirement from the Stooges, as a result of these medical complications, came at the relatively young age of forty-three. His final appearances are nonetheless reminiscent of many other actors whose advancing years and/or reduced mobility became visible in their work, often at odds with the supposed vitality of the star image still projected by the narrative. For all human stars, the body—as a professional tool—will eventually fail. Conceptions of live-action stardom have thus explicitly presumed that even the most glittering career will be concluded by the performer's death.

With animation, however, the situation is a little different. Despite the tongue-in-cheek vision of the future in *The Old Grey Hare*, images of Bugs and Elmer produced in 2000 and beyond do not present them as old and ravaged, subject to the laws of human mortality. Unlike his live-action contemporaries, Bugs Bunny has the capacity to appear just as sprightly now as he was more than seventy years ago.

During the studio era, some cartoon stars were assigned an official "birthday," usually derived from the release date of their cinematic debut (see, for instance, "Mickey Mouse Celebrates a Birthday" 8). For most of the twentieth century, milestone years were given a great deal of publicity. The fiftieth birthday prompted the publication of coffee-table book biographies of several animated personalities, including Donald Duck and Bugs Bunny (O'Brien, *Walt Disney's Donald Duck*; Adamson, *Bugs Bunny*), while Mickey Mouse's seventieth birthday was even accompanied by an *auto*biography, "as told to his good friend Russell Schroeder" (Mouse and Schroeder). Although the passage of time was acknowledged, the general approach was to suggest continuity, contextualizing (and "authenticating") all the disparate media texts about the cartoon star as part of his or her lengthy career as an actor.

In recent years, however, celebrations of birthdays have been comparatively muted. As these characters approach ages that fall into the terminal range of human mortality—and in some cases even begin to exceed them—there appears to be a degree of uncertainty about how to justify the continued existence of the studio-era animated star. There have been attempts over the past few decades to suggest a degree of maturity and growth within certain cartoon personalities. For the most part, though, these attributes—particularly the visual consequences of aging—have been avoided or reversed. The traditional live-action star system no longer offers any clear models for emulation. All concepts of filmic stardom are, in fact, currently in a state of negotiation—and possibly even crisis. Emerging computer-generated (CG) techniques offer possibilities for images of human performers that challenge the conventional assumptions of linear corporeality, and it may be the case that, at the crossroads of digital production, previously divergent figures such as Mickey Mouse will become ever more valuable in helping to determine what truly constitutes a star.

The Parental (Figure) or Old Master

In traditional approaches to live-action film, it is inevitable that human actors will eventually be unable to convincingly embody youthful characters. For many performers across the twentieth century, the physical inability to maintain an established image has proven detrimental to box-office appeal. The stars who have enjoyed significant longevity have tended to be those who can adapt to these changing circumstances, accepting what might be considered "age-appropriate" (and often secondary, rather than lead) parts in an attempt to retain at least some presence on the screen. The actress Mary Astor, for instance, claimed to have been consigned to almost nothing but motherly characters as she grew older (Becker 24). Although Hollywood has displayed hypocrisy with its male stars—note the romantic pairing of sixty-nine-year-old Sean Connery and thirty-year-old Catherine Zeta-Jones in *Entrapment* (1999) (see Sontag, "The Double Standard")—even most leading men have belatedly transitioned into paternal roles during the final stages of a lengthy career.

The revival of studio-era animated stars on television during the late 1980s and early 1990s responded to this trope by creating scenarios in which these "older" protagonists were explicitly placed into a new phase of "life," one of authority and adulthood, usually through juxtaposition against newly created child characters. While the mere presence of children was by no means original—both Donald Duck and Popeye had already found themselves occasionally saddled with nephew characters from the late 1930s onward—many of these later productions posit the stars themselves as actual parents, rather than just babysitters, and establish this as a fixed situation across the entirety of the series. *Popeye and Son* (1987–1988), for instance, presents the sailor and Olive Oyl as definitively married in every episode—contrary to their inconsistent relationship status in the earlier Fleischer shorts—and introduces their son, Junior. In *Goof Troop* (1992–1993), Goofy moves back to his hometown and acts as a single parent to his offspring, Max. In publicizing the former series, a spokesman noted that "what we were trying to do was to bring Popeye to a new generation by getting together a new character with some of the attributes of Popeye" (qtd. in Billen 3). As such, it is Junior, rather than his father, who is frequently called upon to save the day in these new episodes. Similarly, Max is the focus of *Goof Troop*, with Goofy's slapstick antics given comparatively less attention.

Parallels with live-action films can be found in, for instance, *Indiana*

Jones and the Kingdom of the Crystal Skull (2008) and *Tron: Legacy* (2010), which saw the return of popular characters more than two decades after the previous installment. These deferred sequels partnered the main star of the franchise, Harrison Ford and Jeff Bridges, respectively, both in their sixties at the time of production, with a previously unseen son in his twenties. In these films (just as in *Goof Troop* and *Popeye and Son*), the younger characters take center stage in most of the action sequences, at the expense of screen time for the returning actors. The presence of the original stars is maintained to avoid alienating long-running fans, but they are essentially pushed into the background while new characters usurp their leading roles.

Tiny Toon Adventures (1990–1995) avoids the direct theme of parenthood, but in practice, the effect is the same. The series repurposes existing protagonists, such as Bugs Bunny and Daffy Duck, to represent a *previous* generation of cartoon stardom—in this case, depicting them as mentors at an educational facility called Acme Looniversity. The "professors" are venerated as the founding fathers of animated comedy, and the series makes frequent reference to the lengthy history of *Looney Tunes* productions: one line in the show's theme song, for instance, notes that "the teaching staff's / been getting laughs / since 1933."[1] However, the focus is primarily on the institution's young students, each broadly analogous—but, in this instance, not biologically linked—to one of the "older" characters (Buster Bunny to Bugs, Plucky Duck to Daffy, and so on). Buster admires his teachers greatly, and in the episode "Prom-ise Her Anything" (transmitted 8 October 1990), he even studies an actual Bugs Bunny film, *Hot Cross Bunny* (1948), in order to learn the older rabbit's techniques. However, Buster is largely offering a pastiche of Bugs's routine, channeling the familiar pleasures of the older star through a new character designed to appeal to a new generation of children. As with the father-son series, the dramatic range of the *Looney Tunes* characters is severely limited. The likes of Bugs and Daffy are appearing "as themselves," as the *former* stars of earlier Warner Bros. cartoon films, whose newfound scholastic responsibilities prevent them from assuming a broad range of roles. In *Tiny Toon Adventures*, Buster can be the host of a wacky game show in one installment and part of a *Star Wars* parody in another. For the most part, Bugs can only sit on the sidelines and reminisce.

Any anxiety that studio-era animated stars were too "old" to lead a franchise seems to have been short-lived, however. Following the conclusion of *Tiny Toon Adventures*, Bugs Bunny has appeared in many subsequent productions—from *Space Jam* (1996) to *The Looney Tunes Show* (2011–2014)—without any evocation of Buster. Indeed, of the new child characters, only Goofy's son Max has enjoyed a minor afterlife in a handful of other Disney releases, and Goofy has continued to play active roles—such as in *Mickey, Donald, Goofy: The Three Musketeers* (2004), a feature-length adaptation of the Alexandre Dumas novel—that negate his status as a father. Cartoon stars have thus shown much greater flexibility than most aging human performers to "escape" the parental and/or mentorship responsibilities often imposed upon later-in-life movie characters. This is undoubtedly an instance in which the visual freedom of animation offers certain benefits: despite suggesting the emotional maturity of theatrical characters in shows such as *Popeye and Son* and *Tiny Toon Adventures*, the animated star body was not significantly altered from past evocations.

Continuing, and Returning to, Youth

The notion of a decrepit-looking Bugs persisting into the year 2000 would likely have been amusing to the artists who produced *The Old Grey Hare*, a film that was made in the 1940s when the rabbit was (in cinematic terms) just a few years old and by no means assured of such a legacy.

Over time, however, Warner Bros. has become increasingly cautious about such humor. For instance, the co-directors of the independent film *A Political Cartoon* (1974) note that, even in the 1970s, there were already concerns about addressing the potential repercussions of Bugs's longevity:

> One of our favorite gags was the idea of a well-known cartoon character behind the scenes . . . [gazing] skyward with wrinkled eyes and [reminiscing] about the old days . . . . Our first script had . . . a withered and weathered Bugs, wheezing in an old chair [like Joseph Cotten as Jedediah Leland in *Citizen Kane* (1941)], peering over his dark glasses and prodding his febrile memory for recollections of tranquility: "Sometimes I see our old films on the TV. . . . I like to see us, so young and everything. . . . It's hard to remember back that far."

Although Bugs does appear briefly in the finished version—a rare example of a post-studio-era production that managed to get the star on a loan-out—the directors note that their plans for the above scene were politely, but firmly, denied. The New York Warner Bros. office "sent us a very nice letter informing us that they could not allow 'an ageless Bugs Bunny aged' in a movie that children might see" (Stone, Adamson, and Morrow 20–21).

One of the few recent studio-approved representations of a physically maturing cartoon star can be found in the paintings of the long-serving Disney artist John Hench, who was Mickey Mouse's *official* portrait artist during his final decades with the corporation. The image commissioned for Mickey's sixtieth birthday, produced in 1988, subtly features a pair of reading glasses on a table in the background. The seventieth birthday image, released a decade later, makes this even more explicit: Mickey is wearing the glasses on his head, has noticeable forehead wrinkles, and even shows a slight amount of "gray at the temples" (Hench and Van Pelt 143–144).

Since Hench's death in 2004, however, the Mouse has rarely, if ever, been evoked in a similar manner by other Disney artists. For the most part, the approach has been to crystalize the appearance of animated stars, rather than mimic the linearity of human aging. Indeed, there has sometimes even been a tendency to *reverse* the process. The biologist Stephen J. Gould has argued that, as Mickey Mouse got "older" over the course of the twentieth century, his on-screen appearance actually became increasingly childlike: "Measurements of three stages in [Mickey's] development revealed a [progressively] larger relative head size, larger eyes, and an enlarged cranium—all traits of juvenility." Gould suggests that the Mouse's regressing state may exploit certain traits of human evolution that prompt feelings of "tenderness" and compassion toward creatures with "babyish features" (242–243). David Forgacs similarly posits that the growing cuteness of Disney characters has proven valuable not only in driving sales of its films, but also in increasing the appeal of ancillary products, such as plush dolls (363).

Although most of the tweaks in Mickey's screen image across the decades have been relatively slight, one more recent trend in animation pushes this concept to its extreme. Examples of "babyfication" include television series such as *Tom and Jerry Kids* (1990–1994) and *Baby Looney Tunes* (2002–2005), which explicitly present the characters as toddlers (Goodman). Other studios have produced entire merchandising lines on the same principle. The Baby Popeye & Friends and Disney Baby franchises, for instance, purport to depict the (previously unseen) formative years of the popular stars. For instance, a press release on the Baby Popeye website notes:

Popeye wasn't always a squint-eyed old sailor and Olive Oyl didn't start out as a skinny (albeit glamorous) beanpole. Once upon a time, they were both cuddly babies who had the world at their feet. . . . But destiny is a funny thing and this crew of cute kiddies is already showing signs and characteristics of the superstars they are to become in the future. ("Baby Popeye")

The problem with such an assertion is that, just as animated stars appear to lack a definitive end in a human sense, they also have an ambiguous beginning. As indicated above, the "birthday" of the animated star has traditionally been taken from the release of his or her first film. The notion of this "birth" occurring in conjunction with the star entering public consciousness offers a revealing point of divergence from live-action. All human stars have a period of existence before their appearance in film; animated characters do not. Although there is generally a degree of "gestation" in the first few cartoons as the star image is refined, cartoon stars such as Bugs Bunny and Mickey Mouse debuted on screen (and "came to life") essentially as fully formed adults or adolescents. Furthermore, the underlying implication of the babyfication process is that the Bugs Bunny of *Baby Looney Tunes*—clearly set in the 2000s, due to the presence of computers and cell phones—is, somehow, the same Bugs Bunny we see as an adult character in the theatrical cinematic shorts of the 1940s and 1950s (fig. 8.2). This clearly shatters the usual perceptions about the linear career progression of a star. It is easy to accept, for example, Jodie Foster as a teenager in *Taxi Driver* (1976) and then as a mother in her late thirties with a teenage daughter of her own in *Panic Room* (2002) if one checks the production years of the two films against Foster's birth date. The notion of a sixty-something actor (Bugs's "age" at the time of production on *Baby Looney Tunes*) appearing as a baby is much harder to reconcile.

The hyperbolic possibilities of babyfication nonetheless speak to a wider obsession with youth within the Hollywood system. Cynthia Felando suggests that, in the 1920s, studios were already beginning to isolate and privilege a younger audience, which had a direct impact upon the ongoing viability of its personnel. "More than two-thirds of film actors and actresses of that era were less than thirty-five years old, [and] three-fourths of actresses were less than twenty-five years old" (89, 99). A 1927 *Photoplay* article that ridiculed the "passé personalities" of the 1910s is representative of the often-callous manner in which the industry has continued to

FIGURE 8.2. Babyfication of the *Looney Tunes* characters in *Baby Looney Tunes* (episode "A Secret Tweet," transmitted 3 June 2001).

reject its established heroes in favor of a newer (but, over time, just as vulnerable) generation of fresher-faced performers (Waterbury 46). The prevalent rumors of actors altering their reported birthdates or submitting to cosmetic surgery highlight the perceived need to "turn back the clock" in order to defer replacement. Although creating the *illusion* of youth is, of course, easier to achieve with cartoon characters, it has undoubtedly been a pressing concern of the mortal stars of the screen as well.

Animated Stars and the Synthespian: Looking to the Past and the Future

Richard Linklater's feature *Boyhood* (2014) offers potential for interpretation as a celebration (and maybe even a forceful reiteration) of cinema's link to indexicality. Filmed intermittently between 2002 and 2013, *Boyhood* dramatizes the life of a boy, Mason (played by Ellar Coltrane), as he journeys through childhood and adolescence and into young adulthood. The uncommonly lengthy production gives the work an uncanny metanarrative: the audience is clearly shown that it is not just the characters but also the "real-life" actors who are growing noticeably older between scenes. The "spectacle" (of sorts) comes from the realization that—if claims regarding its aesthetic are to be believed—the sequences featuring a six-year-old Coltrane could have been filmed *only* in the early 2000s and that scenes showing him in his mid- to late teens could have been filmed *only* a decade later.

Theories of photography have, of course, frequently been rooted in this idea that the artifact serves as a record of an irretrievable (and increasingly distant) past. The image in the photograph does not age, and yet the real-life subject moves ever closer to death (see, for instance, Barthes, *Camera Lucida* 96). In addition to seemingly offering evidence of a human's basic existence, the photograph can also be seen as something mournful: an apparent confirmation of the linear process of mortality. As Barbara Creed suggests, this is particularly maximized in Hollywood stardom, where a performer's erotic potential is so heavily commodified, and yet these images simultaneously invoke "the opposite, the threat of loss of beauty brought about by [aging]" (85).

The production of *Boyhood* across the early years of the twenty-first century seems especially appropriate because it occurred simultaneously with the rise of new digital technologies that appear to rebut many of cinema's ontological claims. The "synthespian"—a photorealistic computer-generated human character—permits a substantial transformation of the subject's body. *The Curious Case of Benjamin Button* (2008) garnered attention for its self-reflexive demonstration of these possibilities, casting Brad Pitt in the title role of a man born with an aging defect that causes him to live his life in reverse, from old man to baby. Computer effects were used to incorporate Pitt's facial features throughout Button's life, allowing the star to make an acting contribution in scenes where the character's appearance vastly differs from his own. Perhaps the most striking sequence is not one that sees the character at the point either of birth or death, but rather the section of the film in which Button returns to his love interest, Daisy, in the 1980s, having abandoned her a few years previously. This presents Button in his early twenties, roughly the same age as Pitt at the early stages of his stardom—as the youthful sex symbol in films such as *Thelma and Louise* (1991) and *Legends of the Fall* (1994). *Benjamin Button* provides a glimpse into the ability of technology to reverse the textual appearance of human aging, essentially matching the flexibility of the animated star.

A number of recent blockbuster movies have become increasingly reliant upon such tools. In the Marvel Cinematic Universe, for instance, *Ant-Man* (2015) features a prologue set in the late 1980s, using a de-aged version of Michael Douglas, while *Captain America: Civil War* (2016) contains a scene in which Robert Downey Jr.'s Tony Stark uses a computer simulation of his teenage self to relive a traumatic family event. Unlike in *Boyhood*, where the actor's changing appearance serves as apparent confirmation of the approximate date of shooting, these synthespian sequences suggest a chance to revisit—and reimagine—any past stage of a performer's life.

Jason Sperb argues that CG technologies create a star image that is now theoretically "open-ended," rather than finite: a claim most evocatively borne out by the increase in *posthumous* appearances in contemporary Hollywood films (45). It is possible to trace "performance completions" back to at least the 1930s when MGM attempted to salvage *Saratoga* (1937) after the untimely passing of its star, Jean Harlow, midway through production. However, these earlier examples were almost exclusively in service of finishing a project that had begun with the actor's cooperation during his or her lifetime, serving as "final performances rather than new ones" (Bode, "No Longer Themselves?" 50–51). By contrast, *Sky Captain and the World of Tomorrow* (2004) digitally resurrects Laurence Olivier's likeness to create the character of Dr. Totenkopf—a role produced without his knowledge, several decades after his death. *Rogue One: A Star Wars Story* (2016) contains an extended, new CG "performance" from the late Peter Cushing, reprising his characterization of Grand Moff Tarkin from the original *Star Wars* film.

In many pre-digital posthumous completions, there are often unavoidably *visible* signs of the disjunction between existing (pre-death) footage and the various techniques—body doubles, obtuse camera angles, and so on—used to imply the continued presence of the now-absent star. The Ed Wood film *Plan 9 From Outer Space* (1959), for instance, has frequently been mocked for the ineffective use of a stand-in for the late Bela Lugosi. *Rogue One*, by contrast, contains few overt indications of the manufactured nature of the posthumous performance—no awkward cutaways or style changes between shots. Richard Dyer, drawing on the work of Bela Belazs, suggests that the photographic or cinematic close-up, by virtue of its intimate proximity to the subject, purports to reveal "the unmediated personality of the individual," and by extension "a belief in the 'capturing' of the 'unique' 'person' of a performer" (*Stars* 15). *Rogue One* is thus particularly bold in its willingness to allow the camera to linger on the details of Cushing's digital body and face. Whether or not computer technology has yet reached *complete* seamlessness between the constructed and photographed image, there seems to be a confidence in many recent productions that it is certainly "good enough" to avoid detection by the unprimed viewer. Lisa Bode's study of Nancy Marchand's CG-enhanced appearance in the third season of *The Sopranos* (1999–2007)—giving her character, Livia, a final scene after the actor's death—proves enlightening in this regard. Bode discusses showing the footage to a number of "colleagues and friends [who had] no prior knowledge that it was posthumously constructed" and notes that they claimed to have experienced it purely as a conventionally photographed scene ("No Longer Themselves?" 55n40).

The indefinite provenance of a digital and/or posthumous star's performance has at times generated negative publicity of a sort that has largely been avoided by the traditional cartoon star—and even by overtly stylized CG-animated characters such as Woody and Buzz from *Toy Story* (1995). Both scholarly and fan discourse still contain frequent allusions to what Dan North terms "the Frankenstein myth, embodying our own fear of replication and obsolescence, our replacement by digital constructs capable of outstripping our every capability and nuance" (155). Jessica Aldred offers valuable insight into the changing approaches that Hollywood has taken toward the evocation of these virtual beings. She notes that one of the earliest attempts to promote an extended "performance" from a photorealistic CG character—that of Aki Ross from the feature *Final Fantasy: The Spirits Within* (2001)—appears to have failed because of the emphasis placed on the star's total "artificiality," contrasted against her simultaneously evoked humanity. For many viewers, Aki Ross fell into the uncomfortable realm of the uncanny—a perceptually believable character who claims to express personal agency and yet, due to seeming deficiencies in the film's aesthetic and/or extratextual materials, is exposed as a soul-less automaton. As Aldred notes, "director Hironbu Sakaguchi and lead animator Roy Sato took turns positioning themselves as Aki's controller/operator; both men repeatedly joked in interviews about Aki's near-robotic obedience to their every artistic whim, especially in comparison to the unruly, self-governing troublemaker that is the human star" (2).

In this regard, personalities such as Mickey Mouse and Bugs Bunny may actually have offered some guidance: as I have repeatedly indicated, the inherent subservience of the animated character was almost always playfully undermined in order to emulate—rather than deny—the expectations of live-action stardom. Even though there were attempts to cultivate an off-screen "existence" for Ross—such as her controversial appearance in a bikini in *Maxim* Magazine's 2001 "Hot 100" issue (Aldred 2–3)—these ran the risk of being ineffectual because, unlike a living actor (and even Bugs and Mickey), there was never any suggestion of an underlying person whose private self could be revealed.

Aldred suggests that, in the wake of the box-office disappointment of *Final Fantasy*, the industry has generally tried to "re-instate a more traditional nexus . . . between 'real' human star, character and spectator," advocating that the synthespian originates primarily from an actual performance by a human actor, usually recorded with motion-capture technology. Far from the seemingly empty void of Aki Ross, then, the implication is that these later performances have been physically crafted by the star—such as Tom Hanks playing numerous CG characters in *The Polar Express* (2004) or Robert Downey Jr. as the young Tony Stark in *Captain America: Civil War*—with the actor's contribution somehow remaining "virtually 'present'" in the final product (Aldred 2, 7; Barry King, "Articulating Digital Stardom" 249, 255). Even with digital posthumous performances, there appears an attempt to authenticate the star's authorship *in absentia*: the producers of *Rogue One*, for instance, have been keen to stress how the representation of Peter Cushing takes inspiration from (and remains respectful of) his acting choices in previous roles, as well as noting Cushing's stated wish to appear in another *Star Wars* project during his lifetime (Pulver).

Despite this desire to reorient engagement back to the physical, the synthespian marks a less directly embodied mode of performance than those in most previous live-action cinematic productions, creating parallels with the cartoon star-as-auteur model discussed in chapter 5. Indeed, just as the labor of traditional animators was frequently downplayed in the studio era in order to emphasize the vitality of the main protagonist, the synthespian has also served to relegate the visual effects artist to the status of "below-the-line" worker. Tom Sito argues that Hollywood publicity—including the highly visible (if as-yet unsuccessful) attempts to get the actor Andy Serkis recognized by the Academy Awards committee for one of his motion-captured roles—regularly perpetuates the erroneous impression that animators are almost unnecessary to the process. The truth, he suggests, is very different, citing one practitioner's claim that "mocap [usually] gets us [only] 60–70 percent there," with most sequences still requiring "extensive reworking" by digital artists before it constitutes a finished "performance" (*Moving Innovation* 212). In other instances, an actor's involvement may be even more passive: Sperb notes, for example, that Arnold Schwarzenegger did nothing for the production of *Terminator Salvation* (2009) other than grant the use of his virtual likeness, and yet—despite being "narratively excessive"—his digital "cameo" was seen as extremely valuable in suggesting continuity with other installments of the franchise (39). As with the cartoon character, the importance is not so much the reality of a physical performance, but more the *illusion* of authorship in terms of how the star's persona is expressed.

The Schwarzenegger example also highlights how transferrable a human image can be in the digital age. In the studio era, the loan-out of a live-action star required the completion of a physical performance in front of a camera, perhaps even undertaken at another studio's backlot. Today, however, the synthespian loan-out—as in *Terminator Salvation*—can theoretically occur with about as much direct personal involvement from the star as, say, Walt Disney's loaning of Mickey Mouse to MGM for *Hollywood Party* in 1934 (discussed in chapter 6). Although, as noted above, the ability to tout the actor's contribution in the form of, for instance, motion capture has been viewed as preferable, it is by no means a prerequisite and can still be exaggerated or obfuscated in surrounding publicity. Even the underlying permission to recreate the virtual body can at times be supplied by a third party, especially in the case of posthumous "appearances" conceived *after* the invoked actor's death. The 1985 California Celebrities Rights Act decreed that the rights to a star's image would no longer conclude with his or her passing and that ownership could instead be transferred to the subject's estate (see Fowles 250; Gaines, *Contested Culture* 175–207). Such legislation has often been framed as an attempt to *protect* postmortem rights. California's subsequent passing of the Astaire Celebrity Image Protection Act in 1999, for instance, was in response to a complaint by Fred Astaire's widow about the unauthorized use of her husband's image on a "video that proclaimed 'Fred Astaire Teaches You How to Dirty Dance'." Yet, there remains debate as to whether entrusted family members will always act in accordance with the departed performer's wishes—assuming, of course, that these are even known (Petty and D'Rozario 42–43).

The "management" of dead stars has become an industry in itself. In the early 2000s, Virtual Celebrity Productions secured the digital rights to a number of studio-era stars, such as Clark Gable, W. C. Fields, and Bing

Crosby, from their respective estates (Laurens 114). Another organization, CMG Worldwide, acts as an "agent" for the likes of James Dean and Jean Harlow and even, as Lisa Bode notes, works to rehabilitate the fading image of "lesser" stars of yesteryear, such as Gene Tierney and Virginia Mayo, "whose heirs pay [CMG] a percentage." Although there are undoubtedly valid and well-meaning reasons for wishing to keep someone in the popular memory, Bode suggests that often "this kind of consecration occurs wherever a star name or image can be financially leveraged" ("Fade Out/Fade In" 90).

It is possible to find numerous examples in which actors have been digitally resurrected—particularly for the purpose of advertisements, rather than dramatic performances—in ways that have caused some viewers to cry foul. For instance, a recent Dove commercial, which presented a young Audrey Hepburn eating a square of dark chocolate, attracted criticism for its apparent degradation of the star's rarefied image. While Dove's PR department drew attention to the approval granted by Hepburn's sons, who claimed, "[O]ur mother loved rewarding herself with a piece of chocolate, but it always had to be dark chocolate," the underlying implication is that there were other factors at play besides simply wishing to celebrate Hepburn's apparent snacking ritual (Hiltzik).[2]

The concerns regarding the use of Hepburn echo how viewers have responded to certain "comebacks" for animated stars. For instance, the prerelease publicity for *Loonatics Unleashed* (2005–2007) gave the (ultimately false) impression that the series would be transplanting existing *Looney Tunes* characters into a post-apocalyptic science-fiction narrative. This generated a significant number of complaints to Warner Bros.— in essence, the "executors" of Bugs Bunny's "estate"—claiming that the "edgy" theme served as an affront to the star's comedic legacy (Gustines). In the case of both Bugs and Hepburn, these later evocations appeared at least emotively "real" enough to encourage protest from certain fans, who felt the need to speak up for the performer in his or her absence.

The digital commodification of live-action performers still relies, to some degree, on the basis of a (once-)living person, and yet the star is treated increasingly as a "brand," whose ongoing existence—like that of the animated star—may now be entirely textual, rather than physical. In such a scenario, where death no longer appears to offer a guarantee of finality and closure, the "end" of a performer's career becomes virtually impossible to either predict or confirm. Mary Flanagan has suggested that, in a digital realm, the greatest threat becomes obsolescence rather than mortality (81). A star has the potential to appear forever young in synthespian form, but this does not guarantee that consumers will always remain interested. Indeed, in a theoretical Hollywood system that has the potential to choose *any* performer, past and present, the competition for viewer attention only intensifies. Consider the theatrical cartoon star, for whom this kind of longevity has always technically been possible: for every Mickey Mouse that endures, there are numerous Colonel Heeza Liars cast aside in favor of trying something new. Even the most successful animated figures and synthespians will falter at some point in the future due to the still-inevitable mortality of existing fans and will functionally "die" as a result of being forgotten (even if the option always remains for rediscovery and yet another comeback).

With every subsequent generation, however, the star image becomes ever more loaded with varied expectations, making it harder to appear authentic to a past self while also successfully moving with the times. Both Bugs Bunny and Audrey Hepburn may eventually (assuming they have not already) come to be seen less as stars—whose various appearances form the basis of a diverse, but linear, screen "career"—and more akin to literary and cinematic characters. Figures, for instance, such as Sherlock Holmes or Batman remain "distinctly identifiable commodit[ies]" but have been "rebooted" so frequently (and often simultaneously) in so many different forms of media that their respective identification as singular beings who could (somehow) make sense of it all has become impossible (Uricchio and Pearson 1). Will Brooker notes that Batman, unlike Holmes, is at least "still tethered to a multinational institution, rather than floating freely in the public domain" (10–11), with this notion of a corporate author providing some (shaky) anchorage to the character's existence.

Disney has been particularly aggressive in its attempts to retain ownership of its animated creations, successfully lobbying for the Copyright Term Extension Act (1998), a law "that extended copyright protection for an additional twenty years, rescuing Mickey from his original copyright expiration date of 2003" (Grainge 51). The Astaire Celebrity Image Protection Act, enacted in California the following year, prolonged the heirs' exclusive postmortem rights to the deceased star's image from fifty to seventy years (Laurens 128). The ongoing coherence of the synthespian—like the cartoon character—is arguably rooted much more in its status as a legal entity, as protected intellectual property, than in the apparent "truth" of a physical body, as foregrounded in earlier accounts of live-action stardom. At the time of writing, at least, these rights still remain finite, and so it is very possible that any given star will—at some point—come to be owned by everybody, creating the potential for an even greater multiplicity of representations that will place further strain on an already-precarious framework of meaning. As Barry King suggests, if the "branding function of the star" is removed and *anyone* can legitimately evoke or embody the subject, then this may "lead to the end of stardom" itself ("Articulating Digital Stardom" 257). There is undoubtedly a point at which contradiction in the star image becomes a liability rather than an intrigue.

Of course, synthespian technology is still in its infancy, and so making pronouncements about stars being *wholly* consumed by virtual avatars risks looking as foolish as the space-age vision of the year 2000, replete with ray guns and flying cars, in *The Old Grey Hare*. As Sperb notes, however, the "not yet" of future speculation "seems perpetually in tension with the 'always already' . . . , the once unimaginable possibilities that have already come to pass . . . The very notion of a 'posthuman' form of labor, or of (sometimes literally) dead and stored human capital, highlights how objects of consumption [have already] become further removed from their original modes of production" (41, 51). In 2001, Lev Manovich infamously suggested that, as film "enters the digital age, . . . cinema can no longer be clearly distinguished from animation" (295). While there are undoubtedly caveats to this oft-cited quotation, Manovich's claim has been extremely useful in forcing live-action theory to acknowledge and account for the cartoon medium, something that has often been underplayed in previous generations of scholarly work. Indeed, reflecting Sperb's notion of the "always already," several critics have argued that the so-called digital revolution actually serves to expose many of the tensions and contradictions that were already present within analog cinema (see Bode, "No Longer Themselves?" 49–50). The studio-era animated star reiterates that *at no point* in film history has objective ontological truth, or a definitive moment of birth and death, been an absolute necessity for the operation of stardom: a textual simulacrum of these traits—if evoked appropriately—has generally proven an acceptable substitute. As North suggests, the synthespian can actually be seen "as the logical extension of an industry that has developed, over decades, the art of manufacturing star images: the replacement of the actual, physical star body with a digital construct is a minor detail because the rest of the manufacturing process is still the same" (156). Rather than being a belated or inferior model of stardom, the traditional animated protagonist has been somewhat prophetic of the diverse ways in which it is now possible to engage with a "human" live-action performer. By accepting cartoon characters as stars, there is the potential not just to add nuance to our engagement with cinema's digital future, but also to make sense of the flexible boundaries of its celluloid past.

Notes

Introduction

1. This does not necessarily deny that protagonists from other types of animated texts—including Disney's classic features, such as *Snow White and the Seven Dwarfs* (1937); television cartoons, such as *The Flintstones* (1960–1966) or *The Simpsons* (1989–); and even comparatively recent computer-generated features, such as *Toy Story* (1995)—can also be considered as stars. This volume contends, however, that short theatrical animation generated a particular type of star image that has not been completely replicated in these other productions.

2. One can identify a few exceptions. Fleischer Studios produced three two-reel Popeye cartoons in the 1930s: *Popeye the Sailor Meets Sindbad the Sailor* (1936), *Popeye the Sailor Meets Ali Baba's Forty Thieves* (1937), and *Aladdin and His Wonderful Lamp* (1939). These were still accompaniments to a live-action feature, but were heavily advertised as special attractions. The Disney Studios also produced a few "package" films—feature-length but comprising several separate stories—involving short film stars. For example, *Saludos Amigos* (1942) contained two segments featuring Donald Duck and one starring Goofy.

3. To illustrate Gunning's point, see, for instance, Kracauer (vii, 89), who admits from the outset that his book "neglects the animated cartoon" and subsequently

notes that "what holds true of photographic film does of course not apply to animated cartoons."

4. Hand-drawn animation is sometimes referred to as "traditional" or "two-dimensional" because of the recent prevalence of three-dimensional, computer-generated (CG) production. Some other animation techniques were also developed during the twentieth century, but not to the same degree as hand-drawn filmmaking. For instance, stop-motion was notably used in George Pal's *Puppetoons*, a series of short cartoons released in the United States between 1940 and 1947.

5. See also E. Jenkins.

6. At least, Daffy *aspires* to be Robin Hood. A lot of the cartoon's humor involves his failure to live up to the mythology.

7. The outtakes imply that the movie is being filmed on a live-action set. A number of the mishaps involve a boom microphone appearing in the shot or the camera knocking into an object, rather than animation errors (which would have been closer to legitimate mistakes that occurred during production).

8. This contradicts Kristin Thompson's assertion that, unlike live-action, "virtually everything written on animated films throughout their history has concentrated on the 'how-to' aspects" (110). While it is true to say that some—but certainly not all—writings from this period displayed an interest in the underlying technology, even many of these approached this via the fame of the star (note, for instance, the titles of "production-focused" articles such as Braver-Mann, "Mickey Mouse and His Playmates," and Boone, "When Mickey Mouse Speaks").

9. Reflecting the range of media texts surrounding any given star, at least one purported "interview" with Donald Duck—albeit not one officially endorsed by Disney Studios—shows Donald addressing and taking issue with Adorno and Horkheimer's reading. See Wagner 11–19.

Chapter 1: Silent Animation and the Development of the Star System

1. Even release dates and titles of cartoons are often incomplete. Denis Gifford's *American Animated Films: The Silent Era, 1897–1929* provides the most comprehensive filmography of silent animation yet published, although it is not without its own omissions and errors. All film titles and dates referenced in this chapter correspond to those provided by Gifford, except where sufficient additional evidence reveals the information to be inaccurate.

2. Crafton qualifies his approach to stardom and authorship in his later book, *Shadow of a Mouse*, although the volume focuses less on silent-era characters.

3. Much of the paraphernalia surrounding the Yellow Kid and other early comic strip creations was unauthorized, prompting artists and publishers to clearly define their copyright entitlements. This served to establish the comic strip character as a valuable commodity in terms of selling both newspapers and lucrative ancillary products. The licensing of Outcault's subsequent comic creation, Buster Brown, was much more tightly controlled, spawning a large selection of official

merchandise and advertising endorsements featuring the character. For a detailed analysis of comic strip merchandising, see Gordon 31–33, 43–58.

4. For examples of this trope in live-action discourse, see Stamp 338.

5. *Moving Picture World* 27.3 (15 January 1916): 483.

6. *Moving Picture World* 29.11 (9 September 1916): 1657.

7. *Moving Picture World* 27.8 (26 February 1916): 1265.

8. *Motion Picture News* 20.14 (27 September 1919): 2544, 2549.

9. As the punning name may suggest, the protagonist is a bumbling old man whose recollections of events often comically exaggerate his own capability and contribution.

10. *Moving Picture World* 26.13 (18 December 1915): 2133.

11. *Motion Picture News* 13.10 (11 March 1916): 1377.

12. See, for instance, *Motion Picture News* 24.26 (17 December 1921): 3142.

13. *Film Daily* 31.22 (27 January 1925): 6.

14. Felix is also indicative of a general shift from human to (usually anthropomorphized) animal protagonists within animated filmmaking. Although animals became somewhat prominent in cartoons from the mid- to late 1910s onward, Felix's success is considered to have had an influence on other studios developing their own "animal heroes" in the 1920s and beyond. See Crafton, *Before Mickey* 287–289, 321–322.

15. *Moving Picture World* 45.1 (3 July 1920): 4.

16. Bray Studios had previously experimented with the production of promotional comic strips featuring some of its screen creations, such as Colonel Heeza Liar and Farmer Al Falfa, in 1916. However, this early endeavor was not a success: the series appears to have been run by only a small number of regional newspapers and was quickly discontinued (see Holtz).

17. *Film Daily* 25.53 (2 September 1923): 16.

Chapter 2: Stars and Scandal in the 1930s

1. Mickey does claim that some of the engagements were partly as a result of misunderstandings on behalf of publicists.

2. The article also ends with the startling announcement that Minnie was pregnant and that, during the reporter's visit, gave birth to eighteen children—an event that clearly has not subsequently become part of Mickey's authorized biography (McEvoy 97). The presence of professional-looking images of the Mouse within this article (and several of the others mentioned earlier) suggests that there had been some cooperation with Disney, but whether or not the studio had any input into the writing or got to approve the text before publication is unclear. Even Mickey's on-screen persona was not particularly well established at this stage, and so there appears to have been more flexibility for journalists to take liberties with his backstory in the early 1930s than in subsequent years.

3. See, e.g., Smith and Wright 153; H. Jenkins, *The Wow Climax* 132–134. Paul McDonald's research into fake photo websites, where "star faces are grafted on to

naked bodies," examines a more recent subculture of fandom contemplating the sexuality of various celebrities—usually without the sites trying to "deceive visitors into believing what they see is real" ("Stars in the Online Universe" 37). Reni Celeste has argued that the supposed "truth" of nudity in relation to famous people is not necessarily "identity or correspondence but the play between concealment and exposure": the act of revelation itself is perhaps the most important element (31).

4. Hays became fairly synonymous with censorship during the late 1920s and early 1930s, as indicated by the unflattering namecheck in the aforementioned Tijuana bible "Nuts to Will Hays" (Ever). In his 1930 "interview" with Cedric Belfrage, Mickey Mouse says, "I think Mr. Hays is doing great work in trying to make the movies an influence for good, and I am behind him with every bone in my body and curl in my tail." However, as befitting the boisterous tone of these early fan magazine articles, any apparent sincerity is quickly undermined in favor of delving into the Mouse's colorful private life. Mickey apologizes for his digression, and admits that "Mr. Hays has no place in an interview on my intimate moments, or, for that matter, on anybody else's. Much as I admire the man, I would not try to make it appear that I was ever really intimate with him" (Mouse and Belfrage 68).

5. For a historical account of the PCA's formation, see Vasey, *The World According to Hollywood* 126–131; Doherty, *Hollywood's Censor* 58–67.

6. See chapter 5 for further discussion of the imitative aspects of Mickey's persona.

7. Karl F. Cohen's full-length study of animation censorship in the United States lists only one confirmed instance during the silent era. At the behest of the Pennsylvania Censorship Board, various scenes involving alcohol consumption were removed from the 1925 Disney short *Alice Solves the Puzzle* (10–11).

8. It was really only with the rise of Saturday morning television that studios began to explicitly target children to the *exclusion* of an adult audience. This does not appear to have been the case during the 1930s. Indeed, one report of an "all-cartoon show" children's club in the journal *Film Daily* noted that such events were still "apt to bring out a lot of grownups as well" ("Special Stunts" 14).

9. This version of the Mickey Mouse Club is separate from the television series of the same name, discussed in chapter 7.

10. In this example, Mickey is again not specifically complicit in the controversial material. During the cartoon, he even utters a chiding "For shame" upon discovering the horse's inebriation.

11. The article admittedly tries to argue that the cinematic adaptation could be educational. Mickey praises the "wonderful moral" of the film and posits that it may have influenced "a few kiddies and grown-ups to stop doing business with bad bootleggers." However, despite the Mouse's suggestion that readers should respect Prohibition, he implies that he personally continues to consume alcohol. He even concludes the interview by offering the journalist a glass of Canadian gin, which has seemingly been illicitly imported into the country: "You couldn't get such quality in this town" (Mouse and Belfrage 68, 96).

12. A major issue throughout the 1930s and 1940s was the lack of a definitive version of the Code. Several drafts existed from different collaborators, each with varying levels of detail about what could be addressed on-screen (see Doherty, *Hollywood's Censor* 351; Maltby, "Documents" 33). The quotations attributed to the Code in this chapter are taken from the draft that was signed by the boards of directors of both the Association of Motion Picture Producers and the MPPDA in 1930.

13. See the article "Hollywood Censors Its Animated Cartoons" as one of the few contemporary discussions of the cartoon's position within the wider hierarchy of Hollywood content regulation. Hendershot suggests that archival PCA records related to short films no longer survive, and, given the lack of step-by-step attention that these works received relative to features, there may not even have been a great deal of documentation produced at the time ("Secretary" 129n10).

14. Walter Lantz, head of the studio that created Woody Woodpecker, was reportedly especially conscious of this, believing that "animating anything that might be cut by a censor was a waste of money" (Cohen 26).

15. The *Mickey Mouse* series did admittedly persist until 1953, but failed to maintain the momentum of its first decade, with the Mouse's screen time heavily diminished in many of the later installments.

16. See Sampson for an extensive inventory of racial imagery in theatrical short cartoons.

17. Conversely, restrictions can also be loosened as time passes. The recent Mickey Mouse short *Get a Horse!* (2013), which begins as a pastiche of the aesthetic of late-1920s Disney animation, features visual gags about Clarabelle Cow's udders, as well as a sequence in which Mickey accidentally jumps out of his shorts, leaving him temporarily "naked." The film was screened ahead of the PG-rated feature *Frozen* (2013) and attracted no significant complaints about its content.

Chapter 3: The Second World War

1. For instance, Howard Greer (94) proclaims that Mickey Mouse was of greater interest to filmgoers throughout Europe than any live-action performer, including Greta Garbo ("the best known woman in the world"). Henry F. Pringle similarly dubs Mickey "far and away, the most popular American star abroad" (28). Whether or not this can be dismissed as hyperbole, it is certainly the case that viewership for American animation extended far beyond the United States during this period. Richard Schickel notes that Mickey "was available in one form or another in thirty-eight of the world's nations by 1937" and that the Disney Studios had established several offices overseas to aid in this lucrative distribution effort (165, 167). Other studios enjoyed a similarly international fan base: Betty Boop was so popular with Japanese viewers that Fleischer produced an entire cartoon—*A Language All My Own* (1935)—in which Betty travels to Japan and performs to a large, enthusiastic crowd.

2. A few exceptions can nonetheless be identified. The *Looney Tunes* short, *Bosko's Picture Show* (1933), is an early example of a cartoon presenting a negative,

if still comedic, image of Hitler. In a parody of a newsreel, a caricature of the Nazi leader is briefly seen, somewhat bizarrely, chasing the Hollywood star Jimmy Durante with an axe. The aforementioned interview with Mickey Mouse also becomes surprisingly opinionated, with Mickey claiming to be interested in the Stimson Doctrine, which urged American nonrecognition of territorial changes in China as a result of Japanese military intervention. The Mouse's stated reason for supporting Stimson was the fear that Japan's actions would have a negative impact on the box-office appeal of his films in China (Fairbanks 44–45). On the whole, though, studios were rarely this overt about discussing international politics in films or in surrounding publicity throughout much of the 1930s.

3. Popeye continued to be shown in his naval uniform after the war ended, right up until his theatrical cartoon series was discontinued in 1957.

4. Many dramatic films from this period feature character actors portraying Nazis, but these roles were not taken by famous stars. However, live-action comedy performers were given freedoms similar to those of Donald. Charlie Chaplin, for instance, portrayed Adenoid Hynkel, a ruthless parody of Hitler, in *The Great Dictator* (1940). Jack Benny also appeared in Nazi uniform in the comedy *To Be or Not to Be* (1942).

5. Mickey was briefly shown in a soldier's uniform in the cartoon *Out of the Frying Pan into the Firing Line* (1942), implying he was fighting on the front lines, but these battles were never presented on-screen.

6. Waschman's text refers to Oswald the Rabbit rather than Bugs, but the context of the article strongly indicates that the latter was the intended point of reference.

7. For examples of criticisms of the expenditure on the film, see Shale 31; Smoodin 178–179.

8. It should be reiterated, though, that these star-led training films were still a relatively small sub-genre, compared to the limited animation films such as *Four Methods of Flush Riveting*.

9. Unfortunately, the Trigger Joe films are now believed to be lost, and so the analysis here draws from written sources about the character.

10. It is also significant that these characters tended to be represented as human beings, rather than animals. Whether existing animal stars such as Donald Duck would have been just as suitable here remains inconclusive. Although Donald had appeared in a number of army-based entertainment films, it is possible that his star image would have conflicted with the "everyman" approach. Snafu and Trigger Joe are perhaps closer to the "Mr. Average Taxpayer" (or, in this case, "Mr. Average Soldier") that Morgenthau had originally wanted for *The New Spirit*.

11. Although Culbert mistakenly attributes the Snafu films to Disney Studios, the rest of his article is based on careful research of military archives.

Chapter 4: The Comedian Comedy

1. One particularly notable exception is the *Superman* series, produced between 1941 and 1943, initially by Fleischer Studios and continued for a short

run by Famous Studios (formed by Paramount after the Fleischer brothers were ousted). The series operated primarily in the action-adventure genre, with little humorous content, but proved too costly and was canceled after seventeen installments. United Productions of America (UPA) also tried to diversify into some noncomedic films, including *The Tell-Tale Heart* (1953), a somber adaptation of the Edgar Allan Poe story. As Adam Abraham notes, Steve Bosustow (one of the founders of UPA) "recalled that audiences were habituated to laughing at animated cartoons; thus, they found *The Tell-Tale Heart* rather funny. To alter this reaction, UPA prepared a set of opening-title cards. These explain the source material . . . and suggest that what follows is perfectly serious" (107–108).

2. Seidman briefly suggests possible continuities between cartoons and comedian comedies, but unfortunately neglects to develop this thought further (29–30).

3. For an insightful diachronic account of aesthetic and industrial changes across the theatrical era, see Klein. However, this approach is not without its own generalizations, given the vast range of different studios and film series in operation.

4. Embracing these contradictions in noncomedic genres runs the risk of alienating audience members who are unable to accept the star as inhabiting the character believably, leading to accusations of miscasting. For the most part, then, acting in classical Hollywood cinema conforms to what James Naremore defines as "expressive coherence . . . maintaining not only a coherence of manner but also a fit between setting, costume, and behavior" (68–69).

5. Even the simple existence of, for instance, a credit sequence reminds us that a film is explicitly manufactured.

6. Certain animated stars, such as Felix the Cat and Mickey Mouse, did nevertheless attract the attention of surrealists and intellectuals while simultaneously enjoying popular acclaim. See, for instance, Leslie; see also Hansen.

7. Several later animated shorts humorously push this manufactured "relationship" even further. In *A Date to Skate* (1938), Popeye turns to the "camera" and asks, "is there any spinach in the house?" because he forgot to bring his own supply. There is a sound of murmuring and a man emerges at the bottom of the frame, rendered in animation but presented as a silhouette to give the impression that an actual patron in the cinema was standing up and blocking the projection of the film. He shouts "Here you are, Popeye!" and throws a can of spinach "into" the scene for the sailor to consume. A number of *Looney Tunes* and *Merrie Melodies* cartoons include similar audience "interaction" gags. In *Daffy Duck and Egghead* (1938), for instance, a silhouetted latecomer appears to be obscuring part of the screen. After repeated attempts to ask the man to sit down and be quiet, Egghead finally loses patience and shoots him dead.

8. As noted in chapter 1, some early cinematic cartoon stars had a preexisting textual history from appearances in comic strips, but such adaptations were largely phased out by the late 1910s.

9. For a wider discussion of animation and vaudeville, see Crafton, *Shadow of a Mouse* 99–143.

10. Reflecting the cartoon star's existence in yet another medium, a number of cartoons also explore and parody animation production. Examples include *The Tom and Jerry Cartoon Kit* (1962) and *Cartoons Ain't Human* (1943), in which Popeye attempts to make his own animated film.

11. An exception in the actor's filmography is *Son of the Sheik* (1926) because it is explicitly presented as an official sequel to *The Sheik*. The film acknowledges the events of the first installment and develops the narrative further, with Valentino reprising the role of Hassan, as well as taking on a second role as the Sheik's son.

12. In some cases, films that transport the character well beyond usual scenarios are briefly concluded with a segment that *does* explain this deviation. For instance, Chaplin's appearance as a caveman in *His Prehistoric Past* (1914) contains a short coda in which a passing policeman wakes the present-day Tramp on a park bench. Similarly, Mickey Mouse's horrific experience in *The Mad Doctor* (1933), culminating in him being strapped to a gurney to be cut apart with a buzz saw, is revealed to be a nightmare in the closing moments. Such endings are by no means uncommon in both live-action comedies and cartoons, but many films do not bring the protagonist back to a recognizable "reality."

13. Despite Disney's assertion, no cartoon produced up to this point explicitly defines Mickey and Minnie as a married couple, although their romantic relationship appears much more serious in some cartoons than in others. In fact, *Mickey's Nightmare* (1932) sees the Mouse dream that he and Minnie have been wed, but he becomes overwhelmed when the stork delivers more than twenty children to the couple. At the end of the cartoon, Mickey wakes up and rejoices that he is still single.

14. *Customers Wanted* (1939) presents Popeye and Bluto as penny arcade proprietors at a fairground, each exhibiting scenes from their "pictures." In *Doing Impossikible Stunts* (1940)—a title mimicking the sailor's speech patterns—Popeye vies for a job as a stuntman by showing a director some action sequences from earlier films, only to lose out to Swee'Pea who sneaks in a clip of his own bravery taken from *Lost and Foundry* (1937). See also *Spinach Packin' Popeye* (1944) and *Popeye's Premiere* (1949).

15. Roy Hoopes recounts a story of Groucho Marx traveling with a group of famous performers for a war bond rally during the Second World War. On one occasion, the star was not wearing his false moustache and eyebrows. When he attempted to rejoin his companions, a policeman denied him entry to the celebrity area, refusing to believe that he was who he claimed to be. Hoopes notes that "for the rest of the trip, Groucho wore his stage makeup in public" at all times to avoid any further confusion (119–120).

16. Even the rare examples of studio-era human cartoon stars tend to have rather bizarre aspects to their bodies, such as Popeye's bulging forearms and Betty Boop's oversized, infant-like face.

17. See Bordwell, Staiger, and Thompson 174–176. Critics have often noted that Disney Studios broadly moved away from the rubber-hose style as the 1930s

developed, with its new approach (termed the "illusion of life") aiming to render animated characters in a more corporeal and plausible state. Nonetheless, many other studios, in series such as *Looney Tunes* and *Tom and Jerry*, continued to present their protagonists' bodies as malleable and capable of withstanding a great deal of punishment. Indeed, Thompson has argued separately that even Disney's "impulse towards realism" has been overstated in some histories and that the most extreme occurrences were largely restricted to the studio's features, rather than to the more fanciful star-led short subjects (110). See also Crafton, *Shadow of a Mouse* 295.

Chapter 5: Authorship

1. See, for instance, "Bud Fisher's Mutt and Jeff for the Screen" 385; Milne 2214.

2. Chuck Jones made similar claims about *Looney Tunes* producer Edward Selzer (Adamson, "Chuck Jones Interviewed" 139).

3. It should still be acknowledged that these figures performed a valuable business administration role, even if their artistic input has been overestimated.

4. One exception is the coverage given to numerous labor disputes and animator strikes that occurred throughout the studio era, such as the strike at Disney Studios in 1941.

5. For a concise overview of the rise of animation studies, see White.

6. Even the rabbit's point of origin is complicated. While many view Tex Avery's *The Wild Hare* (1940) as the first truly recognizable appearance of Bugs, several earlier cartoons—such as *Porky's Hare Hunt* (1938) and *Prest-O Change-O* (1939), directed by Ben Hardaway and Chuck Jones, respectively—can be seen to contain prototypes of the character.

7. For a discussion of contemporary sources that posit Mickey Mouse as Disney's "son," see Apgar 11; Sammond 294.

8. For a detailed list of gags that were adapted from Oswald cartoons (and even ones from the earlier *Alice* series), see Kaufman, "The Shadow."

9. See, for instance, Greene and Greene 72; Gabler 150.

10. The privileged status that Mickey Mouse enjoyed in critical and popular discourse of the 1930s has helped ensure that the films remained carefully preserved and available to new generations of audiences. By contrast, the relative neglect of silent animation and of the work of some of Disney's competitors means that many of these texts have been lost or survive largely by chance. There is currently very little academic work available on Van Beuren Studios, and no "official" home video releases (although the independent DVD distributor Thunderbean Animation has recently produced some high-quality collections featuring titles that have fallen into the public domain).

11. This becomes even more complicated when one considers the post-Mickey trajectory of several series that existed *before* the Mouse was created. The character of Krazy Kat, which had already been redesigned in 1925 to capitalize on the success of Felix, shifted even further in the 1930s from George Herriman's original comic strip

concept toward an approximation of the *Mickey* series. Note, for instance, Krazy's falsetto voice and less-pointed ears in *Hollywood Goes Krazy* (1932). Similarly, Merritt and Kaufman argue that "when Mickey Mouse eclipsed Oswald, the rabbit Mintz had taken away from Disney was streamlined to look as much as possible like the new Disney mouse" (*Walt in Wonderland* 118). In essence, then, both can be seen to have influenced Mickey, and then Mickey in turn influenced them.

12. As Paul McDonald notes, the Screen Actors Guild does not permit two members to have the same name, reflecting the importance of this identifier to the performer's overall "brand." For instance, "to preserve distinctions and avoid confusion, the actors Stewart Granger and Michael Keaton adopted assumed names as their originals—James Stewart and Michael Douglas—were already taken by other actors" (*Hollywood Stardom* 49–50).

13. Ferguson actually name-checks Chaplin directly, claiming that Mickey and Minnie Mouse "are distinct and individual character mice, just as much, for example, as the characterization of Charles Chaplin in motion pictures is a distinct and individual character of a man, or type of man" (qtd. in United States Circuit Court of Appeals 61).

14. For more information about the various stages of the Kane-Fleischer trial, see "Helen Kane Asks $250,000"; "The 'Boop' Song Is Traced"; and "Miss Kane Loses Suit."

15. See, for instance, Van Beuren's *The Farmerette* (1932) and *Tight Rope Tricks* (1932).

16. *Film Daily* 59.60 (10 June 1932): 3.

17. Stars could be "loaned" from one producer to another during this period, but the decision was entirely down to the studio that had the star under contract. See chapter 6.

18. Such an approach was also used in many other animated star series. In his analysis of the title sequences of the *Betty Boop* cartoons, Eric Smoodin states that "these cartoons celebrate Betty herself as [synonymous] with film entertainment—with her name on the proscenium—and, indeed, as the virtual creator of it" (31).

19. Despite the suggestiveness of this quotation, it should be noted that Corliss, reflecting the prevalent academic approach of the period, still deems Bugs "the cartoon director's alter ego" (18).

20. A follow-up cartoon, *Rabbit Rampage* (1955), is curious as it places Bugs in the same position as Daffy, being tortured by an animator. Bugs's tormentor is revealed at the end of the film to be his nemesis Elmer Fudd, who rejoices: "I've finally got even with that scwewy wabbit [*sic*]." While Bugs does not suffer quite as much as Daffy and has some power to conclude his torment by pulling down a "The End" screen, the cartoon has generally been received poorly due to the perceived mistreatment of its protagonist. According to Maltin, "the concept of the film is all wrong. We don't enjoy Bugs' frustration as we do Daffy's; it's an unlikely defeat for a normally indefatigable character" (*Of Mice and Magic* 263). Although a number of *Looney Tunes* films develop a great deal of comedy from purposely miscasting the

stars, such as Daffy Duck's attempt at playing a cowboy in *Drip-Along Daffy* (1950), there is an argument to be made that Bugs has been *accidentally* miscast in this film. However, as Dyer suggests, films that are rejected by the audience as a "problematic fit" between star and character can nonetheless "serve to reinforce the authenticity of the star image as a whole" (*Stars* 129; "*A Star Is Born*" 136).

21. The one exception was the 1938 winner, *Ferdinand the Bull*. Not technically part of the *Symphony* series, *Ferdinand* was a one-off film produced by Disney that did not feature a recognizable star (Merritt and Kaufman, *Walt Disney's Silly Symphonies* 214).

22. The film has subsequently risen in critical estimation (see A. Davis).

23. The studio did release several "package features" during this period, linking together a collection of shorts into one larger text. *Cinderella* (1950) marked Disney's return to the production of more ambitious single-narrative features.

24. As this chapter has indicated, this still has the potential to be reductive. Claiming that Walt Disney *was* Mickey Mouse, or that Chuck Jones *was* Bugs Bunny, undermines the huge amount of collaboration that occurred in the production of these films, regardless of whether (or not) those figures actually had the most creative input overall. Some recent scholarship has attempted to flesh out the roles played by other personnel—including musicians, layout artists, and voice actors—whose recurring contributions across a series, when considered at all, may previously have been seen as occurring purely in service of the director's vision.

Chapter 6: The Studio System

1. *Kinematograph Weekly* 102.956 (13 August 1925): 26–27.

2. Pat Sullivan's untimely death in 1932 presented a further barrier to the Cat returning to the big screen. It was discovered that agreements Sullivan had made with external companies to produce Felix merchandise did not always adequately protect his control over the character (Canemaker, *Felix* 137–140). While the latter stages of the silent era (and particularly the rise of Felix) had established the value of animated "intellectual property," it was not until the dominance of the major studios in the 1930s that a more stringent process of documenting and protecting these rights became routine.

3. Some animation was released independently during this period, but these films rarely achieved popular success. For instance, after MGM terminated its contract with Ub Iwerks, he formed his own distribution company, but "had neither the resources nor the contacts" to attract enough exhibitors to remain profitable (Iwerks and Kenworthy 122).

4. Of the majors, only United Artists failed to establish its own animation department and/or develop an enduring partnership with an external short cartoon producer during the 1930s and 1940s.

5. Such images were undoubtedly pervasive: Clark notes that even trade journals such as *Variety*—which approached most accounts of "labor-management conflict" with relative seriousness—generally dismissed "player 'outbursts' as a comical staple of industry life" (75).

6. "Hollywood Chatter" appeared regularly in the *Walt Disney's Comics and Stories* series in the early 1940s.

7. One exception was a doll modeled after child star Shirley Temple, which reportedly "accounted for almost a third of all doll sales" in 1934 (Cross 116–117).

8. As discussed in the next chapter, television subsequently commodified its live-action stars in similar ways to animation. Even many film contracts, especially following the success of franchises such as *Star Wars* (1977), now require stars to sign over their likenesses for a range of products—action figures, life-size cardboard cut-outs, and playable avatars in video games, for instance—that invoke the performer more directly than in earlier decades. Carrie Fisher, who portrayed Princess Leia in the *Star Wars* series, noted that George Lucas (before his sale of Lucasfilm to Disney) owned her image rights, joking that "every time I look in the mirror I have to send him a couple of bucks!" She also humorously discussed the strange experience of having her face and body turned into everything from a PEZ dispenser to a bar of soap to a watch, and even to an "anatomically correct" doll, usually without any advance consultation (86–87).

9. Another Fleischer star, Popeye, also appeared on radio from 1935 to 1938. However, because the sailor was a rare 1930s example of a comic strip character adapted to animation, it appears that the series was not a direct spin-off of the cartoons, but rather a separate production arranged by the original strip's owner. Certainly, the surviving episodes make no reference to the Fleischer films, and Popeye's characterization is also somewhat different in the radio series—in particular, he derives his strength not from spinach, but from Wheatena cereal, the program's sponsor (Grandinetti 136–137).

10. For further information on American moviegoing habits during this period, see May 121–122, 289–290; Schatz, *Boom and Bust* 68–71. Schatz notes one survey of cinema attendance during 1941 in New York City—"the nation's largest and most important movie market"—that suggested that the average viewer saw approximately one film each week. Almost 10 percent of respondents claimed to attend ten or more screenings per month (*Boom and Bust* 71).

11. For histories of Hollywood acting unions, see Ross; Clark.

12. See Sito, *Drawing the Line* for a history of animation unions in the United States.

13. Seemingly proving Powdermaker's point, the purposely formulaic opening of this cartoon does, in fact, contain reused footage from *All This and Rabbit Stew* (1941), an earlier Bugs film.

14. Animation in fact played a wider role in perpetuating these reductive views of top live-action Hollywood performers. During the 1930s and 1940s, a number of studios produced caricature cartoons, one-off texts that saw a variety of top live-action celebrities (rendered in animation) enjoying leisure time, often at a function or event. Most of these films lacked a cohesive narrative, simply cutting

to each figure in turn and making a gag about his or her behavior. As Crafton notes: "Each celebrity is identified by an 'attribute,' in the art-historical sense, a synecdoche in which that part represents the whole person. . . . If we accept Richard deCordova's definition of a star as an actor whose personal life affects his or her on-screen persona, then these films seem to neutralize that stardom by denying their off-screen existence as 'ordinary' or 'real' folks" ("The View" 109). For instance, in *Hollywood Steps Out* (1941), a *Merrie Melodies* cartoon, Johnny Weissmuller, star of the *Tarzan* films, arrives at the famous Hollywood restaurant Ciro's wearing a tuxedo, but presents this to the coat check girl, revealing his character's famous loincloth underneath. Similarly, James Cagney, Humphrey Bogart, and George Raft are characterized solely as "wiseguys," seemingly planning a dangerous crime spree, but the overall joke is that they are actually preparing for a game of pitching pennies.

15. One can identify a couple of exceptions. Felix the Cat, for instance, appeared in three films for the Van Beuren studio in 1936, after the rights issues with Pat Sullivan's estate had been resolved. The *Looney Tunes* star Bosko was briefly revived at MGM in 1934 (although this was partially a result of the character's creators, Hugh Harman and Rudolf Ising, moving studios). Several stars—including Felix—were also revived on television, sometimes years after disappearing from the big screen.

16. An earlier version of the Paramount case had been tried in 1938, but studios continued to circumvent its rulings, and the outbreak of war delayed any further action.

17. Some animation units initially tried adding new (and often costly) elements, but without any long-term success. This included producing films in the CinemaScope widescreen aspect ratio and, in rare cases, experimenting with stereoscopic 3-D effects.

18. The use of stock footage from old films, again as a cost-saving measure, can also be identified in a number of *live-action* theatrical shorts of the same period, most notably in many of the later entries in the *Three Stooges* series (Forrester 81, 91).

19. Disney maintained full control of its properties on television, unlike many of the other studios. Warner Bros. has regained the *Looney Tunes* films sold to syndication via a series of complicated acquisitions: A.A.P. was eventually sold to United Artists, which was later acquired by MGM, whose library was then purchased by Turner Broadcasting System, which in 1996 merged with Time Warner. Universal bought all the rights to Woody Woodpecker from Walter Lantz in 1985 (Cawley and Korkis 209). As Paul Grainge indicates, the use of Mickey Mouse, Bugs Bunny, and Woody Woodpecker on the respective studio logos in recent years can be read as an attempt to establish "brand nostalgia," implying that the values of "old Hollywood" are retained even though the studios now exist as part of conglomerate entities with many and varied business concerns (72–79).

Chapter 7: The Animated Television Star

1. See, for instance, Gomery, "The Coming of Television."

2. Although some of the biggest stars chose to break away from long-term contracts in an attempt to achieve greater autonomy, the wider decline in the number of contracted actors was due to the new economics of studio production.

3. Despite the impact that television is perceived to have had in reinvigorating Buster Keaton's late career, many biographies reference it only briefly, usually just a few pages before mentioning his death. See, for instance, McPherson 240–248; Dardis 259–261.

4. For a survey of such responses, see Becker 4–6.

5. The dates supplied for each program in this chapter refer only to a show's first, unbroken run of production. *The Mickey Mouse Club*, for instance, was subsequently revived for new series in the 1970s and late 1980s, while the original episodes have also been repeated on several stations since the original airings. A variant of *The Bugs Bunny Show* existed on television for more than forty years, but jumped among different networks and appeared in various formats (sometimes under new umbrella titles such as *The Bugs Bunny/Road Runner Hour*, which first ran between 1968 and 1971). For an exhaustive, if now somewhat outdated, guide to the different airings of these series, see Woolery. See also Erickson; Cotter.

6. Animation was not quite as heavily restricted to these dates as live-action productions, but studios still generally refrained from releasing their newest cartoons to television during this period.

7. Most of the hosted segments of *The Bugs Bunny Show* appeared only while the series ran during primetime (between 1960 and 1962). Many later versions, airing on Saturday morning and other parts of the schedule, still retained certain elements of the variety show format, including the song-and-dance title sequence, and the character commercials for sponsors (see Woolery 53).

8. A 1957 publication, *TV Scandals*, emphasized the potential for catastrophe in the format of *This Is Your Life*: "Week after week, people tune in to the show hoping that one of these days [the] fancy 'element of surprise' will blow up right in Ralph Edwards' face. What then? What if the victim simply refuses to go through with the noisome spectacle, . . . [leaving] Edwards holding his impotent mike[?]" (qtd. in Desjardins 128). Donald Duck seems to echo this response in his delight at the missing guest in the Disney version, stating: "Wow! . . . I knew this would happen someday! I wouldn't miss this for anything!"

9. As previous chapters have indicated, of course, animated characters already *were* at times presented in hyperbolically "revealing" and "unflattering" states during the studio era—unlike, generally, their live-action counterparts—but this particular sequence sees the rhetoric altered because of its specific links to the broadcast medium.

10. One character in *A Face in the Crowd* even coldly states that television is "the greatest instrument for mass persuasion in the world." Christopher Anderson suggests: "TV audiences imagined by these movies are oblivious to the false appeals taking place on the TV screen and to the machinations taking place just off-screen.

As cinema spectators, however, moviegoers are able to recognize such dissimulations because the movie narratives provide privileged access to the characters' motives, revealing the hidden schemes that are masked by commercial television's obsession with surface detail" (17–18). These films reverse the notion that authenticity can easily be found directly in the televisual text, suggesting instead that its address is too facile and prone to manipulation.

11. Although a fictionalized account, Goofy actually *was* first known as "Dippy Dawg" in his earliest cartoon appearances. The episode further rewrites the star's filmography by implying that he got his "big break" in the cartoon *Moving Day* (1936), when he had actually been appearing in Disney cartoons for several years by this point.

12. A similar gag is presented in the *Disneyland* episode "A Day in the Life of Donald Duck" (transmitted 1 February 1956). Walt Disney claims that "Donald, like any other average cartoon character, lives a simple, unassuming life, in a quiet residential section of Beverley Hills. He resides in a modest little cartoon house." The camera, though, pans back to reveal that Donald's estate also contains a castle and many other amenities.

13. These beer commercials were made in the late 1950s, before cartoon stars were explicitly marketed toward children. Similarly, in the first few years of *The Flintstones* primetime run, Fred and Barney extolled the virtues of Winston cigarettes, the program's sponsor.

14. As with all stars (particularly drawn ones), it is still possible for a brand mascot to be appropriated and parodied in "unofficial" media texts. Even characters created solely to embody the values of a brand can still accrue negative connotations, such as the accusations of racial stereotyping surrounding the Frito Bandito, the late-1960s mascot for Fritos Corn Chips (see Nuiry).

15. As Christopher Lehman notes, such lobbying had the unintended effect of removing not only problematic images but also virtually all appearances of African American (and other nonwhite) characters (99, 119). Over the course of the 1970s and 1980s, pressure groups campaigned for a more diverse range of characters in children's programming, but as Hendershot has noted, this initially prompted only token responses from studios, presenting minority characters in limited (if now broadly "positive") roles (*Saturday Morning Censors* 106–107).

16. Critics have nonetheless argued that certain films, although not consciously made to be distasteful, frequently drew on and perpetuated reductive stereotypes of marginalized people (see, for instance, Sampson vii). Furthermore, as the discussion on wartime animation in chapter 3 indicates, racial images generated by hatred were by no means beyond the realm of cartoon producers.

17. The "public" in this instance was seen as children, "voting" with viewing figures. Parental groups argued that this led to networks responding to what children want, rather than what they necessarily need. Cy Schneider has emphasized that, unlike publicly funded broadcasting, such as the BBC in the United Kingdom or

PBS in the United States, the main networks are "first and foremost a business" and that educational programming has historically struggled to survive under these commercial pressures (5, 169).

18. Some of these "fad" personalities, such as He-Man, have actually returned in new series in recent years, although this tends to occur as a cyclical "rebooting" of the franchise, rather than as another entry in the star's ongoing career (as it often is with the theatrical cartoon star).

19. For instance, a 22 January 1962 advertisement in *Broadcasting: The Businessweekly of Television and Radio* notes that one station, WPIX-11, had begun "playing the NEW Popeye Cartoons—and only the new ones—the Popeyes that King Features is now producing specifically for TV." It claims that, as a result, the ratings were "BIGGER THAN EVER," eclipsing the older theatrical shorts that had previously been aired (21).

20. *Broadcasting: The Businessweekly of Television and Radio* (12 January 1959): 57.

21. The television special *Daffy Duck and Porky Pig Meet the Groovie Goolies* (transmitted 16 December 1972) is often cited as the nadir of several *Looney Tunes* stars' television appearances, featured here alongside characters produced by the Filmation Studio (see, for instance, S. Schneider 133). Discussions surrounding the new *Popeye* and *Tom and Jerry* television series, outlined earlier, similarly indicate a perceived lack compared to the stars' cinematic careers.

22. Despite the increased budgets and "auteur" creators, many of these series still outsourced the animation work overseas, rather than reestablishing in-house production (Perlmutter 200). Erickson also acknowledges that the celebrated texts from this era have perhaps overshadowed the degree to which some schedules were still "littered with hangovers from past seasons," such as "copycat programs" (knock-offs trying to capitalize on the success of another series) and product personality cartoons (1:36). Still, the fact that critics were now focusing on what was good about animated television, rather than outlining its faults, indicates a significant shift from previous decades.

Chapter 8: The Death of the Animated Star?

1. This seemingly recognizes the point at which Leon Schlesinger established his animation unit directly on the Warner Bros. lot, even though he had actually been producing cartoons for the studio (with Hugh Harman and Rudolf Ising) since 1930 (Crafton, "The View" 103).

2. Indeed, this explanation does not justify an alternate version of the ad produced for Dove's equivalent, Galaxy, in the United Kingdom, where Hepburn is instead seen enjoying a bar of *milk* chocolate, seemingly because it is a more marketable flavor in that region.

Works Cited

Abraham, Adam. *When Magoo Flew: The Rise and Fall of Animation Studio UPA*. Middletown, CT: Wesleyan University Press, 2012.

Academy of Achievement. "Chuck Jones: Animation Pioneer." *Chuck Jones: Conversations*. Ed. Maureen Furniss. Jackson: University Press of Mississippi, 2005. 156–167.

Adams, T. R. *Tom and Jerry: Fifty Years of Cat and Mouse*. London: Pyramid Books, 1991.

Adamson, Joe. *Bugs Bunny: Fifty Years and Only One Grey Hare*. London: Pyramid Books, 1990.

———. "Chuck Jones Interviewed." *The American Animated Cartoon: A Critical Anthology*. Ed. Danny Peary and Gerald Peary. New York: E. P. Dutton, 1980. 128–141.

———. "A Talk with Dick Huemer." *The American Animated Cartoon: A Critical Anthology*. Ed. Danny Peary and Gerald Peary. New York: E. P. Dutton, 1980. 29–36.

———. *Tex Avery: King of Cartoons*. New York: De Capo, 1975.

———. *The Walter Lantz Story*. New York: G. P. Putnam's Sons, 1985.

Albert, Katherine. "Let's Get This 'Going Hollywood' Business Straight." *Modern Screen* 5.5 (April 1933): 28–30, 98.

Alderman, Harold. "The Place of Comedy." *Man and World* 10.2 (1977): 152–172.

Aldred, Jessica. "From Synthespian to Avatar: Re-framing the Digital Human in *Final Fantasy* and *The Polar Express.*" *Mediascape* (Winter 2011): 1–12. www.tft .ucla.edu/mediascape/Winter2011_Avatar.pdf.

Anderson, Christopher. *Hollywood TV: The Studio System in the Fifties*. Austin: University of Texas Press, 1994.

"Animated Cartoons in Motion Pictures." *Moving Picture World* 24.1 (3 April 1915): 54.

Apgar, Garry. *Mickey Mouse: Emblem of the American Spirit*. San Francisco: The Walt Disney Family Foundation Press, 2015.

"The Ascendency of Mr. Donald Duck." *New York Times* 23 June 1940: X4.

"Baby Popeye." *King Features*, n.d. kingfeatures.com/licensing/licensed-brands /baby-popeye.

Balio, Tino. *Grand Design: Hollywood as a Modern Business Enterprise, 1930–1939*. Berkeley: University of California Press, 1995.

———. "Retrenchment, Reappraisal, and Reorganization, 1948-." *The American Film Industry*. Rev. ed. Ed. Tino Balio. Madison: University of Wisconsin Press, 1985. 401–447.

———. "Stars in Business: The Founding of United Artists." *The American Film Industry*. Rev. ed. Ed. Tino Balio. Madison: University of Wisconsin Press, 1985. 153–172.

Barbas, Samantha. *Movie Crazy: Fans, Stars, and the Cult of Celebrity*. New York: Palgrave, 2001.

Barker, Martin. "Introduction." *Contemporary Hollywood Stardom*. Ed. Thomas Austin and Martin Barker. London: Arnold, 2003. 1–24.

Barnouw, Erik. *Tube of Plenty: The Evolution of American Television*. Rev. ed. Oxford: Oxford University Press, 1982.

Barrier, Michael. *The Animated Man: A Life of Walt Disney*. Berkeley: University of California Press, 2007.

———. *Hollywood Cartoons: American Animation in its Golden Age*. New York: Oxford University Press, 2003.

Barrier, Michael, and Milton Gray. "Bob Clampett: An Interview with a Master Cartoon Maker and Puppeteer." *Funnyworld* 12 (Summer 1970): 12–37.

Barthes, Roland. *Camera Lucida: Reflections on Photography*. London: Vintage Books, 2000.

———. "The Death of the Author." *Image Music Text*. Ed. Stephen Heath. London: Fontana Press, 1977. 142–148.

Basinger, Jeanine. *Silent Stars*. New York: Alfred A. Knopf, 1999.

Bazin, André. *What is Cinema?* Vol. 2. Berkeley: University of California Press, 1972.

Bean, Jennifer M. "The Art of Imitation: The Originality of Charlie Chaplin and Other Moving-Image Myths." *Slapstick Comedy*. Ed. Tom Paulus and Rob King. New York: Routledge, 2010. 236–261.

———. "Technologies of Early Stardom and the Extraordinary Body." *Camera Obscura* 16.3 (2001): 8–57.

Becker, Christine. *It's the Pictures That Got Small: Hollywood Film Stars on 1950s Television*. Middletown, CT: Wesleyan University Press, 2008.

Beckman, Karen. "Animating Film Theory: An Introduction." *Animating Film Theory*. Ed. Karen Beckman. Durham, NC: Duke University Press, 2014. 1–22.

Bell, Elizabeth, Lynda Haas, and Laura Sells. "Introduction." *From Mouse to Mermaid: The Politics of Film, Gender and Culture*. Ed. Elizabeth Bell, Lynda Haas, and Laura Sells. Bloomington: Indiana University Press, 1995. 1–17.

Bendazzi, Giannalberto. *Cartoons: One Hundred Years of Cinema Animation*. London: John Libbey, 1994.

"Betty Boop and Popeye Pickets [*sic*] for Cartoonists." *Daily Worker* [New York] 16 May 1937: 10.

"Betty Boop in 'Hot Pants.'" Tijuana Bibles Collection. David M. Rubenstein Rare Book and Manuscript Library, Duke University, Durham, NC.

"Betty Boop Picnic Lands Six-Column Smash for Waite." *Motion Picture Herald* 111.7 (12 August 1933): 70.

Billen, Andrew. "Popeye's Son Upsets Purists." *Times* 7 September 1988: 3.

Birdwell, Michael. "Technical Fairy First Class? Is This Any Way to Run an Army? Private Snafu and World War II." *Historical Journal of Film, Radio and Television* 25.2 (June 2005): 203–212.

Blandford, Steve, Barry Keith Grant, and Jim Hillier. *The Film Studies Dictionary*. London: Arnold, 2001.

Blitz, Marcia. *Donald Duck*. London: New English Library, 1980.

Boddy, William. *Fifties Television: The Industry and Its Critics*. Urbana: University of Illinois Press, 1993.

Bode, Lisa. "Fade Out/Fade In: Dead 1920s and 1930s Hollywood Stars and the Mechanisms of Posthumous Stardom." *Celebrity Studies* 5.1–2 (2014): 90–92.

———. "No Longer Themselves? Framing Digitally Enabled Posthumous 'Performance.'" *Cinema Journal* 49.4 (Summer 2010): 46–70.

Boone, Andrew R. "When Mickey Mouse Speaks." *Scientific American* 148.3 (March 1933): 146–147.

"Boop Pic Nix in Eng." *Variety* 114.7 (1 May 1934): 13.

"The 'Boop' Song Is Traced." *New York Times* 2 May 1934: 24.

Bordwell, David, Janet Staiger, and Kristin Thompson. *The Classical Hollywood Cinema: Film Style and Mode of Production to 1960*. London: Routledge, 1985.

Bowes, Mick. "Only When I Laugh." *Understanding Television*. Ed. Andrew Goodwin. London: Routledge, 1990. 128–140.

Bowser, Eileen. *The Transformation of Cinema, 1907–1915*. New York: Scribner's, 1990.

Braver-Mann, Barnet G. "Mickey Mouse and His Playmates." *Theatre Guild Magazine* (March 1931): 14–18.

Brooker, Will. *Batman Unmasked: Analyzing a Cultural Icon*. New York: Continuum, 2001.

Brown, Harry. "Road Runner and Wile E. Coyote: The Bird and the Bushwhacker." *Close-Ups: The Movie Star Book*. Ed. Danny Peary. New York: Fireside, 1988. 41–43.

Brownlow, Kevin. *Behind the Mask of Innocence*. Berkeley: University of California Press, 1992.

——. "Buster Keaton." *Buster Keaton: Interviews*. Ed. Kevin W. Sweeney. Jackson: University Press of Mississippi, 2007. 173–218.

Bruce, Scott. *Cereal Boxes and Prizes, 1960s: A Tribute and Price Guide*. Chamblee, GA: Flake World Publishing, 1998.

"Bud Fisher's Mutt and Jeff for the Screen." *Motion Picture News* 13.3 (22 January 1916): 385.

Burrows, Jon. "Near Broke, but No Tramp: Billie Ritchie, Charlie Chaplin and 'That Costume.'" *Early Popular Visual Culture* 8.3 (2010): 247–262.

Cabarga, Leslie. *The Fleischer Story*. Rev. ed. New York: DeCapo, 1988.

Cagney, James. *Cagney by Cagney*. London: New English Library, 1976.

Caldwell, John Thornton. *Production Culture: Industrial Reflexivity and Critical Practice in Film and Television*. Durham, NC: Duke University Press, 2008.

Callahan, David. "Cel Animation: Mass Production and Marginalization in the Animated Film Industry." *Film History* 2.3 (September–October 1988): 223–228.

Canemaker, John. *Felix: The Twisted Tale of the World's Most Famous Cat*. New York: De Capo, 1996.

——. *Winsor McCay: His Life and Art*. Rev. ed. New York: Harry N. Abrams, 2005.

——. "Winsor McCay's *Little Nemo* and *How a Mosquito Operates*—Beginnings of 'Personality' Animation." *The Art of the Animated Image: An Anthology*. Ed. Charles Solomon. Los Angeles: AFI, 1987. 27–36.

Capino, José B. "Filthy Funnies: Notes on the Body in Animated Pornography." *Animation Journal* 12 (2004): 53–71.

Carr, Harry. "The Only Unpaid Movie Star." *American Magazine* (March 1931): 55–57, 122.

"Cartoonist Pat Sullivan Signs Contract with Famous Players." *Moving Picture World* 43.12 (20 March 1920): 1927.

Castonguay, James. "Myrna Loy and William Powell: The Perfect Screen Couple." *Glamour in a Golden Age: Movie Stars of the 1930s*. Ed. Adrienne L. McLean. New Brunswick, NJ: Rutgers University Press, 2011. 220–244.

Cavell, Stanley. *The World Viewed: Reflections on the Ontology of Film*. Enlarged ed. Cambridge, MA: Harvard University Press, 1979.

Cawley, John, and Jim Korkis. *The Encyclopedia of Cartoon Superstars*. Las Vegas: Pioneer Books, 1990.

Celeste, Reni. "Screen Idols: The Tragedy of Falling Stars." *Journal of Popular Film and Television* 33.1 (Spring 2005): 29–38.

"The Censor!" *New York Times* 16 November 1930: X5.

"Censorship Invades the Animal Kingdom." *TV Guide* (4 January 1958): 12–15.

Chaplin, Charlie, and Harry C. Carr. "Charlie Chaplin's Story." *Photoplay* 8.2 (July 1915): 26–31.

Cholodenko, Alan. "(The) Death (of) the Animator, or: The Felicity of Felix, Part II." *Animation Studies* 2 (2007): 9–16. https://journal.animationstudies .org/the-death-of-the-animator-or-the-felicity-of-felix.

———. "*Who Framed Roger Rabbit,* or The Framing of Animation." *The Illusion of Life: Essays on Animation.* Ed. Alan Cholodenko. Sydney: Power Publications, 1991. 209–242.

Clark, Danae. *Negotiating Hollywood: The Cultural Politics of Actors' Labor.* Minneapolis: University of Minnesota Press, 1995.

Clayton, Alex. *The Body in Hollywood Slapstick.* Jefferson, NC: McFarland, 2007.

Clissold, Bradley D. "*Candid Camera* and the Origins of Reality TV: Contextualizing a Historical Precedent." *Understanding Reality Television.* Ed. Su Holmes and Deborah Jermyn. London: Routledge, 2004. 33–53.

Cohen, Karl F. *Forbidden Animation: Censored Cartoons and Blacklisted Animators in America.* Jefferson, NC: McFarland, 2004.

"Comments on the Films." *Moving Picture World* 16.9 (31 May 1913): 919–922.

Corliss, Richard. "Warnervana." *Film Comment* 21.6 (November–December 1985): 11–19.

Corrigan, Timothy. *A Cinema Without Walls: Movies and Culture After Vietnam.* New Brunswick, NJ: Rutgers University Press, 1991.

Cotter, Bill. *The Wonderful World of Disney Television: A Complete History.* New York: Hyperion, 1997.

Crafton, Donald. *Before Mickey: The Animated Film, 1898–1928.* Rev. ed. Chicago: University of Chicago Press, 1993.

———. *Emile Cohl, Caricature, and Film.* Oxford: Princeton University Press, 1990.

———. *Shadow of a Mouse: Performance, Belief, and World-Making in Animation.* Berkeley: University of California Press, 2013.

———. "The View from Termite Terrace: Caricature and Parody in Warner Bros. Animation." *Reading the Rabbit: Explorations in Warner Bros. Animation.* Ed. Kevin S. Sandler. New Brunswick, NJ: Rutgers University Press, 1998. 101–120.

Crawford, Ben. "Saturday Morning Fever." *The Illusion of Life: Essays on Animation.* Ed. Alan Cholodenko. Sydney: Power Publications, 1991. 113–130.

"Creator of Looney Tunes Here to Seek Role in War Effort." *Washington Post* 11 December 1942: 18.

Creed, Barbara. "The Cyberstar: Digital Pleasures and the End of the Unconscious." *Screen* 41.1 (Spring 2000): 79–86.

Cross, Gary. *Kids' Stuff: Toys and the Changing World of American Childhood.* Cambridge, MA: Harvard University Press, 2001.

Crowther, Bosley. "McBoing Boing, Magoo and Bosustow." *New York Times* 21 December 1952: SM14–15.

———. "Up and at Them: Time Is Fleeting, and a Broad Program of Morale Films Has Yet to Be Laid Out." *New York Times* 15 February 1942: X5.

Crustycrotch, Iva. "Betty Boop in 'Flesh.'" *Tijuana Bibles: Art and Wit in America's Forbidden Funnies, 1930s-1950s.* Ed. Bob Adelman and Richard Merkin. New York: Simon and Schuster, 1997. 28–30.

Culbert, David H. "Walt Disney's Private Snafu: The Use of Humor in World War II Army Film." *Prospects* 1 (1976): 81–96.

Culhane, Shamus. *Talking Animals and Other People: The Autobiography of One of Animation's Legendary Figures.* New York: St. Martin's, 1986.

Curry, Ramona. "Mae West as Censored Commodity: The Case of 'Klondike Annie.'" *Cinema Journal* 31.1 (1991): 57–84.

"D. Duck Joins Up." *New York Times* 22 February 1942: SM20.

Dalton, Susan Elizabeth. "Bugs and Daffy Go to War." *The American Animated Cartoon: A Critical Anthology.* Ed. Danny Peary and Gerald Peary. New York: E. P. Dutton, 1980. 158–161.

Daly, Phil M. "Along the Rialto." *Film Daily* 59.72 (24 June 1932): 3.

———. "Along the Rialto." *Film Daily* 92.39 (25 August 1947): 3.

Dardis, Tom. *Buster Keaton: The Man Who Wouldn't Lie Down.* Minneapolis: University of Minnesota Press, 2002.

Davis, Amy M. "The Fall and Rise of *Fantasia.*" *Hollywood Spectatorship: Changing Perceptions of Cinema Audiences.* Ed. Melvyn Stokes and Richard Maltby. London: BFI, 2000. 63–78.

Davis, Bette. *The Lonely Life: An Autobiography.* London: Macdonald, 1963.

Davis, Ronald L. *The Glamour Factory: Inside Hollywood's Big Studio System.* Dallas: Southern Methodist University Press, 1993.

deCordova, Richard. "The Emergence of the Star System in America." *Stardom: Industry of Desire.* Ed. Christine Gledhill. London: Routledge, 1991. 17–29.

———. "The Mickey in Macy's Window: Childhood, Consumerism, and Disney Animation." *Disney Discourse: Producing the Magic Kingdom.* Ed. Eric Smoodin. London: Routledge, 1994. 203–213.

———. *Picture Personalities: The Emergence of the Star System in America.* Rev. ed. Urbana: University of Illinois Press, 2001.

———. "Tracing the Child Audience: The Case of Disney, 1929–1933." *Prima dei Codici 2: Alle Porte di Hays.* Venice: Realizzazione Fabbri, 1991. 217–221.

Delporte, Christian. "Humour as a Strategy in Propaganda Film: The Case of a French Cartoon from 1944." *Journal of European Studies* 31 (September 2001): 367–377.

Deneroff, Harvey. "'We Can't Get Much Spinach!': The Organization and Implementation of the Fleischer Studio Strike." *Film History* 1.1 (1987): 1–14.

Desjardins, Mary. "Maureen O'Hara's 'Confidential' Life: Recycling Stars through Gossip and Moral Biography." *Small Screens, Big Ideas: Television in the 1950s.* Ed. Janet Thumim. London: I. B. Tauris, 2002. 118–130.

"Detroit News." *Film Daily* 66.63 (14 September 1934): 4.

Disney, Walt. "The Cartoon's Contribution to Children." *Overland Monthly and Out West Magazine* 91.8 (October 1933): 138.

———. "Mickey Mouse Is 5 Years Old." *Film Pictorial* 4.84 (30 September 1933): 36.

Dix, Andrew. *Beginning Film Studies.* Manchester: Manchester University Press, 2008.

Dobbs, G. Michael. *Escape! How Animation Broke into the Mainstream in the 1990s.* Albany, GA: BearManor Media, 2007.

Doherty, Thomas. *Hollywood's Censor: Joseph I. Breen and the Production Code Administration.* New York: Columbia University Press, 2007.

———. *Projections of War: Hollywood, American Culture, and World War II.* Rev. ed. New York: Columbia University Press, 1999.

Dotz, Warren, and Masud Husain. *Meet Mr. Product: The Art of the Advertising Character.* San Francisco: Chronicle Books, 2003.

Dyer, Richard. *Heavenly Bodies: Film Stars and Society.* Basingstoke, UK: Macmillan, 1987.

———. "*A Star Is Born* and the Construction of Authenticity." *Stardom: Industry of Desire.* Ed. Christine Gledhill. London: Routledge, 1991. 132–140.

———. *Stars.* New ed. London: BFI Publishing, 1998.

Eaton, Mick. "Laughter in the Dark." *Screen* 22.2 (1981): 21–28.

Eckert, Charles. "The Carole Lombard in Macy's Window." *Movies and Mass Culture.* Ed. John Belton. London: Athlone, 1999. 95–118.

Edelstein, Michael. "War and the American Economy in the Twentieth Century." *The Cambridge Economic History of the United States.* Vol. 3. Ed. Stanley L. Engerman and Robert E. Gallman. Cambridge: Cambridge University Press, 2000. 329–406.

Editors of *Look* Magazine. *Movie Lot to Beachhead: The Motion Picture Goes to War and Prepares for the Future.* New York: Arno, 1980.

Ellis, John. "Stars as a Cinematic Phenomenon." *Star Texts: Image and Performance in Film and Television.* Ed. Jeremy G. Butler. Detroit, MI: Wayne State University Press, 1991. 300–315.

Erickson, Hal. *Television Cartoon Shows: An Illustrated Encyclopedia, 1949 through 2003.* 2nd ed. 2 vols. Jefferson, NC: McFarland, 2005.

"Europe's Highbrows Hail 'Mickey Mouse.'" *Literary Digest* (8 August 1931): 19.

Eustis, Morton. "Custard Pie to Cartoon." *Theatre Arts Monthly* 22.9 (September 1938): 674–681.

Ever, Hardon. "William Powell and Myrna Loy in 'Nuts to Will Hays!'" *Tijuana Bibles: Art and Wit in America's Forbidden Funnies, 1930s-1950s.* Ed. Bob Adelman and Richard Merkin. New York: Simon and Schuster, 1997. 88.

Fairbanks Jr., Douglas. "An Exclusive Interview with Mr. Mickey Mouse." *College Humor* (February 1933): 44–46.

Faris, Jocelyn. *Jayne Mansfield: A Bio-Bibliography*. Westport, CT: Greenwood, 1994.

Farley, Rebecca. "From Fred and Wilma to Ren and Stimpy: What Makes a Cartoon 'Prime-Time'?" *Prime Time Animation: Television Animation and American Culture*. Ed. Carole A. Stabile and Mark Harrison. London: Routledge, 2003. 147–164.

Felando, Cynthia. "Hollywood in the 1920s: Youth Must Be Served." *Hollywood Goes Shopping*. Ed. David Desser and Garth S. Jowett. Minneapolis: University of Minnesota Press, 2000. 82–107.

Felix the Cat. "Me and Pat Sullivan." *The Picturegoer* 10.59 (November 1925): 18.

"The Felix Vogue." *Film Daily* 28.35 (11 May 1924): 16.

Ferris, Kerry O. "Ain't Nothing Like the Real Thing, Baby: Framing Celebrity Impersonator Performances." *Text and Performance Quarterly* 20.1 (January 2010): 60–80.

Fidler, James M. "A Mouse in a Million!" *Screenland* 30.4 (February 1935): 51, 76–77.

"Films Swell Enlistments." *Film Daily* 82.94 (13 November 1942): 1, 10.

Fisher, Bud. "'Here's How!'—Says Bud." *Photoplay* 18.2 (July 1920): 58.

Fisher, Carrie. *Wishful Drinking*. London: Simon and Schuster, 2008.

Flanagan, Mary. "Mobile Identities, Digital Stars, and Post-Cinematic Selves." *Wide Angle* 21.1 (January 1999): 77–93.

Forgacs, David. "Disney Animation and the Business of Childhood." *Screen* 33.4 (Winter 1992): 361–374.

Forrester, Jeffrey. *The Stooge Chronicles*. Chicago: Contemporary Books, 1981.

Forster, E. M. "Mickey and Minnie." *Spectator* (19 January 1934): 81–82.

Fowles, Jib. *Starstruck: Celebrity Performers and the American Public*. Washington, DC: Smithsonian Institution Press, 1992.

Fox, Julian. "Felix Remembered: Being the Affectionate Portrait of a Unique Star Who Just Kept on Walking." *Films and Filming* 21.2 (November 1974): 44–51.

Franklin, Mortimer. "The Art of Mickey Mouse." *Screenland* 27.4 (August 1933): 26–27, 96.

———. "Confessions of Mickey Mouse." *Screenland* 24.4 (February 1932): 52–53, 116–117.

———. "The Love Life of Betty Boop." *Screenland* 26.3 (January 1933): 62–63, 96.

Furniss, Maureen. *Art in Motion: Animation Aesthetics*. Rev. ed. Eastleigh, UK: John Libbey, 2007.

Gabler, Neal. *Walt Disney: The Triumph of the American Imagination*. New York: Vintage Books, 2007.

Gaines, Jane M. *Contested Culture: The Image, the Voice, and the Law*. London: BFI Publishing, 1992.

———. "The Showgirl and the Wolf." *Cinema Journal* 20.1 (Autumn 1980): 53–67.

Garvie, Charles. *The Betty Boop Book*. London: Bootlace Publications, 1984.

Gehring, Wes D. *Personality Comedians as Genre: Selected Players*. Westport, CT: Greenwood, 1997.

Geltzer, Jeremy. *Dirty Words and Filthy Pictures: Film and the First Amendment*. Austin: University of Texas Press, 2015.

Geraghty, Christine. "Re-Examining Stardom: Questions of Texts, Bodies and Performance." *Reinventing Film Studies*. Ed. Christine Gledhill and Linda Williams. London: Arnold, 2000. 183–201.

Gifford, Denis. *American Animated Films: The Silent Era, 1897–1929*. Jefferson, NC: McFarland, 1990.

———. *The Great Cartoon Stars: A Who's Who!* London: Bloomsbury Books, 1988.

Gomery, Douglas. "The Coming of Television and the 'Lost' Motion Picture Audience." *Journal of Film and Video* 37.3 (Summer 1985): 5–11.

———. *The Hollywood Studio System*. Basingstoke, UK: Macmillan, 1986.

Goodman, Martin. "Baby Steps." *Animation World Network*. October 2002. www.awn.com/animationworld/baby-steps.

Gordon, Ian. *Comic Strips and Consumer Culture, 1890–1945*. Washington, DC: Smithsonian Institution Press, 2002.

Gould, Michael. *Surrealism and the Cinema*. London: Tantivy, 1976.

Gould, Stephen Jay. "A Biological Homage to Mickey Mouse." *Juxtapositions: Connections and Contrasts*. Ed. William Vesterman. Mountain View, CA: Mayfield Publishing, 1996. 240–249.

Grainge, Paul. *Brand Hollywood: Selling Entertainment in a Global Media Age*. Abingdon, UK: Routledge, 2008.

Grandinetti, Fred M. *Popeye: An Illustrated Cultural History*. 2nd ed. Jefferson, NC: McFarland, 2004.

Greenberg, Alex, and Malvin Wald. "Report to the Stockholders." *Hollywood Quarterly* 1.4 (July 1946): 410–415.

Greene, Katherine, and Richard Greene. *The Man Behind the Magic: The Story of Walt Disney*. New York: Viking, 1991.

Greer, Howard. "Europe's Favorite!" *Photoplay* 38.6 (November 1930): 94.

Griffin, Sean. *Tinker Belles and Evil Queens: The Walt Disney Company from the Inside Out*. New York: New York University Press, 2000.

Griffiths, David. "Interview by David Griffiths." *Walt Disney: Conversations*. Ed. Kathy Merlock Jackson. Jackson: University Press of Mississippi, 2006. 67–71.

Grossman, Gary H. *Saturday Morning TV*. New York: Dell Publishing, 1981.

Gunning, Tom. "The Cinema of Attractions: Early Film, Its Spectator and the Avant-Garde." *Early Cinema: Space, Frame, Narrative*. Ed. Thomas Elsaesser. London: BFI, 1990. 56–62.

———. "Moving Away from the Index: Cinema and the Impression of Reality." *differences: A Journal of Feminist Cultural Studies* 18.1 (Spring 2007): 29–52.

———. "'Now You See It, Now You Don't': The Temporality of the Cinema of Attractions." *Silent Film.* Ed. Richard Abel. London: Athlone, 1996. 71–84.

Gustines, George Gene. "It's 2772. Who Loves Ya, Tech E. Coyote?" *New York Times* 6 June 2005: E3.

Hagopian, Kevin. "Declarations of Independence: A History of Cagney Productions." *Velvet Light Trap* 22 (1986): 16–32.

Hansen, Miriam. "Of Mice and Ducks: Benjamin and Adorno on Disney." *South Atlantic Quarterly* 92.1 (Winter 1993): 27–61.

Harvey, R. C. "Getting Our Pornograph Fixed." *The Tijuana Bibles: America's Forgotten Comic Strips.* Vol. 1. Ed. Michael Dowers. Seattle: Eros Comix, 1996. 4–6.

"Hays Discusses Trade Problems, Practices." *Motion Picture Herald* 126.10 (6 March 1937): 38.

Heide, Robert, and John Gilman. *Disneyana: Classic Collectibles, 1928–1958.* New York: Disney Editions, 1994.

———. *Mickey Mouse: The Evolution, the Legend, the Phenomenon!* New York: Disney Editions, 2001.

"Helen Kane Asks $250,000." *New York Times* 4 May 1932: 23.

Hench, John, and Peggy Van Pelt. *Designing Disney: Imagineering and the Art of the Show.* New York: Disney Editions, 2008.

Hendershot, Heather. *Saturday Morning Censors: Television Regulation before the V-Chip.* Durham, NC: Duke University Press, 1998.

———. "Secretary, Homemaker, and 'White' Woman: Industrial Censorship and Betty Boop's Shifting Design." *Journal of Design History* 8.2 (1995): 117–130.

Henderson, Brian. "Romantic Comedy Today: Semi-Tough or Impossible?" *Film Quarterly* 31.4 (Summer 1978): 11–23.

Hills, Matt. "Putting Away Childish Things: Jar Jar Binks and the 'Virtual Star' as an Object of Fan Loathing." *Contemporary Hollywood Stardom.* Ed. Thomas Austin and Martin Barker. London: Arnold, 2003. 74–89.

Hilmes, Michelle. *Hollywood and Broadcasting: From Radio to Cable.* Urbana: University of Illinois Press, 1990.

Hiltzik, Michael. "Introducing the Creepiest TV Commercial Ever Made." *Los Angeles Times* 4 March 2014. articles.latimes.com/2014/mar/04/business /la-fi-mh-creepiest-tv-commercial-20140304.

Hoban, Charles F., and Edward B. Van Ormer. *Instructional Film Research: 1918–1950.* New York: Arno, 1970.

Hollis, Tim. *Hi There, Boys and Girls! America's Local Children's TV Programs.* Jackson: University Press of Mississippi, 2001.

"Hollywood Censors Its Animated Cartoons." *Look* 17 January 1939: 17–21.

"The Hollywood Who's Who—and What the Film Famous Are Doing in the Movie Capital." *New Movie Magazine* 4.1 (July 1931): 30–31, 93.

Holt, R. G. *Little "Dirty" Comics.* Reseda, CA: Socio Library, 1971.

Holtz, Allan. "Obscurity of the Day: The Paramount-Bray Animated Cartoon

Promotional Comic Strip." *The Stripper's Guide* 24 June 2011. strippersguide
.blogspot.co.uk/2011/06/obscurity-of-day-paramount-bray.html.

Hoopes, Roy. *When the Stars Went to War: Hollywood and World War II.* New York: Random House, 1994.

Horkheimer, Max, and Theodor W. Adorno. *Dialectic of Enlightenment: Philosophical Fragments.* Stanford, CA: Stanford University Press, 2002.

"House Forbids OCD Funds for 'Dancers,' Donald Duck." *New York Times* 7 February 1942: 1, 9.

Hovland, Carl I., Arthur A. Lumsdaine, and Fred D. Sheffield. *Experiments on Mass Communication.* New York: John Wiley and Sons, 1949.

Hu, Tze-Yue G. *Frames of Anime: Culture and Image-Building.* Hong Kong: Hong Kong University Press, 2010.

Hubley, John, and Zachary Schwartz. "Animation Learns a New Language." *Hollywood Quarterly* 1.4 (July 1946): 360–363.

Huettig, Mae D. *Economic Control of the Motion Picture Industry: A Study in Industrial Organization.* Philadelphia: University of Pennsylvania Press, 1944.

Hyland, Dick. "Mickey Mouse: His Life and Art." *New Movie Magazine* 1.6 (May 1930): 36–37, 128–129.

Inge, M. Thomas. *Comics as Culture.* Jackson: University Press of Mississippi, 1990.

"Italy Grants Stay to Mickey, Popeye." *Motion Picture Herald* 133.8 (19 November 1938): 14.

Iwerks, Leslie, and John Kenworthy. *The Hand Behind the Mouse: An Intimate Biography of Ub Iwerks.* New York: Disney Editions, 2001.

"J. Wellington Wimpy in 'Back to His First Love.'" *Tijuana Bibles: Art and Wit in America's Forbidden Funnies, 1930s–1950s.* Ed. Bob Adelman and Richard Merkin. New York: Simon and Schuster, 1997. 21.

Jackson, Kathy Merlock. "Autographs for Tots: The Marketing of Stars to Children." *Disneyland and Culture: Essays on the Parks and Their Influence.* Ed. Kathy Merlock Jackson and Mark I. West. Jefferson, NC: McFarland, 2011. 207–214.

———. "Mickey and the Tramp: Walt Disney's Debt to Charlie Chaplin." *Journal of American Culture* 26.4 (December 2003): 439–444.

Jacobs, Lea. "Industry Self-Regulation and the Problem of Textual Determination." *Controlling Hollywood: Censorship and Regulation in the Studio Era.* Ed. Matthew Bernstein. New Brunswick, NJ: Rutgers University Press, 1999. 87–101.

———. *The Wages of Sin: Censorship and the Fallen Woman, 1928–1942.* Rev. ed. Berkeley: University of California Press, 1995.

Jacobs, Lea, and Richard Maltby. "Rethinking the Production Code." *Quarterly Review of Film and Video* 15.4 (March 1995): 1–3.

Jamison, Barbara Berch. "Of Mouse and Man, or Mickey Reaches 25." *New York Times* 25 September 1953: SM26–27.

Jenkins, Eric. "Seeing Life in Disney's Mutual Affection-Images." *Quarterly Review of Film and Video* 30.5 (2013): 421–434.

Jenkins, Henry. "'This Fellow Keaton Seems to be the Whole Show': Buster Keaton, Interrupted Performance, and the Vaudeville Aesthetic." *Buster Keaton's "Sherlock Jr."* Ed. Andrew Horton. Cambridge: Cambridge University Press, 1997. 29–66.

———. *What Made Pistachio Nuts? Early Sound Comedy and the Vaudeville Aesthetic.* New York: Columbia University Press, 1992.

———. *The Wow Climax: Tracing the Emotional Impact of Popular Culture.* New York: New York University Press, 2007.

Jenkins, Henry, and Kristine Brunovska Karnick. "Acting Funny." *Classical Hollywood Comedy.* Ed. Kristine Brunovska Karnick and Henry Jenkins. New York: Routledge, 1995. 149–167.

———. "Introduction." *Classical Hollywood Comedy.* Ed. Kristine Brunovska Karnick and Henry Jenkins. New York: Routledge, 1995. 1–13.

"Joan's Calls For D-Urante." *Tijuana Bibles: Art and Wit in America's Forbidden Funnies, 1930s-1950s.* Ed. Bob Adelman and Richard Merkin. New York: Simon and Schuster, 1997. 85.

Kaufman, J. B. "The Shadow of the Mouse." *Film Comment* 28.5 (September 1992): 68–71.

———. *South of the Border: Walt Disney and the Good Neighbor Program, 1941–1948.* New York: Disney Editions, 2009.

Kenner, Hugh. *Chuck Jones: A Flurry of Drawings.* Berkeley: University of California Press, 1994.

Kerr, Walter. *The Silent Clowns.* New York: Da Capo, 1980.

Kindem, Gorham. "Hollywood's Movie Star System: A Historical Overview." *The American Movie Industry: The Business of Motion Pictures.* Ed. Gorham Kindem. Carbondale: Southern Illinois University Press, 1982. 79–93.

King, Barry. "Articulating Digital Stardom." *Celebrity Studies* 2.3 (2011): 247–262.

———. "Articulating Stardom." *Screen* 26.5 (September 1985): 27–50.

———. "The Hollywood Star System: The Impact of an Occupational Ideology on Popular Hero Worship." PhD diss. London School of Economics and Political Science, 1984.

———. "Stardom as an Occupation." *The Hollywood Film Industry.* Ed. Paul Kerr. London: Routledge, 1986. 154–184.

King, Rob. *The Fun Factory: The Keystone Film Company and the Emergence of Mass Culture.* Berkeley: University of California Press, 2009.

Kinsey, Anthony. *Animated Film Making.* London: Studio Vista, 1970.

Klaprat, Cathy. "The Star as Market Strategy: Bette Davis in Another Light." *The American Film Industry.* Rev. ed. Ed. Tino Balio. Madison: University of Wisconsin Press, 1985. 351–376.

Klein, Norman M. *7 Minutes: The Life and Death of the American Animated Cartoon.* London: Verso, 1993.

Kline, Stephen. *Out of the Garden: Toys and Children's Culture in the Age of TV Marketing.* Toronto: Garamond, 1993.

Kompare, Derek. *Rerun Nation: How Repeats Invented American Television.* New York: Routledge, 2005.

Koppes, Clayton R., and Gregory D. Black. *Hollywood Goes to War: How Politics, Profits, and Propaganda Shaped World War II Movies.* London: I. B. Tauris, 1988.

Korkis, Jim. "Secrets of *Steamboat Willie.*" *Hogan's Alley* 3.4 (2004): 57–63.

———. *The Vault of Walt: Unofficial, Unauthorized, Uncensored Disney Stories Never Told.* N.p.: Ayefour Publishing, 2010.

Korkis, Jim, and John Cawley. *Cartoon Confidential.* Westlake Village, CA: Malibu Graphics Publishing, 1991.

Kracauer, Siegfried. *Theory of Film: The Redemption of Physical Reality.* New York: Oxford University Press, 1960.

Krämer, Peter. "Derailing the Honeymoon Express: Comicality and Narrative Closure in Buster Keaton's *The Blacksmith.*" *Velvet Light Trap* 23 (1989): 101–116.

Krutnik, Frank. "The Clown-Prints of Comedy." *Screen* 25.4–5 (1984): 50–59.

———. "A Spanner in the Works? Genre, Narrative and the Hollywood Cinema." *Classical Hollywood Comedy.* Ed. Kristine Brunovska Karnick and Henry Jenkins. New York: Routledge, 1995. 17–38.

Kurson, Robert. *The Official Three Stooges Encyclopedia: The Ultimate Knucklehead's Guide to Stoogedom.* Lincolnwood, IL: Contemporary Books, 1998.

Lafferty, William. "Feature Films on Prime-Time Television." *Hollywood in the Age of Television.* Ed. Tino Balio. Boston: Unwin Hyman, 1990. 235–256.

Lamarre, Thomas. "Coming to Life: Cartoon Animals and Natural Philosophy." *Pervasive Animation.* Ed. Suzanne Buchan. New York: Routledge, 2013. 117–142.

Langer, John. "Television's 'Personality System.'" *Media Culture and Society* 3.4 (October 1981): 351–365.

Langer, Mark. "Animatophilia, Cultural Production and Corporate Interests: The Case of Ren and Stimpy." *A Reader in Animation Studies.* Ed. Jayne Pilling. London: John Libbey, 1997. 143–162.

———. "The Reflections of John Randolph Bray." *Griffithiana* 53 (May 1995): 94–131.

"Laurel and Hardy Steal MGM's 'Hollywood Party.'" *Hollywood Reporter* 20.16 (29 March 1934): 3.

Laurens, Rhett H. "Year of the Living Dead: California Breathes New Life into Celebrity Publicity Rights." *Hastings Communications and Entertainment Law Journal* 24.1 (September 2001): 111–147.

"Leading Short Subjects." *Showmen's Trade Review* 44.1 (19 January 1946), sec. 2: 39–41.

Lehman, Christopher P. *The Colored Cartoon: Black Representation in American Animated Films, 1907–1954.* Amherst: University of Massachusetts Press, 2007.

Leslie, Esther. *Hollywood Flatlands: Animation, Critical Theory and the Avant-Garde*. London: Verso, 2004.

Levin, Bob. *The Pirates and the Mouse: Disney's War Against the Counterculture*. Seattle: Fantagraphics, 2003.

Lotz, Amanda D. *The Television Will Be Revolutionized*. New York: New York University Press, 2007.

"The Love Guide." *Tijuana Bibles: Art and Wit in America's Forbidden Funnies, 1930s-1950s*. Ed. Bob Adelman and Richard Merkin. New York: Simon and Schuster, 1997. 144–149.

MacKay, John. "Walter Benjamin and Rudolf Arnheim on Charlie Chaplin." *Yale Journal of Criticism* 9 (1996): 309–314.

Madden, David. *Harlequin's Stick, Charlie's Cane: A Comparative Study of Commedia dell'Arte and Silent Slapstick Comedy*. Bowling Green, KY: Bowling Green University Popular Press, 1975.

"Mae West and Popeye." *Little "Dirty" Comics*. Ed. R. G. Holt. Reseda, CA: Socio Library, 1971. 138–153.

Majumdar, Neepa. *Wanted Cultured Ladies Only! Female Stardom and Cinema in India, 1930s-1950s*. Urbana: University of Illinois Press, 2009.

Mallory, Michael. "The Case of the Copycat Concerto." *Animation Magazine* (11 August 2011). www.animationmagazine.net/top-stories/the-case-of-the-copycat-concerto.

Maltby, Richard. "Documents on the Genesis of the Production Code." *Quarterly Review of Film and Video* 15.4 (March 1995): 33–63.

———. "The Genesis of the Production Code." *Quarterly Review of Film and Video* 15.4 (March 1995): 5–32.

———. *Hollywood Cinema: An Introduction*. Oxford: Blackwell, 2000.

———. "The Production Code and the Mythologies of 'Pre-Code' Hollywood." *The Classical Hollywood Reader*. Ed. Steve Neale. London: Routledge, 2010. 237–248.

———. "The Spectacle of Criminality." *Violence and American Cinema*. Ed. J. David Slocum. New York: Routledge, 2001. 117–152.

Maltin, Leonard. *Of Mice and Magic: A History of American Animated Cartoons*. Rev. ed. New York: Plume, 1987.

———. "TV Animation: The Decline and Pratfall of a Popular Art." *Film Comment* 11.1 (January–February 1975): 77–81.

Mann, Denise. "The Spectacularization of Everyday Life: Recycling Hollywood Stars and Fans in Early Television Variety Shows." *Camera Obscura* 6.16 (January 1988): 47–77.

Manovich, Lev. *The Language of New Media*. Cambridge, MA: MIT Press, 2001.

Marchand, Roland. *Advertising the American Dream: Making Way for Modernity, 1920–1940*. Berkeley: University of California Press, 1986.

Maslon, Laurence, and Michael Kantor. *Make 'Em Laugh: The Funny Business of America*. New York: Hachette, 2008.

Massa, Steve. "Billie Ritchie: The Man from Nowhere." *Chaplin: The Dictator and the Tramp*. Ed. Frank Scheide and Hooman Mehran. London: BFI, 2004.

May, Lary. *The Big Tomorrow: Hollywood and the Politics of the American Way*. Chicago: University of Chicago Press, 2000.

McCabe, John. *Charlie Chaplin*. London: Robson Books, 1992.

McConnell, Frank D. *The Spoken Seen: Film and the Romantic Tradition*. Baltimore, MD: Johns Hopkins University Press, 1975.

McCord, David Frederick. "Is Walt Disney a Menace to Our Children?" *Photoplay* 45.5 (April 1934): 30–31, 92, 103.

McDonald, John. *The Game of Business*. New York: Doubleday, 1975.

McDonald, Paul. *Hollywood Stardom*. Malden, MA: Wiley-Blackwell, 2013.

———. *The Star System: Hollywood's Production of Popular Identities*. London: Wallflower, 2005.

———. "Stars in the Online Universe: Promotion, Nudity, Reverence." *Contemporary Hollywood Stardom*. Ed. Thomas Austin and Martin Barker. London: Arnold, 2003. 29–44.

McEvoy, J. P. "The Love Life of Mickey Mouse." *New Movie Magazine* 6.5 (November 1932): 46–47, 97.

McGilligan, Patrick. *Cagney: The Actor as Auteur*. South Brunswick, NJ: A. S. Barnes, 1975.

———. "Robert Clampett." *The American Animated Cartoon: A Critical Anthology*. Ed. Danny Peary and Gerald Peary. New York: E. P. Dutton, 1980. 150–157.

McPherson, Edward. *Buster Keaton: Tempest in a Flat Hat*. London: Faber and Faber, 2004.

Merritt, Karen, and Russell Merritt. "Mythic Mouse." *Griffithiana* 34 (December 1988): 58–71.

Merritt, Russell, and J. B. Kaufman. *Walt Disney's Silly Symphonies: A Companion to the Classic Cartoon Series*. Rev. ed. Glendale, CA: Disney Editions, 2016.

———. *Walt in Wonderland: The Silent Films of Walt Disney*. Baltimore, MD: Johns Hopkins University Press, 2000.

"Mickey Mouse and Donald Duck." *Tijuana Bibles: Art and Wit in America's Forbidden Funnies, 1930s-1950s*. Ed. Bob Adelman and Richard Merkin. New York: Simon and Schuster, 1997. 41.

"Mickey Mouse Celebrates a Birthday." *National Board of Review Magazine* 10.7 (September–October 1935): 8–9.

"'Mickey Mouse' Sues to 'Save Reputation.'" *New York Times* 1 April 1931: 26.

"Mickey Mouse's Fourth Birthday Finds Organization Worldwide." *Motion Picture Herald* 109.1 (1 October 1932): 42–43, 51.

Mikulak, William A. "The Canonization of Warner Brothers Cartoons, or How Bugs Bunny Came to the Museum of Modern Art." *Journal of American Culture* 19.1 (Spring 1996): 21–28.

Mills, Brett. *Television Sitcom*. London: BFI Publishing, 2005.

Milne, Peter. "Bud Fisher's *Mutt and Jeff* Pictures." *Motion Picture News* 13.5 (15 April 1916): 2214.

"Miss Kane Loses Suit Over 'Boop' Singing." *New York Times* 6 May 1934: 5.

Mittell, Jason. *Genre and Television: From Cop Shows to Cartoons in American Culture.* New York: Routledge, 2004.

———. "The Great Saturday Morning Exile: Scheduling Cartoons on Television's Periphery in the 1960s." *Prime Time Animation: Television Animation and American Culture.* Ed. Carole A. Stabile and Mark Harrison. London: Routledge, 2003. 33–54.

"*Momotaro's Sea Eagle* Ad Gallery." *The Roots of Japanese Anime Until the End of World War II.* Zakka Films, 2008. DVD.

Morley, Patrick. *"This Is the American Forces Network": The Anglo-American Battle of the Air Waves in World War II.* Westport, CT: Praeger, 2001.

Mouse, Mickey, and Cedric Belfrage. "My Love Life and Other Things." *Motion Picture Classic* 31.6 (August 1930): 68–69, 96.

Mouse, Mickey, and Hal Horne. "Mickey Mouse's Movie-Go-Round." *New Movie Magazine* 8.5 (November 1933): 54–55.

Mouse, Mickey, and Russell Schroeder. *Walt Disney's Mickey Mouse: My Life in Pictures.* New York: Disney Press, 1997.

"Movie Magic & Mysteries: The Making of *Sherlock Jr.*" *Sherlock Jr. and Three Ages.* Kino International, 2010. DVD.

Murray, Susan. *Hitch Your Antenna to the Stars: Early Television and Broadcast Stardom.* New York: Routledge, 2005.

Musser, Charles. "Work, Ideology and Chaplin's Tramp." *Radical History Review* 41 (Spring 1988): 37–66.

Nardone, Mark. "Robert McKimson Interviewed." *The American Animated Cartoon: A Critical Anthology.* Ed. Danny Peary and Gerald Peary. New York: E. P. Dutton, 1980. 142–149.

Naremore, James. *Acting in the Cinema.* Berkeley: University of California Press, 1988.

Neale, Steve. *Genre and Hollywood.* London: Routledge, 2000.

Neale, Steve, and Frank Krutnik. *Popular Film and Television Comedy.* London: Routledge, 1990.

"New Effects in Bray Comedies: Trick Photography Introduces Novelty with 'Colonel Heeza Liar.'" *Motion Picture News* 26.27 (30 December 1922): 3390.

Newman, Kim. "Flamboyantly Insane." *Sight and Sound* 14.11 (November 2004): 30–33.

"The New Pictures." *Time* 39.6 (9 February 1942): 36.

Ngai, Sianne. *Ugly Feelings.* Cambridge, MA: Harvard University Press, 2005.

North, Dan. *Performing Illusions: Cinema, Special Effects and the Virtual Actor.* London: Wallflower, 2008.

Nugent, Frank S. "That Million-Dollar Mouse." *New York Times* 21 September 1947: 22, 60–62.

———. "The Slapstick Professor." *New York Times* 5 May 1935: X3.

Nuiry, Octavio Emilio. "Ban the Bandito!" *Hispanic* 9.7 (July 1996): 26–32.

O'Brien, Flora. *Walt Disney's Donald Duck: 50 Years of Happy Frustration.* Tucson, AZ: HP Books, 1984.

———. *Walt Disney's Goofy: The Good Sport.* London: Ebury, 1985.

"Paramount Magazine." *Moving Picture World* 47.7 (18 December 1920): 910.

Patten, Fred. "Some Notes on *Crusader Rabbit*." *Animatrix* 6 (1992): 29–36.

Peary, Danny. "Reminiscing with Walter Lantz." *The American Animated Cartoon: A Critical Anthology.* Ed. Danny Peary and Gerald Peary. New York: E. P. Dutton, 1980. 192–200.

Perkins, V. F. *Film as Film: Understanding and Judging Movies.* London: Penguin, 1974.

Perlmutter, David. *America Toons In: A History of Television Animation.* Jefferson, NC: McFarland, 2014.

Petty, Ross D., and Denver D'Rozario. "The Use of Dead Celebrities in Advertising and Marketing: Balancing Interests in the Right of Publicity." *Journal of Advertising* 38.4 (Winter 2009): 37–49.

Pierce, David. "'Senile Celluloid': Independent Exhibitors, the Major Studios and the Fight over Feature Films on Television, 1939–1956." *Film History* 10.2 (1998): 141–161.

Pisney, Salt. "Mickey Mouse in 'Of Mice and Women.'" *Sex in Comics: A History of the Eight Pagers.* Vol. 4. Ed. Donald H. Gilmore. 79–80.

Powdermaker, Hortense. *Hollywood, the Dream Factory: An Anthropologist Looks at the Movie-Makers.* London: Secker and Warburg, 1951.

Prince, Stephen. "True Lies: Perceptual Realism, Digital Images, and Film Theory." *Film Quarterly* 49.3 (Spring 1996): 27–37.

Pringle, Henry F. "Mickey Mouse's Father." *McCall's* August 1932: 7, 28.

"Prolific Profits from Popeye." *Broadcasting: The Businessweekly of Television and Radio* (12 August 1957): 64, 66.

"Protests and Benefits in Show Business Follow Nazi's Attacks." *Motion Picture Herald* 133.9 (26 November 1938): 17.

Pulver, Andrew. "Rogue One VFX Head: 'We Didn't Do Anything Peter Cushing Would've Objected To.'" *Guardian* 16 January 2017. www.theguardian.com /film/2017/jan/16/rogue-one-vfx-jon-knoll-peter-cushing-ethics-of-digital -resurrections.

Ramsaye, Terry. "Mickey Mouse: He Stays on the Job." *Motion Picture Herald* 109.1 (1 October 1932): 41.

———. "Terry Ramsaye Records." *Motion Picture Herald* 102.9 (28 February 1931): 10.

Rawls, Walton. *Disney Dons Dogtags: The Best of Disney Military Insignia from World War II.* New York: Abbeville Publishing Group, 1992.

Raymond, Otis. *An Illustrated History of Sex Comic Classics.* Vol. 1. New York: Comic Classics, 1972.

"Reviews of Sound Shorts." *Film Daily* 58.7 (10 January 1932): 10.

Riblet, Douglas. "The Keystone Film Company and the Historiography of Early Slapstick." *Classical Hollywood Comedy.* Ed. Kristine Brunovska Karnick and Henry Jenkins. New York: Routledge, 1995. 168–189.

Robbins, L. H. "Mickey Mouse Emerges as Economist." *New York Times* 10 March 1935: SM8, 22.

Roberts, Randy, and James S. Olson. *John Wayne: American.* New York: Free Press, 1995.

Ross, Murray. *Stars and Strikes: Unionization of Hollywood.* New York: AMS Press, 1967.

Rosten, Leo C. *Hollywood: The Movie Colony, The Movie Makers.* New York: Arno, 1970.

Saler, Michael. *As If: Modern Enchantment and the Literary Pre-History of Virtual Reality.* Oxford: Oxford University Press, 2012.

Sammond, Nicholas. *Birth of an Industry: Blackface Minstrelsy and the Rise of American Animation.* Durham, NC: Duke University Press, 2015.

Sampson, Henry T. *That's Enough, Folks: Black Images in Animated Cartoons, 1900–1960.* Lanham, MD: Scarecrow, 1998.

Sargeant, Amy. "Dancing on Fire and Water: Charlot and *l'Espirit Nouveau.*" *Slapstick Comedy.* Ed. Tom Paulus and Rob King. New York: Routledge, 2010. 193–206.

Sargent, Epes W. "Exploitation." *Variety* 107.13 (6 September 1932): 19, 31.

Schatz, Thomas. *Boom and Bust: American Cinema in the 1940s.* Berkeley: University of California Press, 1999.

———. "The Studio System and Conglomerate Hollywood." *The Contemporary Hollywood Film Industry.* Ed. Paul McDonald and Janet Wasko. Oxford: Blackwell, 2008. 13–42.

Scheuer, Philip K. "Mickey Mouse Charged with Death of 'Live' Comedians." *Los Angeles Times* 26 November 1933: A1.

Schickel, Richard. *The Disney Version: The Life, Times, Art and Commerce of Walt Disney.* 3rd ed. Chicago: Ivan R. Dee, 1997.

Schneider, Cy. *Children's Television: The Art, the Business, and How It Works.* Lincolnwood, IL: NTC Business Books, 1989.

Schneider, Steve. *That's All Folks! The Art of Warner Bros. Animation.* London: Aurum, 1994.

Schwarz, Ted. *Marilyn Revealed: The Ambitious Life of an American Icon.* Lanham, MD: Taylor Trade Publishing, 2009.

"Screen News." *Screenland* 23.5 (September 1931): 86–91, 127–129.

Segrave, Kerry. *Movies at Home: How Hollywood Came to Television.* Jefferson, NC: McFarland, 1999.

Seidman, Steve. *Comedian Comedy: A Tradition in Hollywood Film.* Ann Arbor, MI: UMI Research Press, 1981.

Sellors, C. Paul. *Film Authorship: Auteurs and Other Myths*. London: Wallflower, 2010.

Sesonske, Alexander. "The World Viewed." *Georgia Review* 28.1 (Winter 1974): 561–570.

Shale, Richard. *Donald Duck Joins Up: The Walt Disney Studio During World War II*. Ann Arbor, MI: UMI Research Press, 1982.

Shales, Tom. "A Duck for All Seasons: 50 Years in Pursuit of Happiness." *Washington Post* 24 June 1984: H1, H5.

Shindler, Colin. *Hollywood Goes to War: Films and American Society, 1939–1952*. London: Routledge, 1979.

"Short Reels." *Film Daily* 19.35 (5 February 1922): 20.

"Shorts: 'The New Spirit.'" *Film Daily* 81.20 (29 January 1942): 7.

"Showmen's Reviews." *Motion Picture Herald* 110.9 (25 February 1933): 37, 40–41.

Simensky, Linda. "The Revival of the Studio-Era Cartoon in the 1990s." *Funny Pictures: Animation and Comedy in Studio-Era Hollywood*. Ed. Daniel Goldmark and Charlie Keil. Berkeley: University of California Press, 2011. 272–291.

Sito, Tom. *Drawing the Line: The Untold Story of the Animation Unions from Bosko to Bart Simpson*. Lexington: University Press of Kentucky, 2006.

———. *Moving Innovation: A History of Computer Animation*. Cambridge, MA: MIT Press, 2013.

Slafer, Eugene. "A Conversation with Bill Hanna." *The American Animated Cartoon: A Critical Anthology*. Ed. Danny Peary and Gerald Peary. New York: E. P. Dutton, 1980. 255–260.

Slide, Anthony. *Inside the Hollywood Fan Magazine: A History of Star Makers, Fabricators, and Gossip Mongers*. Jackson: University Press of Mississippi, 2010.

Smith, Conrad. "The Early History of Animation." *The American Animated Cartoon: A Critical Anthology*. Ed. Danny Peary and Gerald Peary. New York: E. P. Dutton, 1980. 3–11.

Smith, Phillip, and Ellen Wright. "A Glimpse Behind the Screen—Tijuana Bibles and the Pornographic Re-Imagining of Hollywood." *Skandal w tekstach kultury*. Ed. Marian Ursel, Magdalena Dąbrowska, Joanna Nadolna, and Malgorzata Skibińska. Warsaw: Wydawnictwo DiG, 2013. 149–169.

Smoodin, Eric. *Animating Culture: Hollywood Cartoons from the Sound Era*. Oxford: Roundhouse, 1993.

Sobel, Raoul, and David Francis. *Chaplin: Genesis of a Clown*. London: Quartet Books, 1977.

Solomon, Charles. *Enchanted Drawings: The History of Animation*. Rev. ed. New York: Wings Books, 1994.

———. "Live From Trumps." *Chuck Jones: Conversations*. Ed. Maureen Furniss. Jackson: University Press of Mississippi, 2005. 130–145.

Sontag, Susan. "The Double Standard of Aging." *On the Contrary: Essays by Men and Women.* Ed. Martha Rainbolt and Janet Fleetwood. Albany: State University of New York Press, 1982. 99–112.

———. *On Photography.* London: Penguin, 2008.

"Special Stunts for Holiday Time." *Film Daily* 66.135 (8 December 1934): 14.

Sperb, Jason. *Flickers of Film: Nostalgia in the Time of Digital Cinema.* New Brunswick, NJ: Rutgers University Press, 2016.

Stacey, Jackie. *Star Gazing: Hollywood Cinema and Female Spectatorship.* London: Routledge, 1994.

Staiger, Janet. "Seeing Stars." *Stardom: Industry of Desire.* Ed. Christine Gledhill. London: Routledge, 1991. 3–16.

Stalling, Penny, and Howard Mandelbaum. "Moonlighting with the Stars." *American Film* 4.2 (November 1983): 40–46.

Stamp, Shelley. "'It's a Long Way to Filmland': Starlets, Screen Hopefuls, and Extras in Early Hollywood." *American Cinema's Transitional Era: Audiences, Institutions, Practices.* Ed. Charlie Keil and Shelley Stamp. Berkeley: University of California Press, 2004. 332–351.

Stewart, Garrett. "Modern Hard Times: Chaplin and the Cinema of Self-Reflection." *Critical Inquiry* 3.2 (Winter 1976): 295–314.

Stone, Dave, Joe Adamson, and Jim Morrow. "Shooting *A Political Cartoon.*" *Filmmakers Newsletter* 8.3 (January 1975): 18–22.

"Stories of the Films." *Moving Picture World* 30.10 (9 December 1916): 1542–1552.

Strauss, Theodore. "Mr. Terry and the Animal Kingdom." *New York Times* 7 July 1940: X3.

Stuart, Fredric. "The Effects of Television on the Motion Picture Industry: 1948–1960." *The American Movie Industry: The Business of Motion Pictures.* Ed. Gorham Kindem. Carbondale: Southern Illinois University Press, 1982. 257–307.

Telotte, J. P. *Disney TV.* Detroit, MI: Wayne State University Press, 2004.

———. "Disney's Cows, the Mouse, and the Modernist Movement." *Screen* 51.3 (Autumn 2010): 219–231.

Terrace, Vincent. *Radio Programs, 1924–1984.* Jefferson, NC: McFarland, 1999.

Thew, Harvey F. "Colonel Heeza Liar's Waterloo." *Motion Picture News* 13.3 (22 January 1916): 394.

Thomas, Bob. *Building a Company: Roy O. Disney and the Creation of an Entertainment Empire.* New York: Hyperion, 1998.

Thomas, Sergeant Franklin. "The Cartoon and Training Films." *Writers' Congress: The Proceedings of the Conference Held in October 1943 under the Sponsorship of the Hollywood Writers' Mobilization and the University of California.* Berkeley: University of California Press, 1944. 133–137.

Thompson, Kristin. "Implications of the Cel Animation Technique." *The Cinematic Apparatus.* Ed. Teresa De Lauretis and Stephen Heath. London: Macmillan, 1980. 106–120.

Tieman, Robert. *The Mickey Mouse Treasures.* New York: Disney Editions, 2007.

United States Court of Appeals for the Ninth Circuit. *Pathe Exchange, Inc.,*
a Corporation, and the Van Beuren Corporation, a Corporation, Appellants, v. Walt
Disney Productions, Ltd, a Corporation, Appellee: Transcript of Record, upon Appeal
from the United States District Court for the Southern District of California, Central
Division [Case No. 6493]. Los Angeles: Parker, Stone and Baird, 1931.

United States Congress. *Congressional Record.* Vol. 88. Washington, DC: GPO,
1942.

Uricchio, William, and Roberta E. Pearson. "Introduction." *The Many Lives of*
the Batman: Critical Approaches to a Superhero and His Media. Ed. Roberta E.
Pearson and William Uricchio. New York: Routledge, 1991. 1–3.

Vasey, Ruth. "Beyond Sex and Violence: 'Industry Policy' and the Regulation
of Hollywood Movies, 1922–1939." *Quarterly Review of Film and Video* 15.4
(March 1995): 65–85.

———. *The World According to Hollywood, 1918–1939.* Madison: University of
Wisconsin Press, 1997.

"The Voice Behind the Mouse." *Mickey Mouse in Living Color.* Vol. 2. Buena Vista
Home Entertainment, 2005. DVD.

Wagner, Dave. "Donald Duck: An Interview." *Radical America* 7.1 (January–
February 1973): 1–19.

Walker, Alexander. *Stardom: The Hollywood Phenomenon.* Harmondsworth, UK:
Penguin, 1974.

Wallace, Irving. "Mickey Mouse, and How He Grew." *Colliers* (9 April 1949):
20–21, 35.

Warren, Doug, and James Cagney. *James Cagney: The Authorized Biography.*
London: Robson Books, 1983.

Waterbury, Ruth. "Youth." *Photoplay* 32.6 (November 1927): 46–47, 134–135.

Watkin, Lawrence Edward. "Mickey Mouse: Disney's Stand-in." *Close-Ups:*
The Movie Star Book. Ed. Danny Peary. New York: Fireside, 1988. 502–504.

Wells, Paul. *Animation and America.* Edinburgh: Edinburgh University Press,
2002.

———. "To Affinity and Beyond: Woody, Buzz and the New Authenticity."
Contemporary Hollywood Stardom. Ed. Thomas Austin and Martin Barker.
London: Arnold, 2003. 90–102.

———. *Understanding Animation.* London: Routledge, 1998.

"What the Picture Did for Me." *Motion Picture Herald* 111.7 (13 May 1933):
53–57.

White, Timothy R. "From Disney to Warner Bros.: The Critical Shift." *Reading*
the Rabbit: Explorations in Warner Bros. Animation. Ed. Kevin S. Sandler. New
Brunswick, NJ: Rutgers University Press, 1998. 38–48.

Whitney, Simon N. "Antitrust Policies and the Motion Picture Industry." *The*
American Movie Industry: The Business of Motion Pictures. Ed. Gorham Kindem.
Carbondale: Southern Illinois University Press, 1982. 161–204.

"Winsor McKay [*sic*]." *Moving Picture World* 8.16 (22 April 1911): 900.

Woll, Allen L. *The Hollywood Musical Goes to War*. Chicago: Nelson-Hall, 1983.

Wollen, Peter. "Films: Why Do Some Survive and Others Disappear?" *Sight and Sound* 3.5 (May 1993): 26–28.

Woolery, George W. *Children's Television: The First Thirty-Five Years, 1946–1981, Part I: Animated Cartoon Series*. Metuchen, NJ: Scarecrow, 1982.

Yeck, J. L. "In the State of California: de Havilland (Plaintiff) vs. Warner Brothers (Defendant): A Trial Decision That Marked a Turning Point." *American Classic Screen* 6.3 (1982): 34–37.

York, Cal. "Cal York's Monthly Broadcast from Hollywood." *Photoplay* 41.5 (April 1932): 38–41, 84, 86, 92–111.

———. "Inside Stuff: Cal York's Gossip of Hollywood." *Photoplay* 23.02 (July 1943): 4–15.

Zhang, Yingjin, and Mary Farquhar. "Introduction: Chinese Film Stars." *Chinese Film Stars*. Ed. Mary Farquhar and Yingjin Zhang. New York: Routledge, 2010. 1–16.

Index